Presidents and Protesters

STUDIES IN RHETORIC AND COMMUNICATION
General Editors:
E. Culpepper Clark
Raymie E. McKerrow
David Zarefsky

"Hear O Israel":
The History of American Jewish Preaching, 1654–1970
Robert V. Friedenberg

A Theory of Argumentation
Charles Arthur Willard

Elite Oral History Discourse:
A Study of Cooperation and Coherence
Eva M. McMahan

Computer-Mediated Communication:
Human Relationships in a Computerized World
James W. Chesebro and Donald G. Bonsall

Popular Trials:
Rhetoric, Mass Media, and the Law
Edited by Robert Hariman

Presidents and Protesters:
Political Rhetoric in the 1960s
Theodore Otto Windt, Jr.

Copyright © 1990 by
The University of Alabama Press
Tuscaloosa, Alabama 35487–0380
All rights reserved
Manufactured in the United States of America

∞
The paper on which this book is printed meets the minimum
requirements of American National Standard for Information
Science-Permanence of Paper for Printed Library Materials,
ANSI Z39.48–1984.

Library of Congress Cataloging-in-Publication Data

Windt, Theodore.
    Presidents and protesters : political rhetoric in the 1960s /
Theodore Otto Windt, Jr.
        p.   cm. — (Studies in rhetoric and communication)
    Includes bibliographical references.
    ISBN 0-8173-0506-8 (alk. paper)
    1. United States—Politics and government—1961–1963. 2. United
States—Politics and government—1963–1969. 3. Rhetoric—Political
aspects—United States—History—20th century. 4. Presidents—
United States—History—20th century. 5. Vietnamese Conflict.
1961–1975—Protest movements. 6. Peace movements—United States—
History—20th century. I. Title. II. Series.
E841.W55 1990
808.53′0883512—dc20   90-35831
                                                                              CIP

British Library Cataloguing-in-Publication Data available

Theodore Otto Windt, Jr.

Presidents and Protesters

Political Rhetoric in the 1960s

The University of Alabama Press   Tuscaloosa and London

—————————

For my wife,
Beth,
and my sons,
Ted III and Thad

Contents

Preface

In his critique of the published papers from the Temple University conference on genres of political discourse, Richard A. Joslyn, a political scientist, observed: "some of the analyses of political discourse in this volume strip the rhetoric of its political meaning. Political beliefs, worldviews, ideologies, and intentions are occasionally mentioned, but only in passing, in favor of attention to the more stylistic aspects of the discourse. While this is not uniformly true of all or even most of the chapters in this volume, it is troubling when political discourse is depoliticized so thoroughly."[1] Earlier in his essay Joslyn listed a series of topics that an examination of political discourse ought to reveal: the rhetor's political worldview, the rhetor's behavioral intentions, the locus and intensity of political conflict, the locus and legitimacy of political power, and the role of the public. Taken together, these topics are quite different from the constellation of topics addressed by many of the participants at the conference. In his critique Joslyn made the political perspective even more specific by posing questions under each topic that he believed anyone concerned with political discourse ought to address. Among these questions:

1. What does the discourse reveal about the belief system of the rhetor?
2. How may we characterize the belief system of the rhetor—pop-

ulist, progressive, liberal, libertarian, conservative, anarchist, internationalist, and so forth?

3. What does the discourse reveal about the predispositions of the rhetor?
4. What does the discourse reveal about the holding and exercise of power in political systems?
5. What expectations or norms about popular participation are revealed and encouraged in political discourse?
6. Can the mode of analysis distinguish the rhetoric of liberals from conservatives, of moralists from pragmatists, of ideologues from nonideologues, or of isolationists from internationalists?[2]

These questions, direct questions about politics and political discourse, are some of the questions addressed in this volume.

Presidents and Protesters is about political rhetoric in the 1960s. All the chapters are bound together by the fact that they deal with the 1960s, a time of passionate politics and resounding rhetoric. The resounding rhetoric is the focus. I have attempted to deal with both the rhetoric of authorities and the rhetoric of protest. Thus, the first part consists of five chapters on presidential rhetoric, or to be more precise, an introductory chapter on presidential rhetoric and four chapters on aspects of the rhetoric of Presidents Kennedy, Johnson, and Nixon. The second part concentrates on the rhetorical development of protests during the 1960s, specifically on an analysis of the political stances that people took toward protest and the rhetorical genres they used or created as consequences of those stances.

It cannot be stressed strongly enough that these critiques are about political rhetoric only during the 1960s, not the 1970s or 1980s. Those are topics for other books. My interest here is in analyzing some of the significant rhetorical efforts of one decade and, following Joslyn, describing the political significance of those efforts. It is always tempting to see the past through the lens of the present, especially when one considers the presidents and the protests, but I have sought not to succumb to that temptation.

But this book is also bound together by critical perspectives and methods that are brought to bear on the study of political rhetoric. Each chapter examines different *political stances* that various people and groups took toward issues, events, and even politics itself during the decade. The political rhetoric originates in those stances and the events or attitudes that created them. It is the political stance or the way someone views and interprets events and issues that generates the rhetoric intended to justify that stance and to persuade others that such an interpretation should be believed and supported. Examination of the political stance an advocate takes is the first step in rhetorical criticism. The chapters on protest examine four different political stances toward protest.

The second step in criticism is to analyze the *public discourse.* My analysis draws heavily on the theory of rhetorical genres, that is, the notion that some forms of persuasive argument are repeated, either by others in similar situations or by a particular person.[3] Genre analysis of the public discourse requires the critic to elucidate the various *topoi* or lines of argument that constitute and define that genre and to understand the politics and psychology that inform those *topoi*. In the case of President John F. Kennedy, I examine the various forms of "crisis" rhetoric that he used when speaking as president, noting as well the occasions when he did not resort to such a rhetoric. President Nixon, I believe, presents a different case. Much of his rhetoric came from his mind-set about how politics functions. Thus, in his case one is looking at a psychopolitical genre that differs considerably from other forms of political rhetoric. In the analysis of protest, I have sought to delineate a number of different forms that came from the political stances that people took toward issues and politics. However, I do not feel that genre or any other method of criticism ought to be a critical straitjacket. In the case of President Johnson's opening statement at his July 1965 press conference, I am more interested in the ways in which he used the prevailing anticommunist ideology to defend his policy of massive escalation of the war and the ways he sought to deflect public attention from that decision. Nonetheless, it is the lines of argument that people use to attempt to persuade that most interest me as a critic and that provide a means of studying both the techniques and the content of persuasive acts.

The third step in criticism is the analysis of *symbolic acts* committed to confirm a rhetorical effort. Anyone who depends on rhetoric as a resource of political power must also depend to a large extent on personal credibility to make the rhetoric work. Symbolic acts are part and parcel of the rhetorical process. Thus, advocates often act in symbolic ways to demonstrate their sincere (and serious) commitment as well as their willingness to act upon what they have said. Such a critical approach does not minimize the results that may come from such actions. And there may be dire consequences. One thinks of the revolutionary orator who plants a bomb to demonstrate his or her commitment to revolution. That people may be hurt or maimed or even killed by such an action should never be ignored. But what I believe is equally important, especially to understanding rhetoric, is that such a bomb generally does not create a revolution, but instead demonstrates commitment to revolution and thus gives authentic identification to that revolutionary orator.

Furthermore, in a mass society and in a nuclear world, one sometimes can act only symbolically or may want to act only symbolically. For example, President Kennedy viewed the missiles Premier Khrushchev put in Cuba in 1962 as a threat to the United States. That was Kennedy's rhetorical stance. But he was whipsawed by the choices he had. He wanted the missiles removed, but he did not want to start World War III. Therefore, after demanding removal of the missiles, he acted symbolically to demonstrate to Khrushchev that he meant business. The evacuation of Americans from Guantanamo, the naval quarantine of Cuba, and the other decisions he announced on October 22, 1962, were intended to demonstrate that he meant what he said without going directly to war with either Cuba or the Soviet Union. All of these acts were fraught with danger, but they turned out to be essentially symbolic; they were meant to convince Khrushchev how seriously Kennedy viewed the situation and how deliberately he intended to act. As one reads these chapters, one should realize how important such symbolic acts are to the rhetorical process. Put quite simply, people commit such acts to be taken seriously. Indeed, wasn't the American war in Vietnam fought principally to prove to the communist world that the United States would resist communist expansion? For policy makers, this symbolic or proxy war was a realistic alternative to all-out war with the Soviet Union or the People's Republic of China.

Finally, the critical process requires a judgment about rhetorical efforts. Political rhetoric mandates political judgments. Politics is not science or philosophy, although each may play a role within the practice of politics. But still, politics is politics, and that is often forgotten. And just as scientists and philosophers would be greatly offended by having their work judged by political standards, so too politicians are sensitive to having their work judged by standards other than political ones. I have tried to take that into account.

So, too, I have tried to rescue political rhetoric from the current fashion, to analyze it by using literary methods ("metaphoric" and "cultural" criticism) or sociological methods (theories of "social movements") and so on. Instead, the view presented here is a political-historical view of a very political decade and the categories of rhetoric used for analysis are therefore political ones.

A political perspective mandates a significant change in the rhetorical critic's conception of "audience." In the long ago day before mass media, a speaker spoke to *an* audience that had assembled to hear the speech. It was quite appropriate under those circumstances to talk about "the audience" in the singular. But with the rise of mass communication the singular usage is obsolete. There are multiple audiences for every public presentation. And with multiple audiences there are multiple responses. Therefore, throughout these chapters I talk about different audiences (or to put it in strictly political terms, different constituencies) and how they responded to rhetorical efforts.

In making judgments through the course of this book, I have employed varying standards (except when it comes to the issues of human rights and the possibility of human extinction), inasmuch as the very different kinds of political rhetoric considered here demand such diversity. One judges a specific presidential speech differently from the way one judges ideological discourse, especially when one is dealing with genres of protest rhetoric. Many of these differences will become clear as one reads the essays. However, let me orient the reader by citing a few differences.

In the case of a presidential speech, the critic asks whether the speech presented a plausible definition of the situation, whether reasonable arguments were marshaled in response to the situation, whether language was used well or misused, what the effects of the speech were, and a variety of other questions depending on the speech, the speaker, and the occasion.

But can a critic ask the same kinds of questions of an ideologue? What does one say when a feminist ideologue, for instance, says, "All men have oppressed women"? Or how does the critic respond to a contrary truth claim, "The history of all hitherto existing society is the history of class struggles"? How does one prove or disprove such statements? Indeed, how does the judicious critic deal with the entire history of "all hitherto existing society" or with "all men" and "all women"? How does the critic determine whatever it is that "history proves"? How does a critic respond to "all" statements, be they statements made by the left or the right? Quite simply, either the critic accepts or rejects such statements, or the critic asks different kinds of questions for ideological claims than one asks when dealing with truth claims about individual incidents or events.

When it comes to ideological rhetoric, then, I take my critical cue from Henri Lefebvre, who wrote: "The Marxian sociologist will study the emergence of forms, the way forms react on contents, structures on processes. The results of the processes of change illumine the latter retrospectively on the one hand, and modify them on the other."[4]

If "rhetorical critic" is substituted for "Marxian sociologist," one will have an apt distillation of the approach I am using to ideological and cynical rhetoric: the study of the forms and structures of that discourse and their interaction with content and with each other in the process of protest and change.

In attempting to distinguish ideological rhetoric from other forms of political rhetoric, the critic runs into a fundamental problem. The problem is in the very word and concept *ideology* itself. What does it mean? There seem to be as many meanings for the word as there are people to use it.[5] Add to this problem another that occurs even when ideologues agree upon what it means. Alvin Gouldner noted that Marxism, as an ideology, can be used as a scientific critique (theory) or as a guide to action (practice).[6] In the 1960s the search for an ideology had both as its goals. However, in the past ten years or so (at least in the United States) the use of ideology as critique has been more dominant than ideology as a practical plan of action. In dealing with the rhetoric of the 1960s, these different uses can become confusing.

Lest the reader be misled into thinking that ideology is the sole province of the left, let me say that the right has had its share of ideologies. The most insidious of these certainly was fascism. In America the most prominent and powerful ideology is anticommunist. Michael Parenti wrote: "Endowed with an imposing ideology, and a set of vivid images and sacred dogmas, it commands the psychic and material resources of the most potent industrial-military arsenal in the history of mankind. Its forces are deployed on every continent, its influence is felt in every major region, and it is capable of acts which—when ascribed to the communists—are considered violent and venal. Our fear that communism might someday take over most of the world blinds us to the fact that anti-communism already has. If America has an ideology, or a national purpose, it is anti-communism."[7] Reactionary groups, such as the John Birch Society, and particular individuals, such as Joseph McCarthy, took the anticommunist ideology as a creed, one that explained every foreign and domestic failure (and some triumphs as well) in American life.

But this analysis is about protest in the 1960s, and that protest was led by the left. Therefore, I have not analyzed the ideology or rhetoric of the right, except as it was expressed by authorities justifying policies or used by other authorities in responding to protests.

Although the word and concept *ideology* is used in the chapters on presidential rhetoric (especially in connection with anticommunist ideology), it is not carefully defined until Chapter Six and then expanded upon in Chapter Nine. I have chosen to define the concept in a narrow sense of a doctrinaire discourse that strives for a universal apprehension of social and political reality, its major agents for change and reaction to change, and the motivations that compel agents to act as they do. This choice was not arbitrary. Ideology has been defined and used in that manner by radicals and reactionaries during much of the twentieth century. But I would be remiss not to note that it was probably from my early studies of Khrushchev's rhetoric that I was influenced in this direction rather than another. Even more important, however, much of the discourse that came out of one segment of the protests in the 1960s was in form and structure very much like the doctrinaire uses of ideology in the past. That structure of discourse set itself off from other kinds of protest rhetoric in definitive ways that are analyzed and distinguished in some of these chapters.

In dealing with ideological rhetoric, my attempt has not been to resolve the controversies over the term, or to come to some definitive answer about what ideology really is. That subject is so vast and the writings on ideology so extensive that to attempt a full scholarly treatment of it would require—at the very least—another volume. Instead, I have chosen to use one concept of ideology consistently as a clarifying concept in contradistinction to other forms of political discourse. In addition, I have often used the designation *doctrinaire* with *ideology* to remind the reader that my use of it is different from the more expansive and elastic uses of the term by other scholars. For whatever theoretical weaknesses this traditional conception of ideology has, it helps illuminate several forms of political discourse that emerged during the 1960s.

This book is both an analytical and a personal book.

Let me conclude with the personal. What I have written is informed as much by my history as it is by my study of the period. I came of age in the 1960s, and in more ways than one. I was involved in the civil rights movement, in the free speech battle at Ohio State, in the black power movement, and in the antiwar protests. During that time I signed petitions, gave speeches, attended long strategy sessions, and participated in sectarian debates. The decade was intensely political, and I—like so many other young people at the time—became intense about my politics.

When the Cambodian invasion occurred and the protests against that invasion seemed to have little effect on President Nixon, I "retired" from active participation in protest. (And I mean the last part of the previous sentence with all the ironic ambiguity that precision in language can muster.) I began instead to teach courses in presidential rhetoric and the rhetoric of American radicalism in my attempts to understand the tumultuous decade I had lived through. Soon thereafter, I added a course in cynicism. Now, two decades later, I focus my efforts on scholarship in my professional field—rhetoric—

to present part of the results of thinking and teaching about the 1960s.

Some of the chapters in this book were first published as independent essays, but each has been revised for this volume. The analysis of Kennedy's rhetoric surrounding the test-ban treaty was previously published in a slightly different form ("Seeking Detente with Superpowers: John F. Kennedy at American University") in *Essays in Presidential Rhetoric*, edited by Theodore Windt with Beth Ingold, 2nd ed., (Dubuque, Iowa: Kendall/Hunt, 1987), pp. 71–84, and is used by permission. The analysis of Kennedy's rhetoric after the Bay of Pigs was previously published in a slightly different form also in *Essays in Presidential Rhetoric*, pp. 77–82, and is used by permission. The chapter on administrative rhetoric first appeared as "Administrative Rhetoric: An Undemocratic Response to Protest" in *Communication Quarterly* 30 (1982): 245–250, and is used by permission.

Chapter 10 on the diatribe requires special mention. A different version was previously published under the title "The Diatribe: Last Resort for Protest" by the *Quarterly Journal of Speech* 58 (February 1972): 1–14. (Used by permission.) However, my thinking about cynicism has changed so much over the years that this chapter is almost an entirely new essay. I had originally believed cynicism to be a form of ideological rhetoric and took that line in the original essay. I no longer believe that. Rather, I now see cynicism as an entirely different kind of thinking from both procedural political thinking and ideological thinking. This new version then incorporates those changes.

There are several people I wish to thank for their encouragement and assistance. James Chesebro and Karlyn K. Campbell read an early draft of the chapters on protest back in 1974 (I believe it was) and offered valuable criticism. More important, the professional encouragement they extended developed into close friendships that have grown over the years. I want to thank Ray E. McKerrow and Robert V. Friedenberg for their careful and insightful critiques of the current manuscript. Mrs. Sally Samuels typed the bibliography and saved me enormous headaches by so doing. Barbara B. Reitt did a superb job of copyediting that not only caught errors but also sharpened style.

Needless to say, none of these is responsible for what is written in the following pages, but I do value greatly their contributions.

The dedication says it all about what I owe to my family, and even that is not enough.

The decade of the 1960s was a time of great passion. Passionate oratory resonated throughout the land. The diversity of events and people created and very nearly exhausted an equally diverse set of rhetorical forms and ideas. This volume attempts to note and examine those many different forms, as well as analyze some of the ideas they contained. I do not presume that these chapters are the final or definitive word on the resounding rhetoric of the period. But I do hope they are a contribution to a better understanding of some things that were thought and spoken during that time.

Theodore Otto Windt, Jr.
Pittsburgh, Pennsylvania

Presidents

1

Presidential Rhetoric
Perspectives

Political rhetoric creates the arena of political reality within which political thought and action take place. Among the politicians who seek to erect this linguistic colosseum, none is more powerful than the president of the United States. In national affairs presidents establish the terms of discourse. Presidents speak with an authority, especially in foreign affairs, that no senator or representative or citizen can match. Moreover, modern presidents have instant access to television to present their messages to the public and thus can set the initial terms for argument about issues and politics. Their messages create the arenas in which others will do rhetorical and political battle.

Equally important, discourse is a source of power for presidents.[1] Contemporary presidents now have the option of "going public" over the head of Congress and directly to the American people to marshal public support for their policies.[2] In doing so, presidents attempt to build the most persuasive case possible for the policies they advocate or the positions they defend. Politics is not an academic seminar. A president is not a distinguished professor occupying an endowed chair of American government. And the primary purpose of presidential rhetoric is not to educate, but to assist in governing, to provide one part of presidential leadership. Every recent presidency has been accused of "news management."[3] Often, this accusation has been made by journalists and others because presidents have presented only their side of an issue before the public. David Gergen, director of communications in the first Reagan administration, answered this criticism succinctly: "Mr. Gergen [said] that, whereas the news media had an obligation to 'describe reality' and air all viewpoints, a president did not. 'He has several responsibilities,' Mr. Gergen said. 'One is to describe reality, and one is to lead.' He then said that Mr. Reagan's use of one-sided anecdotes helped him 'lead, show direction, emphasize and advocate a point of view.'"[4] Such a description of the function of presidential discourse is a distinctly rhetorical description. But it is not merely the use of one-sided anecdotes that makes up presidential rhetoric. It is the entire way in which presidents present their case: from the choice and definition of issues to the political ways in which they describe those issues to the arguments they marshal to support positions to the audiences they choose to address. Giandomenico Majone noted that "public policy is made of language and . . . argument is central in all stages of the policy process."[5]

But political language cannot be used capriciously. Politicians, especially presidents, are both liberated and imprisoned by language. They are free to define issues within the context of their political beliefs, traditions, circumstances, past history, and political affiliations. Once having spoken for the public record, they have to defend their words and the policies that issued from them. Other politicians, journalists, and the public (on occasion) demand consistency. Thus, political language and rhetoric become a two-edged sword.

Two of the most powerful weapons in the rhetorical arsenal of modern presidents are: (1) the power to define issues; and (2) the ethos (or what political scientists call the "prestige") of the presidential office. Let us examine these two in more detail.

The Power of Definition

The starting point for any study of presidential rhetoric is the political definitions that presidents assign to events, policies, and people. These definitions come from presidential beliefs, from unique worldviews, from individual political psychologies, from their political history, from advice given by advisers, and from a multitude of other sources both conscious and not so conscious. Such definitions can reinforce the prevailing view about politics and issues or can modify or change—if the rhetoric is successful—that prevailing view.[6] Presidents may also define an issue in such a way that heightens the importance given one issue over another. Put it another way, political language gives political meaning to events that might otherwise be seen or interpreted outside a political context.

Scholars often talk about television as creating mediated realities. That is, television news, in particular, picks and chooses what events or people to broadcast and thus assigns significance to each. But at a deeper level all language does the same. By choosing to describe an event or an experience with one word or set of words rather than others, a person has chosen to assign a certain meaning to that event or experience rather than other meanings. Specific words and language, in general, provide the link between experience and meaning, and it is the choice of what words to use that creates meaning.

To explain what I mean, let me use a specific example that will serve not only to illustrate my point but also will give an opening perspective on the two chapters on President Kennedy's crisis rhetoric. Let me begin with an examination of the rhetorical nature of political crises.

Crisis is one of those politically evocative words that became popular during the Kennedy years as an inflated description of the making of hard decisions. But *crisis* is only a word, a descriptive word applied to an event or series of events to give them meaning. Events rarely carry their own meaning with them. People use words to apply meaning to events. And *crisis* is a singular word that Kennedy used repeatedly to describe and give meaning to selected events during his administration. What, then, are the characteristics of political crises pertinent to understanding how definition works in rhetoric and to understanding the crisis rhetoric of President Kennedy?

First, *political crises are primarily rhetorical.* Presidents announce to the people, usually over national television, that a situation "critical" to the United States exists. They contend that the situation requires decisive action and call upon Congress and the public for full support. Invariably, the policy advocated is elevated from a political decision to an issue involving world peace (in foreign affairs) or an attack on the public interest (in domestic affairs). Situations rarely create crises. Rather, presidents' perceptions of situations and the rhetoric they use to describe them mark events as crises. Because modern presidents have immediate access to television to give their interpretations of "critical" situations, usually they can implement policies with a minimum of opposition. In fact, a "crisis" speech is often given to announce actions already taken by the president.

The second characteristic of a political crisis is that *presidents can depend on tremendous public support for whatever policy they pursue in situations they deem "critical."* Nelson Polsby observed: "Invariably, the popular response to a President during international crises is favorable, regardless of the wisdom of the policies he pursues."[7] Letters and telegrams will range from 2-1 upward in support of presidents and their actions. People support the president overwhelmingly in these situations because they see the president as the personification of the country.

One can further discern the rhetorical nature of crises by noting the time that elapses between a precipitating event and the "crisis." Generally, dictionaries describe a crisis as a "turning point," "a decisive moment." With the Truman Doctrine speech of March 1947 (surely a crisis speech), three weeks elapsed (February 21–March 12) between the time the British government informed the Truman administration that it could no longer provide aid to Greece in that civil war and the time of Truman's speech. In the Cuban missile crisis, six days passed (October 16 to 22) between the time when President Kennedy was first informed about the missiles and the time of his crisis speech. With President Nixon's Cambodia speech, no concrete timetable can be given about when he received information about a specific external event or set of events that caused his crisis speech. Indeed, only ten days before he announced the invasion of Cambodia, Nixon had assured the American public in a nationally televised address that the policy of Vietnamization was progressing so well that he could withdraw an additional 150,000 troops from Vietnam. If the "events" that provoked the "crisis" had been inherently so critical, there would not have been this long time elapsing between information about those events and the speech— that is, if the situation itself defined the crisis. Certainly, when the Japanese bombed Pearl Harbor, President Roosevelt took only one day before he rushed to Congress to request a declaration of war. *Thus, a "crisis" that does not involve a direct external military attack on the United States is a political event rhetorically created by the president in which the public predictably rallies to his defense.* But only presidents can create such crises, and the reason for that lies in the ethos of the office, the second major weapon in the presidents' rhetorical arsenal.

The Ethos of the Presidency

In the conduct of foreign affairs, the American presidency, originally conceived as a democratic executive office, has evolved into an elected monarchy, a striking example of modern Caesarism. The multitude of writings about the office and the popular perceptions of it have created a reverence for the presidency to the point that the office and the person who occupies it are frequently confused with the true and only destiny of the nation. During the debates about the federal Constitution, Charles Pickney stated that he supported a strong federal executive, but he feared prophetically that extending to the president the powers over war and peace "would render the Executive a monarchy, of the worst kind, to wit an elective one."[8]

In the popular mythology, and even in scholarly circles, the presidents are different from any other political officials. More is expected of them even as less is suspected about them. They personify American government. The president is "President of all the People." In the words of Clinton Rossiter in his popular book on the presidency: "He reigns, but he also rules; he symbolizes the people, but he also runs their government."[9] There is a reverence that surrounds the presidency, and much of this reverence comes from the fact that people believe that the president has superior information and knowledge about national affairs. James MacGregor Burns and Jack W. Peltason, certainly not unsophisticated scholars of the presidency, wax romantic about this aspect of the presidency: "The President has not only the authority but the capacity to act. For example, he has at his command unmatched sources of information. To his desk come facts channeled from the entire world. Diplomatic missions, military observers, undercover agents, personal agents, technical experts gather tons of material which are analyzed by experts in the State Department and elsewhere. Since the President draws on the informed thinking of hundreds of specialists, *his pronouncements have a tone of authority.*"[10] Inherent in these descriptions of the president, regardless of who that person is, is a predisposition to believe the president, a predisposition that does not exist in the same extreme degree for any other official. In the words so often used in letters to editors in newspapers, "the President knows best." The psychology persistent here makes the presidential decisions seem wise and prudent even when they turn out to be stupid. The aura of reverence shapes a "will to believe" presidents when they speak, and more often than not, places the burden of disproving any presidential statement upon those who disagree.[11] George Reedy, former press secretary to President Johnson, concluded: "The President's ability to place his views before the public is important primarily because he can usually set the terms of the national debate— and anyone who can set the terms of debate can win it."[12]

Nowhere are the advantages of presidential rhetoric more dramatically seen than in foreign policy issues that may involve Americans in military conflict. When such events erupt, political definitions, the ethos of the office, and the president's unique rhetorical arsenal converge to create a mighty force for action. A brief explanation may clarify what I mean.

The conventional view of the Constitution is that Congress declares war and presidents make war through their powers as commander in chief. The corollary is that presidents can commit American military to conflicts only after Congress declares war.[13] However, the legal status of the presidential warmaking powers is not so simple.

Supreme Court decisions have greatly expanded the president's powers in ways that impinge on rhetoric and also depend on rhetoric. The most significant of these decisions was the decision rendered in the *Prize* cases argued before the Court between February 10 and 25, 1863. The constitutional issue in this case that concerns us was President Lincoln's authority to commit acts of war (the blockade of southern ports) for three months prior to Congress's declaration of war on July 13, 1861. By a 5–4 decision, the Court proclaimed: "If a war be made by invasion of a foreign nation, the President is not only authorized but bound to resist force by force. He does not initiate the war, but is bound to accept the challenge without waiting for any special legislative authority."[14] This landmark decision set a precedent for presidents to wage defensive wars without waiting for declarations from Congress.

Over the years presidential power in this area has greatly expanded. The authority claimed by President Truman to commit troops to Korea, where the United States had not been invaded by a foreign nation, was most important. The legal rationale for Truman's actions were spelled out by the Department of State: "The President, as Commander in Chief of the Armed Forces of the United States, has full control over the use thereof. He also has authority to conduct the foreign relations of the United States. Since the beginning of United States history, he has, on numerous occasions, utilized these powers in sending armed forces abroad."[15] These claims that form the basis of modern presidential authority to commit troops in support of foreign policy objectives were claimed on the basis of plenary presidential power and inherent powers independent of Congress. Rossiter concluded: "The entry into Korea was an unalloyed act of independent power."[16]

During the 1960s presidents expanded this warmaking power through additional grants of authority or through claims of inherent power based on these precedents.[17] In doing so, they made a prophet of James M. Carlisle, who argued against President Lincoln's assertion of authority in the *Prize* cases. He stated that the argument for deciding that the president had acted legally was "founded upon a figure of speech, which is repugnant to the genius of republican institutions and . . . to our written Constitution." In his prophetic mood, he concluded: "It makes the President . . . the impersonation of the country, and invokes for him the power and right to use all the forces he can command to *'save the life of the nation.'* The principle of self-defense is asserted, and all power is claimed for the President. This is to assert that the Constitution contemplated and tacitly provided that the President should be dictator, and all constitutional government be at an end whenever he should think that 'the life of the nation' is in danger."[18] Regardless of what one thinks about the decisions of the Supreme Court and subsequent presidents' warmaking actions, one cannot escape recognizing the role *definition* plays in the assumption of authority and the need for a persuasive (rhetorical) justification for that definition. And since the *Prize* cases established the president's authority to act defensively, presidents have found an irresistible justification in the argument that they are acting "to protect American lives that are in danger."[19] Buttressed by the immense prestige and mystique of the ethos of the office, such arguments are compelling. In foreign policy, especially during the 1960s, these propositions provided presidents with enormous latitude for action.

But even as we assert the importance of the discourse presidents use, we also have to confront questions about the authenticity of that discourse. Is it actually the president's words or only the words of professional speechwriters put in the president's mouth? Is the rhetoric intended to reflect accurately the ideas and policies of the administration or is it "mere rhetoric" intended to distort reality and fool the public? These are serious questions that require serious answers.

Speechwriters and the Authenticity of Presidential Discourse

Speechwriting has become a contentious issue in scholarship on presidential rhetoric.[20] The conventional wisdom is that speeches written for presidents are inauthentic, that they are merely words put into presidents' mouths that presidents dutifully mouth. That is an important problem for the critic of presidential rhetoric, and it should be confronted directly.

The conventional wisdom says that no one can write faithfully or truly for another, and therefore rhetorical transactions between a president and the public are corrupted when the president does not write his own speeches. This view finds an impressive advocate in Roderick Hart in his book *The Sound of Leadership.* He even goes so far as to call these "speeches-for-hire" and voices prevailing conventional attitudes by writing:

Most of the speeches analyzed in this book [*The Sound of Leadership*] were the products of ad hoc thinking, not careful deliberation. They were delivered by persons who had no time to write their own speeches and hence who could never fully embrace the thoughts they spoke, thereby producing the mechanical speech-for-hire often observed here. These speeches rarely have the marks of thoughts newly thought or of passions recently felt because they were produced according to a formula and adjusted to a political calender. There is an interminable sameness to them, a lack of what the ancient rhetoricians called "invention." The setting of a speech now dictates what a president will say. Or presidential staffs do. Or audience composition does. Or political traditions do. Or media coverage does. The thoughts and feelings *of presidents themselves* rarely do.[21]

Hart concludes: "Each day, presidents are instructed by their staffs to think of how audience predispositions can be exploited rather than of how citizens' needs can be met."[22]

One who would write seriously about presidential speeches has to answer some of these conventional simplicities. First of all, presidential speeches are not given merely to hoodwink the public. They have many purposes. One purpose certainly is to persuade people to support a president in a policy decision or when a president is defending himself. But the public is not the only audience for a major speech. Allies and adversaries are also listening, and listening carefully to speeches on foreign policy. Members of the president's own administration are listening to speeches on domestic issues trying to determine what the president wants them to do in their departments or agencies.

Nowhere was this more directly noted than by Donald Regan, President Reagan's secretary of the treasury during the first administration: "In the four years I served as Secretary of the Treasury I never saw President Reagan alone and never discussed economic philosophy or fiscal and monetary policy with him one-on-one. From the first day to the last at Treasury, I was flying by the seat of my pants. The President never told me what he believed or what he wanted to accomplish in the field of economics. I had to figure these things out like any other American, *by studying his speeches* and reading the newspapers."[23] If the secretary of the treasury had to learn what the president wanted him to do on the most pressing issues facing the administration by studying the president's speeches, how could he have carried out a coherent policy if the president were merely attempting to exploit public predispositions instead of explaining policies? And if the secretary of the treasury, a major official in the Reagan administration, had to resort to these means for getting direction, what about the secretaries of lesser departments and the heads of various agencies with whom the president rarely, if ever, met? It is this audience that Hart ignores when voicing his skepticism about presidential rhetoric. As any speechwriter knows, writing a speech for a public official means putting that official on the record and sending specific messages to members of the administration or to other branches of government about the intentions and policies of the public official.

Furthermore, presidents and other officials in the public arena know that, in this age of media politics, speeches have become the major standard of accountability for public officials. Lyndon Johnson lost credibility because he "mis-stated" himself in public, and his promise "not to send American boys to do the fighting that Asian boys ought to do for themselves" in Vietnam was repeatedly thrown in his face.[24] On May 22, 1973, Richard Nixon issued his definitive statement saying that he had not attempted to implicate the CIA in Watergate nor had he tried to cover up the Watergate scandal. That statement and his denials became the standard used by various congressional committees as they tried to unravel the scandal. When it was shown that Nixon had lied, the House Committee on the Judiciary voted to impeach the president.[25] So, too, President Reagan's problems with the Congress and the public exploded because he had said he would never bargain with terrorists. When it was learned in 1986 that he had condoned an "arms for hostages" deal with the Iranians, he lost support. These are only a few dramatic examples of how their public statements have come back to haunt presidents. And these statements came back because journalists, politicians, and the public took them seriously and took them to be truthful. Quite simply, prominent politicians are today held more accountable than almost any other group in America. Their public rhetoric has become one major standard by which they are held accountable. In this new age presidents (and even presidential candidates) who deliberately lie in public statements or deliberately attempt to distort beyond the limits of plausible partisan argument run the risk of having their credibility as leaders damaged or destroyed. The fantasy meetings of presidents and their staffs *each day* to figure out how to manipulate the public does not occur in the way in which Hart describes it.

But let me not leave an impression of naive idealism. Staff members concerned with communications or speechwriting do meet to try to figure out ways to get a message out in the most publicized and most persuasively favorable manner. When difficult situations develop, they do meet to see how they can put the best face on a bad situation. That is part of what rhetoric is all about. Even Demosthenes knew that. Sometimes, they succeed. Sometimes, they fail. Sometimes, they get their facts right. Sometimes, they don't.

Even more to the point, the executive branch of government is different from the other two branches. From our courts we expect majority and dissenting opinions. From Congress we expect partisan battles as Democrats and Republicans give different versions of bills before them and therefore different arguments to sustain their versions. But the executive branch is headed by one person—the president. All others in the executive work under that one person. One goal of every contemporary president is to have a single, consistent message coming from the White House. After all, it is the president's policies that other members of the administration are expected to carry out, not their own policies. They have not been elected. The president bears primary and sole responsibility for the policies and authoritative messages of the White House. Little wonder, then, presidents do not want conflicting statements coming from other members of the administration.[26] Beginning with President Nixon, contemporary presidents have used the Office of Communication to establish this consistency.[27] To attribute base motives to people for trying to do their jobs is to issue a blanket indictment without qualifications or specificity. It is argument from principle rather than argument from example.

Some—especially Hart—who use the existence of speechwriters to condemn the corruption of political discourse find themselves in muddled waters when they have to deal with specific speeches to demonstrate this corruption. For example, Hart contrasts an eloquent speech by President Johnson (the "voters' rights" speech to Congress on March 15, 1965) with the usual run of presidential speeches to show that genuine eloquence can be achieved:

[Johnson] was eloquent [on this occasion] despite *his* homespun imagery and ordinary language. He was eloquent because on this occasion *he* shook loose the cobwebs of *his* highly political mind and thereby risked audience disfavor. *He* linked *his* intellect with *his* words and then with *his* feelings and urged his suspicious, sometimes hostile, listeners to throw off their old ways and to reach for something new and better. . . .

One senses in *his* remarks a special kind of rhetorical sensitivity because *he* knew how difficult it would be for many of his listeners to accept what *he* had to say.[28]

After lavishly praising and quoting from this eloquent speech, Hart goes on to castigate presidential speechmaking since 1945 as a product of ad hoc thinking and as speeches for hire.

However, the reality of the creation of this speech is quite different. President Johnson's great speech was not written by him, but by Richard Goodwin in an eight-hour burst of writing on the day it was delivered. According to Goodwin, only one draft was done, and it was so rushed that there was little time for consultation with the president or for revisions in the draft, an unusual occurrence in speechwriting.[29] By his account, it was an ad hoc speech dictated by the occasion and written by a speechwriter without revisions. And yet Hart is correct: It was eloquent and it captured precisely Lyndon Johnson's commitment to equal rights under the law.

Let me not be too harsh on Hart or others who have suspicions of speechwriters. There is a very real problem that scholars have to contend with. Speechwriters, for obvious reasons, seldom are willing to talk about what they do or how they do it.[30] Conversely, few scholars ever have tried their hand at political speechwriting; fewer still have been professional speechwriters. Thus, they are denied the primary evidence or experiences they use in other areas of scholarship to form considered judgments. Let me quote directly from Richard Goodwin about how the process works:

It is not the prerogative of the speechwriter to insert his own ideas, mannerisms, and sensibilities into the president's mouth, to make him something other than what he is. Indeed, it can't be done. Not well. Not without sacrificing all hopes of effective eloquence. The gap between the man and his expression cannot be concealed and, inevitably, degrades the quality of the performance to the memolike prose that is now so dominant in American life. On the other hand, my job was not limited to guessing what the president might say exactly as he would express it, but to heighten and polish—illuminate, as it were—his inward beliefs and natural idiom, to attain not a strained mimicry, but an authenticity of expression. I would not have written the same speech in the same way for Kennedy or any other politician, or for myself. It was by me, but it was for and of the Lyndon Johnson I had carefully studied and come to know.[31]

This is not only an impressive statement about how Goodwin worked to write an eloquent speech for Johnson, it is also an accurate statement about how political speechwriters generally work to write speeches for others.

I have spent considerable space on speechwriting because I am disturbed by the misconceptions that abound about what speechwriters do.[32] And I am concerned with the critical processes. If the text of a speech a critic is studying is not authentic—even in the sense that Goodwin uses the word *authentic*—then how authentic can criticism of those speeches be? In these essays on presidential rhetoric I have taken the public statements as authentic discourse between the president and the public and tried to hold presidents accountable for what they have said, all the while recognizing the ambiguity that is inherent in some uses of language and argument.

Conclusion

The basic principle upon which these chapters rest is: *"Political discourse creates the framework within which political thought and action proceed."*[33] In other words, I take the public language, arguments, and rhetoric that people involved in politics use as a guide to their thought and action. The skeptic might say that such a position is to be expected of a rhetorician, of someone who has devoted much of his professional life to studying political discourse. The skeptic might add that political rhetoric, especially as used by officials in power, is merely a screen to mask real intentions, a soothing public relations set of gimmicks to fool the gullible, or a cynical manipulation of lies and half-truths to maintain power. For a professional rhetorician to respond to such beliefs may seem a special form of special pleading. Therefore, let me turn to the historian Michael H. Hunt and quote him at length as he states with remarkable clarity the position I share:

> But such a skeptical view may be too clever by half. Public rhetoric is not simply a screen, tool, or ornament. It is also, perhaps even primarily, a form of communication, rich in symbols and mythology and closely constrained by certain rules. To be effective, public rhetoric must draw on values and concerns widely shared and easily understood by its audience. A rhetoric that ignores or eschews the language of common discourse on the central problems of the day closes itself off as a matter of course from any sizable audience, limiting its own influence. If a rhetoric fails to reflect the speaker's genuine views on fundamental issues, it runs the risk over time of creating false public expectations, and lays the basis for politically dangerous misunderstanding. If it indulges in blatant inconsistency, it eventually pays the price of diminished force and credibility. Public rhetoric is tainted evidence for the historian seeking a widely shared ideology only when it violates these rules and falls unpersuasively on the ears of its ostensible audience. Indeed, comparisons of public rhetoric with private statements, a sensitive test that cynics might justifiably insist on, suggest that the policy elite do recognize the cost of violating these rules and do generally observe them.[34]

It is this perspective that is taken in the chapters that follow.

The next two chapters concern President Kennedy's uses of crisis rhetoric during his administration, the issues he applied it to and the times when it was applied. President Kennedy's rhetoric deserves extended treatment because he used so many different forms of presidential rhetoric and because he set the themes for a decade. I divided this examination of Kennedy's rhetoric into two separate chapters to draw as dramatically as possible the differences between the ways in which Kennedy treated issues rhetorically during his first two years and his last year. During the years 1961–1962 Kennedy saw issues in crisis terms, with the exception of events concerning civil rights. In the final year he changed the direction of his administration by trying to wind down the critical atmosphere he had created in Soviet-American relations. At the same time he began to recognize the growing force of the civil rights movement and eventually placed the full force of the presidency behind that movement. It was as if there were two different Kennedy administrations, and so they are considered separately.

The third chapter concerns a neglected rhetorical event of great importance to the presidency of Lyndon Johnson and to the history of the United States, his announcement of our escalation of American participation in the war in Vietnam. "Americanizing the Vietnam War: President Johnson's Press Conference of July 28, 1965" is my small contribution to the study of Johnson's rhetoric. Kathleen J. Turner's excellent book *Lyndon Johnson's Dual War* and David Zarefky's comprehensive essays and his book *Lyndon Johnson's War on Poverty* seem to me to cover Johnson so well that my essay is merely a footnote to their work.

"Understanding Richard Nixon" takes a very different approach to presidential rhetoric. In this chapter Nixon's public statements are used to develop a psychological study of the political Nixon. Even though I have not developed the theory very fully, I believe that one can predict a president's general uses of rhetoric by studying the kinds of rhetoric used in the prepresidential years. In this chapter I attempt to show that the campaign rhetoric Nixon developed in his prepresidential years carried over into the first part of his administration, making his promise to "bring us together" merely another unkept campaign promise. I also try to get at another way of analyzing the psychology of presidents beyond the Freudian-influenced psychobiographies and histories. In this age of televised politics, politicians now have created public personalities that are at least as important as their private personalities, and they have had public or political experiences that are as traumatic and influential in forming those public personalities as their childhood experiences were. If I am correct, then standard psychoanalytic methods are less useful in probing the psyches of public figures than we generally assume. This examination of Nixon is an initial step in developing another method for understanding Richard Nixon, this time from a rhetorical viewpoint stressing his public persona.

These chapters form the first section of this book. They are informed by an admonition from Hunt: "Interpretive naivete may reside not in taking rhetoric seriously but rather in failing to listen carefully for its recurrent themes and values."[35] It is the recurrent themes, values, and policies that are taken with critical seriousness in this examination of presidential rhetoric.

2

The Crisis Rhetoric of
President John F. Kennedy
The First Two Years

John F. Kennedy's presidency was a *crisis* presidency. If one reads
Theodore Sorensen's or Arthur Schlesinger's accounts of the Kennedy administration, one will soon learn about the Laos crisis, the
crisis in the Congo, the balance-of-payments crisis, the steel crisis,
the Cuban missiles crisis, the civil rights crisis, and so on and on. In
fact, Sorensen lists no fewer than fifteen crises the Kennedy administration faced in the *first eight months* it was in office.[1]

In his first State of the Union address Kennedy warned Congress
that the nation was entering a period of persistent crises, especially
in international relations: "Each day the crises multiply. Each day
their solution grows more difficult. Each day we draw nearer the
hour of maximum danger, as weapons spread and hostile forces grow
stronger."[2] Crisis—both in domestic and foreign affairs—was the
theme of the Kennedy administration and set the tone for his leadership. Beyond that, Kennedy's insistence on crises helped establish
the political atmosphere for the entire decade.

This is an examination of the crisis rhetoric of President John F.
Kennedy. Central to its thrust is the belief that the "crises" in the
postwar period seldom were actual events, but rather that they were
descriptions of events that the president had chosen—from a multitude of possible events or actions—to accentuate for Congress and
the public as critical. Furthermore, these "crises" were often more a
threat to a president's political leadership or his policies than they
were to the nation as a whole. Thus, recognizing the rhetorical

nature of "crises" and the "events" that precipitated them is essential to understanding and analyzing the rhetoric that accompanied them.

More specifically, this chapter is concerned with President John F. Kennedy's use of various forms of rhetoric that either created or sought to diffuse situations he saw as posing threats to his leadership or to the nation. To understand the president's uses of these rhetorical forms requires a brief examination of several incidents in the 1960 campaign that set the stage for his perception of events during his administration. It also requires an examination of Kennedy's inaugural address, which contributed to the atmosphere of threat and urgency. The bulk of this chapter, however, is devoted to the major speeches Kennedy delivered—both on foreign and domestic affairs—that addressed what he perceived as crises.

The substance of Kennedy's rhetoric is important because he set the themes for a generation of presidents during his brief, tragic tenure in office. Equally important, Kennedy used a wide range of rhetorical forms that other contemporary presidents have found frequent occasions to use or emulate. In this sense, Kennedy provides one model of presidential speeches in the 1960s, especially crisis speeches.

But it should also be noted that Kennedy rarely relied on televised speeches as an instrument of governing. He had no long-range plan for utilizing the rhetorical dimension of the presidency effectively. In fact, he preferred press conferences to nationally televised speeches. According to Sorensen, the president "saw no sense in dividing the country, or alienating the Congress, or squandering his limited political capital, or feeding the fires of extremism, or wearing out his welcome and credibility, by making major appeals for public support" through televised speeches.[3] When he did use television in this way—such as his report to the nation on the Berlin crisis or his address about the missiles in Cuba—he heightened the drama and urgency of these situations in ways that previous presidents could not. With the Kennedy presidency the exaggerated ethos attached to the office combined with Kennedy's exceptional rhetoric and the emergence of television to create a "crisis" presidency.

But for the most part, his uses of important speeches during his administration were reactive, not proactive. That is, he often gave his speeches, especially during his first two years in office, to respond to actions by others rather than to shape public opinion for future action of his own. His early speeches then became discrete rhetorical acts occasioned by some event or events to which the president responded. It was not until the third year that President Kennedy began to realize how speeches could be used to form a climate of favorable public opinion in preparation for policy initiatives. His most effective use of presidential speeches came in 1963, beginning with his address at American University that paved the way for the limited nuclear test-ban treaty, and these speeches will be analyzed extensively.

Before proceeding to an analysis of President Kennedy's crisis rhetoric, I need to provide a brief summary of several events in the 1960 presidential campaign to place the rhetoric of his administration in political context.

Background: The 1960 Presidential Campaign

In accepting the Democratic nomination for president in 1960, John Kennedy promised to usher in the era of the New Frontier. He said the New Frontier was "not a set of promises," but a "set of challenges." In seeking his claim to the presidency, Kennedy faced two major challenges of his own. First, he had to overcome the lead Richard Nixon enjoyed at the outset of the campaign; and second, he had to say what he would do about the "communist menace" in Cuba, only ninety miles from our shores.

The rhetorical high point of the campaign was a series of four televised debates between the two candidates, of which the first was the most important. More than 70 million Americans viewed that first debate. In it, Kennedy demonstrated that he had a grasp of the issues equal to that of Vice President Nixon, thus diminishing Nixon's claim to superior experience in government, one of Nixon's central campaign themes. Equally important was the contrast in appearance between the two candidates. Nixon looked pale and wan next to the suntanned and vigorous Kennedy. The consensus of those who saw the debate was that Kennedy had won handily. Public opinion polls showed a shift among voters, especially those undecided, toward Kennedy. Although the race remained close, the "Great Debates" were a turning point, when Kennedy shed his underdog role and gained momentum in the campaign.[4]

Although much attention has been devoted to the appearances of the two candidates during the first debate, less attention has been given to what was said. For our purposes, Kennedy's opening statement is revealing of his mind-set about the Soviet challenge to Western democracies. In that statement, which he had carefully prepared, Kennedy said:

In the election of 1860, Abraham Lincoln said the question was whether this Nation could exist half slave and half free.

In the election of 1960, and with the world around us, the question is whether the world will exist half slave or half free, whether it will move in the direction of freedom, in the direction of the road that we are taking or whether it will move in the direction of slavery.

I think it will depend in great measure upon what we do here in the United States, on the kind of society that we build, on the kind of strength that we maintain.

We discuss tonight domestic issues, but I would not want that to be—any implication to be given that this does not involve directly our struggle with Mr. Khrushchev *for survival*. . . .

If we do well here [in the United States], if we meet our obligations, if we are moving ahead, then I think freedom will be secure around the world. If we fail, then freedom fails.[5]

The importance of this statement is twofold. First, Kennedy divided the world into two warring camps: one of free people and one of slaves. It was a classic description of political confrontation drawing its sustenance as much from the Truman and Eisenhower foreign policies toward the Soviet Union as from the anticommunist mentality of the postwar period. Second, Kennedy heightened the urgency of the contest between these warring powers by contending that America's very survival was at stake. Not only America's survival, but the survival of the entire free world hung in the balance. It was extravagant statements such as these repeated throughout the campaign that created the atmosphere of crisis that his administration would act upon. And one place where that contest would be joined was in Cuba.

Castro's Cuba played a major role in the campaign. Ever since Fidel Castro had come to power little more than a year before, Americans had voiced serious concerns about the establishment of a communist regime "only ninety miles from our shores." For Kennedy, Cuba became an example of the failure of the Eisenhower administration's foreign policy toward communism. On October 6—a day before the second televised debate between the two presidential candidates—Kennedy delivered an important address in Cincinnati, Ohio, devoted solely to the issue of Cuba. He began with a hard-line assessment of the Cuban situation:

I want to talk with you tonight about the most glaring failure of American foreign policy today—about a disaster that threatens the security of the whole Western Hemisphere—about a Communist menace that has been permitted to arise under our very noses, only 90 miles from our shores. I am talking about the one friendly island that our own shortsighted policies helped make communism's first Caribbean base: the island of Cuba.

Two years ago—in September of 1958—bands of bearded rebels descended from Cuba's Sierra Maestra Mountains and began their long march on Havana—a march which ended in the overthrow of the brutal, bloody, and despotic dictatorship of Fulgencio Batista. . . .

But in the 2 years since that revolution swept Fidel Castro into power, those promises have all been broken. There have been no free elections—and there will be none as long as Castro rules.[6]

Kennedy went on to detail the threat Castro posed not only to the United States and Latin American countries but to the world as well. The Cincinnati speech was jingoistic and right wing. Even some of Kennedy's advisers objected to it. But the speech was delivered, and after that, the principal question was what to do about the threat Castro posed. On October 20 Kennedy answered that question with a statement on Cuba. The third point of the statement was particularly revealing: "[W]e must attempt to strengthen the non-Batista democratic anti-Castro forces in exile, and in Cuba itself, who offer eventual hope of overthrowing Castro. Thus far these fighters for freedom have had virtually no support from our Government."[7] This commitment to assist in the overthrow of Castro would lead directly to the disastrous Bay of Pigs invasion, which crippled Kennedy's presidency in its infancy, and to the other more dangerous crises that would follow.

The 1960 presidential contest between Kennedy and Nixon resulted in the closest election of the twentieth century. Although Kennedy won 303 electoral college votes, he defeated Nixon by only one-tenth of 1 percent of the popular vote. Kennedy gained the presidency, but he did not gain a mandate from the people. Indeed, his narrow victory would be one severe political constraint on his ability to act once he assumed office.

It may be helpful at this point to preview how these two chapters will proceed. This first chapter begins with the inaugural address, which set many of the themes of the administration and exemplifies Kennedy's style at its best. The chapter proceeds in chronological order through the events that provoked Kennedy's crisis rhetoric and responses: the Bay of Pigs fiasco, the Berlin "crisis," the steel "crisis" of 1962, and the Cuban missile "crisis." The next chapter then considers how Kennedy sought to wind down his crisis rhetoric about Soviet-American relations and move to a more pragmatic interpretation of those relations.

Omitted from this original chronology are Kennedy's speeches on civil rights, which are also treated in the next chapter. To introduce the civil rights issues in their chronological sequence would be to disrupt the relationship among these different crises. Furthermore, there was a great change in Kennedy's rhetoric in 1963. During the first two years he treated the leading issues he chose to address in formal speeches as "crisis" issues, especially in the realm of foreign policy. But in the third year, after the midterm election, he sought to wind down this crisis rhetoric in foreign affairs. Civil rights is examined separately because Kennedy treated this issue in the reverse of other issues. During the first two years he seldom spoke on the issue. But when he was forced to do so, he did not treat it as a crisis. In his speech on integration at the University of Mississippi, he defined the issue as a legal issue and strove to defuse the powerful emotions that James Meredith's admission to the university aroused. However, after the midterm election he changed. In 1963, when he had to confront the obstruction of Governor George Wallace over integration of the University of Alabama, Kennedy raised the issue to "crisis" proportions. The contrast between these two important civil rights speeches again dramatically illustrates this change in Kennedy's rhetoric. Kennedy's rhetorical management of civil rights demonstrates his slow evolution from regarding it as a pragmatic political issue to raising it to the level of a moral crisis of American society.

Thus, this chapter advances chronologically from inauguration to the Cuban missile crisis. The next chapter picks up the analysis with the test-ban treaty and then doubles back to consider Kennedy's handling of civil rights.

The Presidency

Inauguration: January 20, 1961

On January 20, 1961, John Fitzgerald Kennedy delivered one of the few memorable inaugural addresses in American history. Although a number of people contributed to the final version, Theodore Sorensen was the principal writer of the address.[8] Sorensen had been with Kennedy during both his Senate years and during the presidential campaign. As a speechwriter, Sorensen held a unique position. Not only was he the primary writer for most of Kennedy's important speeches, he was also a close adviser, confidant, and at times, alter ego. Seldom has a speechwriter had as much influence in an administration as Sorensen had in the Kennedy administration.

Kennedy's reputation as a speaker of uncommon ability rests primarily on his inaugural address. In substance and style, it is the best representative of Kennedy's rhetoric. The speech is a mixture of *idealism* and *crisis*. Being the first president born in the twentieth century, Kennedy proclaimed that the torch of leadership had been passed to a new generation "born in this century, tempered by war, disciplined by a hard and bitter peace, proud of our ancient heritage—and unwilling to witness or permit the slow undoing of those human rights to which this nation has always been committed, and to which we are committed today at home and around the world."[9] In his most memorable and idealistic phrase, he called upon Americans to "ask not what your country can do for you—ask what you can do for your country."

Critics of Kennedy's inaugural address point out that Kennedy had spent the entire campaign arguing that the national government was not doing enough for people and should do more, such as provide medical care for the aged, increase the minimum wage, act against poverty in America, and assure civil rights for blacks. Patrick Anderson wrote that the inaugural address moved from "pose to pose" in a litany of "banalities." About this most memorable phrase, Anderson concluded: "The only man in recent presidential politics who could legitimately have admonished the nation to 'ask not what your country can do for you' was Barry Goldwater, who really wanted individuals to do more and the government to do less."[10] However, Anderson's opinion remains a minority opinion. Most who responded to this clarion call believed the new president was calling them to patriotic public service, rather than presenting a philosophy of government policy. Certainly, the rush to join the Peace Corps during Kennedy's administration attests to this reading of the celebrated passage.

The style of the speech enhanced this idealistic challenge. Successive paragraphs begin with parallelisms: "Let both sides explore," "Let both sides . . . formulate," "Let both sides seek." Rhythmic alliterations abound: "bear any burden, pay any price." Finally, the most distinctive device marking the Kennedy style, the balanced and antithetical sentences or phrases: "Let us never negotiate out of fear. But let us never fear to negotiate."

As for Kennedy's grand style, there still remains controversy. For example, James Golden wrote: "Kennedy, in sum, was a connoisseur of the written word designed to produce a persuasive effect. His love of ideas that have permanent relevance and his use of a clear, concise, and vivid style gave evolutionary power to his discourses."[11] On the other hand, there is Garry Wills, not known for great affection for the Kennedys. In concluding *The Kennedy Imprisonment*, Wills compared Kennedy's speeches with those of Martin Luther King, Jr.: "The famous antitheses and alliterations of John Kennedy's rhetoric sound tinny now. But King's eloquence endures."[12] Whether one agrees with one or the other of these assessments may depend on one's taste in oratorical style. Undoubtedly, one additional reason for its acclaim was how starkly and favorably Kennedy's speeches compared with those of his predecessor. Eisenhower's speeches were prosaic and uninspiring, often lending themselves more to parody than praise.[13] At the time, however, Kennedy's inaugural address struck a responsive chord in the public, both for its grand style and its idealism.

But the idealism of the address was counterbalanced by an acute sense of critical urgency about the state of the world, in stark contrast to posture of the Eisenhower administration. Kennedy had a far different view of the world and thus a far different message. Kennedy expressed this new view in somber words: "In the long history of the world, only a few generations have been granted the role of defending freedom in its hour of maximum danger. I do not shrink from that responsibility—I welcome it." The ominous words—*maximum danger*—were not intended as a rhetorical flourish or exaggeration, as his later rhetoric and actions would amply demonstrate. Indeed, his promises to do something about overthrowing Castro and his belief that Americans actually lived in a time of maximum danger would join to put him on the road to the Bay of Pigs crisis, the Berlin crisis, the creation of the Green Berets, and the introduction of more advisers into Vietnam, and would eventually culminate in the Cuban missile crisis, when he took the world to the brink overlooking the abyss of nuclear war. The poet Carl Sandburg rightly observed about Kennedy's inaugural address: "Around nearly every sentence of it could be written a thesis, so packed is it with implications."[14]

The euphoria created by the inaugural address did not last long. In his first State of the Union address Kennedy presented a laundry list of measures he wished Congress to enact. However, he was to be sorely disappointed. Still dominated by the old seniority system and unimpressed by Kennedy's narrow victory in the election, Congress was in no mood to enact these programs.[15] And the disastrous Bay of Pigs invasion, an invasion personally approved by the president, ended any honeymoon period with Congress that the president might have hoped for.

The Bay of Pigs: April 1961

On April 17, 1961, 1,400 anti-Castro Cubans attempted to invade Cuba at Zapata swamp in the Bay of Pigs. The invaders were quickly captured or killed, with only a few escaping.[16] Just as quickly the world learned that the Kennedy administration had armed and transported the Cubans to the Bay of Pigs, and that the United States had given both approval and active support to the abortive attempt to overthrow Castro. When these facts became known, both Republicans and Democrats, adversaries and allies, criticized the invasion. Clearly, less than three months after he had assumed the presidency, Kennedy had a full-scale military and political disaster on his hands. To repair, or at least to contain, some of the damage done by the failed operation, President Kennedy delivered two important speeches devoted to the American failure in Cuba. In each speech Kennedy was on the defensive, and his rhetoric was constructed to defend his administration and his actions.

KENNEDY'S SPEECH TO NEWSPAPER EDITORS.   On April 20 Kennedy sought to justify the invasion of Cuba in a hastily written speech before the American Society of Newspaper Editors.[17] He opened by saying: "The President of a great democracy such as ours and the editors of great newspapers such as yours, owe a common obligation to the people: an obligation to present the facts, to present them with candor, and to present them in perspective."[18] But even as he stated this as his purpose, Kennedy immediately went on to distort the facts, evade responsibility, and lie about American involvement: "I have emphasized before that this was a struggle of Cuban patriots against a Cuban dictator. While we could not be expected to hide our sympathies, we made it repeatedly clear that the armed forces of this country would not intervene in any way." These words are incredible. The invasion had been planned by the CIA, and the CIA had trained the Cuban invaders. American ships had carried the invaders to Cuba, and American planes had carried out air strikes over Cuba. In fact, an American flyer had been killed in these operations. These statements by the president were not statements of "fact" and "candor," but highly misleading.[19]

But the president continued with this line of defense to soothe his liberal critics: "Any unilateral American intervention, in the absence of an external attack upon ourselves or an ally, would have been contrary to our traditions and to our international obligations." The only conceivable reason for these blatant misstatements of fact and intention had to be Kennedy's sensitivity to the protests by allies and domestic liberals over intervention in Cuba. This short sentence was aimed at pacifying them.

But with the next sentence, Kennedy turned his attention to his conservative critics and to the Russians:

Should it ever appear that the inter-American doctrine of noninterference merely conceals or excuses a policy of nonaction—if the nations of this Hemisphere should fail to meet their commitments against outside Communist penetration—then I want it clearly understood that this Government will not hesitate in meeting its primary obligations which are the security of our Nation!

Should that time ever come, we do not intend to be lectured on "intervention" by those whose character was stamped for all time on the bloody streets of Budapest!

Thus, in the course of three short paragraphs, Kennedy had denied American involvement in the invasion (which he had previously taken personal responsibility for), stated a principle of nonintervention (a misrepresentation of what had occurred but useful nonetheless to soothe his liberal critics), and then turned a complete about-face and threatened to intervene without hesitation if he decided to do so in the future (a provocative threat intended to show his conservative critics that he could be tough on communism). He even drew upon the Soviet invasion of Hungary as an analogy for these threats against Cuba and presumably any other Latin American country that might flirt with communism.

Although this section of the speech makes little logical sense, it makes considerable political sense. Kennedy was being attacked from all sides and needed to protect himself from his critics. Therefore, the president made contradictory statements to appeal for support from different and opposing audiences. In this section, then, there's something for everyone, depending on what one might be listening for.

Next, Kennedy moved from the particular issue of Cuba and the threat it posed to the Western Hemisphere to the general issue of communism and the threat it posed to the world. Kennedy treated the disaster as if it were a learning experience in the course of his political education. He drew three lessons to be learned (by whom was unclear in the speech) from the fiasco:

First, it is clear that the forces of communism are not to be underestimated in Cuba or anywhere else in the world. . . .

Secondly, it is clear that this nation . . . must take an ever closer and more realistic look at the menace of external Communist intervention and domination in Cuba. . . .

Third, and finally, it is clearer than ever that we face a relentless struggle in every corner of the globe that goes far beyond the clash of armies or even nuclear armaments.

These "lessons" were hardly new or profound. In fact, they are just more jingoistic words about the monolithic communist threat to the world, certainly little new that the general public had to grasp. Who, for example, had ever "underestimated" the threat of communism? In fact, the United States had just emerged from a period in which the communist threat—especially domestic communism—had been grossly exaggerated, a period we now call the McCarthy era. Furthermore, *who* had not taken a "closer look" at the "menace of external Communist intervention and domination in Cuba" than Kennedy and the American people ever since Castro came to power? Literally thousands of editorials and articles had been written about the threat of communism "only 90 miles off our shores." And finally *who* in that staunchly anticommunist period had not thought it clear that the United States faced a "relentless struggle in every corner of the globe"? That had been the abiding assumption and cornerstone of both the Truman and Eisenhower foreign policies, and was now becoming the central motivating force in Kennedy's foreign policy. Kennedy's words taught no lessons but, rather, read back the most strident moralisms of the then-current anticommunist textbooks. In fact, Kennedy's speech was not that far removed from the hysterical writings of the John Birch Society when it engaged in strident denunciations of communism.

Kennedy concluded his address by returning to one of the main themes of his inaugural address: we live in a time of maximum danger. But now, he spelled out the extent of that danger:

We dare not fail to see the insidious nature of this new and deeper struggle [with the communist world]. We dare not fail to grasp the new concepts, the new tools, the new sense of urgency we will need to combat it—whether in Cuba or South Viet-Nam. And we dare not fail to realize that this struggle is taking place every day, without fanfare, in thousands of villages and markets—day and night—and in classrooms all over the globe.

The message of Cuba, of Laos, of the rising din of Communist voices in Asia and Latin America—these messages are all the same. The complacent, the self-indulgent, the soft societies are about to be swept away with the debris of history. Only the strong, only the industrious, only the courageous, only the visionary who determine the real nature of our struggle can possibly survive.

Richard J. Walton pointed out the apocalyptic nature of Kennedy's language and vision and noted that it represented a continuation of the Acheson-Dulles view of the world: "Kennedy, after the humiliation of the Bay of Pigs, looked and saw around him a hostile and threatening world. The Visigoths were at the gate. There was only one solution: gird for a long struggle and take the offensive. But this was *not* the world as it existed in 1961; it was a construct of fact, fear, and fantasy. The pragmatist was basing his decisions on the Book of Revelations according to Dean Acheson and John Foster Dulles."[20] But such language and vision were part of the Kennedy style of leadership. He saw crises everywhere. The Bay of Pigs disaster was not an international crisis, as Kennedy and Sorensen portrayed it, but a political crisis for Kennedy because he had approved a stupid plan to overthrow Castro and was catching political flak from its failure. In this sense, the word *crisis* became devalued because it was applied so indiscriminately.

Thus, the grand, elevated style Kennedy had used in his inaugural now became an apocalyptic style in service of defending the president in *his* hour of maximum political danger. It is not coincidental that the president used this platform before an audience of newspaper editors to lecture them and the country about his belief that a severe crisis confronted the nation. Newspaper editors and their reporters, he believed, had not grasped the importance of this "new challenge," and he believed he had to describe it vividly to them. A week later he would elaborate upon this "new challenge" and its consequences for the press.

KENNEDY'S SPEECH TO NEWSPAPER PUBLISHERS. On April 27 Kennedy spoke before the American Newspaper Publishers Association and devoted all his remarks to the relationship between the president and the press. He stated that the United States faced an unprecedented threat to our security, to our survival, and to our future. This threat, he contended, was unique to our history: "Today no war has been declared—and however fierce the struggle may be, it may never be declared in the traditional fashion. Our way of life is under attack. Those who make themselves our enemy are advancing around the globe. The survival of our friends is in danger." And he continued: "For we are opposed around the world by a monolithic and ruthless conspiracy that relies primarily on covert means for expanding its sphere of influence—on infiltration instead of invasion, on subversion instead of elections, on intimidation instead of free choice, on guerrillas by night instead of armies by day." Kennedy's references to a different kind of war was a direct result of two statements that had recently come out of the Soviet Union. In November 1960 a statement was issued from a meeting of communist leaders of eighty-one countries held in Moscow. Very shortly, it was known in the West as the *Mein Kampf* of the party.[21] The other was Khrushchev's January 6, 1961, speech, which Kennedy advised all his aides to read; it was one of the most important speeches Khrushchev gave while in office.[22] Essentially, Khrushchev said that world wars among major powers in a nuclear age were no longer thinkable. Instead, in the new epoch of the 1960s wars would be wars of national liberation and anticolonial wars because that was the nature of the new historical era that lay ahead. The colonial era was dying, and such wars would be necessary to bury it. He said that the Soviet Union would be on the side of the progressive anti-colonial forces in the world.

Kennedy understood Khrushchev's words to mean that he intended to exploit unrest in the Third World and especially in Central and South America, to further the Soviet aims of world domination. For Kennedy, this meant a new Soviet strategy more dangerous than the threat of open hostilities between the two superpowers. After all, the United States still had a vast superiority over the Soviet Union in nuclear weapons. Kennedy believed Khrushchev's speech signaled this significant change from world war to worldwide sub-version, and Cuba was only the first step in that direction. Thus, he believed he would have to respond with a more flexible military force to counteract this strategy. The Green Berets were one tactical military innovation that Kennedy created as a response to the threat of Soviet guerrilla "wars of national liberation," and his calls for enormous increases in defense spending on conventional forces was a strategic response. However, I believe Kennedy misunderstood Khrushchev's speech. Khrushchev was saying that these anti-colonial uprisings were going to occur because the world was enter-ing an anticolonial era. And he was saying that the Soviet Union intended to be on the side of the anticolonialists. No doubt, Khru-shchev intended to exploit *some* of these disturbances when he was able and when it was in Soviet interests. But as he told Kennedy at Vienna in the spring of 1961, he was not behind all the uprisings or turmoil in the world and warned Kennedy not to blame him for each and every one or else he would have to respond in a similar fashion, and that could lead to a Soviet-American confrontation, something both powers sought to avoid.

But Kennedy's beliefs were more important than what Khru-shchev actually said. A new threat was on the horizon and ne-cessitated major changes: "[This new threat] requires a change in outlook, a change in tactics, a change in missions—by government, . . . by every newspaper. For we are opposed around the world by a monolithic and ruthless conspiracy that relies primarily on covert means for expanding its sphere of influence."[23] Thus, the world *circa* 1961 according to John F. Kennedy: a world in which the United States is locked in a deadly struggle with communism, a struggle so great and so intense that our entire way of living requires radical changes to insure the possibility of survival. But now the Soviet Union had changed its strategy and tactics. It no longer sought a direct conflict with the United States, but intended instead to pick off small nations one by one, by exploiting internal turmoil within those countries. This new strategy posed an even greater threat from the communists than those Truman and Eisenhower had faced. It was within this extreme and perilous political reality—invoked rhetorically by Kennedy—that the president got to the heart of the matter of the relations between the president and the press.

Kennedy's new reality demanded that newspapers change their outlook and their mission to join with the administration in its crusade against communism: "This deadly challenge imposes upon our society two requirements of direct concern to the press and to the President—two requirements that may seem almost contradictory in tone, but which must be reconciled and fulfilled if we are to meet this national peril. I refer, *first*, to the need for far greater public information; and *second*, to the need for far greater official secrecy." The uninitiated may ask how one can have "far greater public information" and at the same time have "far greater official secrecy," but that contradiction seemed to bother Kennedy very little. He denied he intended to establish a new Office of War Information or that he intended to impose government censorship, despite the assertion that the country was involved in a new kind of war. Instead, he called for self-restraint on the part of the news media. He reiterated that restraint was essential because the country facing such an unprecedented peril: "If the press is awaiting a declaration of war before it imposes the self-discipline of combat conditions, then I can only say that no war ever posed a greater threat to our security. If you are awaiting a finding of 'clear and present danger,' then I can only say that the danger has never been more clear and its presence has never been more imminent." If the news media did not impose self-restraint, Kennedy predicted that publications might undermine American national security:

> For the facts of the matter are that this nation's foes have openly boasted of acquiring through our newspapers information they would otherwise hire agents to acquire through theft, bribery or espionage; that details of this nation's covert preparations to counter the enemy's overt operations have been available to every newspaper reader, friend and foe alike; that the size, the strength, the location and the nature of our forces and weapons and our plans and strategy for their use, have all been pinpointed in the press and other news media to a degree sufficient to satisfy any foreign power.

In chastising the press in this fashion, Kennedy appeared to be saying that the press was irresponsible or perhaps worse, unwitting collaborators with the nation's enemies. In fact, the *New York Times*, as well as some other newspapers and magazines, had information about the Cuban invasion in advance of its actual execution and had agonized over whether to publish that information. When the *Times* did finally publish a small story, it was sanitized, using few details, and it was handled undramatically.

But if Kennedy ruled out official censorship in favor of self-censorship, on what basis were publishers to make decisions about what to print? Kennedy readily provided an answer, one that presidents have resorted to repeatedly. And he did so more forthrightly than other recent presidents: "Every newspaper now asks itself with respect to every story: 'Is it news?' All I suggest is that you add the question: 'Is it in the interest of national security?'" Kennedy assured the publishers that if the press agreed to voluntary "self-discipline," his administration would cooperate "whole heartedly" in establishing specific new guidelines or machinery to help determine what stories were consistent with the national interest. Needless to say, the audience applauded only once during the speech.

Kennedy's speech was remarkable for the clarity with which he stated what most presidents devoutly believe: the national interest must supersede constitutional liberties in times of peril. Had the country truly been at war, Kennedy's requests might not have sounded unreasonable. Indeed, publishers, editors, and reporters probably would have rushed to avoid compromising American national security and would have considered such actions their patriotic contributions to the war effort.

But the nation was not at war. At the time of the speech there was no visible threat to American national security. No Pearl Harbor had been bombed, nor had there been even a North Korean invasion of South Korea. What had happened was that the president had foolishly approved a stupid invasion of Cuba that had failed miserably, and now the president had a political disaster on his hands. What Kennedy seemed to be saying was that the press was to blame for the disaster because it had published information that he did not believe it should be publishing. But in his speech Kennedy did not cite any leaks about the fiasco in Cuba, but instead recounted other examples that he considered inappropriate.

The president called for self-restraint in news in the name of "national security." At the time, the phrase *national security* had not been so overused as it is today. Nonetheless, Kennedy's use of it is typical of contemporary presidents. Kennedy made his foreign policies synonymous with "national security." And he seemed to be implying that publishing anything that undermined *his* foreign policies would be a violation of national security interests. In this context and given subsequent statements by Kennedy, this use of *national security* was a blatant example of using words primarily for political purposes rather than for purposes of clarifying ideas.

Because little evidence existed of a direct threat to the United States in terms of specific and concrete actions taken by an enemy, Kennedy turned to a more abstract world reality of imminent dangers in which ideological angels do mortal combat with ideological demons. This apocalyptic rhetoric featured a world irreconcilably divided between communism and freedom, with the enemy banging at the gates, a world where everyone within is called upon to unite behind the president. More important, this ideological world that Kennedy portrayed as consistently dangerous transcended the actual world of the differences between the United States and Cuba. Those who accepted this rhetorically transformed world could imagine that the dangers were urgent and world-shaking. It was this rhetorical transformation that allowed Kennedy to make the claims that he did in his speech. It was within this rhetorically created political reality that Kennedy could call for self-restraint and self-discipline on the part of the press, even to the point of asking the press to relinquish part of its First Amendment rights. But to have Kennedy's recommendations taken seriously required that the press share his view of the reality of the struggle between communism and freedom. That is where the speech lost its effectiveness.

Editorial responses were cautious and ranged the political gamut. William Randolph Hearst, Jr., ambiguously said: "Having been a war correspondent, I can well understand the need for security."[24] Benjamin M. McKelway, editor of the *Washington Star* and president of the Associated Press, stated: "I know of no responsible newspaper which would print material damaging to the interests of this country. The old problem is: What is it that is damaging to the interests of this country?"[25] The *New York Times* took an editorial stance that was soon adopted by most others: "For the preservation of our democratic society in this time of 'clear and present danger' it is more essential than ever that the people be fully informed of the problems and of the perils confronting them. This is a responsibility as much of the press as of the President."[26]

Nonetheless, the Publishers Association appointed a committee to study the questions, problems, and recommendations voiced by President Kennedy. On May 9 they held a seventy-minute meeting with the president and told him that they did not see an imminent peril so great as to merit restricting the First Amendment and therefore saw no need for an official organization to assist the press in guarding vital security information. However, that is not to say the press rejected Kennedy's view that communism posed a significant threat to the United States. In fact, much of the prestige press shared his assumptions about communism and the need for the United States to contain it. What they rejected was Kennedy's intense sense of crisis and his call for self-censorship. Felix McKnight, representing the American Society of Newspaper Editors, said the group believed that only a "declaration of a national emergency," or something like that, "would warrant considering some kind of machinery for dealing with issues of national security and freedom of the press."[27] Kennedy could not cite any specific events that warranted such action. Without the declaration of a "national emergency," the publishers and editors were unwilling to submit to Kennedy's recommendations for self-censorship.

According to memoirs written by close advisers, Kennedy was sorely disappointed with the response of the press. He was never again to speak publicly at such length about his criticism of the press. Instead, he would cancel his subscription to the *New York Herald Tribune* when it offended him, and, as Sorensen reported, he would inform his friends in the press of stories which he liked and disliked through "phone calls, notes, and staff relays." He would remind reporters privately of their responsibilities (as he saw them), and he would seek to prevent "the publication of information harmful to the security of the United States" by requesting "newspapers to hold off printing stories their reporters had uncovered."[28] He thought the press had misunderstood him and the world as well. In fact, they had understood the president all too well and only had a different view of danger in the world and its relationship to their responsibilities as journalists.[29]

There are two footnotes to be added to this examination of this remarkable speech. First, during the cold war years the media had almost always behaved exactly as Kennedy was recommending. Almost all major newspapers were overwhelmingly anticommunist and hard-line. Rarely did journalists in main-line publications give much attention to a searching examination of the cold war or the assumptions upon which American foreign policy was based. Even the *New York Times* suppressed certain facts in its story on the Bay of Pigs before the invasion. What Kennedy was calling for—self-discipline and self-restraint—were already the standard practice.

Second, even as President Kennedy was meeting with the committee from the Publishers Association and berating the *New York Times'* representative, he turned aside to Turner Catledge and said: "If you [the *New York Times*] had printed more about the operation, you would have saved us from a colossal mistake."[30] Eighteen months later, only a little more than a month before the Cuban missile crisis, Kennedy told Orvil Dryfoos of the *New York Times*: "I wish you had run everything on Cuba . . . I am just sorry you didn't tell it at the time."[31] What this all boiled down to is this paradox. On the public level Kennedy suggested that the press shared the blame for the Bay of Pigs because it leaked information. But on the private level, Kennedy implied that the press could have helped the country avert a major disaster by printing even more information than it did. Thus, although the president took full responsibility for the tragedy, he also was shifting responsibility to the press in a variety of ways that were not too subtle.

The invasion of Cuba at the Bay of Pigs was a shattering event for the Kennedy administration. The administration viewed it as a "learning experience," as both Sorensen and Schlesinger make clear.[32] It led to a shake-up, known as the "Thanksgiving Day Massacre," in both the Oval Office and other executive offices. Chester Bowles, who had opposed the operation, was removed as under secretary of state and given the title the President's Special Representative and Adviser on African, Asian, and Latin American Affairs. George W. Ball replaced him as under secretary. Walter W. Rostow moved from the White House to become assistant secretary for policy planning at the State Department. Richard N. Goodwin also moved from the White House to State to become deputy assistant secretary for Latin American affairs.[33]

The disaster also seemed to confirm the charge made by Richard Nixon and the Republicans during the 1960 campaign that Kennedy was inexperienced and immature in foreign policy. These suspicions hurt members of the administration, who prided themselves on being tough and pragmatic. Not only were these highly prized personal virtues suspect, the leadership of the president was also suspect. To reassert his leadership Kennedy enforced a hard-line policy toward those he thought would seek to take advantage of him. There followed three crises that when taken together helped to reestablish credibility of Kennedy's leadership: the Berlin crisis, the steel crisis, and the Cuban missile crisis. Each arose from certain external events, to be sure, but each also developed to a crisis level because Kennedy perceived each as a challenge to his personal and political leadership. There is a direct line from the Bay of Pigs to each of these crises, one that cannot be ignored if one is to understand Kennedy's reactions to each of these so-called crises.

But most important of all, the administration was signaling a change in American foreign policy. Kennedy was shifting attention from direct Soviet-American conflicts to symbolic conflicts between communism and the free world in small countries. He was reviving the Truman Doctrine, but with a new twist. Kennedy saw the Soviets as embarking upon a new strategy of world conquest in which the Cuban revolution was the most conspicuous first move. The Soviets, he thought, would instigate or exploit internal unrest in other countries to achieve the long-range goals, and they would do so with "guerrillas by night" rather than "armies by day." Therefore, Kennedy believed it should be the policy of the United States to stop this subversion.

But how was he to justify using the great military might of the United States against this clandestine menace? The issue had to be raised rhetorically to the level of a worldwide battle between communism and the free world, in which events in small countries were symbolic of a much greater struggle. Thus, the hysterical tone of his speeches on Cuba, where he had sought to have Castro overthrown though there had been no attack on the United States or even a direct threat to the country. Americans had to be alerted to the new challenge posed by the Soviet Union, and "scaring hell" out of the country had its rhetorical antecedents. In the next crisis, that is exactly what the administration did.

The Berlin Crisis: June–September 1961

The Berlin "crisis" of the summer of 1961 is a curious crisis. Reflecting on it now twenty-nine years later, one is hard-pressed to understand what the crisis was all about, except that during the first year of Kennedy's presidency everything was viewed as critical. The Berlin "crisis" was unique because it was principally a crisis based on words and symbolic actions. It was precipitated by Khrushchev's proposals at Vienna, fueled by belligerent speeches by Khrushchev and Walter Ulbricht, raised to a fever pitch by Kennedy's rocket-rattling address to the American people in July, brought to a climax with the building of the Berlin Wall, and finally concluded through an agreement to sit down and discuss differences between the United States and the Soviet Union. In sum, the Berlin "crisis" was a rhetorical crisis.

The narrative of events that led to the Berlin "crisis" is not as familiar as that of the Bay of Pigs and therefore needs a bit more exposition. Kennedy met Khrushchev on June 3 and 4 in Vienna, not to negotiate any major agreements, but to "gain as much insight" as possible "on [Khrushchev's] present and future policies."[34] Three specific issues dominated the discussions: a test-ban treaty, the situation in Laos, and the status of Berlin. Khrushchev made a commitment to pursue a negotiated settlement to the strife in Laos, which was the most important and most neglected achievement of the meeting. Nothing was accomplished about a nuclear test-ban treaty. That would have to wait for two more years. It was Berlin, particularly West Berlin, that caused the tumult and hysteria that was to follow. Khrushchev resurrected his three-year-old demands for a settlement of what he called the "Berlin Question." He demanded that the World War II allies meet and negotiate a peace treaty with the two Germanys within six months, a treaty that would recognize the existence of a separate East and West Germany. If the United States and its allies refused, Khrushchev told Kennedy that the Soviet Union intended to sign the treaty unilaterally with East Germany that would terminate all commitments stemming from the original surrender agreement. Furthermore, Berlin would be made a "free city," and responsibility for Western access to West Berlin would pass from the Soviets to the East Germans.

Kennedy replied that the United States had every legal right to be in Berlin and, equally important, Berlin was essential to American national security. He told Khrushchev he did not intend to abandon Berlin, nor would he allow the United States to be expelled from that city so vital to our defense of western Europe. Kennedy adamantly insisted on American occupation rights in West Berlin. Although Khrushchev tried to explain to Kennedy that he was only proposing a peace treaty to normalize the existing situation (that is, the existence of two separate Germanys), Kennedy continued to insist that American rights were not negotiable.

The discussions of Berlin ended on harsh notes. Khrushchev said that the Soviet Union would sign a separate treaty by December and would turn all territory and access rights over to the East Germans. And he warned, "if there is any attempt to interfere with these plans . . . there will be war."[35] Kennedy ended the discussion by responding ruefully: "It will be a cold winter."[36]

Kennedy's reactions to Khrushchev's demands led to the Berlin "crisis," to an apocalyptic presidential speech on July 25, and to a new nuclear war scare of frightening proportions. Kennedy's reactions caused the Berlin crisis, for two reasons.

First, Kennedy treated Khrushchev's proposals about Berlin as if they were entirely new proposals. But this was not the first time Khrushchev had issued these same demands over Berlin. On November 10, 1958, Khrushchev had called for such a treaty and threatened to sign a separate treaty if the Western allies did not agree to a conference to negotiate this treaty.[37] During a press conference on November 27, 1958, he proposed that allied occupation forces be withdrawn from Berlin, as part of the treaty, and that it be made a "free city."[38] A six-month deadline was placed on the demand. Eisenhower, president at the time, unlike Kennedy did not panic. He recognized that Khrushchev had not threatened military action, but proposed negotiations. Eisenhower told Dulles, his secretary of state, that he was willing to study the possibility of making Berlin a free city if that included both West *and* East Berlin. Most important for rhetorical purposes, Eisenhower did not want to raise the issue to the level of a public crisis. As he wrote in his memoirs, "there was no reason for an immediate public reply . . . ; too much eagerness to counter Khrushchev's statement would give the impression that our government was edgy."[39] In fact, Eisenhower delayed eleven days in replying publicly. When he did, he did it not with an important public speech, but through his press secretary, James Hagerty, during a routine briefing of the press. Eisenhower's response was deliberate, not hasty; low keyed, not panic stricken; through a brief statement by his press secretary, not through a speech to the American people. On May 27, 1960, the six-month ultimatum was due, and nothing happened.

Khrushchev revived the peace treaty demand and another six-month ultimatum when he arrived in the United States in September 1959. He made it a leading issue in each of his speeches during his tour of the United States. But after visiting with Eisenhower at Camp David at the end of his trip, he once again dropped the ultimatum and settled instead for a joint communique between himself and Eisenhower agreeing to more exchanges and better relations between the two nations.[40] Again, Eisenhower did not panic, but let Khrushchev play out his demands until he dropped them. But Kennedy was no Eisenhower.

Second, Kennedy's reaction stirred the "crisis" because Kennedy overreacted to the situation. He perceived Khrushchev as attempting to use Berlin to break up the NATO alliance or to "destroy the freedom of West Berlin."[41] In other words, he saw Khrushchev's proposals for negotiations as a threat to go to war over Berlin and believed that he had to respond strongly to that threat.

On June 6 in his "Report to the Nation" on his meetings with Khrushchev, Kennedy focused special attention on the issue of Berlin. He said: "But our most somber talks were on the subject of Germany and Berlin. I made it clear to Mr. Khrushchev that the security of Western Europe and therefore our own security are deeply involved in our presence and our access rights to West Berlin, that those rights are based on law and not on sufferance, and that we are determined to maintain those rights *at any risk*, and thus meet our obligation to the people of West Berlin, and their right to choose their own future." He added, "Generally, Mr. Khrushchev did not talk in terms of war."[42] But Kennedy was thinking of the possibility of war, war over Berlin.[43] Two questions became immediately important. Should the president or someone else respond directly to Khrushchev's calls for negotiations over Berlin? If so and if it should be the president, what should his response be?

On June 12 Walter Ulbricht, head of the East German government, held a press conference in which he blustered against the West and said that all access routes to West Berlin would come under the control of East Berlin once the proposed treaty was signed. A few days later, on June 21 (the twentieth anniversary of the German invasion of the Soviet Union) when Khrushchev publicly appeared in military uniform to announce an increase in military spending, he raised the possibility that the Soviet Union would resume nuclear testing in the atmosphere if provoked by the West and repeated the need to sign a peace treaty with Germany before the end of the year. Khrushchev's speech seemed to be decisive. The symbolism of the military uniform coupled with the announcement of increased military spending and the call for the peace treaty came together to convince Kennedy that Khrushchev meant to take some direct action against Berlin.

But an entirely different interpretation of the symbolism of the occasion and of Khrushchev's speech might have led to a very different reaction by President Kennedy. It appears to me that Khrushchev's statements were meant as a warning to West Germany not to unleash another war against the Soviet Union. Furthermore, the military uniform probably was intended as symbolic of Khrushchev's resolve to make certain that never happened. If all this hoopla was directed at West Germany rather than the United States, which seems plausible, then Kennedy once again misinterpreted Khrushchev. He then acted upon this misinterpretation.

From this point on, there was only one answer in Kennedy's mind to the first question, should someone respond to Khrushchev's call for negotiations? Unlike Eisenhower, Kennedy personally would provide the response to Khrushchev. But what to do?

This second question, however, created a schism within the administration. One group, led by Dean Acheson, argued for a strong military response to Khrushchev, including sending a division up the autobahn to West Berlin.[44] The other group, led by Arthur Schlesinger, urged a diplomatic response, one in keeping with the diplomatic initiative by Khrushchev.[45] The Acheson view, though modified somewhat by the president, prevailed. Acheson argued that Khrushchev's proposals for negotiation had little to do with Berlin, that in reality, Khrushchev was using Berlin to test American "will," as the Soviets always tested a new American president to see what manner of man they were dealing with.[46] Thus, the initiatives by Khrushchev were seen as symbolic, and they required a military, war-like response rather than a diplomatic response. Had Kennedy interpreted the call for negotiations literally, he might have leaned toward Schlesinger's diplomatic response. But he saw the Soviet leader's words as symbolic of a larger meaning involved in Berlin.

Kennedy interpreted Khrushchev's proposals as a pretext to test American power and, more significantly, to test the president's willingness to wage nuclear war. Summarizing Kennedy's interview with James Wechsler of the *New York Post*, Schlesinger wrote: "What worried [Kennedy] was that Khrushchev might interpret his reluctance to wage nuclear war as a symptom of an American loss of nerve. Some day, he said, the time might come when he would have to run the supreme risk to convince Khrushchev that conciliation did not mean humiliation."[47]

Acheson's hard-line views dovetailed Kennedy's predispositions about Berlin. On October 7 during the 1960 presidential campaign, Kennedy had stated:

the next President of the United States, *in his first year* is going to be confronted with a very serious question on our defense of Berlin. Our commitment to Berlin. There's going to be a test of our nerve and our will. There's going to be a test of our strength and because we're going to move in '61 and '62, partly because we have not maintained our strength with sufficient vigor in the last years. I believe that before we meet that crisis that the next President of the United States should send a message to Congress asking for revitalization of our military strength because *come Spring or later in the winter*, we're going to be face to face with the most serious Berlin crisis since 1949 or '50.[48]

In sum, Kennedy was predisposed toward Acheson's position, and the events of June and July 1961 served not as events to be evaluated on their own terms, but as events to be understood symbolically that confirmed this predisposition.

KENNEDY'S SPEECH.   On July 25, 1961, President Kennedy made one of his rare nationally televised speeches to the American people. The subject was Berlin; the rhetoric was war-like, apocalyptic. He began by describing the "immediate threat." He posed it not merely as a threat to our legal rights in Berlin, which he said Khrushchev's peace treaty proposal was, but also as a "worldwide" threat. As he had with the Cuban problem, Kennedy linked the crisis over Berlin to a monolithic threat throughout the world, from Berlin to Souheast Asia ("where the dangers of communism [are] less apparent to those who have so little") to the Western Hemisphere and "indeed [to] wherever else the freedom of human beings is at stake."[49] Thus, the Berlin issue became a multiple issue: a literal threat to Berlin and a symbolic threat to American power and will to resist communism throughout the world. But it was the symbolism that overwhelmed everything else.

Having presented the issue as a symbolic one and having linked it to a worldwide communist conspiracy, Kennedy turned to explain the exact nature of the Berlin symbolism:

> For West Berlin—lying exposed 110 miles inside East Germany, surrounded by Soviet troops and close to Soviet supply lines, has many roles. It is more than a showcase of liberty, a symbol, an island of freedom in a Communist sea. It is even more than a link with the Free World, a beacon of hope behind the Iron Curtain, an escape hatch for refugees.
>
> West Berlin is all of that. But above all it has now become as never before—the great testing place of Western courage and will, a focal point where our solemn commitments stretching back over the years since 1945, and Soviet ambitions now meet in basic confrontation.

Kennedy described the "basic confrontation" in military, not diplomatic terms. In fact, he portrayed the crisis as one that might lead to war between the United States and the Soviet Union. At every turn he described the situation and our potential response to it in military language and in terms of war:

> I hear it said that West Berlin is militarily untenable. And so was Bastogne. And so, in fact, was Stalingrad. Any dangerous spot is tenable if men—brave men—will make it so.
>
> We do not want to fight—but we have fought before. And others in earlier times have made the same dangerous mistake of assuming that the West was too selfish and too soft and too divided to resist invasions of freedom in other lands. Those who threaten to unleash the forces of war on a dispute over West Berlin should recall the words of the ancient philosopher: "A man who causes fear cannot be free from fear."
>
> We cannot and will not permit the Communists to drive us out of Berlin, either gradually or by force.

Such rocket-rattling and war-like speeches had become commonplace in the cold war rhetoric. Had Kennedy ended his speech with such statements, he undoubtedly would have aroused concern among the American people watching on national television, but not hysteria. He produced hysteria because he did not stop with this provocative rocket-rattling. He went on to enumerate a series of concrete military and civil defense actions he intended to propose or to take that led the American people to believe the country was on the brink of nuclear war with the Soviet Union. Kennedy had once told Arthur Schlesinger, "That son of a bitch [Khrushchev] won't pay any attention to words[.] He has to see you move."[50] And "move" he did.

After defining the Berlin issue in military terms and talking about the threat of war, Kennedy announced what appeared to be preparations for imminent war: (1) an additional $3.247 billion in appropriations for the armed forces; (2) another 125,000 men for the Army, raising our standing force to one million men; (3) an increase of 29,000 men for active duty in the Navy and 63,000 for active duty in the Air Force; (4) doubling and tripling the draft, and requesting authority to order to active duty reserve units, as well as authority to order air transport and tactical air squadrons to active duty; (5) canceling orders for many ships and planes headed for retirement and instead reactivating them; (6) $1.8 billion for procurement of non-nuclear weapons, ammunition, and equipment. Coming on the heels of his war-like description of the current situation in Germany, these specifically military announcements sounded for all practical purposes like a preparation for war. What other reason could there be for such drastic actions?[51] He drove this point home in a chilling section asking an additional $207 million for civil defense:

Tomorrow, I am requesting of the Congress new funds for the following *immediate* [emphasis added] objectives: to identify and mark space in existing structures—public and private—that could be used for fall-out shelters in case of attack; to stock those shelters with food, water, first-aid kits and other minimum essentials for survival; to increase their capacity; to improve our air-raid warning and fall-out detection systems, including a new household warning system which is now under development; and to take other measures that will be effective at an early date to save millions of lives if needed.

In the event of an attack [emphasis added], the lives of those families which are not hit in a nuclear blast and fire can still be saved—*if* they can be warned to take shelter and *if* that shelter is available. We owe that kind of insurance to our families—and to our country. In contrast to our friends in Europe, the need for this kind of protection is new to our shores. But the time to start is now. In the coming months, I hope to let every citizen know what steps he can take without delay to protect his family in case of attack. I knew that you will want me to do no less.

Now, Kennedy was not only preparing the military for military action, he was also preparing the American people for the possibility of a nuclear attack upon them.

After summarizing the effect that his civil defense requests would have on the federal budget, the speech took a bizarre twist. Kennedy spent the next four paragraphs talking about domestic economic matters. He proudly announced that the country was recovering from the recession and that consumer prices were only one-fourth of 1 percent higher than the previous October. He noted that America's gold position had improved and the dollar was more respected abroad. What these paragraphs about America's financial situation had to do with the threat in Berlin was unclear.

One point should be made. Kennedy did say, "We do not intend to abandon our duty to mankind to seek a peaceful solution." But this diplomatic initiative was tepid and obscure in comparison with the hawkish threats to unleash a nuclear war over Berlin. The threats and fears dominated the speech, and the press played them up in its reporting.

All in all, the July 25 speech was frightening. In his retrospective about the speech, Sorensen—the chief author of the address—wrote: "It was not, however, a weak speech. Its delivery was hampered by an overcrowded, overheated office. Its domestic economic references were out of place. Its civil defense references were out of perspective. But its basic message was firm and urgent without resort to threats or fear."[52] If one did not know Sorensen better, one would think the last sentence was deliberately ironic because the speech created widespread fear in the United States that a nuclear war with the Soviet Union was not only inevitable, but imminent. (One shudders to think what kind of speech Sorensen might have written had he wanted to produce "threats or fear.") The private fall-out shelter business, which had begun in the 1950s, boomed once again. Clergy and intellectual leaders debated the morality of defending one's backyard fall-out shelter from neighbors seeking refuge after a nuclear attack. The television show *The Twilight Zone* broadcast an episode based on that very premise. Yellow and black signs indicating fall-out shelters were quickly put up in public places and remain even today. The August 25 issue of *Time* reported that 12 million American families "have gotten ready for nuclear attack" by building and stocking fall-out shelters. On September 15 *Life* magazine published a cover story under the title "How You Can Survive Fallout. 97 Out of 100 People Can Be Saved." The story was accompanied by an approving letter from President Kennedy himself.

The hysteria and fear were so widespread in the United States that when on August 13 the East Germans began building the Berlin Wall, many expected a nuclear war to result.[53] But cooler heads prevailed.

SYMBOLIC ACTS. In response to the building of the wall, Kennedy acted symbolically as other presidents, past and future, have done. Such actions were prudent, given that direct action against either East Germany or the Soviet Union could have produced a nuclear holocaust. In other words, Kennedy's apocalyptic rhetoric gave way to prudent and symbolic action.[54] Kennedy had two things to prove with these actions: that we had and would keep a commitment to West Berlin, and that we would use force, if the Soviets did, to honor those commitments. To demonstrate our commitment, Kennedy dispatched General Lucius Clay, who had been in command when the Soviets blockaded Berlin in 1947, and Vice President Johnson to West Berlin. To demonstrate our right of access and that we would use force if necessary to defend it, he dispatched a contingent of 1,500 American troops in armored trucks up the autobahn through East Germany to Berlin. Soon thereafter American tanks pulled up on the West German side of the wall that was being built. Khrushchev understood the symbolism perfectly because he did the same thing. To demonstrate his commitment to East Germany, he sent tanks and troops up to the East German side of the wall. And there they stood for a time, each government symbolically demonstrating its strength and its will. Once that was accomplished, the "crisis" wound down, the tanks and troops returned from whence they came, and Johnson and eventually General Clay came home.

On August 21 Kennedy instructed Secretary of State Rusk to inform American allies that the United States intended to commence negotiations with the Soviet Union on the issue of Germany and Berlin, and those talks began informally in September. On October 17 in a six-hour speech to the Twentieth Party Congress, Khrushchev announced that the Soviet Union would not insist on signing a treaty before December 31. That date, however, also passed without any consequences. Eventually, years later during the Nixon administration, an accommodation between East Germany and West Germany was reached, an accommodation approved by both the United States and the Soviet Union.

What then can be said about the Berlin "crisis" of the summer of 1961? Kennedy's admirers and apologists contend that it was a great victory for Kennedy because he protected West Germany and allied rights in Europe. Or at the very least his vigorous action forced Khrushchev to back away from his dangerous plans to take over West Berlin. But that interpretation presumes that Khrushchev did in fact plan some sort of military or other kind of direct action against Berlin. That evidence is lacking. It is clear that Khrushchev used the Berlin situation to force new discussions with a new president about that issue and others. Berlin was a bargaining chip to Khrushchev, and he won. He not only got the Americans to begin negotiations, the "crisis" also led in September to the initiation of a private correspondence between Kennedy and Khrushchev. In the end, it was Khrushchev, not Kennedy, who got what he wanted. What Kennedy got was another installment in his huge military buildup and a wave of war hysteria that swept through the United

States. That must lead one to ask whether the "crisis" was really worth it, since it took the two superpowers to one step away from the brink of nuclear confrontation. But to talk of that is to talk of a tangible situation with tangible results.

Kennedy's handling of the situation is instructive on two points. First, it demonstrates how great a role symbolism played in Kennedy's conduct of foreign policy. Among Kennedy's apologists, Khrushchev's specific proposal for negotiations was seen not for what it was, but for what it symbolized: a testing of American courage and will. Under that interpretation, the Berlin "crisis" was a triumph in domestic politics for Kennedy in that he demonstrated the courage and will to face down Khrushchev. That was important because his leadership had been damaged by the Bay of Pigs disaster. Kennedy's overreaction and tough stand on Berlin helped revive his claim to vigorous leadership.

Second, Kennedy's speech demonstrated the central role rhetoric plays in creating political reality. Quite simply, except on the symbolic level and in Kennedy's perception of Khrushchev's proposal, there was no crisis, at least none comparable to the bombing of Pearl Harbor, and certainly none that called for the kind of speech Kennedy delivered on July 25. The crisis was more a rhetorically induced crisis than a crisis produced by tangible events. But Kennedy's speech was so frightening that it produced a climate of fear and foreboding among Americans. One cannot stress too greatly that it was the rhetoric—not specific acts—that created the effect. Kennedy's rhetoric of symbolism about Berlin—apocalyptic and more concerned with that symbolism than with actuality—must be judged one of the worst of the important speeches of his administration. But then it might have been expected, given Kennedy's statements about Berlin during the 1960 campaign and his penchant for finding crises where none existed. Stewart Udall, Kennedy's secretary of the interior, remarked after talking with Kennedy during this time: "He's imprisoned by Berlin."[55]

The Steel Crisis: April 1962

On April 10 a little before six in the evening, Roger Blough, chairman of the board of the United States Steel Company, announced to President Kennedy that U.S. Steel was raising its prices by $6 a ton. This announcement in the form of a four-page press release that Blough politely allowed the president to see before making it public was a political bombshell. Only four days before, the United Steelworkers had signed a binding three-year contract that Kennedy and especially his secretary of labor, Arthur Goldberg, had coaxed the union into signing with the assurances that the contract was not inflationary and therefore would not result in an increase in the price of steel. Blough's announcement of the price increase made Kennedy feel as if he had been "stabbed in the back."[56]

For Kennedy it was an acute political crisis. He had been elected only by one-tenth of 1 percent of the popular vote, and the union vote had been strongly in his favor. He could not afford to lose that important constituency, given that his national constituency was still so fragile. Furthermore, what credibility would either the president or Goldberg have with other unions in the future if that price increase was not rescinded? Since coming into office, he had sought to revitalize the economy but to avoid an inflation that usually accompanies such revitalization. His means for achieving that dual purpose was to set guidelines for economic development and then "jawbone" with both business and labor to persuade them to work within those guidelines as they set or negotiated wages and prices. The steel contract had been a shining example of the success of Kennedy's policy and methods. But now, if the price increase was allowed to stand, Kennedy's policies, methods, and credibility would be severely damaged.

Kennedy decided to fight the price increase. During the next three days Kennedy mobilized his administration to a war-like precision that struck like a *blitzkrieg* against the steel companies. Kennedy had no constitutional power to require U.S. Steel and the several other companies that also raised their prices to rescind them. He could not wait for Congress to act—assuming that it could or would. If Congress sought to remedy the situation legislatively, it would have to draw up legislation, hold hearings in subcommittees and committees, and debate the issues. The interminable delay would be debilitating and, in the end, ineffective. Therefore, Kennedy decided to take his case to the American people and to use whatever power he could marshal to back up his rhetoric.

Kennedy's handling of the steel "crisis" is an example of domestic crisis rhetoric. It is a model of presidential rhetoric that other presidents have used when faced with what they perceived to be domestic disturbances or immediate threats to their domestic policies. An examination of Kennedy's use of this form also demonstrates the uses of symbolic acts by a president to confirm that the president truly means what he says so that those who have caused the disturbances or pose the threat take his words seriously. Thus, this analysis will be divided into two parts: an analysis of the form of domestic crisis rhetoric and an exposition of the symbolic acts that Kennedy initiated to confirm his rhetoric.

OPENING STATEMENT AT KENNEDY'S PRESS CONFERENCE. On April 11, the morning following his visit from Blough, President Kennedy read a long opening statement at his press conference. His delivery revealed that he was angry:

> Simultaneous and identical actions of United States Steel and other leading steel corporations increasing steel prices by some $6 a ton constitute a wholly unjustifiable and irresponsible defiance of the public interest. In this serious hour in our Nation's history, when we are confronted with grave crises in Berlin and Southeast Asia, when we are devoting our energies to economic recovery and stability, when we are asking reservists to leave their homes and families for months on end and servicemen to risk their lives— and four were killed in the last 2 days in Viet-Nam—and asking union members to hold down their wage requests at a time when restraint and sacrifice are being asked of every citizen, the American people will find it hard, as I do, to accept a situation in which a tiny handful of steel executives whose pursuit of private power and profit exceeds their sense of public responsibility can show such utter contempt for the interests of 185 million Americans.[57]

Kennedy continued his opening statement by cataloging the horrendous consequences that would result if the price rise was not rescinded, among them: a rise in the cost of homes, autos, appliances, and most other family items; a rise in the cost of machinery and tools; an additional $1 billion to the defense budget. He concluded the statement by saying: "Some time ago I asked each American to consider what he would do for his country and I asked the steel companies. In the last 24 hours we had their answer."

There are three basic arguments that make up the genre of domestic crisis rhetoric. First, the president presents his policy as representing the public interest. In other words, he defines a political or economic policy as one that transcends politics or economics and becomes the "public interest." He presents the policy of his opponents as a representation of private interests in direct conflict with the public interest. The force of this definition of the issue comes from the unique position an American president holds in American political life. Other political figures may describe their policies as being in the public interest, but most Americans know that representatives and senators are responsible to narrow constituencies, the district or state they represent. Only the president is elected in a national election, and by virtue of that fact, only the president can invoke the public interest with believable force. Conversely, only the president can name undesirable other policies as "private interests" (or "special interests") and have that designation appear credible. In actuality, of course, Kennedy was fighting to impose his economic policy upon the steel companies, but to say that would have made the battle between the president and the steel companies a partisan battle. To raise the issue to crisis proportions, Kennedy had to say the price increase represented a narrow private interest in conflict with the broad national or public interest, a much stronger and more advantageous rhetorical ground from which to do battle. Kennedy repeatedly used the words *public* and *private* to contrast the two positions and to emphasize this distinction.

The second argument descends from the first. To give legitimacy to his claim that his policy represents the public interest, the president claims that he is supported by the majority of people, whereas his opponents represent only a minority (in this case, "a tiny handful of steel executives"). Thus, the issue is framed a second time as a contest between majority rule and minority obstruction, and draws its persuasive force from the maxim almost sacred to democratic countries: "The majority rules." Invariably in this kind of political battle, the president claims to have majority support while his opponents are only a small minority.

Finally, the president attributes good or ethical motives to himself (after all, he represents not a personal policy, but the public interest) and to the majority that supports him. Likewise, he attributes base or dastardly motives to his opponents (who represent only private or special interests). In this case, Kennedy described all the sacrifices, including the supreme sacrifice of dying, that Americans were enduring to uphold the public interest. He contrasted these noble motives with the base motives of his opponents: the "pursuit of private power and profit." The point of this argument is not merely to discredit the opponents' policy but to discredit the opponents themselves, to make them loathsome usurpers of legitimate authority and beneficial policies. Think for a moment: If one had to choose between a policy that represented the public interest and was supported by the majority of people who acted from decent, loyal motives and a policy that sprang only from private interests initiated by a small band of greedy and power-mad executives, which would one choose? And which would one want to defend after choosing it?

The diagram of domestic crisis rhetoric makes clear the way a president frames the arguments in a set of three dialectically opposed positions (see Figure 1). Once these terms for argument are set, the president proceeds to picture the dire consequences should his opponents triumph. Such predictions are a mainstay of all political rhetoric and therefore should not be considered unique to this form of crisis rhetoric.

FIGURE 1
Domestic Crisis Rhetoric

The President's Policy	*Domestic Opponents*
Public Interest	Private Interests
Majority Support	Minority Opposition
Honorable Motives	Base Motives

Kennedy delivered his opening statement "in an ice-cold but calm [voice], sounding more like Roosevelt indicting the Japanese for Pearl Harbor than a man displaying 'unbridled fury.'"[58] He answered questions from the press, almost all of which focused on the price increase not only by U.S. Steel but by other companies that had followed U.S. Steel's lead.[59]

Kennedy's appearance and language were harsh, some of the harshest language directed at the business community since the days of Franklin Roosevelt's railings against "economic royalists." His invocation of the genre of domestic crisis rhetoric raised the issue of price increases to a crisis level.

But words alone seldom change events. To begin with, Kennedy had no legal or legislative power to force the companies to rescind their price increases. After all, what kind of government would we have if every time a major business increased its prices, the government had authority to rescind them?

Moreover, during the twentieth century steel companies had been relatively immune from influence by the government. They had survived FDR's denunciations, fought free from the economic controls left from World War II, and successfully resisted President Truman's attempt to seize the industry in 1952.[60]

Finally, the nature of political language and rhetoric limited the practical effect of Kennedy's words. In a democracy, political language contains a tension between what the speaker says and how various constituencies interpret his words. Kennedy wanted his words taken literally: the price increase had to be rescinded! But the steel executives could interpret his angry words as merely rhetorical therapy to soothe his union constituents.[61] Therefore, Kennedy had to convince them through specific actions that he meant what he said: the price increase had to be rescinded.

SYMBOLIC ACTS. "He was coldly determined," Schlesinger wrote, "to mobilize all the resources of public pressure and private suasion to force steel to rescind the increase."[62] That was a polite way of saying that President Kennedy and the administration used every form of persuasion, coercion, and intimidation available to it in pursuit of that goal. During the four days of the crisis the administration and others encouraged by the administration did the following, among other things:

- Senator Estes Kefauver denounced the price increase and scheduled an investigation by his anti-trust subcommittee.
- Representative Emmanuel Celler announced that his House subcommittee on anti-trust would hold hearings on the price increase in May.
- Senators Hubert Humphrey, Albert Gore, and Mike Mansfield joined Kefauver in denouncing the increase and called for investigations into whether the Taft-Hartley law had been violated.
- The Department of Justice began an investigation into possible criminal price fixing or monopoly by the steel companies.
- The Federal Trade Commission began investigations of the commercial practices of the steel companies.
- The Department of Defense announced that it would not grant contracts to steel companies that had raised their prices and simultaneously announced the awarding of a contract to Lukens Steel Company, which had not raised its prices.
- The Department of Justice announced that a grand jury had been convened to investigate possible criminal price fixing and that company papers had been subpoenaed.
- Members of the administration initiated an extensive telephone campaign to keep companies that had not announced a price increase from following the lead of U.S. Steel and to line up members of the business community behind the president in denouncing or disapproving the price increase.
- FBI agents, checking out a story that the president of Bethlehem Steel had previously remarked that the price increase was not justified, called the reporter at 3:00 A.M. and arrived at his house to interview him at 4:00 A.M. FBI agents also interviewed other journalists from the *Wall Street Journal* and the *Wilmington Evening Journal* in the course of their "investigations."
- The administration leaked a number of threats and rumors, including the possibilities that the Internal Revenue Service

would audit tax returns, that the administration would seek to break up the large steel companies, and that the administration would seek to impose price controls on the steel industry through legislation.[63]

These acts, along with others, convinced the steel executives that the president really meant that he wanted the price increase rescinded. Not only that, the proposed and rumored investigations demonstrated that if the steel companies did not reconsider their actions, the government intended to act decisively against them. In response to these symbolic acts, on April 13 Roger Blough announced that U.S. Steel was rescinding its price increases, and soon the other companies that had raised their prices followed suit.

For the president, his forceful words and action against the steel companies was a triumph. He asserted presidential leadership in the face of a threat to his economic policies: "He mobilized every fragment of quasi-authority he could find and, by a bravura public performance, converted weakness into strength."[64] But to others, Kennedy's "short war" against the steel companies was disappointing: "Can acts or conditions that are criminal on Tuesday become less criminal by the following Monday? Are crimes by steel and other industries permitted so long as the criminals 'co-operate' with the administration?"[65] Certainly, Senator Kefauver and others, who were ready to investigate the steel companies, were left out on a limb by the president when he canceled investigations after the capitulation. However, from a rhetorical perspective, these acts were necessary to prove to the executives that Kennedy meant what he said. Words alone could not have caused the rescindment. Action, in the form of these symbolic acts, was necessary. And they were *symbolic*, intended to show the steel companies what the administration *could do* if the prices were not rolled back, not what the administration was actually doing as its policy toward the economic community in general, or the steel companies in particular. These acts symbolized the potential consequences if the steel companies did not acquiesce to the president's demands. When they did, the president scored a major political victory for his administration and took a major step forward in reasserting his leadership, even though his use of federal agencies for political purposes was questionable at best.

Though the steel crisis was a serious political confrontation for Kennedy, it did have a humorous aspect in its aftermath. It produced one of Kennedy's finest sustained pieces of wit. Two weeks after the press conference Kennedy spoke briefly at the White House Correspondents Dinner. He was in high humor as he parodied his opening statement from the press conference, a parody that is worth quoting at length:

> I have a few opening announcements.
>
> First, the sudden and arbitrary action of the officers of this organization in increasing the price of dinner tickets by $2.50 over last year constitutes a wholly unjustifiable defiance of the public interest. If this increase is not rescinded but is imitated by the gridiron, radio, TV, and other dinners, it will have a serious impact on the entire economy of this city!
>
> In this serious hour in our Nation's history, when newsmen are awakened in the middle of the night to be given a front page story, when expense accounts are being scrutinized by the Congress, when correspondents are required to leave their families for long and lonely weekends at Palm Beach, the American people will find it hard to accept this ruthless decision made by a tiny handful of executives whose only interest is the pursuit of pleasure! I am hopeful that the Women's Press Club will not join this price rise and will thereby force a recession. . . .
>
> I'm sure I speak in behalf of all of us in expressing our thanks and very best wishes to Benny Goodman and his group, Miss Gwen Verdon and Bob Fosse, Miss Sally Ann Howes, Mr. Reid—who has some talent—and Mr. Peter Sellers. I have arranged for them to appear next week on the United States Steel Hour! Actually I didn't do it; Bobby did it![66]

This example of Kennedy's wit is only one of many. And to talk about Kennedy's rhetoric without mention of it is to ignore one important reason for his persuasive appeal. At times, such as this one, it was so charming that it caused even journalists to laugh about congressional probes of private expense accounts, public threats against businessmen, and the use of the FBI for political purposes rather than for criminal investigations.

About Kennedy's wit, Schlesinger remarked: "For Kennedy wit was the natural response to platitude and pomposity."[67] His remark was especially appropriate to Kennedy's parody. But it appears that Kennedy's delight in satire was not shared by other members of the Kennedy clan. Mort Sahl, according to his account, was threatened by Peter Lawford, Kennedy's brother-in-law, because Lawford and Joseph Kennedy did not appreciate Sahl's satiric monologues about the president. Sahl said Lawford once yelled that if he did not "cooperate," presumably with the image the Kennedys wanted to present of themselves, Ambassador Kennedy would see "he'd never work again in the United States."[68] During the Kennedy administration Sahl found his comic fortunes failing. As an antidote to Schlesinger's account of Kennedy's love of satire and to set Sahl's account into its full context, one might add that the administration did nothing to assist Lenny Bruce, the most creative satirist of the period, when he faced a myriad of troubles during this time.

Nonetheless, in the aftermath of the steel "crisis" Kennedy's high humor served him well. But humor would have no place in the next crisis.

The Cuban Missile Crisis: October 1962

The Cuban missile crisis is so well known that the details of these events need not be recounted.[69] On October 16 McGeorge Bundy informed the president that offensive missile sites were being constructed in Cuba. Kennedy immediately formed an executive committee of the National Security Council to advise him in determining (1) why Khrushchev had decided to place the missiles in Cuba at this time, and (2) what appropriate action the U.S. government should take in response. The committee, meeting in secret, developed five theories about why Khrushchev put the missiles in Cuba:

1. *Cold War Politics.* The missiles were a "test of America's will."
2. *Diverting Trap.* If the United States responded by attacking Cuba, the United States would be discredited in the world and Khrushchev would move swiftly on Berlin.
3. *Cuban Defense.* Khrushchev put the missiles in Cuba to defend it against another invasion by the United States, thus demonstrating the Soviet Union's credibility as a defender of its allies.
4. *Bargaining Barter.* Khrushchev wanted to use the missiles as a "bargaining chip" to force a settlement on Berlin or to force withdrawal of American armed forces overseas.
5. *Missile Power.* The Soviet Union wanted to improve its military position by placing missiles in Cuba that could evade our early warning system.[70]

Although Kennedy believed each had some merit, he decided that the major reason was the first, to "test America's will" to resist Soviet expansionism.[71] No doubt Kennedy had heard reports that Khrushchev thought Kennedy had been "too soft" during the Bay of Pigs invasion, and those reports further inclined him toward his focus on that particular motive.

When it came to an appropriate response to the missiles, the executive committee discussed everything from an invasion of Cuba to doing nothing. Eventually, the options were pared down to two: a surgical air strike against the missile sites, and a blockade of Cuba accompanied by a demand that the Soviet Union dismantle and remove the missiles. Kennedy decided upon the latter, a blockade of Cuba.

On October 22 President Kennedy spoke to the American people, invoking "foreign crisis rhetoric."[72] The president began by asserting his control over the facts of the situation and acknowledging that new facts that had come to his attention constituted a new situation, which he defined as a crisis. Kennedy opened his address with these ominous words: "This Government, as promised, has maintained the closest surveillance of the Soviet military buildup on the island of Cuba. Within the past week, unmistakable evidence has established the fact that a series of offensive missile sites is now in preparation on that imprisoned island. The purpose of these bases can be none other than to provide a nuclear strike capability against the Western Hemisphere."[73] Such an authoritative statement personalizes political leadership. The president has gotten expert information about new facts that have created a new situation that he, in keeping his compact with the people, is sharing with the public. This new situation, he declares, is critical to American national security and demands that he act.

In so personalizing leadership, the president created for himself the right not only to ascertain the new facts but also to define the new situation and give meaning to it. Kennedy told the American people that the intermediate-range missiles in Cuba were dangerous because they were "capable of striking most of the major cities in the Western Hemisphere, ranging as far north as Hudson Bay, Canada, and as far south as Lima, Peru." Arguing that the missiles formed a direct threat to the citizens of the United States was essential to making this genre of rhetoric work effectively. Without arguing that direct threat, the remainder of the arguments would have been less appealing, if credible at all. The presence of missiles in Cuba were not like the Japanese bombing of Pearl Harbor. In the latter instance, the direct act against the United States was obvious, and president Roosevelt did not have to belabor its gravity. Since the missiles were only being constructed, Kennedy had to demonstrate the extent of the threat to the United States from them in order to portray the missiles as directly dangerous to the American people.

Kennedy then defined the situation as critical not only to the United States and the Western Hemisphere, but also to the rule of law in the world: "This urgent transformation of Cuba into an important strategic base . . . constitutes an explicit threat to the peace and security of all the Americas, in flagrant and deliberate defiance of the Rio Pact of 1947, the traditions of this Nation and hemisphere, the joint resolution of the 87th Congress, the Charter of the

United Nations, and my own public warnings to the Soviets on September 4 and 13."

Once Kennedy argued that a crisis existed, he began to narrate the deceptions used by the Soviets to put the offensive missiles secretly in Cuba. Kennedy quoted directly from Soviet authorities, including the Soviet government and Foreign Minister Gromyko, who had denied that they were putting offensive missiles in Cuba or that they had any need to do so. Within this narration is the first main line of argument that characterizes foreign crisis rhetoric: a contrast between the patience and honesty with which the United States had handled the old situation versus the communists' record of duplicity and secrecy in creating the new situation. Throughout the speech Kennedy emphasized this contrast by describing the deployment of the missiles as "secret, swift, and extraordinary" and as "sudden, clandestine," thus concluding: "Our own strategic missiles have never been transferred to the territory of any other nation under a cloak of secrecy and deception; and our history—unlike that of the Soviets since the end of World War II—demonstrates that we have no desire to dominate or conquer any other nation or impose our system upon its people."

The purpose of this first line of argument is to introduce the angel-devil interpretation into the narration of facts: The Soviet communists are secretive and duplistic; the United States is open and trusting. The situation thus becomes moral melodrama, with sinister motives attributed to the Soviets and pure motives to the United States. In fact, there is a subtle shift in the argument, from the act of placing missiles in another country to the means by which those missiles were sent to another country. As Kennedy said, the United States never did such a thing "under a cloak of secrecy and deception." Kennedy did not deny that the United States had ever done the same thing as the Soviet Union, a fact he could hardly have denied since we had placed offensive missiles in Turkey. What Kennedy emphasized was *motive and method*, that we had never done it *secretly and deceptively.*

The second line of argument is built upon the first. Kennedy reminded the public that this incident was one of many in the continual battle between the free world and the communist world, a cold war that had begun after World War II and thus has a history of this kind of duplistic action on the part of the Soviet Union. As he said, American history since then has been very different from that of the Soviet Union; they tried to conquer and dominate other countries, whereas the United States never sought domination or conquest. In speaking directly to the Cuban people Kennedy elaborated on this argument: "And I have watched and the American people have watched with deep sorrow how your nationalist revolution was betrayed, and how your fatherland fell under foreign domination. Now your leaders are no longer Cuban leaders inspired by Cuban ideals. They are puppets and agents of an international conspiracy which has turned Cuba against your friends and neighbors in the Americas." Thus, the president elevated his particular policy to the level of a historical struggle between the free world and the communist world, one in which ideological angels do mortal and moral combat with ideological devils: moral melodrama. Kennedy drew on the language and assumptions permeating the anticommunist ideology of the American public and reminded hearers that they ought to have learned their lesson about appeasing aggression from the events of the 1930s, an obvious reference to Munich and "peace at any price." For any successful attempt at foreign crisis rhetoric, the Munich analogy is mandatory. It has become a central *topos* in such rhetoric and a "God term" analogy.

President Kennedy then described the seven *initial* steps he was taking to meet the crisis. As he announced his policy, he also continued to shift the issue from its obvious military and political context to a moral context: that is, from the consequences of war to a question of American character. That was the third line of argument defining foreign crisis rhetoric. Kennedy stressed that his actions would be a test of American character:

Let no one doubt that this is a difficult and dangerous effort on which we have set out. No one can foresee precisely what course it will take or what costs or casualties will be incurred. Many months of sacrifice and self-discipline lie ahead, months in which both our patience and our will will be tested, months in which many threats and denunciations will keep us aware of our dangers.

The path we have chosen for the present is full of hazards, as all paths are, but it is the one most consistent with our character and courage as a nation and our commitments around the world. The cost of freedom is always high, but Americans have always paid it.

Thus Kennedy's foreign policy decision is transformed for a third time. It began as a simple, if potentially dangerous, American policy in response to the president's perception of extreme danger to American national security.[74] It became a melodramatic struggle between good and evil, between pure motives and sinister motives. It evolved into another historic test in the long struggle between the free world and the communist world, another example of the long and ongoing cold war between the two. Finally, it was elevated to a test of American character. This last transformation is the "bear any burden, pay any price," "my country right or wrong" appeal. The essence of the problem, according to Kennedy, is no longer political or military, but moral. Those who support the president have character and courage, for that is what standing steadfast with him in this hour of "maximum danger" means; those who oppose his policy presumably lack these virtues. Deliberative rhetoric has given way first to melodrama and then to pure epideictic.

Finally, the president had to justify his initiation of an act of war against another nation, for that is what a blockade is: an act of war. Kennedy did what other presidents have done. He engaged in Orwellian Newspeak. He described the blockade as a "quarantine," denied that this act of war was actually an act of war, and insisted instead that it was a step toward "peace and freedom." As Orwell wrote: "War is Peace, Peace is War." Thus, the American people—at least those accustomed to Newspeak—can rationalize support for the president and the possibility of nuclear war over the introduction of a small group of intermediate-range missiles in Cuba. They can do so because political language has become so distorted and mangled by the cold war that words have lost traditional or even legal meanings. They can do so because they want to prove that they have character and courage in the wake of this latest communist threat. They can do so in order to demonstrate their support for the president of the United States during a time of international crisis, even one that the president has created. They can do so because the president has enacted a policy that they cannot change. They can do so because they have no alternative. War is Peace; Peace is War.

The diagram of foreign crisis rhetoric summarizes its major constituents (see Figure 2). By invoking this form of presidential rhetoric Kennedy put the world on a path, not toward peace and freedom, but toward a potential nuclear confrontation between the United States and the Soviet Union.

The confrontation was avoided. Soviet ships stopped in the waters while the Kremlin decided what to do. Eventually, the president allowed several tankers and a passenger ship through the blockade. But later Americans stopped and boarded a Soviet ship, found no weapons, and allowed it to proceed. The five days following the speech were days of furious public and private exchanges that culminated in Khrushchev's private letter to Kennedy in which he offered to resolve the crisis if the United States would give its assurances that it would respect the sovereignty of Cuba.[75] Although the next day another message from the Presidium of the Soviet Union arrived demanding the removal of U.S. missiles from Turkey as well as assurances about Cuba in exchange for the Soviet missiles, Kennedy,

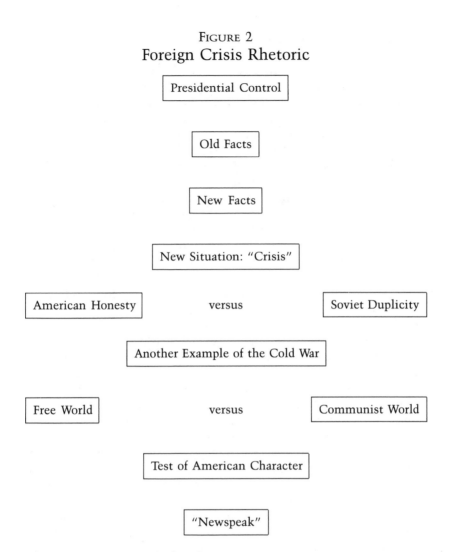

FIGURE 2

Foreign Crisis Rhetoric

Presidential Control

Old Facts

New Facts

New Situation: "Crisis"

American Honesty   versus   Soviet Duplicity

Another Example of the Cold War

Free World   versus   Communist World

Test of American Character

"Newspeak"

upon the sound advice of Robert Kennedy, replied to Khrushchev's original, private proposal, and the crisis wound down.

Viewed from a rhetorical perspective, Kennedy's actions indicate that he meant his demands about the dismantling of the Soviet missiles to be taken *literally*. The blockade was the symbolic act that conveyed that intention. However, his willingness to allow some tankers and a passenger ship through the blockade as well as his choice of a particular ship, which Kennedy had reason to believe was not carrying weapons or material for the missiles, to board and then allow through demonstrated Kennedy's willingness to avoid war and seek a peaceful settlement of the issue. Thus, in the aftermath of Kennedy's October 22 speech, he meant his belligerent actions symbolically and his desire for a peaceful settlement literally.

Once the missile crisis was resolved, Kennedy gained high marks for his handling of it. But since that time people have raised serious questions about his management of the crisis. Such critics as Richard J. Walton, Barton J. Bernstein, and Louise FitzSimons have concluded in various ways that Kennedy ran an unnecessary or vainglorious risk in confronting Khrushchev. Bernstein asked: "What . . . would have happened if Khrushchev had not backed down . . . ? If the missile crisis was Kennedy's greatest triumph, as many scholars and memoirists contend, how many similar victories can America afford to seek?"[76] Walton argued that the offensive missiles in Cuba were not even sufficiently threatening to warrant Kennedy's belligerent response. He wrote that a diplomatic response based on Cuban president Osvaldo Dorticos's statement to the U.N. General Assembly would have been a sufficient response. Dorticos had stated that weapons in Cuba would not be necessary if the United States gave its promise not to threaten Cuba.[77]

Furthermore, the critic might reasonably ask: What right did the United States have to threaten the world with nuclear extinction over an agreement to place offensive missiles in Cuba, an agreement arranged and agreed to by two sovereign nations? After all, the United States had placed offensive missiles aimed at the Soviet Union in other countries, most notably Turkey, and the Soviet Union had not threatened to annihilate the world over them.

In *Robert Kennedy and His Times* Arthur Schlesinger, Jr., answered the critics, especially Walton. He argued that if Kennedy had done nothing about the missiles, Khrushchev would have altered "the balance of world power" and the "sixties would have been the most dangerous of decades." Schlesinger noted an inconsistency in one argument used by the critics. He charged them with saying that Kennedy should have negotiated a settlement rather than overreacting and at the same time saying that Kennedy's weak warnings during the summer of 1962 caused the Soviet Union to honestly misinterpret them as a green light to put the missiles in Cuba, "a view obviously incompatible with their theory [that Kennedy] was on the prowl for confrontation."[78]

But Schlesinger is also vulnerable to the charge of inconsistency. He charged initially that the missiles made a crucial change in the balance of military power, but several pages later he argues that Khrushchev removed the missiles primarily because his military situation was "hopeless." If it was hopeless, then how could the missiles in Cuba radically alter the balance of military power?

Furthermore, even assuming that the missiles contributed to a very small shift in the balance, what sane person would believe they would ever be fired? The Kennedy memoirists and apologists contend that a central concern was that Cubans would have control over the missiles once the Russian technicians completed them. But would Castro have ever even considered firing the missiles in an attack on the United States? That seems absurd, and pathologically removed from reality. The firing of a few missiles against the United States would have resulted in a retaliation that would have obliterated Cuba from the face of the earth. To believe that Castro would have launched the missiles is to believe that he would have been willing to commit mass suicide for himself and his nation.

Kennedy's decision to initiate a nuclear confrontation with the Soviet Union came primarily from two sources: his cold war mentality and his political situation. Kennedy was captive of the cold war mentality that had developed after World War II and had sustained two previous administrations. His references to the communist conspiracy around the globe in previous speeches confirms this, as do his appointments of other cold warriors to positions of authority and influence in his administration. After all, it was Kennedy who first introduced "advisers" into Vietnam and created the Green Berets as a counterinsurgency and counterrevolutionary force. It was Kennedy's political appointees who became Johnson's advisers on Vietnam and led the country down that tragic path. A host of other examples could be cited, but one would be remiss if one did not distinguish Kennedy from earlier cold warriors.

His anticommunist mentality was not as sanctimonious as that of John Foster Dulles and others from the 1940s and 1950s, nor did he extend it to domestic politics when faced with internal adversaries. Nonetheless, it was genuine, and it led him to *perceive* the missiles in Cuba as a real threat to the United States. What is equally significant is that Kennedy moved from questions of *direct* Soviet-American confrontations to the communist threat posed by smaller nations, which *symbolized* the worldwide struggle between democracy and communism. This shift was important both in policy and in rhetoric. It meant that American attention had to be shifted to a variety of nations ("from Cuba to Vietnam") and even cities (West Berlin). The net he cast was far wider than the Eisenhower-Dulles policies in seeing potential confrontations throughout the world, even as Kennedy drew upon the far-ranging treaties that Dulles had negotiated (such as SEATO).

Furthermore, his political situation in October 1962 influenced his decision. Kennedy had been damaged politically by the Bay of Pigs fiasco. Even supporters questioned his leadership. His extravagant response to the Berlin overtures by Khrushchev and his swift, forceful handling of the steel "crisis" had begun to reestablish confidence in his leadership. But in September and early October of 1962 questions were once again being raised in the course of the off-term election campaign about the administration's fortitude and willingness to do something about communist Cuba and the possibility of missiles in Cuba.[79] Clearly, Cuba was becoming a campaign issue in 1962. Kennedy could not afford that. He had committed himself to campaigning vigorously for Democrats and needed their victory to strengthen his hand in Congress. The political pressures were too great not to act against Cuba. The crisis produced a predictable "rally around the president" effect, as foreign crises cause Americans to put aside their partisan feelings momentarily and unify behind the president. When the crisis was resolved, it appeared that Kennedy had "faced down" Khrushchev and emerged victorious. Those feelings apparently spilled over into the elections as the Democratic party lost four seats in the House but gained four in the Senate. More important, breaking even in the election—the president's party typically loses seats—represented a major victory for the president. It demonstrated that he had gained popularity with the public, due in no small amount to the coincidence of the crisis and the election. It demonstrated that he was indeed a forceful and courageous (if not reckless) leader washing out the last smudges from the dirty laundry of the Bay of Pigs.

Above all, it allowed him to move away from the right. For almost two years, ever since the Bay of Pigs, he had had to protect himself politically from attacks by conservatives, and he had done so by being more conservative, it sometimes appeared, in foreign affairs than they were. The confrontation over Cuba and the subsequent results of the election allowed Kennedy to begin to move toward a less rigid rhetorical posture toward the Soviet Union and eventually to seek rapprochement through the nuclear test-ban treaty. Schlesinger concluded the same: "If the nuclear missiles had remained in Cuba, there would have been no American University speech, no test ban treaty, no 'hot line' between the White House and the Kremlin, no relief from the intolerable pressures of the Cold War."[80] After two years of "crises" these events and reactions came together to allow Kennedy the political room to move in different directions. In so doing, he would create a new administration quite different from that of the first two years.

3

The Crisis Rhetoric of
President John F. Kennedy
The Final Year

The final year left to President John F. Kennedy was a year of remarkable changes both in foreign policy and domestic policy. His first two years had been marked by "crises" in foreign policy. They had also been years when he showed little public interest in the struggle for civil rights among black Americans. In the final year left to him, he would reverse this process by attempting to seek detente with the Soviet Union and by putting the force of the presidency behind the civil rights movement.

Seeking Detente with the Soviet Union

In the spring of 1963 President John Kennedy embarked on a policy not to foment crises, but to seek conciliation with the Soviet Union. Instead of confrontation, he sought cooperation. In terms of his "crisis" presidency, Kennedy's political moves toward detente with the Soviet Union reversed the rhetorical process of creating or responding to the "crises" of the first two years of his administration. Now, he went on the rhetorical offensive. During the summer of 1963 he sought to wind down the confrontational mentality that had dominated American-Soviet relations and to replace standard anticommunist rhetoric, at which he had been so adept, with a more conciliatory rhetoric, at least toward the Soviet Union. But how does a president achieve those goals rhetorically, especially after having placed so much emphasis on a hard-line anticommunism during the first two years of his administration? To answer that question, we begin a bit ahead of the story with American attempts to open the doors to the People's Republic of China later in 1963.

In *To Move a Nation* Roger Hilsman chronicled the delicate rhetorical and political maneuvers in 1962–1963 the State Department engaged in as it sought to send a signal to the People's Republic of China that the United States was willing to be more flexible in its policies toward that country if China would reciprocate.[1] More ambitiously, the Kennedy administration sought to change basic assumptions about American-Chinese relations. John Foster Dulles, secretary of state under President Eisenhower, had assumed that the communist regime in China was a "passing and not a perpetual phase" and that it was the responsibility of the United States "to do all that we can to contribute to that passing."[2] These assumptions were much the same assumptions that guided American attitudes and policy toward the Soviet Union during the same period.

The Kennedy administration, according to Hilsman, had reconsidered those assumptions and believed that a new, more realistic approach would include understanding that the communist regime was in firm control of the mainland and that there was little likelihood it would be overthrown. Such a fundamental change in assumptions about foreign policy with a major power required a public announcement and justification. But how to do it?

Hilsman, by then assistant secretary of state for Far Eastern affairs, became the principal spokesperson for this change. He planned to speak at the Commonwealth Club of San Francisco on December 13, 1963. The symbolism of this setting was important because San Francisco with its large Chinese-American population was a traditional place for speeches on China policy and because Dulles had made the "last full statement on the subject in 1957" in that city.[3] Hilsman's speech aimed at being firm, flexible, and dispassionate. He later wrote:

By firmness, we meant firmness in our support for our friends and allies, including the people and government of the Republic of China on Taiwan; firmness in our determination to maintain our strength in Asia and firmness in our determination to meet aggression wherever it occurred. By flexibility, we meant a willingness to seek and carry out initiatives that seemed promising and to negotiate with anyone who sincerely wanted to negotiate, including the Chinese Communists. And by dispassion, we meant analyzing our problems and our policies coolly, without emotion, to discover our own best interests—appealing to the American people to substitute rationality in China policy for the emotionalism of which . . . there had been too much.[4]

Though Hilsman's speech got mixed reviews in the press, it did not change policy—at least, not at that time.[5]

The experiences Hilsman recounted serve as an introduction to the question: how does an American president go about announcing a change in assumptions toward one of the adversary superpowers as a prelude to major changes in policy? And how does he go about persuading the American public to accept those changes, especially when there are vested political and/or psychological interests in maintaining the status quo? For that is exactly what Kennedy had to do in his attempts to gain a nuclear test-ban treaty with the Soviet Union. Instead of reinforcing established attitudes and values, Kennedy sought to change them. Roger Hilsman's experience with the speech on China provides a skeletal outline for the development and presentation of such a rhetoric:

1. An appropriate symbolic setting must be chosen to emphasize the importance of the announcement.
2. The president must persuade the public that the old assumptions are irrational or unrealistic and that the new assumptions are rational and realistic as well as in the best interests of the United States.
3. The president must signal our adversary that the United States is willing to negotiate certain issues based on the new assumptions.
4. The president must reassure the American people as well as interested outside parties (especially our allies) that we will not compromise American national security nor essential agreements with allied governments.
5. The president must act in a concrete way to symbolize that some concrete policy changes will come from these new assumptions.

President Kennedy's dramatic move toward detente with the Soviet Union in the summer of 1963 provides an example of how one president went about changing the rhetoric and policies toward that country. It resulted in the limited nuclear test-ban treaty. And it changed American policy from confrontation with a superpower to one of detente, a policy that was to last through the next four presidents.

The Cuban missile crisis had a sobering effect on President Kennedy. In a variety of ways the president sought to ease tensions between the United States and the U.S.S.R. Kennedy finally decided to deliver an important speech on the topic of peace and decided also that he would announce a unilateral suspension of atomic testing in the atmosphere. Sorensen wrote:

The final step was the American University speech itself, the first Presidential speech in eighteen years to succeed in reaching beyond the cold war. The address had originated in a Presidential decision earlier in the spring to make a speech about "peace." His motives were many. It was, first of all, an expression of his deep personal concern. He had not elaborated his views on this topic since the 1961 address to the U.N. He thought it desirable to make clear his hopes for East-West agreement as a backdrop to his European trip in June. He valued in particular an April 30 letter from Norman Cousins. Cousins suggested that the exposition of a peaceful posture prior to the May meeting of the Soviet Communist Party Central Committee, even if it could not deter an expected new rash of attacks on U.S. policy, might at least make those attacks sound hollow and hypocritical outside the Communist world. That meeting had been postponed until June, and the June 10 commencement at American University appeared to be the first appropriate forum on the President's schedule.[6]

Sorensen worked on the speech and cleared it with the necessary cabinet officials. Appropriate Soviet officials in Moscow and Washington as well as the White House correspondents were briefed in advance that the speech was to be of great importance.[7]

Kennedy's Speech

On June 10, 1963, President John F. Kennedy received an honorary degree from American University and delivered his speech, "The Strategy of Peace." The setting was most appropriate for the message he bore.

When a president delivers a speech on a university campus, his role changes perceptibly. He becomes not only leader of the nation but *teacher* of the nation. All the trappings of the occasion contribute to this change. He is attired in academic regalia. Leaders of the university—administrators, faculty, and outstanding students—share the platform with him, symbolically conferring intellectual approval on him. The academic atmosphere of disinterest permeates the event. Specific and immediate concerns fade as larger issues are discussed. The search for enduring principles that will guide one in day-to-day activities becomes paramount. Indeed, Kennedy recognized the symbolism of the setting when he opened his speech by saying:

"There are few earthly things more beautiful than a university," wrote John

Masefield, in his tribute to English universities—and his words are equally true today. He did not refer to spires and towers, to campus greens and ivied walls. He admired the splendid beauty of the university, he said, because it was "a place where those who hate ignorance may strive to know, where those who perceive truth may strive to make others see."

I have, therefore, chosen this time and this place to discuss a topic on which ignorance too often abounds and the truth is too rarely perceived—yet it is the most important topic on earth: world peace.[8]

Furthermore, commencement is an occasion to look to the future which was precisely what Kennedy intended to do in his speech. The commencement exercises mark a major change in the graduates' lives. The era of being a student ends; life in the work-a-day world begins. So, too, in Kennedy's speech: old Soviet-American antagonisms must ease; new relations must be developed. Finally, the audience at commencement is made up primarily of young people. They symbolize the future. And the speaker will emphasize that the ideas he proposes will make the future safer and better for them. In sum, such a setting is ideal for the president to assume his role as teacher of the nation and to present fresh ideas and new directions for the country.

Kennedy's purpose in this speech, according to Sorensen, was to reach beyond the cold war rhetoric that had prevailed for eighteen years. Equally important, the president intended to prepare the American people for a series of negotiations that eventually would lead to the ratification of the limited nuclear test-ban treaty. To be effective, Kennedy had to discredit the strident anticommunist perceptions of American-Soviet relations that had pervaded those relations for almost two decades. In other words, Kennedy had to establish a new political context within which to view the new initiatives—especially the unilateral cessation of atmospheric nuclear tests and negotiations for the test-ban treaty—so as to marshal public support for these measures. A new political context requires a new political language. It is that new language that creates new "pictures in our heads"; it is a new linguistic lens through which to view events and policies.[9]

Early in his speech Kennedy asked his audience (and the nation as well) to reexamine its attitudes "toward the possibilities of peace, toward the Soviet Union, toward the course of the cold war and toward freedom and peace here at home." The first three would occupy the bulk of the speech and are most pertinent to our subject. Kennedy interwove three lines of argument throughout the speech: (1) specific definitions of the new attitudes he wished Americans to cultivate; (2) incentives for adopting these attitudes; and (3) negative consequences for maintaining the old, outmoded anticommunist attitudes. His organizational and stylistic pattern was antithetical. Part of this pattern is revealed in his answer to his rhetorical question of what kind of peace we seek: "Not a Pax Americana enforced on the world by American weapons of war. Not the peace of the grave or the security of the slave. I am talking about genuine peace, the kind of peace that makes life on earth worth living, the kind that enables men and nations to grow and to hope and to build a better life for their children—not merely peace for Americans but peace for all men and women—not merely peace in our time but peace for all time." Kennedy continued by citing three major incentives for seeking peace: (1) "Total war makes no sense in an age when great powers can maintain large and relatively invulnerable nuclear forces and refuse to surrender without resort to those forces." (2) Continued stockpiling of nuclear weapons "is not the only, much less the most efficient, means of assuring peace." (3) Peace is "the necessary rational end of rational men." These incentives infused the remainder of the speech, as Kennedy continued to discuss the three main topics of his speech.

Kennedy began his reexamination of our attitudes with the idea of peace itself.

Too many of us think it impossible. Too many think it unreal. But that is a dangerous, defeatist belief. It leads to the conclusion that war is inevitable—that mankind is doomed—that we are gripped by forces we cannot control.

We need not accept that view. Our problems are manmade—therefore, they can be solved by man. No problem of human destiny is beyond human beings. Man's reason and spirit have often solved the seemingly unsolvable—and we believe they can do it again.

But Kennedy needed to be more precise about what kind of peace he sought. Beginning negatively, he stated that he was not "referring to the absolute, infinite concept of universal peace and good will of which some fantasists and fanatics dream." No, his kind of peace would be a more limited, more practical, more positive peace "based not on a sudden revolution in human nature but on a gradual evolution in human institutions—on a series of concrete actions and effective agreements which are in the interest of all concerned." This definition of limited steps toward peace dovetailed neatly with the specific, limited proposals he would announce near the end of his address.

But if we were to seek peace, we would also have to change our attitudes toward the Soviet Union, the second topic of the address.

Kennedy began by deploring the distorted view Russians have of the United States, but he used that distortion to warn Americans against falling into the same trap of seeing "conflict as inevitable, accommodation as impossible, and communication as nothing more than an exchange of threats." Instead of these negative and unproductive attitudes, Kennedy sought to emphasize our common human traits:

No government or social system is so evil that its people must be considered as lacking in virtue. As Americans, we find communism profoundly repugnant as a negation of personal freedom and dignity. But we can still hail the Russian people for their many achievements—in science and space, in economic and industrial growth, in culture and in acts of courage.

Among the many traits the peoples of our two countries have in common, none is stronger than our mutual abhorrence of war.

So, to change attitudes toward the Soviet Union, Kennedy sought to shift focus from ideological differences that divide the two nations and will continue, to human traits shared by the two peoples that must be the foundation for resolving some outstanding issues. In the rhetoric of seeking accommodation with adversaries, this separation between a political system and its people is standard.[10] Kennedy reinforced this distinction as well as the shift in emphasis in the most eloquent paragraph of the speech:

So, let us not be blind to our differences—but let us also direct attention to our common interests and to the means by which those differences can be resolved. And if we cannot end now our differences, at least we can help make the world safe for diversity. For, in the final analysis, our most basic common link is that we all inhabit this small planet. We all breathe the same air. We all cherish our children's future. And we are all mortal.

Certainly, if the United States was to seek peace cooperatively with the Soviet Union, a new view of Russians would have to be created. In emphasizing the human bonds that unite us rather than the ideological differences that separate us, President Kennedy found a realistic common ground upon which to begin building that cooperative effort.

Kennedy's charge to change our attitudes toward the cold war came almost as an anticlimax within the speech since everything that preceded it draws the listener to that logical conclusion. If we are to seek peace in a cooperative spirit, then it necessarily follows that the cold war must thaw. And so the president said: "Let us examine our attitude toward the cold war, remembering that we are not engaged in a debate, seeking to pile up debating points. We are not here distributing blame or pointing the finger of judgment. We must deal with the world as it is, and not as it might have been had the history of the last 18 years been different." Kennedy stated that, if we were to achieve these ends, our weapons must be controlled, our military forces committed to "peace and disciplined in self-restraint," and our diplomats instructed "to avoid unnecessary irritants and purely rhetorical hostility."

This entire section of the speech—perhaps the most important part of the speech—was intended to achieve what Hilsman called flexibility, the signal to the Soviets that the United States was willing to negotiate from a new set of assumptions. However, sending a signal to the Soviets was a far easier task than changing American attitudes.

Presidents who offer dramatically new directions for policy (especially foreign policy) must attack and discredit the old linguistic lens, the old slogans, the old rhetoric if they are to have any chance of implementing new policies. "For the most part we do not first see, and then define. In the great blooming, buzzing confusion of the outer world we pick out what our culture has already defined for us, and we tend to perceive that which we have picked out in the form stereotyped for us by our culture."[11] And so President Kennedy sought to redefine relations between the United States and the Soviet Union so that the American people would *see* differently. In treating each of the three major topics of his address, Kennedy contrasted the old definitions with the new and argued that continuing to act upon the old definitions and assumptions would be futile or injurious whereas acting upon the new definitions would be realistic and bring a sliver of hope to the world.

As Hilsman pointed out, flexibility in such a situation always has to be tempered by firmness. By this, Hilsman meant that certain commitments had to be reaffirmed. As Kennedy stated in his speech, "we merely invite discouragement and incredulity" by seeking universal peace and good will immediately. Moreover, such a dramatic change as the one advocated by the president so changes perceptions—if effective—that they may leave the public confused and disoriented. Thus, Kennedy sought to stress his firmness toward the Soviet Union in two ways: (1) by pointing to the differences that still separate the two nations; and (2) by affirming existing American alliances with countries that might be affected by the flexibility he had called for.

Kennedy scored the Soviets for their distorted view of the West and for their aggressive intentions toward other nations. Yet, in both cases the president drew clear positive lessons from these Soviet faults that lent credence to his call for greater cooperation between the two countries. Early in his speech, as he was asking Americans to reexamine their attitudes toward the Soviet Union, the president prefaced his argument by noting the distorted view Soviets have of the West:

It is discouraging to think that their leaders may actually believe what their propagandists write. It is discouraging to read a recent authoritative Soviet text on *Military Strategy* and find, on page after page, wholly baseless and incredible claims—such as the allegation that "American imperialist circles are preparing to unleash different types of war . . . that there is a very real threat of a preventive war being unleashed by American imperialists against the Soviet Union . . . [and that] the political aims of the American imperialists are to enslave economically and politically the European and other capitalist countries . . . [and] to achieve world domination . . . by means of aggressive wars."

Even as Kennedy cited this quotation as typical of Soviet misperceptions, he warned the American public "not to fall into the same trap as the Soviets, not to see only a distorted and desperate view of the other side." Later, Kennedy placed responsibility for world unrest on the communists: "The communist drive to impose their political and economic system on others is the primary cause of world tension today." Thus, even as Kennedy sought to change attitudes, he also reaffirmed certain basic attitudes. Nonetheless, the peace could be assured, Kennedy concluded, if we embarked upon "a new effort to achieve world law—a new context for world discussion," which would be achieved through "increased understanding between the Soviets and ourselves," through "increased contact and communication."

In developing his argument in this fashion, Kennedy accomplished several tasks at once. First, he demonstrated that he was not naive about the Soviet system and the difficulties to be confronted in seeking cooperation with the Soviet leaders. Second, he reinforced the distinction between the communist system (that is aggressive and the leading cause of world tensions) and the Soviet people (who are human and the basis for a cooperative effort between the two countries.) Third, he used these hard-line statements as incentives for changing American attitudes and seeking greater cooperation with the Soviet Union. Thus, firmness gives strength to flexibility, even as the latter tempers the former.

In reaffirming American commitments with her allies, however, there can be no compromise:

Speaking of other nations, I wish to make one point clear. We are bound to many nations by alliances. Those alliances exist because our concerns and theirs substantially overlap. Our commitment to defend Western Europe and West Berlin, for example, stands undiminished because of the identity of our vital interest. The United States will make no deal with the Soviet Union at the expense of other nations and other peoples, not merely because they are our partners, but also because their interests and ours converge.

The rearrangement of perspectives about the Soviet Union does not compel a rearrangement of existing commitments to allies. In this area Kennedy exhibited the firmness essential to maintaining stability within the Atlantic alliance.

It is a commonplace in political rhetoric for speakers to present themselves as rational and their opponents as emotional, just as it is another commonplace to describe one's own proposals as the "plain truth" and opposing proposals as "mere rhetoric." These commonplaces are used even as advocates become emotional about their own rationality, even as they skillfully construct rhetorical arguments to denounce the use of rhetoric by others.

Throughout the address Kennedy presented his definitions of what kind of attitudes Americans ought to adopt as rational and positive and contrasted them with the old attitudes that were consistently described as irrational. Those who think peace cannot be achieved are described as indulging in "dangerous, defeatist" thinking.[12] Those who would continue with the old assumptions about confrontation with the Soviets are described as indulging in a "distorted and desperate view of the other side." The president, moreover, predicted that the consequences of not changing our attitudes would be catastrophic in this nuclear age: the ultimate irrationality. Peace becomes, then, as Kennedy said early in the speech, "the necessary rational end of rational men."

Symbolic Acts

Persuasive arguments are seldom enough to change deep-rooted beliefs or attitudes, among friends or adversaries. Specific acts of good faith are needed to demonstrate to friend and foe alike that one means what one says. Thus, President Kennedy announced two important decisions near the end of his speech:

First: Chairman Khrushchev, Prime Minister Macmillan, and I have agreed that high-level discussions will shortly begin in Moscow looking toward early agreement on a comprehensive test ban treaty. Our hopes must be tempered with the caution of history—but with our hopes go the hopes of all mankind.

Second: To make clear our good faith and solemn convictions on the matter. I now declare that the United States does not propose to conduct nuclear tests in the atmosphere so long as other states do not do so. We will not be the first to resume. Such a declaration is no substitute for a formal binding treaty, but I hope it will help us achieve one.

The first announcement symbolized the beginning of Soviet-American cooperation, though on a small scale—a beginning, nonetheless. The second demonstrated American willingness to take the initiative in making such cooperation the basis for more progressive relations between the two nations.[13] The importance of these announcements lay in their symbolism for the speech. The cessation of testing did not weaken or harm our national security in any perceptible fashion, as Amitai Etzioni later pointed out:

Although [halting nuclear testing in the atmosphere] was dramatic, it was basically a psychological gesture. It did not limit American arms. At the time the U.S. could deliver five times the firepower of the Soviet Union, and its missiles were better protected. The U.S. had conducted about twice as many tests as the U.S.S.R., and needed a one-or-two-year pause to digest the information.

Moreover, American experts agreed that even after two years there was little to be gained from additional testing. Any necessary tests could be conducted underground. Thus, in effect, the President used the termination of testing as a psychological gesture.[14]

The Soviets responded positively to these symbolic acts. The next day they removed their objection to sending observers to Yemen, a Western proposal they had previously blocked. On June 15 Premier Khrushchev made a speech favorable to the Kennedy initiatives and announced that he had ordered a halt to production of strategic bombers.[15] The flow toward detente was underway.

Results

Though Kennedy's speech generally met with favorable editorial response (especially in Europe), it did not have the immediate impact intended.[16] The next day, June 11, Governor George Wallace fulfilled a campaign promise to try to stop school desegregation by blocking the entrance to the University of Alabama when black students tried to enroll. That evening President Kennedy spoke to the nation, justifying his decision to send National Guardsmen to insure the enrollment of black students. In addition, he proposed a new civil rights bill outlawing segregation in public accommodations. Thus, this dramatic confrontation between federal authority and the governor became the top news story of the week, putting the Kennedy peace initiatives on the back pages.

Furthermore, the president left Washington on June 23 for a triumphant tour of Europe. His first stop was in West Germany to reassure its people that his overtures for peaceful settlement of outstanding differences between the United States and the U.S.S.R. would not endanger German security.[17] His appearances were intended to reaffirm American commitments to West Germany.

However, in one of his speeches, Kennedy got carried away. Speaking in the shadow of the infamous Berlin Wall in the Rudolph Wilde Platz, Kennedy orated:

Two thousand years ago the proudest boast was *"civis Romanus sum."* Today, in the world of freedom, the proudest boast is *"Ich bin ein Berliner."*

There are many people in the world who really don't understand, or say they don't, what is the great issue between the free world and the Communist world. Let them come to Berlin. There are some who say that communism is the wave of the future. Let them come to Berlin. And there are some who say in Europe and elsewhere we can work with the Communists. Let them come to Berlin. And there are even a few who say that it is true that communism is an evil system, but it permits us to make economic progress. *Lass sie nach Berlin kommen.* Let them come to Berlin.[18]

This attempt at firmness and reassurances surely went beyond what the occasion required. It was a direct contradiction of what Kennedy had said at American University. After all, it was Kennedy himself who had said—only sixteen days before—that communism permits some economic progress and that "we can work with the Communists." The speech was unfortunate in that it could have torpedoed the earlier peaceful initiatives. Kenneth O'Donnell and David Powers remarked: "Kennedy's fighting speech in Berlin . . . actually was a grave political risk, and he knew it. Such a heated tribute to West Berlin's resistance to Communism could have undone all the success of his appeal for peace and understanding with the Soviets in his American University speech two weeks earlier."[19] Because the speech might have produced this effect on the Russians, Kennedy hastened to the Free University in West Berlin that afternoon to give another speech that returned to the themes of the American University address. But the "Ich Bin Ein Berliner" speech shored up Kennedy's image for firmness in dealing with the Soviets. And it sent a message to his domestic critics in the United States that even though he wanted to seek rapprochement with the Soviet Union, that did not mean he intended to abandon our commitments around the world.

But these two speeches—the American University speech and the Berlin Wall speech—had even greater significance for foreign policy. The juxtaposition of these two speeches represented a juxtaposition of two concurrent policies Kennedy intended to pursue toward the Soviet Union. Because of the destructive power of nuclear weapons, Kennedy sought detente with the Soviet Union so as to avoid another nuclear confrontation. The American University speech eloquently delineated that policy. On the other hand, Kennedy saw the Soviet Union as the source of unrest in smaller countries throughout the world. He had said that explicitly at American University. Therefore, in the Berlin speech he was sending a message that the United States intended to continue to protect nations that it considered objects of communist expansion. Thus, the two speeches represent a two-track foreign policy that Kennedy intended to pursue in regard to the Soviet Union and the communist world. On the one hand, he would continue our policy of nuclear deterrence and also would pursue a policy of detente to assure that those weapons would never be used. Only by finding specific areas of agreement and concluding limited treaties could these objectives be achieved. On the other hand, he intended to pursue a policy of containing communist expansion into smaller nations by fighting limited wars with conventional weapons for political objectives.[20]

This set of complementary policies reconciled two seemingly contradictory speeches. And it set the stage for our involvement in Vietnam. What happened rhetorically was that Kennedy wanted to develop a more pragmatic rhetoric for talking about Soviet-American relations. At the same time, he was not abandoning traditional anti-communist rhetoric in foreign affairs. He applied it vigorously to relations with smaller nations that he believed needed our protection or that he believed represented sources of communist subversion and expansion. Thus, he sought to replace standard anticommunist rhetoric, but only as it applied to relations with the Soviet Union. When it came to other nations, he imposed it upon those situations more emphatically than Eisenhower or Dulles ever had.

These policies became the principal policies of subsequent presidents. They were brought home to the American people vividly in May 1972. At that time President Nixon ordered the mining of Haiphong harbor and a general escalation of the war in Vietnam on the eve of his trip to Moscow to conclude the first Strategic Arms Limitation Talks creating the SALT I treaty. Thus, the American people were treated to contrasting images of our foreign policy all at the same time. On the one hand, television brought home pictures of increased fighting in Vietnam to contain communism. And on the other, it broadcast conciliatory pictures of Nixon and Brezhnev toasting one another in a spirit of cordial cooperation as they concluded the strategic arms limitation treaty. One was an image of conflict; the other an image of cooperation. Each finds its antecedents—both in policy and in rhetoric—in Kennedy's remarkable speeches in June 1963.

Kennedy's Speech on the Treaty

On July 25, 1963, the limited nuclear test-ban treaty was concluded and initialed in Moscow. The next day President Kennedy spoke on national radio and television about the significance of the treaty. The speech was intended to marshal public support for the treaty and to present the president's main arguments to the Senate as it began deliberations over ratification of the treaty. In sum, the president was attempting to set the terms for argument over ratification, knowing full well that whoever sets those terms can usually win the argument.[21]

President Kennedy advanced four reasons or incentives for ratifying the treaty:

First, this treaty can be a step towards reduced world tension and broader areas of agreement.

Second, this treaty can be a step towards freeing the world from the fears and dangers of radioactive fallout.

Third, this treaty can be a step towards preventing the spread of nuclear weapons to nations not now possessing them.

Fourth and finally, this treaty can limit the nuclear arms race in ways which on balance, will strengthen our Nation's security far more than the continuation of unrestricted testing.[22]

Each of these was argued by balancing firmness with flexibility. And the president fully recognized the role symbolism plays in foreign affairs. For example, when Kennedy argued the first advantage of the treaty, he stated:

The Moscow talks have reached no agreement on any other subject, nor is this treaty conditioned on any other matter. Under Secretary Harriman made it clear that any nonaggression arrangements across the division in Europe would require full consultation with our allies and full attention to their interests. He also made clear our strong preference for a more comprehensive treaty banning all tests everywhere, and our ultimate hope for general and complete disarmament. The Soviet Government, however, is still unwilling to accept the inspection such goals require. . . .

But the difficulty of predicting the next step is no reason to be reluctant about this step. Nuclear test ban negotiations have long been a symbol of East-West disagreement. If this treaty can also be a symbol—if it can symbolize the end of one era and the beginning of another—if both sides can by this treaty gain confidence and experience in peaceful collaboration—then this short and simple treaty may well become an historic mark in man's age-old pursuit of peace.

Kennedy concluded the speech by remarking on the symbolic nature of the treaty:

According to the ancient Chinese proverb, "A journey of a thousand miles must begin with a single step."

My fellow Americans, let us take that first step. Let us, if we can, step back from the shadows of war and seek out the way of peace. And if that journey is a thousand miles, or even more, let history record that we, in this land, at this time, took the first step.

Thus, Kennedy established the strongest grounds for argument: ratification of the treaty would be a step toward peace; failure to ratify it might, by implication, be a step away from peace and toward greater tensions between the United States and the U.S.S.R. These grounds were quite favorable ones upon which to wage rhetorical battles for ratification.

On September 24, 1963, by a vote of 80 to 19, the Senate of the United States ratified the limited nuclear test-ban treaty.[23]

Conclusion

Chairman Nikita Khrushchev called Kennedy's speech at American University "the best speech by any American President since Roosevelt."[24] Truly, it was the best speech Kennedy gave during his entire administration. But it was only part of an overall effort to change public attitudes toward reaching the first phase of detente with the Soviet Union. That is, Kennedy began with the principles upon which the United States should seek accommodation with the U.S.S.R., principles he spelled out in full in the American University speech. The speech was a mixture of firmness, flexibility, and rationality. The specific issues to be negotiated were relegated to the conclusion of the speech and were to be seen and understood in light of the principles enunciated earlier in the speech.

The main problem the president faced was assuring both the American public and our allies in Europe that he was as firm in his commitments to national interests and to allies as he was in his call for flexibility in negotiating with the Soviets. His European trip and his tough "Ich Bin Ein Berliner" speech were intended to give those assurances. Furthermore, the two speeches when taken in tandem represented a two-pronged approach to dealing with the communist world in a comprehensive way.

Using the unique presidential pulpit on the eve of Senate debate over ratification, Kennedy established the strongest possible ground for himself in those debates. He gave his supporters arguments to use for ratification as well as arguments to use against opponents. In the end, the treaty was ratified and stands as Kennedy's greatest achievement during his administration.

In conclusion, President Kennedy's rhetorical efforts to change assumptions about policy differences on outstanding issues between the United States and the Soviet Union ushered in the era of detente. It was a masterful political and rhetorical performance, and one that would be emulated by other presidents seeking to change attitudes on controversial foreign policy issues. Above all, Kennedy was now on the rhetorical offensive in exerting leadership, rather than on the defensive in responding to events. In the third year of his presidency Kennedy had begun to realize how public speeches could be used as an instrument of politics to achieve his policy aims.

Civil Rights: 1960–1963

Civil rights was the leading domestic issue facing the United States during Kennedy's administration. During the 1960 campaign Kennedy had dramatically intervened when Dr. Martin Luther King, Jr., was imprisoned on a traffic technicality and helped to free him. He called Mrs. King to express his concern, and then his brother Robert called the judge in the case to plead (successfully as it turned out) for King's release from prison. The result of this intervention was that Dr. King's father, who had previously supported Richard Nixon, publicly switched to Kennedy, saying: "I've got a suitcase of votes, and I'm going to take them to Mr. Kennedy and dump them in his lap."[25] That dramatic gesture seemed to demonstrate Kennedy's personal commitment to civil rights.

On election day Kennedy received 68 percent of the black vote in the election. The black vote was crucial to Kennedy's narrow victory. Theodore White pointed out that in Illinois, which Kennedy carried by 9,000 votes, 250,000 blacks were estimated to have voted for him. Moreover, in Michigan, which he carried by 67,000, another 250,000 blacks were estimated to have voted for him.[26] But as impressive as these numbers were, there was also another story. The 68 percent of the black vote that Kennedy garnered represented the second-lowest percentage of black votes for a Democratic presidential candidate since 1952.[27]

During the campaign Kennedy had scored the Eisenhower administration for not signing an executive order ending discrimination in federal housing. He pledged that his first order of business upon becoming president would be to sign such an order and end housing discrimination "with a stroke of a pen." These words would come back to haunt Kennedy during the first two years of his administration.[28]

John F. Kennedy's presidential record on civil rights is a mixed one. On the one hand, he has been called our "second Emancipator President."[29] On the other, a variety of critics have scored him for his lack of leadership to the most pressing domestic problem confronting his administration.[30] Whichever assessment one agrees with may depend more on one's political views than on any final objective analysis. Despite that limitation, there are several conclusions that can be drawn about Kennedy's approach to civil rights.

First, Kennedy sought to deal with the issue through judicial means (including appointments to the bench) or executive orders instead of through legislative action during the first two years of his administration. Although he delayed issuing the executive order about discrimination in housing until after the midterm election, shortly after his inaugural he signed Executive Order 10925 directing executive agencies to take action to eliminate racial discrimination in hiring. This order also established the president's Committee on Equal Opportunity. In addition to this action, President Kennedy appointed more blacks to the federal bench than all his predecessors and sought to have Congress create a new cabinet department, the Department of Housing and Urban Affairs, to which he wanted to appoint Robert Weaver, a black. Furthermore, the Kennedy Justice Department filed a number of civil rights suits attempting to have the Courts overthrow discriminatory practices.[31] Although the results of these efforts were mixed, they were on the whole more positive than negative.

But in the area of legislative initiatives and public leadership, Kennedy's record was less sterling. No doubt he preferred to address the issue of civil rights through judicial rather than legislative means. No doubt he faced formidable political opposition in Congress for any legislative initiatives in this area.[32] But it is equally evident that Kennedy did not see the sit-ins, the marches, the freedom rides, not even the bombing of the Birmingham church as sufficient—at least during the first two years of his administration—to arouse his well-established proclivity for crisis. During those first two years Kennedy treated civil rights as a legal issue or a typical political issue, sometimes as an isolated incident to be dealt with in its own terms rather than as part of a broad movement in American politics and history. It was not until the third year that he saw the impending crisis and reacted by describing it as a moral crisis. In fact, during the first two years of his administration he repeatedly sought to minimize the emotional aura surrounding civil rights incidents. For the crises of civil rights for black Americans during those years, Kennedy did not employ crisis rhetoric but instead resorted to calm (and sometimes innocuous) statements about the issue, preferring to defuse emotions rather than arouse them. Nowhere was this better demonstrated than in a comparison of two speeches Kennedy delivered in response to two similar situations: James Meredith's enrollment at the University of Mississippi in September 1962 (before the midterm elections) and the integration of the University of Alabama in June 1963 (after the midterm elections).

Desegregation at the University of Mississippi

In 1961 James Meredith, a black who met all the academic requirements for admission to the University of Mississippi, applied for admission to that state university and was refused. He sought redress through the courts, and in September 1962 the courts ordered the University of Mississippi to admit him as a student. On September 30 he was admitted. At the same time rioting broke out on the Oxford campus and continued into the next day. Two people were killed. The president called upon federal troops and National Guardsmen, sworn into federal service, to take control of the violent situation.[33]

In the midst of the rioting on the evening of September 30, President Kennedy spoke over national television and radio about the significance of the events in Oxford in a "law and order" speech. Kennedy defined the issue at Oxford, indeed the entire civil rights issue, as a legal issue that required Americans to abide by the rulings of the court:

All students, members of the faculty, and public officials in both Mississippi and the Nation will be able, it is hoped, to return to their normal activities with full confidence in the integrity of American law.
This is as it should be, for our Nation is founded on the principle that

observance of the law is the eternal safeguard of liberty and defiance of the law is the surest road to tyranny. The law which we obey included the final rulings of the courts, as well as the enactments of our legislative bodies. Even among law-abiding men few laws are universally loved, but they are uniformly respected and not resisted.

Americans are free, in short, to disagree with the law but not to disobey it. For in a government of laws and not of men, no man, however prominent or powerful, and no mob, however unruly or boisterous, is entitled to defy a court of law. If this country should ever reach the point where any man or group of men by force or threat of force could long defy the commands of our court and our Constitution, then no law would stand free from doubt, no judge would be sure of his writ, and no citizen would be safe from his neighbors.[34]

From this point in his address, the president proceeded to justify his actions in sending federal troops into Mississippi, even to the point of expressing his deep "regret" that such action was necessary. He went on to recognize that "the present period of transition and adjustment" (as he called the civil rights movement) was a difficult one for the South and pointed out that the responsibility for the accumulated wrongs of the past one hundred years had been a failure that must "be shared by us all, by every State, by every citizen."

Kennedy then made a special plea to the University of Mississippi and the citizens of that state:

Mississippi and her University . . . are noted for their contribution of talent and thought to the affairs of this Nation. This is the State of Lucius Lamar and many others who have placed the national good ahead of sectional interest. This is the State which had four Medal of Honor winners in the Korean War alone. In fact, the Guard unit federalized this morning, early, is part of the 155th Infantry, one of the 10 oldest regiments in the Union and one of the most decorated for sacrifices and bravery in 6 wars.

In 1945 a Mississippi sergeant, Jake Lindsey, was honored by an unusual joint session of the Congress. I close therefore with this appeal to the students of the University, the people who are most concerned.

You have a great tradition to uphold, a tradition of honor and courage won on the field of battle and on the gridiron as well as the University campus. You have a new opportunity to show that you are men of patriotism and integrity. For the most effective means of upholding the law is not the State policeman or the marshals or the National Guard. It is you. It lies in your courage to accept those laws with which you disagree as well as those with which you agree. The eyes of the Nation and of all the world are upon you and upon all of us, and the honor of your University and State are in the balance. I am certain that the great majority of the students will uphold that honor.

Even as Kennedy spoke, rioting raged in Oxford, and two people were killed that evening.

President Kennedy's speech on the desegregation of the University of Mississippi was curiously restrained. He defined the issue in the narrowest of legal terms and engaged in a rhetoric of supplication toward the white citizens of Mississippi, imploring them to accept reasonably and peaceably the court rulings. But who was the audience for this speech? Certainly not blacks, who found the speech obviously insufficient. Certainly not the white racists of Mississippi. How could they listen to reason and moderation when they were preoccupied with rioting on the Oxford campus?

Sorensen tried to suggest that the president was unprepared for the violence that Meredith's enrollment excited.[35] But that explanation is tepid. For weeks the administration had negotiated with Governor Ross Barnett over the admission of Meredith, and it had tried a variety of ways to have him enrolled that would minimize the event so as not to enrage the white citizenry of Mississippi. One might explain this moderate speech by referring to the national political situation. After all, the confrontation at the University of Mississippi came just two months before the midterm election. One could argue that Kennedy was hoping to avoid the loss of southern Democratic seats in Congress by treating the situation delicately. But that explanation will not suffice. At the time, the South was a one-party region, where Democratic representatives were hardly in danger of losing their seats. One could also argue that, given the slim margin by which he was elected, Kennedy sought to avoid losing personal popularity. But certainly he must have known that *any* action he would take in regard to civil rights would cause white southerners to turn against him. One could finally argue that Kennedy sought not to inflame unduly the passions created by the situation. But if that was his thinking, he was sorely deluded, given the violence that followed.

The plainest explanation for this cautious speech is that Kennedy did not perceive the civil rights struggle as a major or critical issue facing the country. Quite simply, Kennedy was not sensitive to the determination that black citizens felt in attempting to secure their rights and their legitimate participation in American life. And so, in 1962, Kennedy did not place civil rights in the same category as other urgent business with which he had to deal. Navasky observed: "[E]arly Kennedy priorities put civil rights somewhere around the middle of the list—after organized crime, after Jimmy Hoffa, after anti-trust . . . , after juvenile delinquency, but ahead of internal security, ahead of crime in the streets, ahead of such unglamorous fields as civil, lands and natural resources litigation."[36] Kennedy confirmed this assessment in his conclusion to the September 30th speech, when he said: "There is in short no reason why the books on this case cannot now be quickly and quietly closed in the manner directed by the court. Let us preserve both the law and the peace and then healing those wounds that are within we can turn *to the greater crises* that are without and stand united as one people in our pledge to man's freedom" (emphasis added). But the books were not closed, the wounds were not healed, and greater civil rights battles were on the horizon.

Desegregation at the University of Alabama

Less than a year later similar events at the University of Alabama brought Kennedy finally, albeit reluctantly, into the mainstream of the civil rights movement. But between the two speeches Kennedy continued to drag his feet when the issue erupted. After the House Republicans introduced a civil rights bill, Kennedy tried to offset that political move by introducing his own bill. The measure he presented was a modest one calling principally for additional federal funds to help school districts that had embarked on desegregation and for more vigor in prosecution of voting rights cases in the courts. However, the leaders of the movement were not so cautious. In April 1963 Dr. Martin Luther King, Jr., and his Southern Christian Leadership Conference launched a public campaign to test segregation laws in Alabama. They mounted massive demonstrations in Birmingham, which were met with equally massive and brutal responses by police commissioner "Bull" Connor. The televised pictures of police dogs attacking unarmed men, women, and children and the spraying of demonstrators with water hoses enraged the nation. Yet, it was not until the confrontation over integration at the University of Alabama that the president decided to speak out forcefully.

The day after Kennedy's speech on the situation at the University of Mississippi, Governor George Wallace of Alabama publicly pledged to "stand in the doorway" of any schoolhouse if the events in Mississippi were repeated in Alabama.[37] On June 11, 1963, he kept that pledge by blocking the entrance to the admissions building to prevent the enrollment of two black students at the University of Alabama in Tuscaloosa. It was a futile symbolic gesture, but it dramatized the conflict to come. After federal marshals presented the governor with the court orders, he reluctantly stood aside and the students were enrolled.

On the evening of June 11, 1963, President Kennedy spoke to the nation about the events at the University of Alabama. His speech differed radically from his speech of nine months before. Sorensen hurriedly wrote this eloquent speech, and only one draft was completed. He did not begin working on the speech until late in the afternoon that it was delivered, and it was completed only minutes before the president went on television. Sorensen said that Kennedy "wholly extemporize[d] a heartfelt conclusion."[38]

Kennedy opened the speech by recounting the actions that he had taken that afternoon—the deployment of National Guardsmen to the University of Alabama to carry out the court order requiring the admission of black students. But now in 1963, instead of narrowing the issue to the university situation, Kennedy broadened the issue to talk about the plight of black citizens (Negroes, as the prevailing language was at that time) in America. But in concentrating on their plight, Kennedy focused on the social indignities and economic oppression they faced. Drawing upon the struggle for freedom abroad, Kennedy used that struggle to highlight the struggle at home:

Today we are committed to a worldwide struggle to promote and protect the rights of all who wish to be free. And when Americans are sent to Viet-Nam or West Berlin, we do not ask for whites only. It ought to be possible, therefore, for American students of any color to attend any public institution they select without having to be backed up by troops.

It ought to be possible for American consumers of any color to receive equal service in places of public accommodation, such as hotels and restaurants and theaters and retail stores, without being forced to resort to demonstrations in the street, and it ought to be possible for American citizens of any color to register and to vote in a free election without interference or fear of reprisal.

It ought to be possible, in short, for every American to enjoy the privileges of being American without regard to his race or his color. In short, every American ought to have the right to be treated as he would wish to be treated, as one would wish his children to be treated. But this is not the case.

The Negro baby born in America today, regardless of the section in which he is born, has about one-half as much chance of completing a high school as a white baby born in the same place on the same day, one-third as much chance of completing college, one-third as much chance of becoming a professional man, twice as much chance of becoming unemployed, about one-seventh as much chance of earning $10,000 a year, a life expectancy which is 7 years shorter, and the prospects of earning only half as much.[39]

In contrast to the legal approach Kennedy took to the desegregation of the University of Mississippi, Kennedy now defined the issue in more affecting and eloquent terms:

We are confronted primarily with a moral issue. It is as old as the Scriptures and is as clear as the American Constitution.

The heart of the question is whether all Americans are to be afforded equal rights and equal opportunities, whether we are going to treat our fellow Americans as we want to be treated. If an American, because his skin is dark, cannot eat lunch in a restaurant open to the public, if he cannot send his children to the best public school available, if he cannot vote for the public officials who represent him, if, in short, he cannot enjoy the full and free life which all of us want, then who among us would be content to have the color of his skin changed and stand in his place? Who among us would then be content with the counsels of patience and delay?

In contrast with his hopes that the actions at the University of Mississippi could close the books on the issue, Kennedy now called for immediate legislative action "giving all Americans the right to be served in facilities which are open to the public—hotels, restaurants, theaters, retail stores, and similar establishments." This public accommodations section was the distinguishing section of the bill Kennedy sent to Congress eight days after the speech. But it also contained sections prohibiting the use of literacy tests unless those tests were uniformly administered in writing and making a sixth-grade education in English a presumption of literacy. The bill gave the federal government power to halt federal funding for programs that were administered in a discriminatory manner. Furthermore, it established new agencies, such as a permanent Commission on Equal Employment Opportunity and a Community Relations Service, and extended the powers of established departments and agencies to act more aggressively in pursuing lawsuits.

Some have contended that these legislative proposals were merely window-dressing in the light of the magnitude of the wrongs that Kennedy had described in the speech and the actual conditions that existed: economic oppression, unemployment, and voter disenfranchisement. But given the preceding two years of avoiding any progressive legislation in this area, Kennedy's initiative was dramatic. It signaled that the president was coming into the mainstream of the civil rights movement and intended to strike out in a new direction to confront the issue. It signaled a turning point in the federal government's involvement in the issue. In sum, the speech was dramatic and moving. Indeed, some black leaders called it the "Second Emancipation Proclamation." It is one of the oddities of Kennedy's celebrated rhetoric that he delivered his two most eloquent and progressive speeches on successive days: the American University address on June 10 and the Civil Rights speech on June

11. In these back-to-back speeches Kennedy boldly pointed to new directions for Americans in both foreign and domestic policy.

The confrontation at the University of Alabama was the last crisis Kennedy had to face in his short administration. Crisis rhetoric was now employed in the struggle for equal rights in America. But it should be remembered that what called forth this form of rhetoric at this time was not rioting on a university campus, nor a bombing of a black church, nor even the use of police dogs and water hoses against black demonstrators. Instead, the inciting incident was an act of defiance of federal authority by a southern governor. Nonetheless, Kennedy's speech aroused a nation and injected the moral force of the presidency into the civil rights movement. He presented his civil rights bill to the Congress and then watched the movement gather steam, culminating in the great march on Washington on August 28, 1963. Kennedy did not live to see the bill become law, but he had finally established the moral basis for it and for subsequent legislation that President Johnson would present and steer through Congress.[40]

Conclusion

This analysis of Kennedy's crises does not pretend to be a comprehensive study of President John F. Kennedy's rhetoric. It has been limited to his speeches on important issues. It has also been an examination of how and why Kennedy used crisis rhetoric during the first two years of his administration, especially in foreign affairs, and then tried to replace it when it came to Soviet-American relations in the third year. In the civil rights arena, Kennedy reversed the pattern. He originally saw the struggle for equal rights in America as little more than another political issue to manage, usually through judicial means. But in the third year he changed course and elevated civil rights to the level of a moral crisis for American society. Overall, crisis became the rhetorical signature of his administration.

Kennedy's rhetoric was generally conceived and developed as a response, a reaction to situations. Often, in foreign affairs, it was a hysterical reaction, as in the case of the so-called Berlin crisis. But in a certain mystical way these crisis speeches also contributed to a sense of idealism on the part of the American people. Perhaps that was due to the association of crisis with risk, and of risk with idealism. Certainly, actions seem more important when they are taken in a time of "maximum danger" than when they are taken in a time of tranquility.

Kennedy set a political style for his administration that greatly depended on his rhetoric. Kennedy's distinctive political style was far different from his predecessor's. In his farewell address to the American people, given only three days before the inaugural, President Eisenhower also described the world in crisis terms, but he warned against meeting them with "some spectacular and costly action." He cautioned against the rash action of the "emotional and transitory sacrifices of crisis" and proposed the country follow a policy that balanced the "actions of the moment and the national welfare of the future."[41]

President Kennedy ignored these warnings to set his own course, one of urgency and crisis. It was heralded by his rhetoric and carried through in his actions. He sought out "crises," and they were "costly."

The forms of Kennedy's rhetoric are important because they are so varied. During his short three years as president, Kennedy ran through a variety of different forms of presidential address, forms that other presidents would use after him. His inaugural address set the standard for modern presidents. His uses of domestic crisis rhetoric and foreign crisis rhetoric created typical lines of argument that Johnson and Nixon also used, indeed establishing the genres of presidential rhetoric for the postwar period. At the same time, his inaugural address, and his speeches on peace at American University and on civil rights the day after remain eloquent addresses; in them, the famous Kennedy rhetorical style matched the occasion and the issues. Indeed, his American University address remains the finest postwar statement by an American president on the imperative for seeking peace in this dangerous world. It is one speech that all presidents should read and reread as they deliberate on international nuclear issues and ponder courses for the future.

Kennedy's rhetoric also set many of the rhetorical themes for a generation of politicians. During the first two years of his administration he struck strident notes of confrontation: first with the news media over the Bay of Pigs, then with the Russians over Berlin, next with the steel executives over their price hikes, and finally once again with the ultimate confrontation with the Soviet Union over the missiles in Cuba. As he said in his inaugural address, he welcomed the challenge to live in a time of maximum danger. In each of these confrontations he saw *his* will and *his* courage being tested. More often than not, these themes—tests of will and courage— overshadowed specific, tangible policy goals. More often than not, other presidents have followed suit by invoking a crisis rhetoric in which America's will and courage are at stake.

With this emphasis on the symbolism of actions, Kennedy often obscured the actual events and goals. And sympathetic historians have followed suit by concentrating more on the symbolism surrounding the events of his administration than on the events themselves, except as seen through the lens of Kennedy's rhetoric.

But what are we to say of the concrete accomplishments of the Kennedy administration? They are painfully few: the test-ban treaty, the Peace Corps, "the largest and fastest military buildup in our peacetime history," the Alliance for Progress, the educational television act, among others.[42]

More to the point, Kennedy set the stage for triumphs and tragedies to come. He invited young people to participate in politics, and they took him at his word, setting off an explosion of youthful politics and protest that took directions he could never have imagined. His belated recognition of the plight of black citizens finally directed the nation's attention to this persistent national problem. In describing that plight in 1963 as a moral crisis, he prepared the way for the creative and far-reaching accomplishments of the Johnson administration in civil rights.

Yet, he set the stage for more tragedies than triumphs to come. His approval of a unilateral invasion of Cuba, even though only Cuban exiles actually landed, eroded part of our claim to moral leadership in the world, the initial slippage that would become a landslide. His "largest and fastest military buildup in our peacetime history" solidified the place of the military-industrial complex in American politics and society. Taking us to the brink of nuclear war over offensive missiles in Cuba made some Americans and policy makers believe that such confrontations could be successfully managed, even as future presidents and policy makers sought to avoid such direct confrontations. In fact, President Kennedy was the only postwar president to take the country and the world so close to nuclear war.

Richard Walton concluded his study of Kennedy's foreign policy by stating that as president, Kennedy "was Cold Warrior and counterrevolutionary."[43] That is overstated and only partly true. In the area of foreign policy ideas Kennedy certainly deserves great credit for initiating the era of detente that led to the test-ban treaty, to Nixon's opening the doors to the People's Republic of China, and to Reagan's INF treaty as well as the START proposals. The idea of detente with superpowers and the political risks Kennedy took in proposing it at American University were progressive steps quite different from the foreign policies of the two previous administrations in regard to the Soviet Union.

But in this triumph were also the seeds of great tragedies. Even as he called for abandoning the strident anticommunist rhetoric in Soviet-American relations, Kennedy transferred that rhetoric to smaller nations in the world, expanded it, and intensified it. Thus, the only change in traditional anticommunist rhetoric that he made was in attempting to apply it more to Third World nations than to the Soviet Union. And by his sometimes hysterical rhetoric about the challenges America faced in "every corner of the world," as he phrased it in one of his speeches after the Bay of Pigs, he greatly heightened the perception of the importance of Berlin, Cuba, and Vietnam to American national interests. With his creation of the Green Berets and the massive buildup of conventional forces, he set in motion preparations for intervention in smaller countries where he believed that the decisive future battles with communism would be fought. In concentrating so intensely on these nations—especially Vietnam—and in seeing them rhetorically as testing grounds in America's deadly confrontations with communism, he prepared the way for Johnson's escalation of American involvement in the war in Vietnam and the tragedies that issued from that involvement.

In 1961 Kennedy took his stand on Cuba and Berlin. In 1962 he took his stand once again on Cuba. By 1963 he had built the platform for Johnson to take his stand on Vietnam.

Indeed, the two-track or two-pronged foreign policy he pursued became the basic foreign policy of the United States, even now almost thirty years later. If the critic can praise Kennedy for establishing the groundwork that led to progressive treaties and relations with superpowers, the critic can also indict Kennedy for preparing the way for involvement in Vietnam, Cambodia, and Nicaragua.

The Kennedy administration was unfortunately much too short. To paraphrase the title of Lewis Paper's book, there was more promise than performance. During his administration he affected the mood and direction of the United States more than its immediate policies. Thus, he is remembered more for his words than his works. And some of those words were dangerous, some foreboding, some inspiring. That is the political legacy of Kennedy's crisis rhetoric.

4

Americanizing the Vietnam War
President Johnson's Press Conference of July 28, 1965

The early summer of 1965 became a time of decision for President Lyndon Johnson. On the one hand, he desperately wanted peace in Vietnam. On the other hand, he faced what he thought would be a defeat in Asia if he did not do something about the deteriorating situation in Vietnam. Trying to reconcile these two would cause Johnson great anguish. But his anguish would be intensified by his attempts to reconcile his eventual decision to the rhetorical demands of explaining his policy to American opinion makers and the American public. Television and the "bully pulpit" had emerged as crucial elements in national decision making. To put it simply, a president could not make a critical decision without considering how he would explain that decision and where he would announce that decision publicly. This chapter is about how Johnson sought to harmonize all these discordant concerns.

Johnson had campaigned the year before as the peace candidate promising not to send American boys to do the fighting Asian boys ought to be doing for themselves.[1] Since the end of the campaign he had sought peace. He had said it over and over again. Nowhere had he spelled it out more clearly than at Johns Hopkins University on April 7, 1965:

We will never be second in the search for . . . a peaceful settlement in Viet-Nam.

There may be many ways to this kind of peace: in discussion or negotiation with the governments concerned; in large groups or in small ones; in the reaffirmation of old agreements or their strengthening with new ones.

We have stated this position over and over to friend and foe alike. And we remain ready with this purpose for unconditional discussions.[2]

To put the brightest face on this plea for peace, Johnson pledged a "billion dollar investment" for economic development of Vietnam, obviously an enticement (or bribe, if one prefers) for the Viet Cong and North Vietnamese to negotiate a settlement. But negotiations were not forthcoming.

Johnson wanted peace because he wanted to be remembered as the president who tried to end poverty and disease, illiteracy and racial injustice in America. He wanted to build his Great Society where every mind "is set free to scan the farthest reaches of thought and imagination."[3] Already he had gotten the 1964 Civil Rights Act passed, and he was pressing for passage of the new voters' rights bill. In addition, major bills involving his program for the Great Society were proceeding through committees in Congress: Medicare, education bills, bills to reduce poverty and to rebuild the cities. The president needed to focus his considerable legislative skills on these bills to see them through to completion. To do that, he needed peace in Vietnam.

But in the early summer both the military and the political situations in Vietnam were deteriorating. General William Westmoreland had requested another major deployment of American troops beyond the 75,000 who were already there. In fact, he sent his requests saying he needed these substantial increases if the country was to avoid losing Vietnam to the communists. But Johnson was reluctant to make such a commitment at that time. Nonetheless, the time for decision was quickly approaching.

Before he decided, Johnson wanted to explore his options. In mid-July he sent Secretary of Defense Robert McNamara and former ambassador Henry Cabot Lodge to Vietnam on a fact-finding mission to learn firsthand what Westmoreland needed by way of reinforcements. When they returned and submitted their report, Johnson convened a week-long series of meetings with his cabinet officers and advisers to explore his options and to make a decision.[4] To put Johnson's decision in perspective, it may be appropriate here to review briefly Johnson's most important public statements up to this time because it is in July 1965 that Johnson made the fateful decision that was to lead the United States into another war and eventually was to wreck his presidency.

Johnson on Vietnam: 1963–1965

The story of our early involvement in Vietnam has been told many times in many places. What concerns us here are the important public statements by President Johnson leading up to his late July decision on Vietnam.

In his first major speech after the assassination of President John F. Kennedy, Johnson reaffirmed what he took to be American national commitments. In foreign affairs he was specific: "This Nation will keep its commitments from South Viet-Nam to West Berlin."[5] But the kind of commitment he was prepared to make remained vague. Indeed, Johnson focused little public attention, for the most part, on Vietnam in 1964, and our military advisers in Vietnam increased by only 7,000 that year, from 14,000 to 21,000.

There was one important exception. In August 1964 the Tonkin Gulf incident occurred. Johnson went on national television to announce that two American ships had been fired upon by North Vietnamese torpedo boats. In ordering a "positive reply" to these attacks, Johnson announced that a retaliatory bombing of the ports from which the torpedo boats had been launched was being carried out even as he spoke. Furthermore, the president requested a resolution from Congress giving him authority to "take all necessary measures in support of freedom and in defense of peace in southeast Asia."[6] In a speech the following day at Syracuse University and again in a speech before the American Bar Association on August 12, Johnson defended his retaliatory bombing of North Vietnam but insisted that no other country need fear that the United States wanted a wider war in Southeast Asia. In the latter speech Johnson chastised those who wanted stronger action: "Some . . . are eager to enlarge the conflict. They call upon us to supply American boys to do the job that Asian boys should do. They ask us to take reckless action which might risk the lives of millions and engulf much of Asia and certainly threaten the peace of the entire world. Moreover, such action would offer no solution at all to the real problem of Viet-Nam. America can and America will meet any wider challenge from others, but our aim in Viet-Nam, as in the rest of the world, is to help restore the peace and to reestablish a decent order."[7] At the same time Johnson reaffirmed American commitments to the "independence and security" of South Vietnam, to repelling aggression, and to maintaining what he called these "tested principles" that both the Eisenhower and Kennedy administrations had honored. In hindsight, one can see that these goals of repelling aggression but not widening the war were compatible only so long as South Vietnam was capable of defending itself, a political and military situation that was quickly changing. In 1964 Johnson seemed to believe he could carry on this two-track policy without committing significant American resources to the war. By retaliating against North Vietnam but not significantly increasing the American military presence in South Vietnam, Johnson appeared to the American public as a prudent but forceful leader.

After his inauguration in 1965 events began to move swiftly, so swiftly that the president believed they required further action. The pattern for his actions had been set the year before. He would respond with limited retaliation and at the same time pursue his two-track policy of firmness toward "aggression" while seeking a peaceful settlement.

On February 6, 1965, Viet Cong guerrillas attacked the U.S. officers' barracks at Pleiku. Eight Americans were killed and 126 were wounded. Several days later the Viet Cong struck again at Qui Nhom. Johnson's response to each was a retaliatory air strike against targets he selected in North Vietnam. Thus began the bombing war. Soon these retaliatory attacks ("Operation Flaming Dart") evolved into a daily and full-scale bombing of military targets in North Vietnam ("Operation Rolling Thunder"). Near the end of February the administration issued a white paper on Vietnam accusing the North of waging a war of aggression against the South. On March 7 the first fully equipped combat troops landed at Da Nang. But their purpose was officially defensive: limited service in the protection of the perimeters of air bases, as Secretary McNamara described it. Furthermore, McNamara specifically directed these "combat troops" (a significant change in description from the "advisers" who had been in Vietnam for years) not to engage the Viet Cong in battle.[8]

By mid-March these changes in American involvement in Vietnam created protests against them. The first—a university teach-in on Vietnam—ironically occurred at the University of Michigan, where less than a year before Johnson had announced his intention to use his administration to build a Great Society in the United States. These teach-ins soon spread to other campuses and eventually led to a national teach-in protest in Washington scheduled for May.

It was within this context Johnson delivered his famous speech on Vietnam at Johns Hopkins University on April 7.[9] But as much effort as Johnson and his advisers put into the speech, it was principally a "peace" speech restating in sometimes softer language what the president had been saying all along. He wanted peace, not war. But aggression by North Vietnam could not go unpunished or unchecked. Yet, the president made no new announcements about American military intentions, and certainly the president did not announce further escalation of the war. President Johnson emphasized instead what the United States would *not* do: "We will not be defeated. We will not grow tired. We will not withdraw, either openly or under the cloak of a meaningless agreement."[10] The Johns Hopkins speech was a peace speech and an attempt to pacify Johnson's domestic critics. But Johnson had no real fall-back position other than the claims that aggression had to be stopped and that America would not be defeated in Vietnam. This lack of specific goals in Vietnam remained a persistent rhetorical and policy problem. The president compounded these problems by stating our reasons for being in Vietnam in negative terms. In other words, Johnson gave little direction on where the United States intended to go in Vietnam, but at the same time he was closing the back door, leaving no honorable escape from the conflict there.

In May the national teach-in convened in Washington and near the same time Johnson declared a six-day bombing halt to induce North Vietnam to negotiate a settlement. Claiming that he had received no "peace feelers" from North Vietnam during the bombing halt, Johnson resumed the bombing. Both the military and political situations in Vietnam were deteriorating rapidly, leading to the crisis of July 1965 and Johnson's decision to Americanize the war.

The Turning Point

On July 21 President Johnson began a week-long review of U.S. policy in Vietnam. He had two problems to resolve: a policy decision and an announcement decision. He had to decide what to do about U.S. involvement in Vietnam. Once that was decided, he had to determine the best way to announce his decision. Johnson knew time was running out on his two-track "holding" policy, and now a major decision was required.

As Johnson saw it, he had five options:

1. The United States could go in all the way and destroy North Vietnam.
2. The United States could pull out of Vietnam.
3. The United States could continue providing assistance to South Vietnam at the same level as it had been for the preceding months.
4. The United States could increase its involvement significantly but short of an all-out war by giving the commanders what

they needed, by rallying the public through a declaration of a national emergency, by calling up the reserves and National Guard, and by having the president go before Congress for a special request for emergency funds.

5. The United States could increase its involvement significantly (as in option 4) but without the theatrics of calling up the reserves or declaring a national emergency or going before Congress with a major address.[11]

The first three options were hardly considered and quickly discarded. Johnson was not about to go before Congress and ask for a declaration of war against a nation that had not attacked the United States. Indeed, what justification would there be for a declaration of war against North Vietnam or even for a full commitment of American troops to fight a war in Vietnam? And one could forget even thinking about justifications for such an action. Johnson was not about to commit the United States to a full-scale land war in Asia. Or at least so he thought.

The second option was just as quickly dismissed. Only a few days after the assassination of President Kennedy, Johnson had told Ambassador Lodge that he was not going to be the first American president to lose a war. In his public statements he had repeatedly said that America would not desert her ally in South Vietnam. Withdrawing from the conflict was out of the question.

The third option was not really an option at all. The current policy was not working, and that had been the reason for convening these critical meetings. As Johnson later described it, continuing at the same level would require the United States to suffer the terrible consequences of continuing "to lose territory and take casualties. You wouldn't want your own boy to be out there crying for help and not get it."[12]

So the eventual decision narrowed down to a choice between the final two: increasing American involvement and declaring a national emergency, or increasing American involvement but not declaring a national emergency. But increasing American involvement—or, as Johnson later put it, giving "our commanders in the field the men and supplies they say they need"—actually meant Americanizing the war. It meant not only greater involvement. It meant a change in strategy and tactics.[13] Indeed, it meant a change in policy and purpose. American troops would be increased significantly and soon would be allowed to search out and attempt to destroy the enemy. It would mean an additional 50,000 troops immediately and a doubling of the draft. And that was the decision.

At this point, the rhetorical handling of the decision became as important as, if not more important than, the decision itself. Given the way Johnson had phrased options four and five, the options and the accompanying rhetoric to announce or justify them became inseparable from those options. In fact, the most important difference between options 4 and 5 was the difference in impact each would have on the Congress and the American public. Calling up the National Guard or doing any of the other actions of Option 4 would amount to a national crisis and would clearly signal a fundamental change in our policy in Vietnam. That Johnson did not want. But at the same time, he believed he had to increase our involvement significantly or South Vietnam would be lost.

As the discussions on the decision continued, the ways of announcing the decision increased in importance. For example, three of the six items discussed at the afternoon meeting of July 22 concerned how to handle the public announcement:

> How big a change in policy is this, and how do we explain it—in political and military terms?
> Is this policy justified in terms of Vietnam, Asia, or U.S. national interest—or all three?
> What are our war aims? What is the answer to Walter Lippmann's question on this point?[14]

Johnson certainly did not want to make his decision to change the mission of American troops in Vietnam a leading issue for public discussion. Already there were protests against his current policy of bombing the North, and he did not want to fuel them further. Just as certainly he did not want a congressional debate on this issue because that would give conservatives and Republicans an opportunity to delay enacting his Great Society programs.[15] There were a host of other reasons why Johnson decided for option 5, increasing our involvement with as little fanfare as possible.

This was the turning point. Up to this time Johnson had not publicly committed the United States to fight the war in Vietnam for the Vietnamese. Instead, he had committed us to assisting the South Vietnamese, to bombing the North in a futile attempt to make it negotiate a settlement, and to dispatching combat troops for the limited purpose of protecting American air bases from attack. Johnson still could "cut our losses and withdraw," as McNamara had described it. But Johnson decided otherwise. He would not be the first president to lose a war, he thought. Now, he would commit U.S. forces to fighting the war for the Vietnamese by escalating our presence there to 125,000 troops and by doubling the draft in preparation for an extended war. Such an effort by the United States, the most powerful nation in the world, would no doubt soon convince the North Vietnamese to negotiate a peaceful settlement in Vietnam. At least, so it seemed at the time. But such an escalation would also have another effect, more tangible and more far-reaching. Once this decision was announced, the war in Vietnam would no longer be a Vietnamese war, but an American-Vietnamese war. Johnson admitted as much in his memoirs: "Now we were committed to major combat in Vietnam."[16]

The Setting of the Announcement

President Johnson agreed with William Bundy, the assistant secretary of state for Far Eastern affairs, that the message announcing the escalation should be a complete message, not one that would "dribble out bits and pieces of this to the press or to publishers."[17] By July 1965 Johnson was acutely sensitive to the means by which he announced decisions. He had been stung during the Dominican Republic intervention of late April and early May of the same year. At the outset of that crisis Johnson had appeared on television three times in five days, twice interrupting regularly scheduled programming. During that time Johnson had been harshly criticized for the intervention, especially by the "liberal" press, as much for the means he had used to announce his actions as for the actions themselves.[18]

At the same time the president did not want to present the message in prime television time nor to make it an important speech to the nation. These conditions were met, but they worked at cross purposes. Presenting a complete message and keeping it low-keyed were inconsistent.

In a rhetorical sleight of hand Johnson chose to make this momentous announcement, not in a major televised speech in prime time to the American people, but rather in a long, undramatic opening statement at a press conference deliberately scheduled for a little after noon on a Wednesday, July 28, not a time known for gathering a large viewing audience. Furthermore, his long, subdued recitation about why we were in Vietnam, about our war aims, and the announcement of further escalation of our effort served in some respects as a prelude to his announcements that he would be nominating Abe Fortas to the Supreme Court seat that Arthur Goldberg had vacated and that he was appointing John Chancellor as director of the Voice of America. These two announcements came at the end of his opening statement and served two purposes. First, it appeared that Johnson was making rather routine announcements about further troop deployments to Vietnam before getting to the real news of the press conference: the two appointments. By arranging the topics of his statement to proceed from our reasons for being in Vietnam through the other topics and then concluding with the appointments, Johnson seemed to be saying that his appointments were the important news, not Vietnam. By holding the press conference at noon, he seemed to reinforce this impression.

Second, by making the announcements about Fortas and Chancellor, Johnson was offering journalists an alternative headline for news to his announcement of military increases for Vietnam. Thus, even though he could not control what journalists wrote, he could at least give them another story that some might consider as important as the story about Vietnam, and thereby cause them to play down the Vietnamese story as much as he played it down in his opening statement. It was an adroit strategy to avoid a public uproar over the change in American policy toward the war in Vietnam. But by playing it so adroitly and so subdued, Johnson also lost an opportunity to mobilize greater public support for his war effort, a support that is essential to success for any significant foreign policy initiative. Thus, Johnson may have achieved a short-term advantage only to lose a long-term opportunity.

Johnson's Arguments for an American War in Vietnam

President Johnson's speech at Johns Hopkins University in April 1965 was a peace speech. President Johnson's speech at his press conference of July 28, 1965, was a war speech. In a covering memorandum to the president that accompanied one of the final drafts of the speech, Richard Goodwin, author of Johnson's speech, noted that the word *peace* was used only once and the word *peaceably* also only once.[19]

Let us turn then to how President Johnson justified his decision to make the war in Vietnam an American-Vietnamese war. Johnson opened the press conference by reading a portion of a letter he received from a woman in the Midwest saying she did not understand why we were in Vietnam.

The president answered this poignant request by presenting five arguments for our involvement in Vietnam. These became the basic arguments administrative officials and defenders of the war would use repeatedly in the years to come, sometimes directly and sometimes with variations as events or occasions warranted. Therefore, it is worth quoting Johnson at length at this point in our analysis.

The answer [to the question why are we in Vietnam], like war itself, is not an easy one, but it echoes clearly from the painful lessons of half a century. Three times in my lifetime, in two World Wars and in Korea, Americans have gone to far lands to fight for freedom. We have learned at a terrible and brutal cost that retreat does not bring safety and weakness does not bring peace.

It is this lesson that has brought us to Viet-Nam. This is a different kind of war. There are no marching armies or solemn declarations. Some citizens of South Viet-Nam at times, with understandable grievances, have joined in the attack on their own government.

But we must not let this mask the central fact that this is really war. It is guided by North Viet-Nam and it is spurred by Communist China. Its goal is to conquer the South, to defeat American power, and to extend the Asiatic dominion of Communism.

There are great stakes in the balance.

Most of the non-Communist nations of Asia cannot, by themselves and alone, resist the growing might and the grasping ambition of Asian Communism.

Our power, therefore, is a very vital shield. If we are driven from the field in Viet-Nam, then no nation can ever again have the same confidence in American promise, or in American protection.

In each land the forces of independence would be considerably weakened, and an Asia so threatened by Communist domination would certainly imperil the security of the United States itself.

We did not choose to be the guardians at the gate, but there is no one else.

Nor would surrender in Viet-Nam bring peace, because we learned from Hitler at Munich that success only feeds the appetite of aggression. The battle would be renewed in one country and then another country, bringing with it perhaps even larger and crueler conflict, as we have learned from the lessons of history.

Moreover, we are in Viet-Nam to fulfill one of the most solemn pledges of the American people. Three Presidents—President Eisenhower, President Kennedy, and your present President—over 11 years have committed themselves and have promised to help defend this small and valiant nation.

Strengthened by that promise, the people of South Viet-Nam have fought for many long years. Thousands of them have died. Thousands more have been crippled and scarred by war. We just cannot now dishonor our word, or abandon our commitment, or leave those who believed in us and who trusted us to the terror and repression and murder that would follow.

This, then, my fellow Americans, is why we are in Viet-Nam.[20]

Contained in this excerpt from the opening statement are the five lines of argument used to explain and defend the president's decision to make the Vietnam conflict an American-Vietnamese war: (1) argument from definition, (2) argument from existing decisions and from the prestige of the presidential office, (3) argument from analogy, (4) argument from metaphor, and (5) argument from principle. Let us examine each of these.

First, Johnson argued that the war was a war of aggression waged by North Vietnam against the independent nation South Vietnam. This was the crucial argument upon which all other arguments rested. It was the argument or assumption most frequently attacked by antiwar activists. Indeed, the whole war effort rested on the assumption that the United States was coming to the aid of a small nation threatened to be conquered by another nation, or by "Asiatic communism," his more abstract description of the enemy. This argument from definition was the cornerstone of American policy in Southeast Asia. Had the administration defined or seen the war differently—say, as a civil war—none of the other arguments would have had an effective foundation.

Curiously, Johnson did not state this argument directly in his opening statement. Rather, he included it with other goals that he said motivated North Vietnam's aggression, such as "to defeat American power, and to extend the Asiatic dominion of communism." Perhaps Johnson believed that the military aggression by the North was so well recognized that he did not have to press that point at this time. After all, the March white paper on Vietnam had sought to demonstrate the means and methods of North Vietnam's aggression. And at Johns Hopkins two months earlier he had argued this point forcefully and fully by stating that "North Viet-Nam has attacked the independent nation of South Viet-Nam."[21] Of equal importance, Johnson would not have had to argue explicitly the ideological basis for American action. At this time, most people accepted that it was America's responsibility to protect other nations from communism. The anticommunist mentality dominated the thinking not only of policy makers but of the public as well. More probably, he slighted this argument because he was now making a case for active involvement by the United States in the war, not just assistance to the South Vietnamese in fighting against the Viet Cong or the North. Therefore, the great commitment of American troops had to be justified in terms of a larger set of goals, not merely the defense of South Vietnam. A commitment of 125,000 combat troops required grand and worthy goals. By combining the defense of South Vietnam from North Vietnam with the defense of Asia from communism and adding that American power and prestige were at stake, Johnson seemed to define the situation in terms large enough to justify the commitment he was making. Moreover, the combination of these arguments foreshadowed the other arguments he was to present. But defining the war as a war of aggression remained the basic argument for our involvement, and it had to be. Without this argument, what justification could there be for any military commitment of American power and prestige?

Johnson sought to demonstrate that he was not alone in recognizing the great stakes at risk in Vietnam by calling upon his two predecessors as witnesses. This second argument from existing decisions or commitments by previous presidents also was used to assure the public that he was not announcing a basic change in policy, but instead only increasing American military power in Vietnam in pursuit of a long-established policy. He even said so directly in answer to a question: "It [increasing the number of American troops in Vietnam] does not imply any change in policy whatever." This argument coincided with Johnson's description of the war as a war not only of aggression, but also as a war to defeat American power. Thus, even as the president was making a basic change in policy, he either did not see it that way, or he did not want the American people to recognize this significant change. Since the president was doing everything possible to make his announcements as undramatic and subdued as possible, one does not need to be a cynic to believe the latter motivation rather than the former. Furthermore, Johnson was invoking the names of two immensely appealing presidents: the beloved Eisenhower and the martyred Kennedy. To argue against Johnson would require arguing against them as well and, as Johnson framed it, dishonoring their commitments.

The third and fourth arguments were literary arguments and worked in connection with one another: argument from analogy and from metaphor. Johnson imposed the "Munich" analogy upon the situation in Vietnam and revived the "domino theory" to explain the consequences that would come if the United States did not act.[22]

Johnson argued that if the American government did not take a stand against communist aggression, as Great Britain should have done against Hitler instead of appeasing him at Munich, then aggression would continue and would eventually swallow up nearby nations, each of which would fall like dominoes standing in a row.[23] This metaphor and analogy had compelling significance to Johnson and his advisers, who had come to maturity during the days before and during World War II or at the time of the Korean War. In the former case, the Munich analogy was pregnant with historical meaning, opportunities, and fears. In the latter case, the Korean War seemed to justify viewing new conflicts through old lens. Truman's prompt action had prevented the conquest of South Korea, and the world had remained relatively at peace since the end of that war. Johnson and his advisers apparently ignored the fact that Truman had gotten support from our allies and from the United Nations.

Furthermore, both the metaphor and the analogy contributed to the principle of credibility, which was the cornerstone of American foreign policy in reaction to perceived communist threats. Without the powerful appeal of the metaphor and the analogy—and at the time of the press conference in 1965 both were greatly persuasive to the American public[24]—the principle or doctrine of U.S. credibility would not stand. Thus, instead of choosing to view the conflict in Vietnam as analogous to the French experience there in the 1950s, Johnson chose to view it as analogous to the British conflict with Hitler in the 1930s. But as we shall see, the choice was not merely a personal choice but one also dictated by existing foreign policy thinking.

The final argument was the most important, an argument from principle, and the principle was maintaining American credibility throughout the world. Johnson said our prestige as a world power and our credibility as a shield against communist aggression was at stake in Vietnam. If this principle of credibility was not maintained, he warned that "no nation [could] ever again have the same confidence in American promise, or in American protection." The doctrine of credibility was at the center of our effort in Vietnam. In March 1965 James McNaughton, assistant secretary of defense, who specialized in developing the rationale for American involvement in Vietnam, outlined American war aims by writing:

U.S. Aims:
70%—To avoid a humiliating U.S. defeat (to our reputation as a guarantor).
20%—To keep SVN (and the adjacent territory from Chinese hands).
10%—To permit the people of SVN to enjoy a better, freer way of life.[25]

And again in January 1966 McNaughton wrote: "The present U.S. objective in Vietnam is to avoid humiliation. The reasons why we *went into* Vietnam to the present depth are varied; but they are now largely academic. Why we have *not withdrawn* from Vietnam is, by all odds, one reason: (1) to preserve our reputation as a guarantor, and thus to preserve our effectiveness in the rest of the world."[26] This doctrine of credibility, as Jonathan Schell called it, was the real rationale for the war effort in Vietnam.

Of all the reasons Johnson gave for fighting the war in Vietnam, the aim of maintaining American credibility both with our allies and our adversaries proved the most sustaining. As other reasons were attacked or weakened or discredited as persuasive arguments, the doctrine of credibility was the one that defenders of the war fell back on as a last resort.

But the doctrine of credibility was not merely an invented rhetorical justification for this war. It sprang from strategic thinking about the role of the United States in world affairs. It sprang from the need to avoid using nuclear weapons but at the same time demonstrating American determination to prevail when our national interest was at stake or when communist aggression sought to dominate other nations. Jonathan Schell noted that this doctrine was "rooted firmly in the modern experience" and it "formed the basis for all strategic thinking in the nineteen-sixties." He succinctly summarized these strategic reasons:

For it was in the credibility of the nuclear deterrent that the United States had placed its hopes for survival in the nuclear age. The government hoped that by creating a formidable impression of national strength and will in the minds of the nation's adversaries it could deter them from launching a nuclear attack. In its application to Vietnam, the doctrine of credibility found expression in a revised version of the traditional domino theory which might be called the psychological domino theory. According to the traditional domino theory, each nation that fell to Communism would endanger its immediate neighbor; according to the psychological domino theory, the ill effects of a nation's fall would not necessarily be on neighboring nations but would be on nations all over the world, which by merely watching the spectacle would lose their confidence in the power of the United States. Allies, it was said, would be discouraged from relying on American power, and foes would be emboldened to challenge it. The United States would, in a word, lose credibility. In this thinking, Vietnam became a "test case" of the United States' will to use its power in world affairs. If the United States could not muster the "determination" to prevail in Vietnam, it was believed, then it would be showing, once and for all, that it lacked the determination to prevail in any conflict anywhere. And, since in the official view credibility was indivisible, a collapse of credibility in the sphere of limited conflict would cast doubt on the credibility of American power in other spheres of competition as well, including even the all-important nuclear sphere.[27]

Maintaining the credibility of the United States as a vital actor in world affairs became the over-arching goal of our policy in Vietnam, and indeed, in the rest of the world. All other arguments merely contributed to a persuasive rationale for the doctrine of credibility. The reason why the United States stayed on in Vietnam through two presidencies and even after a decision had been made to withdraw and seek a negotiated settlement was the maintenance of American credibility in the rest of the world. The principle was so steadfastly held that all other reasons became secondary. As early as January 1966, in the memorandum already cited that sustaining our "reputation as guarantor" was our reason for being in Vietnam, McNaughton added that we were *not* staying in Vietnam to "save a friend, or . . . to deny the Communists the added acres and heads (because the dominoes don't fall for that reason in this case), or even . . . to prove that 'wars of national liberation' won't work (except as our reputation is involved)."[28]

President Kennedy had created the rationale for this policy in his administration and had put America on this path with his commitment of "advisers" to Vietnam. Now, Johnson chose Vietnam as a symbolic testing ground to demonstrate that the United States would use force to thwart communist aggression in the world and thereby also demonstrate our credibility as a defender of freedom to our allies and adversaries alike. By fighting the war to defend and demonstrate this principle, we changed the nature of the war as inevitably as we changed its goals. This is painfully apparent when one reads the war aims Johnson explained in his statement. This was not a war "to make the world safe for democracy," nor was it a war to be fought for victory and unconditional surrender of the enemy—"a war to end all wars." Instead, he listed two aims for our involvement in Vietnam (1) "to convice the Communists that we cannot be defeated by force of arms or by superior power"; and (2) "once the Communists know, as we know, that a violent solution is impossible, then a peaceful solution is inevitable." In other words, the war was fought to demonstrate our power, not in the sense of how the United States could ravish another nation, but only in the sense that the United States could not be defeated. More important than that even, the war was fought to convince the communist world that the United States had the "will" to use its power even in small wars. Flexing our military muscles in Vietnam was more important than tangible military or security goals.

The thinking that motivated Johnson's commitment of American military might to Vietnam was his belief that the commitment itself would cause the North Vietnamese to see the futility of continuing their efforts to dominate South Vietnam. When that was achieved, a negotiated settlement—probably comparable to the one that ended the Korean War—would be concluded. But more important than the tangible agreement would be the message that the original commitment sent to the entire world. The United States would use its military power to demonstrate its will to contain communist expansion. And with that demonstration of American will power—backed by the enormous military might of the United States in this symbolic war—the communists would be less adventuresome in other areas of the world in the future.

What it all boiled down to was that President Johnson was committing vast resources of troops and money to fight a proxy war for symbolic purposes. That was the real meaning of the war, and that also created the genuine problems of maintaining public support for the war. Johnson did not have a great problem, as some critics have maintained, explaining why we were in Vietnam or what his war aims were. He explained them very well, especially at Johns Hopkins and in his press conference. The problem developed later because few wanted to risk their lives for symbolic purposes. They wanted tangible goals and tangible results. Thus, Johnson later found himself attacked by both liberals and conservatives. The opponents of the war found Vietnam an unworthy place to demonstrate our symbolic efforts and found Vietnam unworthy of the mayhem and death inflicted on Americans, both in the war and on the domestic front. They wanted out. They did not want to be real people in somebody else's symbolic drama. (President Reagan solved this problem without abandoning the principle by creating a proxy army, the Contras, to fight a proxy war in Nicaragua.) Supporters of the war effort found the symbolic goals insufficient and wanted to increase our effort to achieve victory over the North Vietnamese communists.

Johnson did have rhetorical problems in presenting his policies in Vietnam to the American public. But his real problem came from American strategic and military thinking, with applying the doctrine of credibility to the situation in Vietnam. It did not fit. It did not work. It ruined his presidency. Americans grew frustrated, impatient, and angry to the point that Johnson had to seek a negotiated settlement and withdraw from the 1968 presidential campaign.

Conclusion

President Johnson's press conference of July 28, 1965, was important because it announced a new American policy in Vietnam, a policy of Americanizing the war. In fact, Johnson made no bones about what was happening. In speaking about the dissension in South Vietnam, he said: "But we must not let this mask the central fact that this is really war." To that end, Johnson increased the number of combat troops in Vietnam by 50,000 and doubled the draft, two sure indications that America was going to war. In his opening statement Johnson used the main arguments for American involvement that would be used throughout the war to justify our continuing that effort.

Despite what critics have written, Johnson did lay out the arguments for war in explicit terms, that is, in terms of the anticommunist ideology in America. The goal of North Vietnamese aggression, Johnson said, was the dominion of communism over

Asia. He saw Vietnam as symbolic of that ongoing modern battle between the free world and the communist World. Thus, he pulled out the major arguments that sustained that ideology: the Munich analogy, the domino theory, commitments by previous presidents, and American credibility. Only such great stakes could justify the commitment Johnson was prepared to make.

But Johnson also did not want his opening statement to spark public debate about Vietnam and especially about this new policy of Americanizing the war. Only two months before, opponents—although still a very small minority—had staged a successful media event in protest against our involvement at the national teach-in in Washington. Furthermore, this critical decision was coming at a most inopportune time since Congress was considering some of his major domestic programs. Johnson was thus caught in a dilemma. He wanted to make a full statement about our reasons for Americanizing the war, our war aims, and our need to escalate our involvement. Such a statement required an important speech. But Johnson also wanted to play down this turning point in his presidency and indeed in American history by presenting his full statement in the most undramatic fashion possible. These two rhetorical purposes could not be reconciled. So Johnson sought to minimize public reaction to his decision by holding a press conference a little after twelve o'clock noon, by giving a long opening statement to justify the war effort, by insisting that he was merely continuing a well-known policy that had been pursued by three presidents, and by giving alternative headlines through the announcement of the nominations of Abe Fortas to the Supreme Court and John Chancellor to the Voice of America. And in reply to one of the questions at the press conference, Johnson insisted that his announcements about additional troops for Vietnam and increases in the draft did not "imply any change in policy whatever. It does not imply any change in objective."[29] But this self-assessment was misleading. True, Johnson's announcements in the press conference did not indicate any change in principle. Since the days of the Eisenhower administration through Kennedy's and then into the Johnson administration, the United States had been committed in principle to defending South Vietnam. But even as the principle remained consistent, the announcements in this press conference definitely indicated a change in policy. From this time forth, Americans would take over the fighting in Vietnam from the South Vietnamese. No longer would they be "advisers" nor would they be stationed in Vietnam for limited engagements protecting American bases. The immediate increase in American troops to be dispatched and the doubling of the draft made this change in policy clear. Americans would now fight the war for the South Vietnamese.

In essence, Johnson's press conference was a declaration of war, but a most peculiar one. Johnson did not declare war against another country, but declared war on those who would dare to challenge or threaten America's credibility in the world and this particular president's will to maintain that credibility. In terms of the consequences of this decisive turning point, it did represent a fundamental change in policy. Johnson sought to minimize the impact of his decision on Congress and on the public, and for the most part, he succeeded temporarily. But this single decision would ignite the protests that were to wrack American society for the reminder of the decade. That was the tragedy for his presidency, and the tragedy for the country. And it would take a new president whose political psychology made him more committed to his place in history than to his own staunch anticommunism to disengage the country from Vietnam.

5

Understanding Richard Nixon
A Psycho-Rhetorical Analysis

To say that Richard Nixon is a complex mass of contradictions is to repeat a cliché of some thirty-five years' standing. He has worn many masks and played many roles. There is the *sanctimonious* Nixon chastising Harry Truman in 1960 for using foul language in telling Republicans to go to hell; the *expletives-deleted* Nixon telling John Mitchell on one of Watergate tapes, "I don't give a shit what happens. I want you all to stonewall it, plead the Fifth Amendment, cover-up, or anything else, if it'll save . . . the plan; the *homey* Nixon who cherishes a dog named Checkers, whose wife wears a respectable Republican cloth coat, and who loves hamburgers, "Really I do"; the *imperial* Nixon telling David Frost in a TV interview after he left office that when others break the law, it is illegal, but it is not illegal when he, as president, breaks the law; the *hypocritical* Nixon vowing never to give amnesty to draft evaders but accepting a "full and free pardon" for his allegedly illegal acts as president; the *paranoid* Nixon worrying about whether John Dean might not have concealed a miniature tape recorder to tape their conversations, even as he was secretly taping the conversation about his being worried about being taped.

If these paradoxes are not enough, look at the twists and turns of his political beliefs: Nixon, the archetypical anticommunist during his prepresidential years, once he becomes president opening the doors to the People's Republic of China and negotiating the SALT I agreements with the Soviet Union; Nixon, in 1969, pledging never to impose wage-price controls, and Nixon in 1971 imposing wage-price controls; Nixon, the staunch balance-the-budget Republican, after two years in office declaring himself a Keynesian.

Such contradictions would cause severe problems for other politicians because they seem to represent basic changes in beliefs, at best, or hypocrisy in values, at worst. And what about Nixon's constituencies? With all these twists and turns, why did people continue to support Nixon over his long political career? These are not the only questions one needs to ask. What were the psychological and political sources that converged to create these contradictions? What is the relation between words and political reality, especially in the case of Richard Nixon? And what do these tell us about the psychology of political figures in this age of personal, public politics?

These are some of the questions I propose to address. The focus will be on Richard Nixon's rhetoric for a variety of reasons. Scholars and political analysts have been fascinated by him for more than four decades. Having had little political experience before the end of World War II, Nixon is truly a product of the postwar world. He is one of the first of this generation of politicians to recognize and exploit television as a power in modern politics. Nixon saved his political career with his famous "Checkers" speech during the 1952 presidential campaign. Usually, that televised speech is described as one of the earliest exploitations of television for personal political purposes. But equally important was Nixon's so-called last press conference after his loss in the California gubernatorial race in 1962. At that press conference Nixon said: "And I can only say thank God for television and radio for keeping the newspapers a little more honest."[1] Although most commentators have concentrated on Nixon's criticism of the press in this 1962 appearance, what Nixon had discovered during the course of that campaign was that television allowed him to go directly to the people without interference or interpretation from journalists. It was that insight that became unique to his presidency.[2]

Furthermore, it is the consistent structure of Nixon's rhetoric that gave form to his politics and his political personality. Nixon's career has been a rhetorical career. It was his rhetoric that created his reality and laid the basis for reconciling the many apparent contradictions in his career. But I want to begin with a larger picture that focuses on a psycho-rhetorical perspective of Richard Nixon. To start painting this picture, I will summarize the traditional psychological analysis of Nixon and contrast that with the psycho-rhetorical perspective, one I believe is more appropriate to contemporary politicians who live in a media-dominated public arena. The next section concentrates on the relationship of Nixon's rhetoric to his political reality, and it is followed by an examination of the political reality created by Nixon's unique career as a campaigner. The final section deals with the specific structure of Nixon's rhetoric that has created his psychology and his reality. All of these sections work together to provide a richer understanding of Richard Nixon and provide the rudimentary methods for analysis of other presidents in this new era of mediated politics, mediated public personalities, and the predominance of rhetoric in creating both.

Nixon and Psychobiography

Richard Nixon invites psychological analysis. Throughout his public career he has constantly been analyzing himself—his thoughts, his motives, his anticipations, his hopes, and his fears. About his trip to Caracas in 1958, he told one of his biographers his first thoughts on arrival there: "The minute I stepped off the airplane, while getting the salute, I cased the place. (I always do that when I walk out.) I looked it all over and watched the kind of crowd, thinking, where will I make an unscheduled stop, where will we move out and shake hands and so forth . . . . So we walked down the steps from the airplane, and I quickly made a few mental notes and decisions."[3] In his first autobiography, *Six Crises*, Nixon examined not his political development so much as his personal reactions to his personal-political crises. Thus, he wrote that the purpose of the book was "to distill out of my experience a few general principles on the 'crisis syndrome.'"[4] In fact, this remarkable book is almost devoid of any serious political analyses of ideas or policies, devoid of any insight into the inner workings of government, devoid of any real insights into the Eisenhower administration, which he served for eight years. Instead, it is Nixon on Nixon: what he thought, what he felt, how he reacted.[5] Events serve almost solely as a backdrop to the ongoing drama of Richard Nixon, a Horatio Alger story of Nixon struggling up the political ladder in the face of adversity only to reach a broken rung at the top in the form of the defeat to John F. Kennedy.

With this history of self-analysis by Nixon, little wonder that anyone who presumes to write about the former president finds himself wading in the murky waters of psychobiography or psychohistory. Psychoanalysis—whether professional or amateur—is the occupational hazard of a Nixon scholar. Among the professionals who have used this approach and written on Nixon are: David Abrahamsen, Eli Chesen, Bruce Mazlish, and Fawn Brodie.[6] Each uses Freudian or neo-Freudian methods. Each proposes to capture the essential aspects of Nixon's personality. To summarize part of the psychobiographical method, I shall focus on Abrahamsen's analysis of Nixon to note two essential features of the method and to contrast this traditional method with what I shall propose.

The Traditional Analysis of Nixon's Psychology

First, Abrahamsen spends most of his book on Nixon's childhood, adolescence, and early manhood. He devotes seven chapters to these topics. Another chapter concerns Nixon's career from 1945 to 1960; and the final two chapters deal with Nixon's administration including Watergate and Abrahamsen's conclusions. Such an inordinate amount of space devoted to Nixon's prepolitical life (pre-1946) is to be expected from a Freudian. Abrahamsen bases his analysis of Nixon's later life almost exclusively on what he describes as the traumatic events of his childhood. The following excerpt about Nixon's playing poker during World War II demonstrates Abrahamsen's method:

> Yet, we suspect that Nixon may have had conflicting feelings about the game, since playing cards, especially for money, was gambling. Only "tramps" and "bums" did it—*words he must have heard time and time again* from his grandmother, Almira, and his parents. Nixon says of his grandmother . . . that she had "great concern for people who was less fortunate. It was often said . . . that no tramp ever came to the door and got turned away." Tramps were destitute persons. *"Tramp" and "bum" were names Nixon had been called by his impulsive father.* These scolding, hostile expressions *Nixon would use repeatedly against students and others* who between 1967 and 1971 vigorously protested and demonstrated against American involvement in the Vietnam War and the invasion of Cambodia.[7]

In contrast to this version of Nixon's childhood, Stephen E. Ambrose, Nixon's most recent and thorough biographer, came to a different conclusion: "As a youth, [Nixon] was surrounded by trusting people whom he had every reason to trust completely. In this regard, his childhood was so normal as to be dull. No one abused him; there were no traumas, no betrayals, only love and trust."[8] But this excerpt from Abrahamsen typifies the method: the use of childhood experiences to explain various types of adult behavior, and in this instance, even rhetorical usage.

There are real problems with this approach. Abrahamsen *speculates* that Nixon must have heard these words repeatedly from his grandmother and his parents, but there is precious little proof that he did. Second, I cannot find in the many biographies of Nixon proof that his father called him a "tramp" or "bum." That Frank Nixon was impulsive, argumentative, and volatile is clearly established. That he persistently called his son Richard these disparaging names is not. In fact, what emerges from most biographies is that Richard was the peacemaker between his father and his other brothers, and that he sought to avoid arguments or confrontations with his father as much as possible. Moreover, Abrahamsen claims that Nixon used these hostile descriptions "repeatedly against students and others . . . between 1967 and 1971." I can find only one significant occasion in the public record during this period when Nixon used the word "bum." That, of course, occurred on May 1, 1970, outside the Pentagon after the protests over Nixon's invasion of Cambodia. During the midterm election in 1970 Nixon did call demonstrators "hoodlums" and "thugs" but not "bums," a precise description over which Abrahamsen makes much ado. And certainly Nixon did not use these pejorative terms repeatedly.

The second point worth noting is the way in which these analyses and explanations develop to evaluate Nixon's personality and actions. Abrahamsen first chooses a particular event or statement about Nixon, then applies a general psychoanalytic generalization to it, and finally comes to a conclusion about Nixon's personality and the reasons for his actions. This method is repeated to draw a composite portrait of the complexity of the man, even as the sources for that analysis are rather simple. Abrahamsen, for example, devotes a full seven pages to the origins of Nixon's "oral fixation," which finds its release in aggression against others. I quote from the relevant passages:

> In contrast to Harold, his quiet older brother, Richard "was known in the family as a screamer." The first characteristic that impressed Hannah was his "decided voice."
> It certainly is not unusual for children to cry in their early years. But persistent screaming surely indicates a problem.[9]

> To his great-grandmother, Elizabeth, the boy's loud voice meant that he would be either a preacher or a lawyer; a psychiatrist or pediatrician would reason that he was either uncomfortable and needed attention, or felt lonely and wanted company. He was in the first year of his life, in the oral period, which lasts for about one year.[10]

> By crying or screaming loudly, young Richard learned how to get attention, and this pattern continued as he grew older. By crying or seeking attention in other ways, he unconsciously found a way to control his mother and, to a

lesser degree, his father. We can easily believe that his childhood screaming represented a pattern that would cause him in later life to continue to use his mouth, to proclaim his wishes loud and clear, particularly in an emergency or crisis. We see this pattern in his political career; for example, in the Watergate period he said he would "fight the impeachment like hell."[11]

Drawing attention to himself became a predominant trait in young Nixon, one reason why he loved to talk, argue, and debate.[12]

Orally oriented and orally fixated, speech was his way of releasing his aggression.[13]

The leaps from fact to fanciful speculation by Abrahamsen are astonishing in this case. Nixon's screaming during his first year is transformed into "childhood screaming." This is further transformed into a "pattern" of "crying or screaming loudly" that "continued as he grew older." The facts do not agree with these leaps. Abrahamsen himself notes that Nixon had quieted down by his first birthday and does not cite any additional evidence that Nixon followed a pattern of "crying or screaming loudly" later on. In fact, most biographers, especially Ambrose, describe Nixon as quiet, private, shy, and reserved.

At a later point, Abrahamsen argues that it "stands to reason that Nixon's overwhelming desire to become a politician was based not only on his oral fixation but also on a need to control external events and situations." "Politics," he continues, "would help him get away from his inner conflicts . . . and escape his emotional problems."[14]

The screaming incidents take up several pages of Abrahamsen's analysis of Nixon and lay part of the foundation for his interpretation of Nixon's later behavior. In fact, he describes these as representing a pattern for Nixon's political career. Yet, Abrahamsen points out that Nixon had "quieted down" by the time he was one year old.[15] Though there is no way to prove or disprove Abrahamsen's theory, I find it difficult to believe that a few chance remarks about Nixon's having a "decided" or "loud" voice at birth truly established a pattern that would cause him later on to love "to talk, argue and debate." (Does such infant behavior also account for all the high school, college, and university debaters and speech teachers? Were all of them afflicted by this "oral fixation"?) But if Nixon did have an oral fixation that impelled him to attempt to "control external events and situations," politics should have been the last profession to choose, especially national politics, where the politician rarely has control and frequently is at the mercy of rapidly changing external events and situations. But then again, there is no way to prove or disprove any of the theoretical applications of Abrahamsen's method to Nixon's character because it is so tied to and dependent on standard psychoanalytic theory and the psychologist's interpretation of that theory.

As a method, psychobiography entails an intense examination of the subject's childhood and adolescence as a means for interpreting adult character and behavior. It also requires knowing which events (among the innumerable and contradictory events of childhood and adolescence) are significant. Finally, it demands a clear command of psychoanalytic theory to interpret these events meaningfully. Yet the portrait of Nixon that is painted is curiously one-dimensional.

No one would deny the importance of Nixon's or anyone else's childhood and youth upon the development of character. Certainly, the traumas of Nixon's brothers' deaths, his head injury at age three, the absence of his mother from home for two years—all must have had some effect on Nixon. But how are we to know which of these events exerted what effects? For example, both Frank and Hannah Nixon were extremely religious and insisted upon a strict religious regimen and atmosphere in their home. Richard Nixon and his brothers were reared as Quakers. Yet in his adult life his Quaker heritage seems to have had little influence on his political life. During the 1960 campaign Norman Vincent Peale, a staunch Nixon supporter, said he was not as concerned about Nixon's Quaker background as he was about Kennedy's Catholicism because he had never known Nixon's religion to have affected Nixon much one way or another. In viewing Nixon's early life from this perspective, one senses that something very important is omitted or ignored in painting this classic psychoanalytic portrait of him. What it seems is missing are the unique influences that make up the nature of political behavior.

The Psycho-Rhetorical Analysis

Major politicians have dual selves. They have private sides influenced by heredity and by environment, much of that private self being formed during their early years. They also have a public self, much of it created by political opportunities, events, and history and formed during their early years in politics. The two may be closely aligned, the public side being only a sanitized version of the private. Or they may be widely divergent. In one sense, political lives may be inherently schizophrenic, not necessarily in the clinical sense, but metaphorically. Psychoanalytic theory may help interpret the private personality, but when it comes to national political figures and their public lives, it may not be as helpful as its proponents believe. After all, those who practice it have not interviewed or spoken confidentially with the subject, but are dependent on biographies and retellings of early life. They are thus deprived of one of the essential tools of the analysis: asking the person what particular events truly affected him or her and subjecting those and other events to close psychological scrutiny. However, with the public persona, public events that affected the formation of the public self are part of the public record, easily seen and agreed upon. In other words, evidence about these early political events is much more accessible than personal incidents for analyzing the public character of public figures.

A second approach to understanding the psychology of national public figures, particularly presidents, was developed by James David Barber. He was most successful in applying his method to Richard Nixon, especially to the psychological stages of Nixon's crises. He pointed out that Nixon goes through four distinct stages during a crisis: Fastening, Tensing, Release, and Letdown.[16] Barber noted that these stages were created in the formative period of Nixon's career, that is, before his election to the presidency. Indeed, Barber's analysis was so penetrating and accurate that it allowed him to predict that Nixon would have a crisis that would destroy him. But Barber's analysis, as acute and penetrating as it is, was devoted to Nixon's behavior as a public figure in a crisis situation. As a rhetorician, I am interested in a different kind of pattern, a rhetorical pattern of defining, thinking, and speaking—acts that precede and direct behavior.

What I intend to examine is Richard Nixon's public character by examining the role rhetoric has played in creating and developing it. Nixon provides an excellent case study of the divergence of these two selves—private and public—and the place of rhetoric in creating his public self. Indeed, as I will argue, it has been rhetoric that became the means to create the public Nixon and the political world in which he believed he lived. This structure—this persistent pattern—of his public character rested on his rhetoric, and I believe that became more important in establishing his public behavior than the private experiences of his childhood. For example, throughout the Watergate tapes, which reveal the private side of Nixon as he grappled with the intricacies of Watergate, we read or hear him referring back to political, not personal traumas. He tells aides to read *Six Crises* and particularly the chapter on the Hiss case. He reveals repeatedly his concern about Edward Kennedy's opposing him in the 1972 campaign or Kennedy's being behind certain events. He disparagingly refers to Eisenhower's insistence on being as clean "as a hound's tooth." In fact, his talk is almost entirely political when it comes to his concerns, hopes, and fears—even in these private conversations.

Beyond that, I believe that in this new age of public politics, especially the public presidency, the public personality is sometimes more important than the private one in determining political behavior. Sometimes, as in the case of Nixon, the private self is suppressed so that the new public self can emerge. This brief study of Nixon, then, is intended not only to present a different understanding of him, but also to serve as a test model for understanding other presidents who have found themselves living and acting in full public view via television and an incessant press. It is the public character and behavior that contemporary presidents believe they must live up to in order to meet expectations of the public, and that makes this aspect of their personalities more interesting and important to understand.

Richard Nixon: Rhetoric and Reality

In developing our analysis, let us turn again to the most perceptive student of Nixon's behavior, James David Barber. In *The Presidential Character* Barber carefully delineated a structure for Nixon's political behavior, a structure that permitted Barber to predict certain ways in which Nixon would act or react. When it comes to explaining the contradictions or paradoxes in Nixon, however, Barber is on less certain ground. Nonetheless, he provides significant insights, especially for rhetoricians, to begin explaining our complex former president and his speeches.

"Nixon lives rhetorically," Barber observed.[17] A startling insight, and how true. When one thinks of Nixon, one thinks of speeches and debates: the 1946 debates with Jerry Voorhis, the "pink lady" campaign against Helen Douglas, the "Checkers" speech, the kitchen debates with Khrushchev, the Kennedy-Nixon debates, Nixon's "last press conference" in 1962, and so on and on throughout his career. If we were to believe Woodward and Bernstein's *Final Days*, even in face of impeachment Nixon deluded himself into believing one more speech might save him.

Lives rhetorically! At this point, Barber shrewdly noted: "once having [been] spoken, the words must be defended. They tend to become . . . no longer symbols more or less representative of an objective reality, but realities in their own right."[18] Instead of pursuing this idea, Barber veers off into a discussion of the technical ways Nixon prepares his speeches. But his point is well-taken. If the words must be defended, the words must truly and fairly represent the world as Nixon sees it. It is the words and the political ways they describe events that is of supreme importance, not the fragile connection between those words and an objective set of events.

Let me cite an example for clarification. In his 1946 campaign against Jerry Voorhis, Nixon made communism a central issue in the campaign. Yet, in 1955 he told a reporter that "Communism was not the issue at any time in the '46 campaign. Few people knew about Communism then, and even fewer cared."[19] One might think this remark was thoughtless and atypical. But in his memoirs Nixon repeated it: "Despite later—and widespread—misconceptions, communism was not the central issue in the 1946 campaign. The PAC controversy provided emotional and rhetorical excitement, but it was not the issue that stirred and motivated most voters."[20] Nixon goes on in this passage to say that the quality of life was the central issue and continues at length to argue his case. In other words, in later years Nixon decided that making communism such a big issue was not in his best interests. Therefore, he denied it had been a big issue previously. Facts do not matter. Words do. "The words must be defended."

What conclusion can be drawn? *Nixon's rhetoric creates his reality.* Equally important, *the rhetoric he uses creates Nixon*—the Nixon the public knows, or thought it knew until the Watergate tapes became available.

There are two essential points about Nixon that stand out. First, the public Nixon is a rhetorically manufactured Nixon. In *Nixon Agonistes* Garry Wills wrote:

Nixon is a postwar man. Politically, he does not preexist the year 1946. Though he showed an early interest in American history, it was centered moralistically in semimyth—Lincoln and Wilson, the Calvinist saviors who failed. He does not seem to have made the obvious connection between Wilson's domestication of "populism" and Franklin Roosevelt's domestication of "radicalism." For Nixon, the thirties seem not to have taken place. . . .
History ended in 1921, with the death of his boyhood hero Wilson, and did not start up again until 1946.
He was [in 1946], politically a blank slate.[21]

This observation by Wills is especially significant to the case I intend to make. Before 1946 Nixon may have had personal traumatic experiences that influenced his character, but he seems to have had few experiences that created or influenced his public/political character.[22]

Just as a child is born and has experiences that shape character and personality, so too a politician is "born" with the first entry into politics and has political experiences that create the public self and public character: a second childhood and adolescence, a second identity crisis. The new self may become so important (after all, one's career and livelihood are dependent on maintaining it) that the private self may be subsumed into it or separated from it. And what shaped Nixon's early political character? His rhetoric.

Unlike his contemporaries, Kennedy and Johnson, Nixon did not come from a prominent political family. I deem this important because Nixon did not have any political heritage to live up to (as Johnson did) or to live down (as Kennedy did). Before he entered politics Johnson had been deeply influenced by his father's populist beliefs and by what he had experienced as a schoolteacher and as an aide to a congressman.[23] The political activities of the Kennedy family are so well known they need not be repeated here.

Nixon's family did not rate any political importance in Whittier. Frank Nixon, the story is told, became a Republican—though he and his family had been Democrats—because William McKinley admired his horse one day when McKinley came to Frank's hometown in Ohio.

To dramatize the political differences in heritage and development among these three presidents born within a ten-year span of each other, one need only look at what each was doing in the final prewar year, 1940. Johnson was a first-term congressman from Texas campaigning for reelection. At Harvard, Kennedy had completed his senior thesis, *Why England Slept*, and had had it privately published. Nixon was a young lawyer in Whittier courting Pat Ryan, marrying her that year, and failing in a orange juice business venture. He had no history of significant work within the Republican party. He was, as Wills noted, "a blank slate."

Furthermore, public speech became Nixon's road to prominence. His speech before the Committee of 100 in the Twelfth District won him its endorsement and the Republican nomination in 1946. His campaign, run with the assistance of his collaborator—Murray Chotiner—won that election.[24] His "Checkers" speech saved his place on the Eisenhower-Nixon ticket. One could cite example after example of how central a role rhetoric has played in the development and maintenance of his political career, but these well-known examples should suffice.

But if Nixon's rhetoric creates his reality, what kind of rhetoric did Nixon develop in these formative years? The answer to that leads to my second point about Nixon.

Nixon's rhetoric is primarily a campaign rhetoric, drawing its sustenance and direction from Nixon's career as a campaigner before his election in 1968. (Lyndon Johnson once described Nixon as a "chronic campaigner" whose role in politics was "to find fault with his country and with his Government during a period of October every 2 years.")[25] That description may seem innocuous enough, until one recognizes the plain differences between campaigning and governing. These are the two basic arts of politics, arts that every politician must master to be successful. Herbert M. Baus and William B. Ross succinctly summarized the art of campaigning: "War is political campaigning with bullets. Political campaigning is warfare without hardware. War and politics are related in techniques and goals. Both involve a collision of organizations seeking absolute victory; both are fought by the tactics of applied weaponry; and both are won by the grand strategy best combining factors of time plus the ability to win confrontations—surmounting hostile pressure while imposing decision upon the enemy."[26] The comparison is apt. Political campaigns are wars. But once one wins the war or public office, one must alter both style and arguments to accommodate new circumstances—the circumstances of governing. Governing does not require defeating an enemy, but consists primarily of developing and passing legislation. Campaigning means working for personal victory; governing means serving constituencies and gaining legislative victories. The two are not mutually exclusive but rather are distinct in crucial ways. In a campaign, candidates and promises are the issue. When governing, the officeholder and the effects of policies are the issues.

We may distinguish between campaigning and governing by citing particular differences between the two:

1. The metaphor for campaigning is war. The metaphor for governing is negotiation.
2. Campaigning aims at victory over one's enemy within a specific period of time. Governing aims at solving public problems through the passage of legislation. To one who governs, there are no final victories, only more problems to be addressed.
3. In campaigns the enemy is singular and visible. In governing, there are no enemies in this sense. The representative or senator who opposes you on one issue may be the very one who will support you on another issue. A constituency group that supports one policy may oppose you on another policy. Thus, instead of trying to destroy an opponent, as one might try to do in a campaign, one strives to confront one's opponents in a professional manner when governing.
4. In campaigns one must demand loyalty from one's supporters.

When governing, one must deal with supporters who may have divided loyalties.

5. Finally, campaigns involve direct confrontations. Governing involves symbolic confrontations always with an eye to practical accommodation.[27]

If these distinctions between these two political arts are valid, then it follows that the rhetoric constructed to achieve the aims of each will be different also. A campaign rhetoric will be one of either-or choices, a war-like rhetoric seeking defeat of the enemy and victory for the candidate. A governing rhetoric will be one of decorum in which confrontation usually leaves some opening for accommodation. It is the former that Nixon mastered, not the latter. What Nixon did is merge a campaign rhetoric into a governing rhetoric. The reason for that merger lies in the peculiarities of his political career. These peculiarities became the structure of his reality, his way of viewing himself and his opponents, his way of handling issues and events.

Richard Nixon as Political Campaigner

Before his election to the presidency in 1968 Nixon spent his political career mainly campaigning. William Costello, who researched Nixon's record as congressman and senator, found that during that time Nixon was involved in only three causes: (1) the Taft-Hartley Act of 1947 and the 1949 struggle to amend it; (2) the Mundt-Nixon bill; and (3) the Chambers-Hiss case.[28] In his memoir, *RN*, Nixon has surprisingly little to say about his four years as congressman except to dwell at length on the Hiss case, which made him nationally famous, and nothing whatsoever to say about his two years as senator, except to rehash briefly the campaign against Douglas.[29]

Nixon's record as Vice President is even more sparse, though that is not unusual for any vice president. He had few policy responsibilities under Eisenhower. Wills wrote that Eisenhower entrusted Nixon primarily with the duties of "house-keeping work in the Republican party."[30] Emmet John Hughes, an Eisenhower speechwriter, described Nixon's participation in cabinet meetings as "crisp and practical and logical: never proposing major objectives, but quick and shrewd in suggesting or refining methods—rather like an effective trial lawyer, I kept thinking, with an oddly slack interest in the law."[31] Eisenhower used Nixon's strengths. Nixon's responsibilities as vice president were to campaign for Republicans in off-term elections and to campaign against communism and for Americanism abroad on his various trips.

If one examines Nixon's career from 1946 to 1969, one finds Nixon engaged in one campaign after another:

1. In 1946 he campaigned for his first seat in Congress.
2. In 1948 he campaigned for renomination and was reelected.
3. In 1950 he campaigned for election to the Senate.
4. In 1952 he campaigned for the vice presidency.
5. In 1954 he campaigned for Republicans.
6. In 1956 he campaigned for reelection as vice president.
7. In 1958 he campaigned for Republicans.
8. In 1960 he campaigned for the presidency.
9. In 1962 he campaigned for election as governor of California.
10. In 1964 he campaigned for Goldwater and other Republicans.
11. In 1965 he campaigned for Wayne Dumont for Governor of New Jersey.
12. In 1966 he campaigned for Republicans in the off-term election.[32]
13. During 1967–68 he campaigned for the presidency again.

The list becomes more impressive if one adds his campaigning abroad for Americanism as vice president:

1. October 6–December 14, 1953: Far Eastern tour to twenty-one nations.
2. February 6–March 5, 1955: Central American tour to nine nations.
3. January 29–February 4, 1956: Trip to Brazil for the presidential inauguration.
4. June 30–July 12, 1956: Trip to Asia.
5. February 28–March 21, 1957: Tour of nine countries in Africa and to Italy.
6. April 27–May 18, 1958: South American tour to nine nations.
7. July 22–August 5, 1959: Trip to Soviet Union and Poland.[33]

Nixon confirmed this emphasis on campaigning, albeit indirectly. In *Six Crises* he described his reaction to what he considered six significant periods in his political career. With the exception of his actions during the time President Eisenhower was incapacitated (when Nixon gained high marks for doing nothing), each crisis was a campaign of one sort or another. Two chapters deal explicitly with campaigns ("The Fund" and "The 1960 Campaign"). Two chapters deal with his campaigns for Americanism against communism ("Caracas" and "Khrushchev"). His first chapter on "The Hiss Case" is in reality a case study in campaign tactics under different circumstances. The issue was who (Chambers or Hiss?) was one to believe or trust? Nixon chose Chambers early and campaigned heavily to persuade people to believe ("elect") Chambers. When the first trial ended in a hung jury, Nixon attacked the judge, called for an inquiry into whether the foreman of the jury was prejudiced against Chambers, suggested a special prosecutor to replace the original prosecutor, and generally condemned the inconclusive decision all the way around (the equivalent of calling for a recount in a disputed election).[34]

During his fourteen years as representative, senator, and vice president, there was significantly little in the way of legislative action from Nixon. One can believe Emmet John Hughes when he described a cabinet meeting on April 17, 1953, that Nixon chaired. A number of important issues were pending, but Nixon spent most of the meeting planning the 1954 campaign.[35] One can understand why a perplexed Eisenhower, when asked in August 1960 what Nixon's contributions to policy had been in his administration, replied: "If you give me a week, I might think of one." Nixon's contributions to American politics had not been in policy nor in governing, but in refining his own art of campaigning. It was this mind-set and its accompanying rhetoric that Nixon brought to his presidency, especially during the first two years of his administration.

In a seminar at the University of Pittsburgh in 1978 John Ehrlichman, chief domestic adviser to President Nixon, summarized how Nixon decided whether he set specific domestic policies or delegated them to Ehrlichman: "the passion issues: race, religion and pocketbook. These were the domestic issues that [Nixon] was interested in. And they were the ones in which he set policy. Richard Nixon had to be persuaded that there was a correlation between a given domestic issue and votes in the voting booth. If he couldn't see the correlation, then I got to decide it [the domestic issue]. If he could see the correlation, then by golly he was going to decide it, and no fooling."[36] His career as a campaigner created his political character. And that career was created and sustained by his rhetoric.

The Structure of Nixon's Rhetoric

Richard Nixon's career has been a rhetorical career, more so than most of his contemporaries. Equally important, the structure of his rhetoric has been fairly consistent throughout his career, although after the midterm election of 1970 he spent two years above the political fray as much as possible and allowed surrogates to campaign against his opponents for him. Nixon's rhetoric, as Barber noted, creates much of his reality. It was to his own rhetoric that Nixon reacted, and acted upon as if it were the way the actual world is. To put it another way, Nixon announces that something is one way or another and that becomes the reality for him. Nixon's rhetoric and reality form a whole, and each part is part of that whole, all coming together to create a consistent structure. One constituent does not exist without the others, even though one may not find each of the six constituents in every speech. But they are there as unspoken assumptions or conclusions.

Nixon divides nearly every important question or issue into an "either-or" choice. Lynn Hinds and Carolyn Smith described this division as a "rhetoric of opposites," a dialectic of two mutually exclusive positions, but without any synthesis.[37] Meg Greenfield made the same point: "Nixon apparently finds it almost impossible to make a statement that is not, in some manner, an argument. Ideas never quite exist for him until they have been pitted against something else—an extreme danger, a radically different point of view, or a potential attack from some sinister quarter."[38] One would expect such a dialectical rhetoric in a campaign where the electorate must choose between two candidates. But for Nixon, this either-or division is a fundamental habit of his rhetoric and his thinking, rather like scholastic debaters who have never grown up. In his pitch to the Committee of 100 on November 2, 1945, to gain its support for his congressional nomination, Nixon contrasted two conflicting opinions about the nature of our American political system:

One advocated by the New Deal is government control in regulating our lives. The other calls for individual freedom and all that initiative can produce.

I hold with the latter viewpoint. I believe the returning veterans, and I have talked to many of them in the foxholes, will not be satisfied with a dole or a government handout. They want a respectable job in private industry, where they will be recognized for what they produce, or they want the opportunity to start their own business.[39]

Of course, one can expect this kind of limiting of choices in a campaign, but with Nixon it became part of his rhetorical mind-set so that when he entered the presidency, he carried it with him.

In a speech on student revolutionaries at General Beadle State College on June 3, 1969, Nixon contrasted a "vocal minority of our young people" with the vast majority of college students in describing the revolt of the young.[40] A day later, speaking about the importance of military power to graduates of the Air Force Academy, Nixon stated: "When great questions are posed, fundamental differences of opinion come into focus. It serves no purpose to gloss over these differences, or to try to pretend that they are mere matters of degree."[41] He told his audience that *only* two schools of thought exist about how America could keep the peace abroad and secure freedom at home. The one, he designated as "neo-isolationist," and the other he defined as his own.

In his famous November 3, 1969, speech on Vietnam, Nixon gave a repeat performance:

My fellow Americans, I am sure you can recognize what I have said that we really only have two choices open to us if we want to end this war.

I can order an immediate, precipitate withdrawal of all Americans . . . .

Or we can persist in our search for a just peace through a negotiated settlement.[42]

And, of course, Nixon persistently divided the American people into two warring camps: the great silent majority (that supported him) and the small vocal minority (that opposed him).

Such a division in campaigns is understandable. But when he became president, such divisions on major issues did more to distort than clarify those issues. Students fell into a number of different categories, not just the two he described. A variety of different proposals had been made during the Vietnam war days about how American power should be distributed abroad, not just "neo-isolationists" versus Nixon. And certainly there were more than just two options in Vietnam.[43]

In a variation on this tactic Nixon would list three or more "options" available to him, saving the option he had chosen for last in order of presentation. In his August 15, 1971, speech he used this tactic to seek support for his temporary wage and price controls. Nixon used this variation to suggest that he was considering a number of different policies. However, when those "options" are examined, one sees that they are merely a variation on the either-or choice. Nixon would present three "options," label two of them extreme, and then present his own policy, the third option. The choice thus became a choice between either one of two extremes or Nixon's policy, by definition a "moderate" policy. The tip-off to this veneer of considering various possibilities is that Nixon usually listed "doing nothing" as a possibility. "Doing nothing" was no real option since Nixon in whatever topic he was speaking on had already described the crisis or peril that faced the country. "Doing nothing" would amount to irresponsibility, not to a realistic policy option.

A revealing example of this occurred in Nixon's 1970 speech announcing the invasion of Cambodia. In face of what the president called a critical threat to 7 million people in Cambodia, 18 million in South Vietnam, and to American lives, Nixon listed three options: (1) "we can do nothing"; (2) we can "provide massive military assistance to Cambodia itself"; or (3) we can go "to the heart of the trouble," which meant an incursion into Cambodia to clean out "major North Vietnamese and Vietcong occupied territories." Here one has two extremes ("doing nothing" and "massive military assistance") versus Nixon's policy that will go to the "heart of the trouble."

Whether Nixon's either-or choice is presented in pure form or in one of its variations, the dichotomy remains rhetorically fundamental in Nixon's mind-set and leads directly to the second constituent of his rhetoric.

Nixon is always specific about what he opposes. Murray Chotiner, Nixon's political collaborator throughout his career, pointed out the reasons for this negative approach:

There are many people who say we don't want that kind of campaign [a negative campaign] in our State. They say we want to conduct a constructive campaign and point out the merits of our own candidate. I say to you in all sincerity that if you do not deflate the opposition candidate before your own campaign gets started, the odds are that you are going to be doomed to defeat.

Because, if we like it or not, the American people in many instances vote against a candidate, against a party, or against an issue, rather than for a candidate or an issue or a party.[44]

Nixon brought this mentality into the White House. Jeb Stuart Magruder cited a memorandum from Nixon during the early days of the administration that admonished the staff that the "basic need is not PR—it's PO"—a Presidential Offensive.[45]

Quite simply, people become more agitated about what they are *against* than by what they are *for*. Or put another way, as Andrew King and Floyd Anderson did: Nixon relies on the old rhetorical maxim that people "who can unite on nothing else can unite on the basis of a foe shared by all."[46] Negative campaigning produces activity; positive campaigning does not produce the same, either in intensity or in breadth. Thus, it follows, the more the electorate knows about the negative aspects of your opponent (whether actual or attributed), the more it has to be against.

In developing this argument against opponents, Nixon has consistently used two tactics: (1) attributing extreme positions or associations to opponents, or (2) personifying issues by laying the blame for failures on specific people or associations with specific people. In campaigning against Voorhis, Nixon argued: "Five times Jerry Voorhis has had the support of the radical groups because he was at one time a registered Socialist and always supports radical causes. Voorhis has the endorsement of the National Political Action Committee because he voted their viewpoint 43 times out of 46 opportunities during the past four years."[47] In campaigning against Helen Douglas, the Nixon organization issued the infamous "pink sheets" (which served the dual purposes of suggesting that Douglas was a communist fellow traveler and of reminding voters that she was a woman), headlined the "Douglas-Marcantonio Voting Record":

Many persons have requested a comparison of the voting records of Congresswoman Helen Douglas and the notorious Communist party-liner, Congressman Vito Marcantonio of New York. . . .

Mrs. Douglas and Marcantonio have been members of Congress together since January 1, 1945. During that period, Mrs. Douglas voted the same as Marcantonio 354 times. While it should not be expected that a member of the House of Representatives should always vote in opposition to Marcantonio, it is significant to note, not only the great number of times which Mrs. Douglas voted in agreement with him, but also the issues on which almost without exception they always saw eye to eye, to wit: Un-American Activities and Internal Security.[48]

During the 1952 campaign Nixon called Adlai Stevenson "Adlai the Appeaser" and charged that he had earned "a Ph.D. from Dean Acheson's College of Cowardly Communist Containment."[49]

Nixon brought this negative rhetoric to his presidency, especially during the first two years as he sought to expand his constituencies. In his speech at General Beadle State College, he railed against the college student "who invades an administration building, roughs up the dean, rifles the files, and issues 'nonnegotiable demands'"[50] In his speech at the Air Force Academy Nixon contended that the "neo-isolationists" believe in unilateral disarmament, downgrading American alliances with traditional allies, reducing American forces abroad, and "that America will be able to deal with the possibility of peace only when we are unable to cope with the threat of war."[51]

Richard Nixon's rhetoric is a *negative* rhetoric. Certainly, attacking one's opponents is a time-honored part of political rhetoric and may even be valuable in clarifying important issues. But for Nixon it is an essential habit of mind that he needs in order to think and to speak. On important issues Nixon almost always begins with what he is against, not as a means for clarifying issues, but rather as a means for showing what he opposes and thus giving supporters something concrete to be opposed to and thereby a basis for supporting him. In essence, Nixon defines himself *negatively.* That is, he defines himself by what he is against or what he is not, and he is specific in his opposition. In 1968 he even defined his supporters in negative terms: "the nonshouters, the nondemonstrators. They are not racists or sick; they are not guilty of the crimes that plague the land."[52]

If this point about the essential negativism of Nixon's rhetoric is well-taken, then it begins to explain the successive "New Nixons," the mystery of the durability of his support over all these years. Liberals and academicians have always been perplexed about what Nixon stands or stood for. They have been more perplexed about why people continue to support him. Arthur Schlesinger, Jr., summarized this problem, but came up with only a lame conclusion: "His [Nixon's] essence is precisely that he cannot be pinned down. He cannot be identified with high interest rates or with low interest rates, with fixed price supports or flexible price supports, with Keynesianism or budgetary orthodoxy, with protection or free trade, with massive retaliation or balanced defense. His appeal seems almost to reside in this very capacity for eager, emphatic, unlimited flexibility."[53] But Schlesinger misses the whole point. Many people did not support Nixon because he stood *for* something, other than his persistent anticommunism (a negative proposition itself). But then again, almost every politician in the 1950s and 1960s was anticommunist. People supported him mainly because he *opposed specific things.* Realizing that people become politically active when they are agitated about something, Nixon rode the crest of those resentments to the presidency.[54] Nixon was facile and sensitive enough to public resentments to capitalize upon them, bind them up, and express the public's anger, frustrations, and fears about fleeting events and then to make these over into workable and continuing constituencies.

Nixon always is as general as he can be about what he believes. If knowing as much as possible about an opponent gives people reasons to be against that opponent, then it follows that the less they know about you, the less they have to be against. Nixon typically attacks opponents specifically, but, when talking about his own proposals, he resorts to generalizations and platitudes. Thus, in his 1968 acceptance speech, he said:

When the strongest nation in the world can be tied down for four years by a war in Vietnam with no end in sight;

When the richest nation in the world can't manage its own economy;

When the nation with the greatest tradition of the rule of law is plagued with unprecedented lawlessness;

When the President of the United States cannot travel abroad or to any major city at home without fear of a hostile demonstration,—*then it is time for new leadership for America.*[55]

Part of the reason for Nixon's reliance on general statements about what he believes is due to his political career. As vice president he could hardly take positions much different from those Eisenhower took. His responsibility was to support the president. And as I have demonstrated, most of the rest of his career before his election in 1968 was spent campaigning. If he followed Chotiner's advice, as I believe he did, he stayed away from specific statements of policy on controversial issues during those campaigns, and any detailed study of Nixon's campaigns and career up to 1968 demonstrates that conclusion.[56] The important point to note is that Nixon brought this mind-set, rhetorically created, to the presidency. He would be specific about what he opposed but remain general about what he supported. Thus, he could castigate those who called for "precipitate withdrawal" from Vietnam but he could at the same time refuse to describe his policy other than in the general terms of "Vietnamization" and continued negotiations with the North Vietnamese without any timetable for turning over the war to the Vietnamese or for American withdrawal from Vietnam.

Nixon presents his opponents as extremists or part of a minority, usually with sinister overtones. This characteristic of Nixon's rhetoric is unique to him, and probably a residual not only from his early campaigns but from his strident anticommunist days. Other politicians use one or more of the other five constituents of Nixon's rhetoric, and such use therefore is not unusual. But portraying opponents as extremists or illegitimate is not usually a part of other politicians' campaign rhetoric. Only in his two campaigns for the presidency in 1960 and 1968 did Nixon refrain from using this strategy. (Indeed, in the 1968 campaign, Nixon sent one of his staff members to the Agnew staff after Agnew had accused Hubert Humphrey of being "squishy soft on communism.") But once he was in office, Nixon repeatedly described his political opponents as extremists or part of an unworthy—but powerful or vocal—minority. It is a distinctive mark of his rhetoric and his thinking.

Rarely are Nixon's opponents legitimate political opponents.

They are a vocal minority, a conspiratorial few, a fringe element in American society usually bent on destroying American institutions. He characterized Jerry Voorhis as "a former registered Socialist and his voting record in Congress is more Socialistic and Communistic than Democratic."[57] Nixon dubbed Helen Douglas the "Pink Lady" who "did not vote as a Democrat. She did not vote as a Republican. It just so happens that my opponent is a member of the small clique which joins the notorious party liner, Vito Marcantonio of NY in voting time and again against measures that are for the security of this nation."[58] In his 1962 campaign for governor of California, Nixon described Edmund (Pat) Brown as a captive of the California Democratic Council and in a fraudulent postcard mailed to Democrats asked: "What do you feel we can do to throw off the shackles of this left-wing minority, now so powerful it can dictate the course of our party."[59] The group sending out the telegram was a fraudulent "Committee for the Preservation of the Democratic Party in California," a phony committee made up by Nixon's campaign staff. But the existence of a "Democrats for Nixon" organization or some variation thereof is absolutely essential to Nixon's campaigns. Furthermore, it is perfectly logical. Since Nixon's opponents represent only a minority and are illegitimate, they must have come to gain legitimate nominations by some devious manner. Therefore, the Democrats have to be saved from these usurpers. Organizations are then formed by Nixon's people to represent the true, main-line interests of legitimate opponents who can save their Democratic party from the usurpers by voting Republican. These organizations purport to represent "majority" interests. When Nixon became president, he used the same technique in the administration, particularity by Charles Colson. When the *New York Times* criticized Nixon's bombing of Hanoi and Haiphong on the eve of his trip to the Soviet Union, the White House took out an ad in the *Times* entitled "The People vs. the *New York Times*," but without indicating that it had been prepared and written in the White House.[60]

As president, Nixon continued to view his opponents in this light. Speaking about the student protests in 1969, he described protestors as a "vocal minority of our young people [who] are opting out of the process by which civilization maintains its continuity."[61] The "neo-isolationists" were scored for growing weary of the weight of free world leadership and advocating policies that *even they themselves* knew would cause the world to live in terror.[62] Through Vice President Agnew, he attacked the media for being unrepresentative, biased, a tiny handful of executives and anchor-people unresponsive to the people. Agnew proceeded with these themes in his subsequent attacks on media, protesters, political opponents (whom during the

1970 off-term election he dubbed "radical-liberals"), and anyone else who posed political opposition to Nixon.[63] (There has been much speculation about Nixon's influence on Agnew's provocative speeches. In *RN* Nixon began to clarify his own rhetorical relationship with Agnew's Des Moines speech. He wrote: "Pat Buchanan sent me a memorandum urging a direct attack on the network commentators and a few days later he submitted a speech draft that did so in very direct and articulate language. Ted Agnew's hard-hitting speeches had attracted a great deal of attention during the fall, and I decided he was the right man to deliver this one. I toned down some of Buchanan's rhetoric and gave it to Agnew. We further moderated some sections that Agnew thought sounded strident, and then he edited it himself so that the final version would be in his words." If Nixon "toned down" some of Buchanan's rhetoric and then Agnew insisted still more be "moderated," one wonders how "strident" the original version was.)[64]

During the Watergate days Nixon reverted to this strategy by accusing the media of causing his troubles or saying that Watergate was merely an attempt by political opponents to overturn his legitimate election in 1972 (which he had won overwhelmingly).

The central appeal of this argument is to the sacred maxim: *The majority rules.* It is not very subtle. But more important, Nixon sees himself as sole representative of the majority in all matters, and anyone who opposes him represents only a minority or extremist point of view. Because "majority rule" is synonymous with democracy, Nixon perforce represents democracy, and his opponents by definition do not. Thus, an attack on him is an attack on fundamental democratic principles. In other words, he is legitimate; his opponents are almost always illegitimate. In this sense, then, anyone who disagrees with Nixon does not have a legitimate disagreement. And being illegitimate, opponents must have achieved public prominence by some sinister means. Such reasoning makes repeated ad hominem attacks on opponents not only self-justifying but mandatory. Most importantly, opponents are not to be listened to or heeded. That has been the consistent message Nixon has preached to Americans throughout his career, from his beginnings in 1946 to his most recent statements. And it leads to the two final constituents that form the structure of his rhetoric.

Nixon predicts catastrophic consequences should this minority defeat him. Since Nixon's adversaries are seldom legitimate, this argument logically follows. Those who are seduced by an extreme minority will reap disastrous consequences. In chastising the "neo-isolationists," Nixon charged that if they prevailed, America would become "a dropout in assuming the responsibility for defending peace and freedom in the world . . . and the rest of the world would live in terror."[65] In his November 3, 1969, speech, Nixon predicted that if those who believed in "precipitate withdrawal" prevailed, they would "inevitably allow the communists to repeat the massacres which followed their takeover in the North 15 years before." Nixon then drew a grim picture of what those consequences would be; the immediate consequences:

- They [the North Vietnamese] then murdered more than 50,000 people and hundreds of thousands more died in slave labor camps.
- We saw a prelude of what would happen in South Vietnam when the Communists entered the city of Hue last year. During their brief rule there, there was a bloody reign of terror in which 3,000 civilians were clubbed, shot to death, and buried in mass graves.
- With the sudden collapse of our support, these atrocities of Hue would become the nightmare of the entire nation—and particularly for the million and a half Catholic refugees who fled to South Vietnam when the Communists took over in the North.[66]

The long-range consequences:

For the future of peace, precipitate withdrawal would thus be a disaster of immense magnitude.
- A nation cannot remain great if it betrays it allies and lets down its friends.
- Our defeat and humiliation in South Vietnam without question would promote recklessness in the councils of those great powers who have not yet abandoned their goals of world conquest.
- This would spark violence wherever our commitments help maintain the peace—in the Middle East, in Berlin, eventually even in the Western Hemisphere.
Ultimately, this would cost more lives.
It would not bring peace; it would bring more war.[67]

Those who oppose Nixon, then, propose policies that would be catastrophic.
An important variation on this argument is Nixon's "crystal ball" knowledge of his opponents, or what Meg Greenfield called the

"slippery would-have-been."[68] Nixon proclaims that he "knows" what opponents believe and what consequences would result if he had not been there to prevent them from prevailing. These "crystal ball predictions" take two forms: first, "if they had their way," and, second, "if they had won." In campaigning against Helen Douglas, Nixon charged that "if she had her way, the Communist conspiracy would never have been exposed, and Alger Hiss would still be influencing the foreign policy of the United States."[69] Greenfield noted Nixon's warning about what would have happened if Adlai Stevenson had been elected president instead of Eisenhower: "We of course do not know the answer to that question, but of these principles I am sure: indecision, weakness, retreat, and surrender do not bring peace in dealing with dictatorial, aggressive communism."[70]

Of course, one may argue that every politician predicts dire consequences should he or she lose and the opponents win. It's a standard rhetorical tactic in campaigns. But Nixon puts a different twist on this standard technique. He believes these terrible consequences will actually occur should his illegitimate opponents prevail. That led him to believe that he should adopt their illegitimate tactics before they used them on him. William Safire, Nixon's speechwriter during his first term, noted this in Nixon: "When Nixon later spoke of the 'expected excesses' of others as the reason for the excesses of 'us,' he put his finger on the political philosophy of the preemptive strike, which is rooted in an attitude of 'us against them,' a golden rule turned by perverse political alchemists to read: Do it unto others before they do it unto you."[71] Such a position leads to the last constituent of Nixon's rhetoric.

Nixon sees each substantive issue as a moral issue on which he is right. Nixon was the most rigidly moralistic president since Woodrow Wilson. He believed he was right and his opponents were wrong. In contrasting his Vietnam policy to "precipitate withdrawal," Nixon stated: "I have chosen this second course [Vietnamization and negotiation]. It is not the easy way. It is the right way."[72] In justifying the invasion of Cambodia, he said: "I would rather be a one-term President and do what I believe is right than to be a two-term President at the cost of seeing America become a second-rate power and to see this Nation accept the first defeat in its proud 190-year history."[73]

Since Nixon is always right and his opponents illegitimate, he sees no reason for engaging them in debate on issues. The only matters left to discuss are the moral character defects that cause opponents to take positions that are wrong (that is, positions different from Nixon's). This is truly the mark of the self-righteous and of their rhetoric. Those who believe themselves morally right on an issue do not debate with opponents because to do so would be to admit that the other side has some legitimate claim in the debate. To do that diminishes one's moral claim. Therefore, Nixon's speeches and memoirs are filled with charges of hypocrisy about those who have opposed him. In scoring the "campus revolutionaries," Nixon charged: "Some of the more extreme even argue, with a rather curious logic, that there is no majority, because the majority has no right to hold opinions that they disagree with. Scorning persuasion they prefer coercion. Awarding themselves what they call a higher morality, they try to bully authorities into yielding to their 'demands.' On college campuses they draw support from faculty members who should know better; in the larger community, they find the usual apologists ready to excuse any tactic in the name of 'progress.'"[74] In his speech on military power at the Air Force Academy, Nixon asserted that the "neo-isolationists" *knew* that the policies they advocated would cause "the rest of the world [to] live in terror."[75] Reeling from the defeats of his nominations of judges Haynsworth and Carswell to the Supreme Court, Nixon made the same kind of charge against senators who voted against confirmation: "But when all the hypocrisy is stripped away, the real issue was their philosophy of strict construction of the Constitution, a philosophy I share, and the fact that they had the misfortune of being born in the South."[76] In actuality, Nixon was not stripping away hypocrisy. He was charging that senators were hypocritical for opposing his nominees, not because of apparent conflicts of interest or judicial incompetence, but because Haynsworth and Carswell were from the South and believed in a strict interpretation of the Constitution.[77]

The Watergate scandals confronted Nixon with the greatest of all his crises and the greatest challenge to his carefully created world of words. During the campaign of 1972 after the discovery of the Watergate break-in, Nixon relied on surrogates, especially his press secretary Ron Ziegler, to denounce reporters, primarily those from the *Washington Post*, for revelations about White House involvement in Watergate. People who spoke for the administration accused reporters of printing "a collection of absurdities," "a senseless pack of lies," and they charged that reports from Woodward and Bernstein were "a political effort by *The Washington Post*, well conceived and coordinated, to discredit this administration and individuals in it."[78] When, in early 1973, the Senate voted to establish a select committee to investigate illegal activities in the 1972 campaign, Nixon's aides met at Rancho La Costa in California to discuss strategy for responding to the committee. These aides agreed: "The White House will take a public posture of full cooperation but privately will attempt to restrain the investigation and make it as difficult as possible to get information and witnesses. A behind-the-scenes media effort would be made to make the Senate inquiry appear very partisan. The ultimate goal would be to discredit the hearings and reduce their impact by attempting to show that the Democrats have engaged in the same type of activities."[79] That these aides were reflecting Nixon's own strategies became apparent as the president sought every means possible to avoid giving information to the committee or allowing his aides to testify, including: claims to executive privilege and executive confidentiality, legal battles in the courts, the firing of the first special prosecutor, rhetorical attacks on journalists for being biased, and so on and on.[80] The dichotomy between the public statements and private resistance demonstrates once again the dichotomy inherent in the Nixon psyche.

In the end these strategies did not work. Nixon was forced to resign. But even in the resignation Nixon felt compelled to moralize about his administration:

But I want to say one thing: We can be proud of it—5½ years. No man or no woman came into this Administration and left it with more of this world's goods than when he came in. No man or no woman ever profited at the public expense or the public till. That tells something about you.

Mistakes, yes. But for personal gain, never.[81]

Self-righteous to the end. That was one of the reasons for Watergate. The moralists in the White House thought their goals were so important and inherently moral that they justified any means necessary to achieve them, which is typical of strident moralism. And yet, one of the great ironies of the American presidency is that Richard Nixon, who built his career on words and on several occasions saved it through words, was finally brought down by his own words meticulously recorded on his own secret recording system. Public words created Richard Nixon, the politician; private words destroyed Richard Nixon, the president.

Conclusion

In Act IV Hamlet has a remarkable revelation. On his way to England he meets Fortinbras en route to Poland "to gain a little patch of ground / That hath in it no profit but the name." Upon learning Fortinbras's mission, Hamlet imagines twenty thousand dead "for fantasy and trick of fame," "for a plot / Where on the numbers cannot try the cause." In that moment a new Hamlet is born. The private, introspective, philosophic Hamlet entangled in inertia by his own thoughtfulness is transformed into a public, sacrilegious, political Hamlet determined finally to avenge his father's death and seize the crown. His *being* is redefined. "O, from this time forth," he declares, "My thoughts be bloody, or be nothing worth!"

Shakespeare's *Hamlet* is a profoundly tragic drama about the changes wrought in a very private person required by circumstances to become a very public person. He changes from philosopher to politician, and a politician of an unsavory sort, no better than Claudius, upon whom he sought revenge. At the same time, it is a poignant psychological study of how these changes affected Hamlet.

In one very real sense Nixon is a modern Hamlet, a very private, intelligent, and thoughtful man who was forever changed by his choice of politics as a career. His psychology as national leader has always been as fascinating as his policies, sometimes more so. Thus, his career has been repeatedly subjected to psychological analysis.

The standard analysis has been that of psychobiography or psychohistory. Authors of these psychological studies contend that the key to adult behavior lies in childhood experiences that form character and personality. Therefore, they explain adult behavior and even political events through an analysis of childhood experiences. Even as one does not deny the very real impact of those experiences on adult personality, one recognizes that this approach has distinct difficulties. First, one cannot refute psychobiographical studies. They do not abide by the standard rules of evidence and reason since they claim to understand not only the conscious but the subconscious and unconscious as well. In reviewing Fawn Brodie's psychobiography of Nixon, Walter Goodman shrewdly observed that this psychological method "rests less on the evidence than on the intent and ingenuity of the interpreter."[82]

Second, such studies ignore essential facts about public figures, especially Presidents: *they are public figures who must respond to public events, and often it is these events that most shape their public personalities and behavior.* A political figure creates a political personality, a public persona that is guided more by political beliefs, political actions, and reactions to public events than by private or personal experiences. It is these aspects of politicians that psychobiographers often ignore as sources for understanding their public personalities and behavior.

But how are we to understand national political figures? We begin with their political careers, their "rebirth" as public persons. We study their public traumas and persistent patterns of behavior. James David Barber provides an excellent model of this with his examination of Nixon's "crisis syndrome."

My study has been intended for scholars interested in psycho-rhetorical studies of presidents. It establishes a distinctively rhetorical approach to the psychology of a president's persistent rhetoric. Nixon serves as an excellent subject. His career has been built on rhetoric from start to finish. In analyzing the consistent structure of his rhetoric, one penetrates an important part of his reality. In so doing, one learns that there has never really been a "new" Nixon. There has been only one Nixon—rhetorically consistent from the day he entered politics until today. The issues he has embraced over the years have changed, and so, too, on occasion, has his style. As public issues have changed, Nixon has changed to adapt to them. As public resentments have changed, so too Nixon's attacks have changed to capitalize upon them. But there has always been a consistent structure to his attacks and to his rhetoric, and thus to his thought and his public reality.

The essence of Richard Nixon lay not in a set of consistent political beliefs but in a consistent ideology of self. Others have political beliefs that shape their public responses to issues. Nixon was driven by a psychology that often determined the form of his political responses regardless of events, issues, and opponents. Understanding Nixon in this way helps explain why this staunch anticommunist could overcome this long-established stance to extricate the United States from Vietnam, to negotiate SALT I, and to open the doors to China. Indeed, the politics of the decade probably required a Richard Nixon to bring the decade to a close, and to open the vistas to a new decade. After all, before Johnson's dramatic announcement of March 30, 1968, that he would seek an end to the war, Nixon had believed that the United States ought to escalate our war effort in Vietnam. But after Johnson's announcement Nixon changed and proclaimed that he had a "secret plan" to end the war. Once the words were spoken, they had to be defended. The new words became the new reality and would replace the old "hawk" Nixon with the new "peacemaker" Nixon.

Nixon was a negative and moralistic personality who saw his opponents as representing an illegitimate minority who would bring havoc or even destruction to America were they ever to defeat him. His words have been his reality, and he has acted upon them as if they were the truth.

In this sense, the structure of Nixon's rhetoric is also the structure of his reality. Both have a consistency found in few other political figures, from Nixon's initial entry into politics "for a fantasy and trick of fame" to Watergate "Where on the numbers cannot try the cause."

Protesters

6

A Rhetorical Sketch
of Protests
Perspectives

The 1960s will be known in American history as a decade of protest
and remembered for the generation that gave temporary rebirth to a
genuine radicalism. Rebellion after rebellion erupted on campuses
and in streets across the land. People organized into groups demanding their cause be heard. Groups merged into movements, gained
publicity, then splintered into factions, each contending with others
for prominence, power, and truth. Dissension rent the fabric of American society. Public strife threatened political life as Americans
turned upon one another with a vengeance seldom experienced
since the War between the States.

Though protests of one sort or another have been a special feature
of American society since its inception, no previous generation produced such a wide range of sects and so many different rhetorical
forms in such a short period of time. One reason for the proliferation
of these forms may have been the perceived inadequacy of conventional political language to express protesters' concerns and demands. Another reason, one repeatedly charged by protesters, was
that the prevailing political language had become so corrupt that it
was merely a tool to keep officials in power and thus was no longer
relevant to the events it was supposed to explain. As a result, in the
1960s American political language not only expanded, it seemed to
burst apart at the seams. Powerful emotions exploded, and conventional political language seemed inadequate for their expression,
thereby provoking the exploration of a variety of rhetorical forms
that became defining features of the decade.

The sketch of American protest that follows attempts: (1) to establish a critical vocabulary to analyze these different rhetorical forms; and (2) to outline the major lines of argument (*topoi*) that define these various forms of protest discourse. The focus of this work is on liberal or radical protest, not on conservative or reactionary countermovements. The anomaly in this process is administrative discourse that uses liberal ideas for a conservative purpose. To understand these different rhetorical forms we must place them in the political context in which they developed during the protests of the 1960s.

Two Idealized Forms: Procedural Politics and Ideological Politics

People do not give political speeches in a vacuum. Personalities, situations, circumstances, perceptions, ideas contribute to shaping political discourse. But equally important is the advocate's political stance. The way one looks at politics, the way one talks about politics, the way one sees himself or herself in relation to politics and government, the expectations one has from politics—all these further shape and direct discourse. There are two fundamentally different ideas about politics—procedural and ideological—that give rise to fundamental differences in political form, expression, and action. It is not my purpose in this chapter, to indulge in an extended investigation into political philosophy. Rather, it is my purpose to point to certain fundamental differences as a way of creating a *political* perspective for understanding the various rhetorical forms that flowered during the 1960s. These distinctions are important also because they were the prevailing ideas and attitudes about politics at the dawn of the decade. Let me present these two different forms of politics in idealized terms so as to illuminate their differences.

The conflict between ideological politics and procedural politics is as old as Plato and Aristotle, although this particular designation of that conflict is of more recent vintage.[1] The central point of contention is the role ideas are to play in politics. To clarify these two different kinds of politics in this connection, let us turn first to Walter Lippmann. In *The Public Philosophy* Lippmann characterized the liberal democrat (his name for what I am calling the procedural politician) as one committed to laws and rules of society. The liberal democrat, he wrote, "presumes the existence of a state which is already constitutional in principle, which is under laws that are no longer arbitrary, though they may be unjust and unequal. Into this constitutional state more and more people are admitted to the governing class and to the voting electorate. The unequal and the unjust laws are revised until eventually all the people have equal opportunities to enter the government and be represented."[2] In such a system, as described by Lippmann, the government is seen as legitimate, authorities as reasonable and responsive, laws as protective, citizens as disciplined participants (to one degree or another), opportunities limited only by personal talents, and orderly change the order of the day.

Within this system politicians committed to procedural politics believe primarily in form. No matter how firmly beliefs are held, these beliefs must be adjusted to the rules, circumstances, and laws—the *form*—of democratic society. The form, then, sets the perimeters for what action is permissible and practical. If there are policies that procedural politicians believe need to be changed, such changes are effected through the existing structures, either by persuading those in authority to make changes or by voting those authorities out of power and replacing them with people who will be responsive to new concerns.

John H. Bunzel described some of the essential differences that separate procedural politicians from doctrinaire ideologues:

Politics [procedural politics, that is] is concerned with listening to the many diverse and opposing groups in society, conciliating them as far as possible, and giving them the freedom and security to express their own interests so that they can each contribute to the machinery of democratic decision-making. This is the art and business of political rule, and one of its indispensible characteristics is that it does not proceed from a set of rigid principles leading only to absolute goals. A major problem of the Socialist and Communist parties in the United States [doctrinaire ideologues, that is] was that they could never adapt themselves to the "rules of the American game." They preferred to be "right" rather than popular, doctrinaire instead of flexible, intransigent rather than malleable.[3]

Thus, the great democratic machine, a favorite metaphor in the 1960s, is one operated by political engineers who take their direction from citizens who choose to assist by suggesting ways in which cogs in the machine can be made to operate more efficiently and effectively.

In contrast to procedural politics, doctrinaire ideologues believe in the primacy of content:

Ideologies insist on the primary value of the realization of principles in conduct; this is one of the reasons with which they accuse the central value and institutional systems of hypocrisy, the compromise of principles, and corruption by power. Corresponding to this rigorist attitude, the ideologies and their exponents, whether out of power or in central positions of power over society, are relentlessly critical of the inconsistencies and shortcomings of conduct with respect to principles of right and justice in sectors of society over which they do not have complete control. Ideologies demand an intense and continuous observance of their imperatives in the conduct of their exponents.[4]

Doctrinaire ideologues believe primarily in content—their particular doctrines. They seek consistency in matters of justice and righteousness in government. They see inequality and injustice as products of a corrupt system or corrupt ruling class that can be changed only by destroying or radically changing the system. In other words, and especially among revolutionary ideologues, the system itself—not individual laws or rulings—is beyond redemption, and only by gaining power themselves or by overthrowing the system can they redress grievances: "The rulers are to be attacked. They are few. So they are not invincible. They bear the total guilt of all the sufferings and grievances of men. To remove them is then to cure all evil."[5] Their doctrines control their view of politics and speak to the need for changing political systems radically, instead of merely changing specific laws or redressing particular grievances. Injustices or inequalities are only examples of the inherent corruption of the entire system, which must be changed to correspond to the doctrine the ideologue espouses.

In pristine form, procedural politicians and doctrinaire ideologues represent two distinct approaches to politics and thus two distinct systems of political thought. Procedural politicians seek to adjust policies to what they perceive to be public opinion and to the rules and laws by which democratic countries govern themselves. Ideologues demand that society reconstruct itself in line with their fixed ideas which, they claim, are historically or scientifically correct. Furthermore, procedural politicians concentrate on changing specific policies or laws that may eventually alter governmental form and content. Ideologues insist the structure of government must be changed before any real changes in policy can occur.

This is not to say that procedural politicians are so devoted to form that they have no ideas. Quite the contrary. They have a variety of ideas about what policies should prevail and are willing to voice them vigorously. On occasion, they may even adopt ideological ideas. A similar thing can be said about ideologues. They may resort to standard procedural politics at times to further their goals. Much of the history of the Socialist party in America testifies to this attempt to blend socialist doctrine and electoral politics. Procedural politicians and ideologues are two different sides of the same political coin. After all, they are both trying to deal with the same problem: the messy existential world they encounter and the need for a conceptual theory or rationale to confront it coherently. But there is a great difference in emphasis. Among procedural politicians, practice and results are usually more important than theory or rationale, whereas among ideologues, theory is of principal importance. Nonetheless, in their purest sense, the two are distinct in more ways than emphasis, as I have tried to show. They represent different forms of political thinking. The distinction between the two creates the basis for later arguments I shall make in respect to different forms of protest rhetoric.

From the perspective of almost thirty years of hindsight, the polar differences I have drawn between these two forms of political thinking in the 1960s may seem like caricatures. But to that generation this distinction was not arbitrary nor merely speculative. It was real. And it had its roots in the events and the writings about politics in the 1950s. During that time there was a concerted effort by influential writers to "de-ideologize" politics. Liberals had been frightened by the pious orthodoxies that Senator Joseph McCarthy had sought to impose on Americans. Conservatives had been equally frightened by the orthodoxies of socialism and communism. Both had fought against Nazism. Both had been traumatized by Stalinism and the cold war, although in different ways. Both were horrified by the thought of ideologies.

But the drive against ideologies was not solely negative. It was also influenced by admiration—some of it grudging—for President Franklin Roosevelt. He was the model of the nonideological, free-wheeling, imaginative leader. Arthur Schlesinger, Jr., the most persuasive and committed critic of political ideologies, described the rift between Roosevelt and his adviser Raymond Moley in these words: "For Moley . . . national planning tended to be almost an end in itself; for Roosevelt, it was a means to an end. *Seeing people and not ideologies*—specific cases rather than general principles—Roosevelt freely indulged in contradictions which drove logical men to despondency. . . . Roosevelt transcended systems for the sake of a more complex vision of America, which included elements of coordination and of decentralization, of nationalism and internationalism."[6] In his enormously influential book, *Presidential Power: The Politics of Leadership*, Richard Neustadt celebrated the same qualities in contrasting Roosevelt's lack of an ideology and a style of leadership that issued from it with the more rigid styles of Truman and Eisenhower. About Roosevelt, Neustadt wrote: "Political experience and private life created in [FDR] *not an ideology* but a decided feeling for what government should be and where its policies should lead."[7]

By the dawn of the new decade the result of these experiences was the perception of politics, as Garry Wills aptly described it, that was "beyond left and right."[8] It was pervasive, spilling over from politics into all sorts of other intellectual and practical endeavors. In social psychology, it meant the status-politics school of thought and the "organization man"; in sociology, the reconsideration of the problems of individualism symbolized by the "lonely crowd"; in higher education, the multi-university or new Ideapolis of Clark Kerr; in Republican circles, the "New Conservatism"; in Democratic circles, the pragmatic "realists" who occupied "the vital center"; in religion, some of the writings of Reinhold Niebuhr, Norman Vincent Peale's positive thinking, and Harvey Cox's "secular city"; in literary criticism, the triumph of "New Criticism."[9]

Nowhere was the anti-ideological attitude more pronounced than in writings on American history and politics, especially by influential historians. This theme runs from Schlesinger's *Vital Center* (1949) through Daniel Boorstin's *Genius of American Politics* (1953), Louis Hartz's *Liberal Tradition in America* (1955), Raymond Aron's *Opium of the Intellectuals* (1957), on to Richard Hofstader's *Age of Reform* (1955), *Paranoid Style in American Politics* (1965), and *Progressive Historians* (1968). These "consensus" historians dominated the writing and thus the interpretation of American history, but they were also, in the words of Marian J. Morton, "terrified" by ideological politics.[10] The same theme runs through other influential works in which what I call "procedural politics" is contrasted starkly with "ideological politics." In *Political Power: USA/USSR*, Brzezinski and Huntington called them "instrumental" and "ideological."[11] John Bunzel, writing later in the decade, contrasted "real" politics (procedural) with "anti-politics" (ideological).

The whole anti-ideological mood that pervaded the times was summed up with Daniel Bell's famous proclamation in 1960 that Western civilization was witnessing an exhaustion of political ideas, which he felicitously described as "the end of ideology."[12] The "new politician," as the end-of-ideologists saw it, would be the expert social engineer, the expert political manager who "can provide us with the solutions to all of our problems. The benevolence of the social engineer is taken as a foregone conclusion. Being so much more enlightened [procedural, not ideological, that is], he certainly knows what is best for the general welfare. He has been trained to be value-free, to be completely objective."[13] More important, the ideal politician would be the one who defended "democratic" procedures above all else, especially against ideologues and ideologies.

The polarity between procedural and ideological politics had profound consequences. For this analysis of protest movements, four are worth mentioning.

First, it led to an exaggerated idealization of procedural politics. In fact, working within accepted procedures became synonymous with practicing politics to the exclusion of all other forms of politics. Few stated this more emphatically than did Bernard Crick in his 1962 book, *In Defense of Politics*: "*The* political method of rule is to listen to these other groups so as to conciliate them as far as possible, and to give them a legal position, a sense of security, some clear and reasonably safe means of articulation, by which these other groups can and will speak freely. Ideally politics draws all these groups into each other so that they each and together can make a positive contribution towards the general business of government, the maintaining of order."[14] This excessive idealization of political rules and proper practices resulted in perceiving any new procedures (such as the "participatory democracy" advocated by Tom Hayden) as a direct threat to an orderly democracy or as a naive romanticism that violated the "laws" of political realism. Thus, the end of ideology and the exaltation of procedure meant, as Mario Savio would later say, an end to history, an end to political evolution, an end to political imagination.

Second, the excessive fear of ideology led many to confuse political beliefs of the right with political beliefs of the left by seeing them only as mirror images of one another. This lumping of right and left together was a natural consequence of the distinction between procedural and ideological politics. Both right and left violated orderly procedures by insisting on the primacy of ideas and worldviews. For that reason, they were "extreme." At the outset of their book, *The Politics of Unreason*, Lipset and Raab wrote:

> Extremist movements designated "left" and "right" in America have frequently shared the same political technology, such as a working impatience with dissent. They have often moved in the same surface ideological directions, such as isolationism, or opposition to Wall Street banking. If there has been one constant, it has been the perception of extreme rightist movements as those which have risen primarily in reaction against the displacement of power and status accompanying change; while left-wing extremism has been seen as impelling social change, and, in that course, attempting to overthrow old power and status groups.[15]

Even though these differences in political beliefs were noted, the authors still contended that the form of politics practiced by the two was identical, as evidenced in their definition of extremism:

"extremism [is] a specific tendency to violate democratic procedures."[16] It should be remembered that Lipset first coined the phrase "radical right." Historically, the term *radical* had been reserved for left-wing agitators or ideologues; "reactionaries" had been used to describe right-wing agitators or ideologues. However, once the defining point for politics became one's attitude or stance toward procedures, rather than specific political beliefs one held, the mixture of left and right under the rubric of "radical" made perfect political sense. What resulted were repeated denunciations of the extremism of both. Thus, those who did the denouncing presented themselves as nonpartisan, and attacked not political beliefs, but rather the kind of politics "extremists" practiced. This merger of very different beliefs into one category, in turn, gave rise to new ways of talking about political positions: extreme, moderate, militant—all descriptions of attitudes toward procedures, not designations of political beliefs. It even encouraged such convoluted statements as Richard Nixon's attempt to justify his call for firing Professor Eugene Genovese from Rutgers University for saying he would welcome a Viet Cong victory in Vietnam on the grounds that doing so would protect academic freedom: "If we are to defend academic freedom from encroachment we must also defend it from its own excesses."[17] In other words, to preserve the principle of academic freedom of speech and inquiry ("from its own excesses"), one had to deny it to "extremists" who might practice it. From a logical perspective, Nixon's statement is contradictory. But from the perspective of procedural politics, his statement makes eminently good sense.

Third, the shift from political beliefs to political attitudes as the defining feature of what is acceptable or unacceptable meant the devaluation of political ideas, even—on some occasions—modest proposals that were presented through the proper channels. Political procedures took precedence over political ideas. Furthermore, authorities were rarely willing to share their power to interpret and administer rules. After all, they had been elected or appointed to be the guardians of a new "nonideological" society. Administrators were de facto legitimate guardians of the procedures. Thus, ideas that could be converted into specific programs, ideas that were "realistic," ideas, in other words, that would work within accepted procedures and were approved by legitimate authorities were ideas that could be entertained (possibly) for future deliberation and action by those authorities. But ideas that caused people to question basic assumptions, ideas that questioned the efficacy of established procedures, ideas that expanded participation in the decision-making process—ideas, in other words, that required serious critical thinking were usually considered unrealistic, romantic, or potentially subversive. Proposals that would require new policies were received suspiciously because they might call into question the "credibility" of officials and the methods by which they had arrived at existing policies. When protesters challenged basic policies, they often frightened officials into seeing an "ideology" behind the proposal or sinister motives lurking in those who made the proposals.

Admittedly, this characterization is overdrawn. Policies that could be seen as within the "mainstream," simply tinkering with the democratic machine, were often accommodated; or proposals that sought to redress long-standing grievances upon which many in the public agreed need to be redressed reached favorable ears. But ideas that required a rethinking of basic causes or primary ideas or firmly established procedures caused exaggerated reactions from authorities. Conviction had to give way to consensus. And, indeed, what was "conviction" anyway except a romantic ideal or the symptom of a rigid, sublimated ideological system?

Finally, the confluence of the idealization of procedure and the fear of ideology produced a blindness to the American government's own foreign policy ideology: anticommunism. Michael Parenti wrote: "If America has an ideology . . . , it is anti-communism."[18] But few in government or elsewhere, for that matter, saw the policy of containment and its theoretical underpinnings as ideological. The policies that evolved from or into fervent anticommunism had gone through the proper procedures of government. Furthermore, containing communism could not be an ideology, the architects of this policy believed, since it was not "extreme" or "revolutionary," nor was it advocated by "radicals." Containment was instead a "moderate" policy (in comparison with an all-out nuclear war with the Soviet Union or complete capitulation to communism); it was defensive, seeking not territorial conquest but only to thwart the inherent expansion of communism; and it had been created by some of the most respected members of American political society.[19] No, anticommunism was not an ideology, they thought, but a set of coherent beliefs and values that ordered American foreign policy and gave policy makers a clear guide to the motives, tactics, strategies, objectives, and character of our enemies. This political blindness was, in part, a direct result of the polar contrast that had long before been drawn between procedural and ideological politics.

In addition, another ideology was emerging: the ideology of administrative credibility. Procedures that were once meant to promote free discussion of issues were fossilized into a rigid set of beliefs about how such ideas would be discussed and with whom. When protest erupted, administrators who denounced them employed an anti-ideology ideology, a rhetorical form that denounced ideology in the name of a procedural ideology. This "procedural ideology" became one of the most important methods of discrediting protesters in the 1960s.

Deliberative Rhetoric and Ideological Rhetoric

If the differences between the procedural politician and the doctrinaire ideologue are clear, then it must follow that the rhetoric developed by each would also be different. In the *Rhetoric* Aristotle emphasized the connection between political systems and the forms persuasion takes:

> The most important and effective qualification for success in persuading audiences and speaking well on public affairs is to understand all the forms of government and to discriminate their respective customs, institutions, and interests. For all men are persuaded by consideration of their interest, and *their interest lies in the maintenance of the established order*. Further, it rests with supreme authority to give authoritative decisions, and this varies with each form of government; there are as many different supreme authorities as there are different forms of government.[20]

Though Aristotle exhorted his readers to know the various forms of government, he based his *Rhetoric* on a Greek democratic society in which rulers were subservient to laws, rules, and citizen opinion. Citizens come together in this setting to debate and deliberate on issues of state. The rules of the democratic system allow citizens to air disagreements and provides the "marketplace for competing ideas." The essence of the deliberative rhetoric is that it deals with issues of probability. Every issue is open to debate. Each requires a judgment. No one possesses "truth." Persuasion is the central feature of this rhetoric. For those out of power, it means supplication to authorities to redress grievances. For those in power, it means a debate among equals about which course of action is most prudent and expedient.

The rhetoric of the ideologue is much different from deliberative rhetoric. Henri Lefebvre aptly summarized the essence of ideological rhetoric: "Within a group that takes up the ideology, it serves as a pretext for zealousness, sense of common purpose, and then the group tends to become a sect. Adherence to the ideology makes it possible to despise those who do not adhere to it, and, needless to say, leads to their conversion or condemnation."[21] Among ideologues, the relation between ideology and truth or reality is difficult to untangle, both historically and philosophically. Some doctrinaire "true believers" insisted that the ideology is an objectively true representation of reality. Analytic students of ideology are more inclined to believe that ideology cannot actually capture reality, only essential parts of it. For example, Lefebvre contended that ideology is not a reflection of reality, but a refraction of it. But this point of contention, a philosophic question to be argued by ideologues, is only incidentally germane to the rhetorical manifestation of the ideological spirit.

What is important is that the ideological rhetors *present* their ideas as if they are true and demand assent from authorities and followers. Gouldner described this rhetorical stance in pointed fashion when writing about four different aspects of Marxist ideology. Of the four, two are most pertinent to the argument presented here:

(2) There is also the "living" or "plain" Marxism of those for whom Marxism is part of an everyday life and practice, who submit to its grammar, obey its rules, using them to define or pursue political projects, and to organize their own personal identities. This is Marxism as an everyday culture, as a *less* reflexive language, i.e. a "Weltanschauung."

(3) There is a Marxism as a structured network of associations and social relations instrumental to the achievement of its political projects, and actively enforcing its grammar in evaluating its community's projects or its members' performances. Here we deal with Marxism as a "social movement," which may include one of the highly-boundaried, risk-taking, combat parties the movement has developed, i.e. the "vanguard" organization.[22]

In essence, the ideological leaders ("vanguard") actively enforce the ideology upon supporters, who "submit to its grammar" and "obey its rules" and are, in turn, evaluated by how well they conform to the grammar and rules. These also become the standards by which they judge those in authority.

The rhetoric of the ideologue is one of truth explained. The ideology is *true*, not probable. Thus, the veracity of the ideology is not open to argument, except within the closed circle of those committed to the ideology. For ideological protesters, their interests lie not in the maintenance of the established order of government, but in the maintenance of the established order, coherence, and veracity of the ideology. Ideology stands as the secular counterpart of religion. Each makes absolute truth claims. Each has an authoritative book or set of teachings containing the truth. Each has a comprehensive explanation of all reality in its rhetoric. And each is essentially moral. In religion, there are theologians who study doctrine with critical sophistication and preachers who apply the Word to daily living and individual belief. So, too, among ideologues there are those who theorize about ideology and those who use it as a guide for belief and action in the world of practical politics.

What, then, do ideologues advocate? I shall return to this question in more detail later, but for the time being one can say that ideologues must exhort supporters to accept the truth of the ideology, must explain it to them, and must reveal its application to current conditions and circumstances. Ideological rhetoric is deductive, a rhetoric in which basic principles cannot be compromised (at least, in public), but either must be accepted or rejected. Interpretation (or the ideological critique of ideology) or the appropriate strategies for applying the ideology to existing conditions are open to argument only among committed ideologues.

Thus, the differences between deliberative rhetoric and ideological rhetoric become clear. The public speeches and writings of procedural politicians are intended, to use Donald C. Bryant's splendid phrase, to serve "the function of adjusting ideas to people and of people to ideas."[23] Ideologues, on the other hand, are principally concerned—to borrow a definition from Charles Sears Baldwin—of "giving effectiveness to truth" and thus adjusting people to ideas only.[24] The rhetoric of the former is one of persuasion; of the latter, conversion. The rhetoric of procedural politicians is the Aristotelian genre of deliberative public address, that is, the finding of the available means of persuasion in a given case based on expediency and inexpediency. It is an "innovative" rhetoric that "acts with the expectation that the change it demands will not disturb the symbols and constraints of existing values or modify the social [or political] hierarchy."[25] The rhetoric of doctrinaire ideologues, however, is one of truth explained, which requires new symbols and new words to express it and which aims at changing existing values and perceptions so as to change social hierarchies and political thought.

One can imagine a number of serious objections to these distinctions between procedural politics and ideological politics, between deliberative rhetoric and ideological rhetoric, and some of these should be discussed directly.

First, the classical purist may object to inclusion of ideology within the province of rhetoric because it purports to deal with the truth and not the probable. However, if one were to contend that rhetoric must be concerned only with ideas in the realm of probability, then one would have to exclude much of the study of religious rhetoric. After all, religious rhetoric (preaching) is concerned with the conveyance of scriptural truth to believers, and with the attempts at converting unbelievers to that truth.[26] The basis for the truth is the scriptures. The preacher is the interpreter. Ideologues, like religious rhetors, explain and defend their truths and seek to expose falsehoods. For each, rhetorical invention is limited to interpreting scriptures or the "sacred" secular text of the ideology and to finding appropriate methods for applying that truth to specific audiences, circumstances, or events.

A second objection is that all people claim that what they believe is true, and thus the distinctions between procedural and ideological politics are arbitrary, at best, and imaginary, at worst. One can agree with the first part of this objection without necessarily coming to the same conclusion based on that objection. People have beliefs because they are convinced they are true. But from a rhetorical standpoint, the essential differences lie in the ways in which they hold and handle their truths. Procedural politicians may personally believe their policies or ideas are true, but they also believe that they must submit them for public approval and frequently will modify them, if necessary, to suit public moods, needs, circumstances, or events. Ideologues seek to remain consistent in believing their truths are objectively true regardless of public mood, needs, circumstances, or events. They may be willing to modify or shift *strategies* or *tactics* to adjust to public moods, but they remain committed to the basic principles of the ideology. In other words, procedural politicians may be willing to modify ideas to suit audiences or circumstances, whereas ideologues may be willing to modify strategies or tactics to suit audiences or circumstances. Yet, both submit to certain rhetorical requirements imposed by the need to persuade or to convert potential constituencies, even though their political stances may require them to respond in quite different ways.

A third and more serious objection may be that the distinction between procedural politics and ideology is a distinction without a difference. My position is that these are two different kinds of politics. Others would argue that procedural politics is only another form of ideology.[27] Cultural critics, in particular, take this position and argue that the real difference is whether the ideology is explicit or implicit. In fact, they see ideologies lurking everywhere, either embedded or hidden in the discourse and only awaiting excavation or "unmasking." Their argument is seductive. It appeals to the human urge to find a unity in all things, to find a single coherent method for analyzing and resolving all the messy conflicts of life and thought.

However, could one not apply the same process with a different perspective and come to a very different conclusion? Instead of saying all politics is ideological and that the only distinctions occur at different points on an ideological spectrum based on how overt or covert the ideological claims may be, could one not say that all politics is really about Machiavellian machinations of power? The consequence of taking this power position, instead of an ideological position, would be to see both deliberative and ideological rhetoric as merely masks or smoke screens for the naked struggle for power among contending groups or people.[28] Then, procedural and ideological politics would differ only in occupying different places on the power spectrum. And how would they be assigned their respective places? Would they be distinguished by the different ideas they embrace and the different purposes they seek? Or would they be distinguished by their successes or failures in gaining and exercising power? But what if ideologues insisted that they were interested in more than power for its own sake, that power was only an instrument to achieve one goal of ideology, and that the real purpose was to create a critical social theory and perhaps a comprehensive guide to action? Undoubtedly, the Power Cynic (if I may use this description for the moment) would laugh in their faces and say: "Your rhetoric is inauthentic, only a rationalization for your will to power. All you want to do is replace one form of repressive power with another form of repressive power. The only difference between you and procedural politicians is that if you gain power, this time you will be the ones doing the oppressing rather than being oppressed."

The problem with both the ideological and power approaches to politics—presented here—is not so much reductionism, but the attacks on integrity that they require: attacks on the integrity of intentions, attacks on the integrity of language. Each argues that some stated intentions are only masks for the real (usually malevolent) intentions, and some specific uses of language must not be taken literally, but must be unmasked for the ideology or will-to-power they conceal. Such attacks then result in "strawman" arguments rather than engagement with the actual arguments others have advanced.

This examination of protest rhetoric proceeds on the basic assumption that there are different kinds of politics—procedural and ideological—and that they therefore create different rhetorical forms to conform to those politics. Thus far, the argument has been advanced primarily at the conceptual level. An examination of these different rhetorical forms in the following chapters will demonstrate the appropriateness of this distinction.

But before proceeding to a discussion of genres and political movements, we need some definitions. *Radical* will be used to refer to left-wing ideologues.[29] The terms *protester, dissident,* and *agitator* are used to describe those who rely on procedural means for protest. *Ideologue* refers to those who either have an ideological consciousness or who have specific programs for ideological change. The term *revolutionary* is reserved for those who advocate violence as a means for change. Each of these terms has definite historical antecedents, and my use of them in this context is political rather than sociological or psychological. Indeed, the whole thrust of this study of protest is to develop *political* categories for analysis to replace the *sociological* categories that pervade other studies. It should be reemphasized that each of these terms is being used within a rhetorical context; that is, radicalism and the others are seen and so defined through the prism of the use by each of public language on political issues. The public statements, rather than private intentions, are the central materials for analysis and for distinguishing among different forms of political discourse.

Rhetorical Genres and Symbolic Action

The critic who uses generic forms as an analytic tool believes that rhetorical efforts are repetitive, that the choice to use one form or another depends on the rhetor's view of politics and circumstances, that these forms create an organizing principle for scholarship that allows the critic to compare one rhetor's use of a form with another idealized or established description of that form.

Genre criticism is composed of three different elements. First, there are *situational* elements: a particular event or series of events—either action or speech—that are perceived by rhetors as calling for rhetorical activity. The important word here is *perceived*. Things happen or people speak in such ways that others perceive a need to respond.[30] The situation may be limited to a striking event or it may be indicative of a prevailing condition. How the situation is perceived and interpreted by those who respond is what creates the second element of a genre: the *substantive or stylistic characteristics* of the rhetoric. Since different people or groups interpret events in different ways, they will develop or create different arguments to justify those ideas or perceptions. The final element is what has been called the *organizing principle* of the rhetoric genre: "the internal dynamic of the constellation that is formed by the substantive, stylistic, and situational features of the genre."[31] In other words, the interaction of all elements.

But we should not make too much ado over this "modern discovery" of genres. After all, Aristotle first described the three major forms of democratic speeches: deliberative (political), epideictic (ceremonial), and forensic (legal). The general purpose of each are to persuade audiences, and the specific purposes of each are to persuade about specific matters; for example, deliberative discourse concerns itself with expediency and inexpediency, the future, and what is to be done or not done. Each genre has different purposes suited to different circumstances, and therefore has different and distinct strategies and tactics as well as sources for ideas that define its peculiarities. As I noted previously, Aristotle formulated his genres on the basis of his knowledge of governments of his time and cannot be faulted for not anticipating the intellectual revolutions in political thought of subsequent centuries.

The Aristotelian genre of deliberative rhetoric is clearly useful when analyzing procedural protest on single issues. However, it is inadequate—but not irrelevant—as a guide and analytic tool when it comes to some forms of protest rhetoric. First, it is inadequate because ideological rhetoric starts from a different premise than Aristotelian rhetoric: the truth of the ideology rather than ideas in the realm of probability. Thus, the ideas of ideological rhetoric are structured to conform to the tenets of the ideology, as I have already argued, and not by adaptation to circumstances.

Second, in its strictest sense, Aristotelian rhetoric limits its search for ideas and arguments to finding those appropriate in a specific case. Aristotle enumerated the variety of arguments available to apply in a given case. Ideologues speak to broad conditions in which specific cases are only examples of these conditions.

Finally, Aristotelian rhetoric, based as it was on Athenian democracy, presumes a general equality among participants in the rhetorical debate on issues in which all will decide what is to be done in a given case. This rhetorical model is appropriate to describe the situation of parliamentary or congressional debates. But the situation changes dramatically when citizens approach their government, or students confront college administrators, to make changes in policy. This rhetorical situation is not one in which all are equals. Citizens have the power to petition for redress of grievances. But only authorities have the power to change policies. As I shall demonstrate, some authorities see protesters as threats to be suppressed rather than as citizens to be addressed. This perception of protest will give rise to rhetorical forms unimagined by Aristotle. Protesters respond to these dismissals by escalating the intensity of their efforts and by developing new rhetorical strategies and tactics. At this point, ideological critiques become valuable by exposing the interests authorities represent and the unstated premises from which they argue.

In the chapters that follow I describe briefly the political conditions that established various rhetorical situations protesters faced, identify various genres that developed from their perceptions of the kind of politics and rhetoric appropriate to respond to these situations, and finally analyze the particular *topoi* that constitute the internal dynamics of these genres. Such an analysis involves a shift in critical perspective from Aristotelian purpose (persuasion) to structure (genre), a shift not necessarily anti-Aristotelian, but quite different in perspective. Furthermore, this shift in emphasis also means a shift from the study of single speeches or pieces of writings to the study of patterns of persuasion or conversion that make up that genre. It may be that all the elements that constitute a genre may be found in a single work, but not necessarily so. At times, it may be prudent to pick from a variety of statements to find the parts that make up the whole.

The genres chosen by advocates are meant to persuade or to convert or to condemn or to cause people to act, and the symbolic acts they perform after voicing their rhetoric confirms or denies the authenticity of the rhetors' beliefs, or at least measures the extent of their commitment to their politics.[32] Thus, a procedural protester who accepts a jail sentence when arrested by authorities demonstrates authentic belief in procedural politics and therefore achieves authenticity as this kind of political person. A revolutionary who advocates violence and blows up a building demonstrates symbolic, existential commitment to violence as an acceptable tactic for forcing change and thus confirms his or her authenticity as a revolutionary. Those who refuse to act in accordance with their rhetoric deny or diminish their political authenticity.

The Rhetoric of Political Movements

Most writers and scholars describe protest movements as social movements. I want to replace *social* with *political* not so much as a matter of semantics, but rather as a more precise delineation of what the 1960s generation of protesters was all about. They wanted to change political policies or political institutions, which, in turn, would have social ramifications. It is on the political rhetoric that I will concentrate.

Definitions of movements abound. Historians as well as rhetoricians seem confused and at odds with one another about how to define them. The eminent historian Richard Hofstadter complained that historians were interested in movements only so long as they were rhetorical, the subject of public agitation: "Presumably the historians drop the subject of anti-trust at or around 1938 not because they imagine that it has lost its role in society but because after that point it is no longer the subject of much public agitation—in short, because there is no longer an anti-trust movement. The intensity of public concern . . . is a poor guide for historians."[33] But the "intensity of public concern" is a legitimate focus for the rhetorical critic, and a variety of rhetoricians have advanced theories to analyze movements.

Leland Griffin developed the first theory to begin to account for rhetorical movements. He divided the combatants into *pro* and *anti* groups (aggressor and defendant rhetoricians) who progress through a period of inception to a period of rhetorical crisis to a final period of consummation.[34] This framework provided the beginning for studies of movements, but to some later theorists Griffin's model seemed simplistic, lacked specificity, and could not account for the diversity of groups and rhetorical forms that developed in protest movements of the 1960s.

Herbert A. Simons sought to provide that specificity in his influential essay "Requirements, Problems and Strategies: A Theory of Persuasion for Social Movements."[35] Simons took the perspective of procedural politics and invoked the categories that issue from it. He made no distinction between left and right but treated them as mirror images of one another, both being involved in social movements. He divided members of protest groups into "militants" and "moderates" and sought to develop a theory that would address the requirements, problems, and strategies of reconciling militants and moderates to one another so as to create a cohesive social movement. He spelled out the procedural and prescriptive nature of his approach in his celebrated essay.

Robert Cathcart responded to both Griffin and Simons with an ideological definition of social movements.[36] Cathcart sought to lift movements out of their specific historical contexts by defining movements as moral dialectics exemplified by confrontational rhetoric, the defining feature of rhetorical movements. Such an ideological approach deals with essences rather than means and ends and permits the critic to make substantive distinctions that other theories do not, although such distinctions must be made on the ideological level or not at all.

Since these early theories were first presented, dozens of other scholars—as well as the original theorists—have expanded, developed, and refined theories about the rhetoric of movements, but thus far they have not come to any consensus about what constitutes a movement or how to proceed in analyzing one.[37]

The current writings about movements are too extensive to be summarized here.[38] But a symposium published in 1983 delineated four distinct approaches: the historical approach, the confrontational approach, the meaning-center approach, and the functional approach.[39] I intend to attempt to accommodate each of these approaches to some degree in the examination of protest movements of the 1960s.

Within the restricted historical context of the 1960s, the rhetorical genres that were used are related to the political milieu in which they developed. Michael McGee's "meaning-centered" approach provides the defining feature for *when the movement moves*: that is, from one rhetorical period to another. Movements move when rhetors redefine the issues in such ways that new rhetorical forms are called forth to explain the new *meaning* of the issues and the new *meaning* of the protest. Robert Cathcart's insistence on rhetorical form as one central feature of rhetorical movements is shared in this analysis, but his equally intense insistence on confrontational form as the sole defining feature seems too limiting to accommodate the variety of rhetorical forms that developed during the 1960s. Charles Stewart's belief that a theory of movements can be established by studying unique patterns that have different functions within protest movements is a belief with which I agree. In fact, to show that these patterns are recurring, I shall occasionally draw analogs to comparable rhetorical efforts from the past to demonstrate not only the repetitive patterns of these genres but also the predictable ways these genres have emerged.

For our purposes, we can say that a political movement moves from one period to another when the central issues are redefined and the public language protesters use changes so dramatically that new rhetorical genres emerge.[40] To put it another way, we can describe a new rhetorical phase within a movement as a time when advocates discard the prevailing political language and rhetorical genres to create new ones that demand fresh symbolic acts to legitimize them, that give new meaning to the protest, and that, as a consequence, redefine both the protest and the protesters. These changes signal divergent interpretations of goals, strategies, and tactics, and thus create a new rhetorical environment.

Choosing which movements to use as objects of study and which advocates as representative of the various groups presents considerable problems. By distinguishing between radical and reactionary, I consider only left-wing advocates and thereby eliminate such reactionaries as George Wallace and his supporters, George Lincoln Rockwell, and Robert Welch of the John Birch Society. After all, in that turbulent decade, it was the left that created the major movements of the period. The concentration is on the student movement, the antiwar movement, the civil rights–black power movement, and the feminists and women's liberation movement (although this last group actually flourished more in the 1970s and 1980s than in the

1960s). In selecting individual advocates, I chose those who represented generic types of rhetoric that I wanted to examine. I believe they are representative of the rhetoric of the era.

The development of political protest movements during the 1960s may be represented, to borrow Robert C. Tucker's phrase, as a series of concentric circles.[41] Agitation proceeds from an initial period of liberal protest (with primary reliance on deliberative rhetoric) to a period of radicalization (with emphasis on developing or finding an ideological rhetoric) to a period of competing ideologies and competing politics (with each faction rhetorically claiming different interpretations of what the movement ought to be and what it ought to do) to a period of adapting ideological principles to deliberative form. Only the first three periods will be dealt with in these pages. It was during the first three periods that the new genres emerged. In the fourth period rhetors reverted to the deliberative form. To examine that period would be repetitive in a work devoted to genre criticism and therefore is not central to the focus of this analysis.

Two other rhetorical forms are included in this analysis. One is administrative rhetoric, a unique form of response to initial protests. It is included because it is a form unique to liberal authorities of the period and because it helps explain why some procedural protesters turned from deliberative to ideological rhetoric.

The other is the idiosyncratic rhetoric of the cynic. Some, and they were not many, became so disillusioned with both procedural and ideological protest that they went beyond both to another form of thinking, another form of discourse: the cynical diatribe. Cynicism is a response to and an escape from procedural protest and ideological protest. Because it is idiosyncratic, I have devoted a separate chapter to cynicism, and I beg the reader's indulgence as I digress to explain some of its basic tenets as the original cynics created them in ancient Greece.

The protest generation of the 1960s provides the rhetorical critic with an almost unending set of materials for theoretical and critical study. In this introduction I have sought to put my critical vocabulary in order so the reader may more easily follow what comes next.

It should be emphasized that this study is not a history of protest, as history is properly done, nor does it proceed with chronological marching orders. This study instead is a rhetorical history, an analysis of the changes in political language and rhetorical structures. In the following chapters I sketch the arguments that defined the new genres of political rhetoric that emerged during that decade, thus going beyond Aristotle's limited description of deliberative rhetoric as the sole kind of political discourse available to those who participate in politics.

But I would be less than honest if I did not admit that I have a more ambitious aim, which is only partially attempted and certainly only partially realized in this skeletal form. What I believe happened in the 1960s is that the excruciating pressures of the times led some who participated in the protests to race through the three great systems of Western thought in the course of a single decade. In his *Critique of Cynical Reason* Peter Sloterdijk named these three systems: Enlightenment, Ideology, and Cynicism. Enlightenment extols freedom above all values and reason as the method for achieving it. But as Sloterdijk pointed out, when those seeking freedom speak to those in power especially in times of turmoil, these great Enlighteners respond not with reason, but with a crushing power intended to keep the seekers in place. Thus, Ideology arises to unmask the hidden interests that motivated Enlightenment to praise freedom and reason but also to deny freedom to those who challenged Enlightenment officials and to refuse to reason with those who sought redress of grievances. Ideology promises liberation from perfidious Enlightenment and extols equality as the supreme value, but only to those who become subservient to the Ideology. Ideology preaches: "I am your master and liberator, you shall have no other liberator before me! Every liberty you take upon yourself from elsewhere is a petit-bourgeois deviation."[42] The disillusionment Enlightenment and Ideology provoke in some produces conditions for Cynicism, the final system of thought, the last refuge for realistic idealists. Sloterdijk came to the same conclusion I did, although by a different route and for different purposes and with a far greater detail than space affords me at this time.

Let us begin, then, with the beginnings of protest movements in their initial state of procedural politics and deliberative rhetoric as these movements move from enlightenment to ideology to cynicism.

7

Liberal Protest
Procedural Politics and
Deliberative Rhetoric

American protest movements begin reasonably enough. When large numbers of people become disturbed about an issue or policy or event, they turn not to radicalism but to procedural politics, not to ideologies but to practicalities, not to revolution but to reform. They seek to redress grievances through existing legal and legislative channels. Though they may condemn certain authorities and certain political systems (such as the entrenched system of segregation in the South), they appeal to other leaders or higher authorities to right these wrongs. Each of the prominent movements of the 1960s began in this manner, as a movement involved in procedural politics and deliberative rhetoric.

American protest movements also begin as single-issue movements. The civil rights movement concentrated on obtaining basic political and legal rights. The student movement originally began in protest against certain university rules. The feminist movement sought initially to acquire equal rights for women. But they share a common approach: reformist, procedural, parliamentary. They accept the legitimacy of existing institutions and ask mainly that leaders change particular policies regarding issues dissidents are agitated about. Protesters outside the corridors of power organize public meetings to publicize their concerns (peaceful demonstrations, sit-ins, teach-ins, protests against the Miss America contest, marches on symbolic settings). In other words, they combine peaceful appeals for change with direct action that sometimes involves civil disobedience. Sympathizers in power use their authorized forums to question officials responsible for policies in hearings before congressional or other institutional committees, to introduce legislative remedies, or to initiate lawsuits that challenge what they believe to be discriminatory or illegal.

The public discourse is geared to reform within existing procedures: appeals to laws, existing agreements, self-interest, traditional beliefs and ideals, conventional attitudes, acceptable symbols and language, respected authorities. This rhetoric of decorum is one of flattery, supplication, and common ground between the interests of the protesters and the interests of authorities. It has its roots in a shared sense of civility, a respect for reason and self-interest as the prime means for change, and a belief in existing conventions and institutions as susceptible to persuasion.[1] In essence, they use the traditional Aristotelian genres of procedural rhetoric—deliberative, forensic, and epideictic—that the occasion or forum dictates.

Activists seek to establish and maintain a respectable ethos. They present themselves as stable, hard-working, concerned Americans taking time off from their regular jobs to ask the government to stop doing what it is doing or to start doing something that needs to be done. At the 1965 teach-in in Washington, Professor Hans J. Morgenthau described the people who had assembled to protest the war in Vietnam as "respected professors who have raised respectable questions requiring respectable answers."[2] If one were to use *students* or *blacks* or *women* in place of *professors,* one would have an apt description of how protesters in each group sought to present themselves in this initial stage.

To maintain this ethos of respectability, leaders of movements commit symbolic acts that, they say, demonstrate their commitment to a democratic society. Thus, they engage in witnessing that commitment (nonviolent demonstrations) through means that are traditional (picketing or boycotts or debates) and responsible (going to jail when arrested). Though these actions may be misinterpreted or denounced as radical or subversive, they fall well within a long and clearly established American tradition of democratic protest, especially in the American labor movement.[3] These acts are intended by leaders of movements to demonstrate to authorities and opponents alike that activists are not seeking the violent overthrow of the government, but rather are seeking changes in governmental policies or laws. By abiding by accepted political and rhetorical conventions, they seek to establish credibility as respectable Americans "who have raised respectable questions requiring respectable answers."

The emphasis on the reformist nature of protest in this first stage may mislead the reader into assuming that at this stage radicals do not exist or are not important. That would be a serious mistake. The radical's relation to the central part of the movement is ambiguous. On occasion the radical may join in protests, accepting conventional procedures though speaking with an ideological voice, as Isaac Deutscher did during the 1965 teach-in. More often, the radical simply is not part of the dominant movement, or is separated from it, or tends to his or her own organization, or is treated by leaders of the dominant movement and by media as a rhetorical and political liability not to be touched. The treatment radicals receive from media is important to note. Radicals—those who violate the procedural ideals and goals liberals insist upon at this point—are generally ignored or ridiculed or treated as psychotics by the press. Yet, they exist, they speak, they agitate, they endure. Frustrated protesters at a later stage in the development of movements will look back on some of these radicals for fraternity, guidance, and a different view of politics.

The purpose of the dominant group of protesters in this inaugural period is mainly to arouse sympathetic supporters, especially among legislators, the press, and the power elites. They seek to do this by identifying with them, by appealing to them through conventional beliefs, attitudes, and aspirations, and by assuring them that they do not intend to take away anything precious these groups have aspired to or achieved. They want primarily only two things: to participate equally (be it in legal, economic, social, political affairs, or in decision making) as others already can; or to end policies they believe are wrong or counterproductive. Advocates seek to minimize or avoid rhetorical or political acts that would offend these higher power groups even as they take action against lower power groups. But even as procedural politics and deliberative rhetoric govern this period, radicals stand in the background rendering ideological analyses and wait for the day when others catch up to them or realize the futility of their rhetoric of supplication.

My purpose in the following sections is not to provide a conceptual framework for criticizing the rhetoric of various groups during this period nor to analyze that rhetoric vigorously. Deliberative speeches are the ones most commonly criticized by rhetorical critics, and an extensive set of critical scholarship already exists and the methods various critics have developed are quite sophisticated.[4] Instead, my purpose is to demonstrate how protest movements in the United States in the 1960s began, to cite the major themes, and to place the radical protest in this initial stage of protest in political perspective.

The Black Civil Rights Movement

Procedural Protest

Though the civil rights movement was somewhat different from other movements, it was, at the same time, the prototype for the other movements. First of all, the civil rights movement was not new, but possessed a continuous history stretching back almost to the introduction of slavery into North America. As early as 1652 the Society of Friends had spoken forthrightly against slavery.[5] Only the feminist movement with its roots in the suffragette movement of the nineteenth century could lay a claim to such a history.

Second, during this history, blacks and whites had gone through a multitude of struggles experimenting with a variety of strategies and tactics ranging from vocal protest to outright rebellion as means for abolishing slavery and later for attempting to end institutional discrimination. Because of this, civil rights activists had a longer and more varied rhetorical history to draw upon than any other movement, often an oral history handed down from generation to generation and just as often kept alive through the network of black churches.[6]

Finally, the civil rights movement served as the early prototype for other protests. Many who later became active in other movements gained their first exposure to the politics of protest and their first experiences from working in the early civil rights struggle in the South. They would draw much of their language and arguments, their political strategies and tactics, from those experiences. These would become resources of metaphor and analogies as well as the definitive examples of discrimination or oppression in the rhetoric of protest.

By almost every reputable account, the contemporary black civil rights movement may be said to have begun in December 1955 with the Montgomery bus boycott, and it reached its rhetorical heights in this initial period with the speeches given at the march on Washington in August 1963. As their principal goal, activists sought to integrate blacks into American legal and political life through the elimination of institutional discrimination against blacks.[7] Dr. Martin Luther King, Jr., emerged as the movement's most eloquent advocate.

Dr. King insisted on nonviolent protest: "But in our protest there will be no cross burnings. No white person will be taken from his home by a hooded Negro mob and brutally murdered. There will be no threats and intimidation. We will be guided by the highest principles of law and order."[8] Dr. King created the dominant patterns for persuasion by calling upon blacks to reject violence, to suffer and to sacrifice willingly, to accept God's injunction to love one's enemies, and to build a strong coalition among blacks and whites to pressure appropriate power groups to change discriminatory laws and practices. He used nonviolence as a means for achieving reconciliation among the races through direct action: "The non-violent resister must often express his protest through non-cooperation or boycotts, but he realizes that non-cooperation and boycotts are not ends in themselves; they are merely means to awaken a sense of moral shame in the opponent. The end is redemption and reconciliation."[9] In sum, Dr. King personified the dominant rhetoric of this period: a moral plea for blacks and whites to join in a cooperative effort to persuade people in power to live up to the ideals of American society—equality for all, freedom for all under law. Rhetors cited the discriminatory nature of existing laws (in the South), discriminatory actions against blacks, the hypocrisy of professing belief in freedom while denying freedom to blacks as major arguments to justify actions taken to meet the movement's goals. Leaders of the civil rights movement used traditional symbols and attitudes to appeal to those in power to end this systematic discrimination, and they relied on forensic or deliberative rhetoric fueled by a moral fervor to press their case in courtrooms and legislative chambers.

These actions symbolized commitments to the ideas expressed by Dr. King and his supporters. They used peaceful and democratic means for protest: boycotts, sit-ins, freedom rides, public and church meetings. When arrested, they went limp and then went to jail. They worked through law courts and legislatures to have discriminatory laws repealed and to have new laws protecting their citizenship enacted.

In the context of the late 1950s and early 1960s many of these actions caused opponents of the civil rights movement to see it as a grave threat to democracy. They pilloried Dr. King and his associates as "anarchists," "communist-influenced," and "revolutionaries."[10] Friends, such as Julius Lester, saw (in retrospect) a revolutionary in the making:

King represents, in one sense, a transition from the methods of reform to the methods of revolution. Although his ends remained reformist, he moved outside the legal framework of the system and engaged in civil disobedience. He involved the masses of blacks in a fight for the redress of grievances based on the rhetoric of the Constitution for redress of grievances. It was a very short step from nonviolent attacks on mores and the law to violent attacks upon them. King represents the death of reform as an end and the beginnings of disregarding the law as a means.[11]

As much as friends and foes alike might want to agree with Lester's assessment, this interpretation will not stand close scrutiny. Dr. King did not advocate violence. And he denounced those who did. He urged peaceful demonstrations, boycotts, sit-ins, all of which have a long history in the labor movement in the United States. He used the rhetoric of the Constitution, as Lester noted, and he accepted the sovereignty of the law by submitting to authorities when arrested for breaking it.[12]

Finally, civil rights leaders repeatedly relied on epideictic speeches to stir the conscience of sympathetic white Americans. This particular rhetorical form is closely akin to the sermon and thus especially suited to the black ministers and preachers, who often used churches as meeting places for rallies. The topics of an epideictic speech are public virtue (honor) and public vice (dishonor).[13] Civil rights leaders would recite the vices of slavery, exploitation, and discrimination of past and present but would look to the virtue of brotherhood and freedom in the future. At the Lincoln Memorial on August 28, 1963, Dr. Martin Luther King, Jr., gave the greatest epideictic speech of the movement, the greatest speech given to my generation, when he summarized his vision of the future:

So I say to you, my friends, that even though we must face the difficulties of today and tomorrow, I still have a dream. It is a dream deeply rooted in the American dream that one day this nation will rise up and live out the true meaning of its creed—we hold these truths to be self evident, that all men are created equal.

I have a dream that one day on the red hills of Georgia, sons of former slaves and sons of former slaveowners will be able to sit down together at the table of brotherhood.

I have a dream that one day, even the state of Mississippi, a state sweltering with the heat of injustice, sweltering with the heat of oppression, will be transformed into an oasis of freedom and justice.

I have a dream my four little children will one day live in a nation where they will not be judged by the color of their skin but by the content of their character. I have a dream today. . . .

And when this happens, and when we allow freedom to ring, when we let it ring from every village and hamlet, from every state and city, we will be able to speed up that day when all of God's children—black men and white men, Jews and Gentiles, Catholics and Protestants—will be able to join hands and to sing in the words of the old Negro spiritual, "Free at last, free at last; thank God Almighty, we are free at last."[14]

This epideictic speech of reconciliation and brotherhood became the hallmark rhetorical form of the procedural dimension of the civil rights movement. Its remarkable appeal lay in the unique religious and moral suasion that only the eloquent Dr. King could articulate. This conventional rhetorical form so dominated the early movement that not only were black radicals excluded from participation in the major events, such as the march on Washington, but those who would speak more critically were persuaded to tone down their remarks.[15]

Black Radicals

But black radicals did exist. Even as the rhetoric of constitutional redress of grievances dominated this initial stage of protest, black radicals spoke about a different interpretation of the plights of blacks in America. The Black Muslims, led by the Honorable Elijah Muhammad, taught a mystical religious form of Garveyism and called for blacks to unite and separate from the white devils of America. Week in and week out, he preached from his pulpit an altogether different message from that being preached by Dr. King and the mainline civil rights advocates. Malcolm X, a refugee from the Muslims, began to develop a theory of pan-Africanism as a political solution to his Islamic analysis of the struggle of blacks.[16] Le Roi Jones (now known as Amiri Baraka) wrote *The Dutchman* and *The Slave*, in which he dramatized the uselessness of depending on constitutional rights and the goodwill of either the government or white people to achieve freedom (in *The Dutchman*) and then dramatized the need for existential revolution (in *The Slave*).

Based primarily in the northern urban cities, these speakers and writers sharpened a new racial and radical ideology of separatism. Nigel Young pointed out the significance of this development: "The speeches of Malcolm-X, the novels of [James] Baldwin, the theatre of Le Roi Jones, emphasized a bitter, aggressive blackness. Previously, Black Nationalism had been merely the most primitive political expression of this mood, but the separatist instinct was never far from black rhetoric and programmes in the 1960s, or from the projections of 'black power.'"[17]

For their separatist beliefs and radical rhetoric, these blacks who would not accept the political and social creed of the mainline civil rights movement (much less its decorous rhetoric of supplication) were excluded from rallies and vilified or ignored by the various media. Le Roi Jones's *The Dutchman* could not be made into a motion picture in the United States because it was too "controversial" and therefore had to be filmed in England, only to receive negative reviews in this country. To my knowledge, *The Slave* has not been filmed. Reporters described the Muslims as racists or "racists in reverse."[18] Upon his assassination in 1965 and under the title "Death of a Desperado," *Newsweek* described Malcolm X as "a demagogue who titillated slum Negroes and frightened whites with his blazing racist attacks on the 'white devils' and his calls for an armed American Mau Mau."[19] *Nation*, a liberal news weekly, called Malcolm X intelligent and courageous but characterized him as only a "leader of one segment of the Negro lunatic fringe."[20] This pattern of consigning radical speakers to the category of "extreme" or "fringe" or "lunatic fringe" segment of the movement reflected the prevailing political ethos of the time. The political and rhetorical crime these radicals had committed was to violate the conventions of civil protest and to voice ideas that did not reflect the conventional virtues of American life. It was a pattern of media antagonism nearly every radical movement experienced in this beginning stage of protest. And it then established a justification for either attacking radicals or ignoring them and their message.

The Feminist Movement

Procedural Protest

The reemergence of the feminist movement originated with the publication in 1963 of Betty Friedan's *Feminine Mystique*.[21] It became an overnight best-seller and the bible of the early feminist movement. In it Friedan argued that post–World War II back-to-the-home "togetherness" had propagated a myth that "truly feminine women do not want careers, higher education, political rights—the independence and the opportunities that the old-fashioned feminists fought for."[22] As a result of the choices women made on the basis of this mystique, they now were experiencing its consequences—a middle age characterized by emptiness.

The widespread publicity given *The Feminine Mystique* led to a revival of the dormant women's rights movement, active participation by women in a protest movement concerned directly with the quality of their lives, and the creation of the National Organization for Women (NOW). From 1963 to 1968 Betty Friedan was the principal national spokesperson for feminists, and NOW was the central organization. Feminists sought to create an alliance between enlightened women and men to change laws that discriminated against women as well as to assert their rightful place as equal members of American society. During this initial period of development, feminists, like their civil rights counterparts, concentrated on legislative and legal changes to better their situations.

At the first national conference of women in 1967, NOW adopted a bill of rights that called for:

I. Equal Rights Constitutional Amendment
II. Enforce Law Banning Sex Discrimination in Employment
III. Maternity Leave Rights in Employment and in Social Security Benefits
IV. Tax Deduction for Home and Child Care Expenses for Working Parents
V. Child Day Care Centers
VI. Equal and Unsegregated Education
VII. Equal Job Training Opportunities and Allowances for Women in Poverty
VIII. The Right of Women to Control Their Reproductive Lives.[23]

Each issue (right) involved legislative or legal issues, and a series of demands followed this list. NOW requested that the proper authorities enact these demands. There were no calls to overthrow the system, to destroy male enemies, to describe women as exploited as "sex objects," to exclude sympathetic men from the cause. Reflecting upon her perception of the movement, Friedan later wrote: "I now see the women's movement for equality as simply the necessary first stage of a much larger sex-role revolution. I never did see it in terms of class or race: women, as an oppressed class, fighting to overthrow or take power away from men as a class, the oppressors. I knew the movement had to include men as equal members, though women would have to take the lead in the first stage."[24] The distinction Friedan drew between her reformist intentions and rhetoric and that of subsequent radicals was consistently sustained by her and by many chapters of NOW. Procedural politics and deliberative rhetoric governed this first stage in the reemergence of the women's movement, as even radical feminists would admit.[25]

Radical Feminism

The radical feminist voice developed not so much out of experiences within NOW or within the women's rights movement as from frustrating experiences in the civil rights movement, the Students for a Democratic Society (SDS), and the antiwar protests.[26] When radicalism did emerge, it was later than in other movements, primarily in the 1970s. Yet, before the breakthrough to a radical feminism, there were rhetorical rumblings, especially in 1967. In that year Jo Freeman created the Chicago Group.[27] That same year Carol Hamisch, Shulamith Firestone, and others founded the New York Radical Women and later started the journal *Notes from the First Year*.[28] A year later Ti-Grace Atkinson made her celebrated break with NOW and created the October Seventeenth Movement, later called The Feminists.

But Valeria Solanis was the most strident radical in her sexual-political anarchism. In 1967 she created the Society for Cutting Up Men (SCUM) and published a manifesto stating, in part: "SCUM will always operate on the criminal as opposed to a civil disobedience basis, that is, as opposed to openly violating the law and going to jail in order to draw attention to an injustice. Such tactics [procedural politics] acknowledge the rightness of the over-all system and are used only to modify it slightly, change specific laws. SCUM is against the entire system, the very idea of law and government."[29] Solanis called for responsible females "to overthrow the government, eliminate the money system, institute complete automation, and destroy the male sex."[30] Whether the manifesto was a product of the sincere attempt to fuse sexual politics with revolutionary anarchism or of a mentally disturbed political mind, it received little media attention at the time it was issued. However, when Solanis was arrested and eventually confined for shooting Andy Warhol, the media used these events to ridicule and discredit not only her but other segments of the radical feminist movement. Nonetheless, she became a minor cult figure to some feminists, and a martyr to other radicals.[31]

The Antiwar Movement

Procedural Protest

The antiwar movement was quite different from others in this period. It did not have roots in a long-standing grievance nor in rights denied. It developed in response to President Lyndon Johnson's escalation of American participation in the civil war in Vietnam.[32] It would wither with the ending of the draft and the eventual withdrawal of American troops from Vietnam.

As a movement to stop further participation in the Vietnamese war, the protest reached the national public when the National Teach-In convened in Washington on May 15, 1965. A model of democratic debate, organizers of the teach-in invited supporters and opponents of administration policy to debate the expediency of further American involvement in the war. At the meetings deliberative rhetoric prevailed, a civil decorum was maintained.

The speech by Hans J. Morgenthau, who was the most prominent and prolific speaker at the teach-in, amply represented the genre. He stressed two major points: South Vietnam is not a sovereign state under attack by an outside aggressor, and the United States has no binding legal or moral obligation to defend South Vietnam. He selected his proofs from treaty agreements, historical materials, and venerated witnesses of the past as appeals designed to dissuade the administration from pursuing its current policy. He concluded by warning: "So it is . . . a special virtue and a special function of this meeting that it reminds all of us, and especially those who govern us and would rather not be reminded, that our policy is contradicted by facts. If they do not have the wisdom and the courage to adapt their policies to the facts, the facts will overtake them and take a vengeance on them for having been disregarded."[33] Morgenthau's speech exemplified the deliberative rhetoric that pervaded the antiwar movement in its initial stage during the years 1965–1966.[34] This academic protest (with all the ironies intended by that description) sought to show authorities why their perception of the war was mistaken and that therefore, for the sake of expediency, these agents of power should change their policy. By inviting supporters of the administration to debate, protesters demonstrated symbolically their commitment to a democratic society in which truth arises from argument rather than descends from edict.[35]

Radicals at the Teach-In

Though the deliberative genre was the order of the day, a radical rhetoric was voiced at the teach-in. Isaac Deutscher, Trotskyite and biographer of Stalin and Trotsky, rendered an ideological critique of the American anticommunist ideology, which, he contended, served as one of the real causes for our involvement in the war in Vietnam. I. F. Stone commented that Deutscher "spoke a language Washington has not heard in public since the cold war and the witch hunt began two decades ago" and generally praised Deutscher's analysis.[36] Most reporters dismissed Deutscher's remarks as belonging to another time and another place, as irrelevant to current concerns. Instead, they dwelt on Deutscher's animated delivery, his beard, his rushing around from place to place, and his resemblance to Lenin.[37] Yet, in only a short time, Deutscher's ideological critique would seem mild and reasoned in comparison with other voices raised in anguish over the continuation of the war.

Radical Beginnings in Theory: C. Wright Mills and the Students for a Democratic Society

During the 1950s C. Wright Mills, among others, tried to revive radicalism in America and to revise socialist thought to meet the political and economic circumstances of the cold war. He sought to create a new left, one that would avoid Stalinism, on the one hand, and would, on the other, neutralize charges of totalitarianism that opponents of the left had effectively lodged against it during the two previous decades. At the same time Mills wanted to disassociate himself from traditional cold war liberals or the "new conservatives," as he called them.

My purpose here is not to attempt an explication of Mills's thought or to trace its development as it influenced later radicals. Much of that work has been done.[38] Rather, I want to delineate some central ideas that show up in the transition from procedural politics to radicalism.

What Mills developed was a democratic (or existential) socialism in which he identified the liberal establishment (a central part of the power elite) as the primary obstacle to social change. Yet he remained committed to persuasion and procedural politics (as well as scholarship, though with a decidedly polemic bent) as the appropriate means for achieving that change. His was a fresh analysis from the left, clearly distinguishable from old Stalinist or Trotskyite leftists. He sought to change the system not through revolution or through a socialist party, but through a new alliance of intellectuals, who would form a new left. Most important, however, Wright identified the current enemy of change not as Wall Street reactionaries or mossback conservatives or even greedy landowners and bankers. Rather, he pointed to the liberal elites, especially cold war liberals, who had become "conservatives by default" and now controlled the centers of power. Their influence and control had become so pervasive that political life in America after midcentury no longer included a great range or variety of political statements, much less of political alternatives.[39] All politicians, Wright contended, now adopt a liberal rhetoric (the deliberative rhetoric of procedural politics), thus rendering political discussion meaningless: "The intellectual slackness of [America's] political life is such that it does very well with the liberal rhetoric. If, as a rhetoric, liberalism has become a mask of all political positions, as a theory of society it has become irrelevant, and in its operative mood, misleading."[40] What Mills was attacking was the lack of ideas in the "end of ideology" procedural politics of the time. Unfortunately, his attempt to create a new left ideology and rhetoric was cut short in 1962 by his untimely death. That work was left to others, in particular, SDS.

Originally founded in 1960, the Students for a Democratic Society became the chief new organization of the new left. It issued the Port Huron Statement (written principally by Tom Hayden) in 1962, the primary and controlling rhetorical effort in the early days of SDS. The Statement challenged the cold war policies of President Kennedy and indirectly scored the moral and political insensitivity of his administration to black people. The authors hurried to disassociate themselves and the organization from the empty phrases of the old left as well as the "conservative default" of established cold war liberals:

Unlike youth in other countries we are used to moral leadership being exercised and moral dimensions being clarified by our leaders. But today, for us, not even the liberal and socialist preachments of the past seem adequate to the forms of the present. Consider the old slogans: Capitalism Cannot Reform Itself, United Front Against Fascism, General Strike, All Out On May Day, or, more recently, No Cooperation with Commies and Fellow Travelers, Ideologies are Exhausted, Bipartisanship, No Utopias. These are incomplete, and there are few new prophets. It has been said that our liberal and socialist predecessors were plagued by vision with program, while our own generation is plagued by program without vision.[41]

Following the lead of Mills again, the Statement called for an alliance of intellectuals, young people, and minorities to reform society so as to achieve two primary goals: "that the individual share in those social decisions determining the quality and direction of his life; that society be organized to encourage independence in men and provide the media for their common participation."[42] Common participation! That grew into the rallying cry of the 1960s—participatory democracy. Certainly, this new vision was a far cry from the stagnant rhetoric of the old left.

It is difficult to recreate the excitement that attended the writing and publication of the Port Huron Statement now more than twenty-five years later. Not a few otherwise perceptive commentators have cast glances back with a jaded vision that saw nothing new or exciting in it. Milton Viorst noted that the specific proposals—disarmament, increased foreign aid, realignment of the political parties, an antipoverty program—already were on the liberal agenda.[43] Though Viorst tried to recapture the spirit of the times, he failed to appreciate the deep sense of betrayal some young liberals and the fledgling new left felt about Kennedy, about the great chasm they believed existed between his valiant campaign promises and his conservative presidential performance during the first two years of his administration.[44] In his early history of SDS Alan Adelson came to a similar conclusion: "The *Port Huron Statement* was straight out of the old populist tradition. The vision of making society somehow more responsive to its individual members brought with it the idea of breaking down the size of governing institutions so that the people could be heard better. But that's a vague vision that doesn't necessarily challenge the system at all. It could be a foreshadowing of socialism, or it could instead be the sort of rhetoric about listening to the silent, unheard majority which Richard Nixon recites so solicitously."[45] In light of subsequent events and confrontations and manifestos, the statement appears mild, quite palatable to the liberal sensibility. Certainly, by no stretch of the definition of radicalism used in this work can the Statement be seen as radical. It was reformist.

But just as certainly as well, the Statement was distinctly different from the prevailing "realist" liberalism of the Kennedy administration. It was also distinctly different from other manifestos coming from other protest groups in three specific ways. First, the Statement sought to be a comprehensive document ranging over both foreign and domestic issues, from colonialism to deterrence theory, from discrimination against blacks to problems within the university system. It was not a single-issue document. Second, it attacked the strident anticommunist ideology that dominated almost all American thinking on foreign policy at this time. As the Statement announced: "An unreasoning anti-communism has become a major social problem for those who want to construct a more democratic America."[46] In its place, Hayden and his coauthors called for a more self-critical and positive approach to foreign policy. Finally, the Statement urged greater participation by those who had been left out of the decision-making processes that created the rules by which they were governed. It was a direct challenge to institutional hierarchies, from the "best and the brightest" of the Kennedy administration to the doctrine of *in loco parentis* at colleges and universities. But the challenge was not a confrontation until the free speech battle at Berkeley. Instead, it was a request for hierarchies to loosen their grip on decision making and expand their membership to include those affected by decisions.

What, then, can be said about the Port Huron Statement? For our purposes here, it should be noted that the Statement remains within the realm of reformist politics and deliberative rhetoric. Despite the reputation later earned or foisted upon it, SDS began as other protest organizations and movements began in the 1960s, with libertarian goals and committed to established procedures. Moreover, the authors of the Statement continued C. Wright Mills's assault on the liberal establishment by naming liberals as political culprits opposed to the enactment of liberal ideas. But it was more than ideas and accusations, more than policies and positions. The Statement sounded a clarion call from the young people who wrote it to young people around the country to join in a new (young) left that would begin the long march through the 1960s, a march that would go every which way, sometimes helter-skelter, but a march that began with the first step at Port Huron, Michigan.

Conclusion

In the initial stage of protest dissidents turned not to ideology or to radicalism, but to using accepted procedures and conventional language for achieving change. The staff report to the National Commission on the Causes and Prevention of Violence emphasized this point:

The two general phases of the [student] movement—before and after 1965—may be viewed as follows: In phase one, the student movement embodied concern, dissent, and protest about various social issues, but it generally accepted the legitimacy of the existing political community . . . and especially the university. In those years, many students believed that the legitimacy of the existing political structure was compromised by the undue influence of corporate interests and the military. They made far-reaching criticisms of the university and of other social institutions, but their criticisms were usually directed at the failure of the American political system and of American institutions to live up to officially proclaimed values. Thus, despite their commitment to reform and to support for civil disobedience and direct action, the student activists in the first half of this decade generally accepted the basic values and norms of the American political community.[47]

So, too, feminists, civil rights activists, and the antiwar movement.

Instead of radicalism, they focused on specific policies, voiced their belief in the political system and its authorities by appealing to them, and sought to avoid violating or abusing conventional politics and rhetoric. Issues were treated as political or legal, although moral arguments were advanced with other arguments.

At the beginning of protest movements the dominant rhetoric aimed at reform while the less publicized radical rhetoric aimed at criticizing the system. The relationship between the two is dialectical in content, aesthetic in form. It is dialectical because the topics and arguments of procedural dissidents conflicted directly with the topics and arguments advanced by radicals. Those who relied on deliberative methods stressed that the policy they sought to change was harmful. They viewed authorities as rational and thus susceptible to changing their minds, if effective reasons were presented to them. They saw institutions as capable of reforming themselves. They devised arguments to accommodate these considerations. In so doing, these protesters saw themselves in partnership with authorities in striving to achieve through civil persuasion certain alterations in policy, but not necessarily in the system, except as those policies might affect the system. Additionally, procedural protesters limited their concerns to specific issues that affected their supporters. Thus, a black group arose to protest for policies and laws beneficial to blacks. So, too, with feminists and others. The Students for a Democratic Society were an exception, in effect functioning as a transition as the Port Huron Statement cast a wider political net.

Nonetheless, what bound these protesters together was an energetic idealism about the American political system's ability to respond reasonably to their requests for change. Most protesters truly believed the political arena was a "marketplace of ideas" in which truth would eventually triumph if only truth could be presented persuasively. Even black protesters faced with the vile power of white racists in the South believed that the federal government would intervene if an effective alliance with sympathetic whites could be forged. Perhaps one reason for this idealism was that most of these early protesters were college or university educated and had been reared on the political textbooks that extolled the ability of existing procedures and authorities to respond positively to their pleas for change. In this, these protesters were truly academic.

Radicals, on the other hand, contended that specific policies were only symptoms of the real problems: the political and social structures and the intellectual or political assumptions that support them. They believed policies could not be changed until the structure and its assumptions were changed. They viewed opponents not as rational, but as socially, economically, racially, or sexually determined categories and thus probably immune to civil persuasion. Radicals saw themselves in political warfare with political enemies rather than in reasonable disagreement with rational partners. They bound up issues into a series of charges against the system and the authorities who administer it.

Closer examination reveals the arguments advanced by the two different groups to be contrary to one another, in a dialectical relationship. Yet, they coexisted formally in an aesthetic relationship; that is, instead of condemning one another for false ideas, they responded to one another with feelings of awe, wonder, or horror, a variation on the aesthetic principle of "willful suspension of disbelief."

One reason this relational phenomenon occurred was because the two groups—procedural and radical protesters—aimed their arguments at different audiences. The procedural dissident attempted to persuade authorities to change policies, an *external* purpose. The radical hoped to change the consciousness of members of the protesting group itself, an *internal* purpose.

More important, the procedural protesters and radical critics represented two very different systems of political thought. They disagreed on almost every point of protest, except the specific issue that had to be confronted. Here they agreed on opposition to discrimination against blacks and women, and to the war in Vietnam. They disagreed about the appropriate rhetoric to be used. They disagreed about the nature of the protest. They disagreed about the character of their opponents. They did so because they had two different systems of political thought and had different political ancestors. Procedural protesters descended from the tradition of Enlightenment, the tradition of John Locke, Thomas Jefferson, and John Stuart Mill. Radical protesters descended from the ideological tradition of Georg Hegel, Karl Marx, Mikhail Bakunin, and C. Wright Mills. In this chapter, this first system of thought has been explored. The next two examine the transition to and development of ideology, the second system of thought.

8

The Administrative Rhetoric
of Credibility
Changing the Issues

Once protesters march out to voice their grievances, they expect authorities to change policies or procedures to accord with those protests. More sophisticated or veteran protesters may recognize that such changes will be neither simple nor speedy to effect. What they do not expect is the intransigent response they receive from administrators or the kind of rhetoric administrators create to justify that intransigence. In fact, what occurs is that the central issues change from issues of policy to the issue of credibility. To understand this critical development within the dynamics of protest movements, we may concentrate on the example of the Berkeley Free Speech Movement.

College and university students were in the forefront of the protest movements that burst onto the national scene in the 1960s. And Berkeley students were in the vanguard of those students. The Free Speech Movement exploded at the University of California at Berkeley during the fall and winter of 1964–1965. In microcosm, the Berkeley free speech battle contained most of the elements and patterns that would soon become so familiar as other protests wracked the decade. It defined a new era of conflict "leading to mass arrests, a general strike, the involvement of the entire faculty in the dispute, and a continuing atmosphere of crisis and distrust."[1] The Free Speech Movement (along with the Port Huron Statement) set many of the protest themes for the decade and indeed for a generation of young people. It served, actually and symbolically, as a transition from procedural politics to ideology, from deliberative rhetoric to radical rhetoric, from compromise to confrontation, from petitioning for change to demanding change, from theory to praxis.

Though Berkeley has come to symbolize an entire decade of protest, little attention has been paid to the administration's response and rhetoric. If the dissidents at Berkeley represented a new era of conflict, the response of the administration created another new rhetoric that changed the issues and eventually became a model of rhetoric used by administrators faced with protests. The events at Berkeley during the free speech controversy are so thoroughly documented that I shall attempt only a brief summary of them, pointing mainly to those events that bear upon the analysis of administrative rhetoric and the circumstances that provoked it.[2] It is my purpose to examine the response of the administration at Berkeley by delineating the lines of argument that comprise "administrative rhetoric." To achieve this, I have divided the chapter into three parts: (1) the context of the revolt at Berkeley; (2) the administrative response; and (3) other uses of administrative rhetoric in responding to other protests.

The Revolt

The original issue at the University of California at Berkeley was a relatively simple procedural one: the right of students to engage in political solicitation of funds and to advocate political ideas or causes for political action, to be more specific, the right of students to engage in these political activities on campus. For some time students had used a twenty-six-foot slice of pavement at the corner of the Bancroft and Telegraph entrance for such purposes. But on September 14, 1964, as the new fall semester began, Katherine Towle, dean of students, sent a letter to all student organizations informing them that the sidewalk area of Bancroft and Telegraph could no longer be used for setting up tables, raising funds, recruiting members, or generally advocating political causes.[3] From such seemingly prosaic actions do protest movements arise.

Students responded immediately. They formed a United Front among various political organizations, ranging from conservatives to radicals and including Young Democrats and Young Republicans, Youth for Goldwater and the Young Socialist Alliance. In this initial stage of protest they petitioned the administration to restore the area of Bancroft-Telegraph to its former and traditional place as one where students could engage in political activity. They entered into negotiations—with the usual charges of bad faith and poor intentions being leveled against one another—as each side sought some way to extricate itself from the tangled situation.

But events took unexpected twists and turns. On September 30 the administration cited five students for violating its new ordinance against political advocacy. The next day the protesters decided to test the administration directly by moving from Bancroft-Telegraph to Sproul Hall, the administration building. At noon they began setting up tables for political activity at the steps of Sproul and called a mass rally. The police were called in, and they arrested Jack Weinberg, a former teaching assistant in mathematics, for operating a CORE table in violation of the new university rules. But instead of allowing the police to drive Weinberg away after his arrest, students spontaneously surrounded the police car, immobilizing it for thirty-two hours. That action marked a turning point for young white students in the 1960s, a turning point as significant to them as the sit-ins at Greensboro, North Carolina, in 1960 had been for black people.

With this act of defiance the Berkeley protest moved into its second phase: from requesting changes and entering negotiations to denunciations and confrontations, from passive reaction to direct action. Soon, students would extend the protest to the occupation of buildings, disruptions of meetings and of speeches, and calls for amnesty for their actions. These strategic and tactical changes would cause the United Front to splinter, to be replaced by the Free Speech Movement, the FSM. The issues would also change, as is typical in protest movements, from the specific issue of the right to use Bancroft-Telegraph for political advocacy to the more general issue of student rights. In essence, the FSM asked whether students had the same right of freedom of speech and action as every other citizen had. Or did students necessarily give up these rights (or have them taken away) when they became students? Thus, in the second phase of protest—the most crucial period—the issue became one of principle rather than of policy.

From a rhetorical standpoint there was a third, albeit brief, period in the development of the FSM. Once the administration granted that students had a right to freedom of speech, some began to test those limits. This testing became known as the the Filthy Speech Movement. Soon thereafter, so-called Obscenity Rallies were held. Thus was the use of obscenity born as a tactic for public protest in the political rhetoric of movements in the 1960s. These incidents pointed to a different way of thinking and protesting that are considered in detail in the chapter on the cynics and the diatribe.

The final period of the movement, of course, involved a resolution of the issues. Eventually, a series of directives on the rights of students to political advocacy were drawn up, and order was restored to the university.

The crucial period within the movement came when students confronted the police over the arrest of Jack Weinberg. On that occasion students moved away from petitions to confrontation, and they needed a rhetoric not only to marshal support but also to justify this change in strategy and tactics. The search for an effective means for describing the reasons for this change crystalized in Mario Savio's long statement, "An End to History," given to a reporter on December 2, 1964, after demonstrators occupied Sproul Hall. Although given privately to a reporter who asked him what was happening, his long answer was tape recorded, published, and widely circulated.[4]

If one is to attempt a balanced understanding of why students protested at Berkeley, one must read Savio's statement. A number of protesters had previously attempted to explain "what was happening at Berkeley," not the least of whom was Jack Weinberg. Later, he recalled that in his speech on September 30 he had tried "to fit some of what was happening into the theoretical framework—explaining it in terms of these framework [sic] that had been exposited" by Hal Draper in a speech on September 29 when he criticized Clark Kerr's *The Uses of the University.*[5]

But Savio did more than crystalize the meaning of the Berkeley protest. He brought to the fore the crisis of liberal procedural politics in the 1960s. For many of us who participated in the protests, "An End to History" was a more poignant statement of our frustrations and hopes than even the Port Huron Statement.

Savio's statement—widely publicized and reprinted—has three important parts. First, he expanded the meaning of the protest by linking the struggle for political rights at Berkeley to the struggle for civil rights among blacks. He recounted briefly his experiences in battling discrimination in Mississippi the previous summer and concluded that he was battling the same enemy at Berkeley: "In Mississippi an autocratic and powerful minority rules, through organized violence to suppress the vast, virtually powerless, majority. In California, the privileged minority manipulated the University to suppress the students' political expression. That 'respectable' bureaucracy masks the financial *plutocrats;* that impersonal bureaucracy is the efficient enemy in a 'Brave New World.'"

Savio's linking of student protest to the civil rights movement became a familiar theme in protest rhetoric. Indeed, the oppression of blacks would persistently serve as an analogy for the oppression of other groups within the lexicon of various movements.[6] The theme of rights ignored or denied became a major topic of protest rhetoric in the 1960s.

Second, Savio named liberals and the bureaucracies they administered as major obstacles to social and political change, an echo of the writings of C. Wright Mills and a prophesy of the problems activists would confront in the future:

Our attempt to convince any of the administrators that an event had occurred, that something new had happened, failed. They saw this simply as something to be handled by normal University procedures.

The same is true of all bureaucracies. They begin as tools, means to certain legitimate goals, and they end up feeding their own existence. The conception that bureaucrats have is that history has in fact come to an end. No events can occur now that the Second World War is over which can change American Society substantially. We proceed by standard procedures as we are.[7]

This last deadly sentence effectively described Savio's view about the response of authorities to the petitions of the United Front and the FSM. Savio indicted President Clark Kerr, well known as a liberal and as an adviser to the Democratic party, as the principal obstacle to progressive change. (Clark Kerr had attained his national reputation as a liberal when he led a spirited attack upon the loyalty oath that regents of the University of California had sought to impose on faculty members in 1949. He assumed the chancellorship of the university in 1952 and became president in 1958. In the spring of 1964 the American Association of University Professors presented Kerr with the Alexander Meiklejohn Award for "conspicuous contributions to academic freedom.")[8] Whether consciously or not, Savio echoed C. Wright Mills's assertion that political labels were no longer intellectually meaningful, that the liberal rhetoric masked a "conservative default."[9] Whether consciously or not, Savio summarized in these brief words Max Weber's thesis that the starting point for identifying politicians emanated not so much from political creed, but from describing how each responded to the historic development of the postindustrial bureaucratic society.[10] Whether consciously or not, Savio alluded to the generational gap between authorities, whose political beliefs were formed by the Depression and World War II, and the young students, whose political beliefs were just forming from entirely different sources and under much different conditions. But most certainly Savio was acutely aware that he had pinpointed the central problem facing protesters in the 1960s: *convincing liberal authorities that something "new" had indeed happened.*

Finally, Savio was ambivalent about action. In his speech he indicted authorities for being unresponsive and implored them to grant protesters their democratic rights. This section of his speech represents not only the prevailing attitudes and beliefs of the times but also the hopes that existed among most protesters that authorities would relent from their uncompromising position and negotiate. But Savio had joined with others in occupying Sproul Hall. More than likely, that occupation was intended primarily to force the administration to recognize and negotiate the political action issues.[11] Thus, the selective use of confrontation to achieve procedural ends.

Administrative Response

Something new had indeed happened. But administrators at Berkeley did not see the issues in the same light as protesters did. Writing afterward about the Free Speech Movement, Max Heirich observed:

> It is clear from interviews conducted with several members of the university administration after the events that administrators were united in considering this sit-in as a crisis of authority. Both the setting up of tables in the Sather Gate area the day before and the mass appearance for discipline were perceived, first and foremost, as challenges to the authority of the Chancellor's office, one that could not be ignored.
> In contrast, the students saw these events as a crisis of legitimacy. They were claiming the regulation that precipitated them was unconstitutional and therefore not one to be observed.[12]

Thus, the issue became *authority* and *legitimacy.*

Protesters saw the issue originally as a new policy that was wrong or misguided and petitioned to have it rescinded. When it was not, they attacked the legitimacy of the administration for acting arbitrarily and for being unresponsive to legitimate requests for redress of grievances. Administrators saw the issue not as one of policy, but rather as an attack upon their authority and credibility. So they constructed a rhetoric to defend themselves. In so doing, they developed a new rhetorical genre—*administrative rhetoric*—intended not only as an answer to dissidents but also as a means for short-circuiting protesters' ideas and influence.[13] This genre of political administrative rhetoric is a product of historical circumstances (the development of a postindustrial, bureaucratic society) and the then current intellectual assumptions of liberalism.[14] Whether intended or not, those who use this genre give greater impetus to the creation of radicalism than they imagine, and eventually they undermine not so much the efforts of protesters as the protesters' beliefs in the ability of the democratic system to respond to new ideas and to its citizens.

When public protests mount, some officials see demonstrations not as specific issues to be discussed, compromised, and resolved, but rather as insidious attacks upon the authority and credibility of the institution administering those policies. William Petersen, professor of sociology at Berkeley during the free speech battle, denied that freedom of speech was really the issue. He wrote: "If not free speech, what then is the issue? In fact, preposterous as it may seem the real issue is the seizure of power. The guiding principle of the radicals heading the revolt is one of Lenin's favorite aphorisms, which he borrowed from Napoleon: 'On s'engage et puis on voit.' Roughly translated, this appeared on one picket sign as 'Strike now, analyze later.'"[15] Power, indeed, was the issue after the administration refused to rescind its directive about political advocacy and instead took a hardline defense against the original protest. John Searle, professor of philosophy at Berkeley and defender of the administration, succinctly defined the position of the administration: "Each issue [in campus protest] involves a demand which is a direct challenge to the local administration, and which the administration cannot grant without major sacrifice of its authority and prestige. *At Berkeley in the Free Speech Movement crisis, the administration had just enacted new campus rules. How could they back down on these rules in the face of the first direct challenge to their enforcement?*"[16] How indeed?

Posing the questions as Searle and the administrators at Berkeley did *changes the terms for argument, changes,* in fact, *the issue from policy to credibility.* Thus, the meaning of the protest changes. And this change, in turn, obscures or ignores the merits of a specific policy. The invocation of the genre of administrative rhetoric sets in motion a series of dialectic confrontations presented in rhetorical form between protesters and authorities about the nature of policies, politics, and ethos. So insistent were administrators on preserving *procedural form* that they resorted to ideological arguments and the form of ideological rhetoric to denounce those they perceived as attacking standard procedures.

What are the *topoi* of this rhetorical genre? Various statements by President Clark Kerr and Chancellor Edward Strong during the battle for Berkeley can be pieced together to construct the defining arguments that constitute this rhetorical genre of administrative ideology.

(1) Administrators transform the particular issue agitating pro-

testers into a general issue, the authority and credibility of the institution to act as its officials see appropriate.

(2) They contend that protesters represent only a minority, whereas the administration must act in the interests of the majority (thus drawing upon the rhetorical power of the political maxim "The majority rules.")

(3) They attribute base motives to protesters by calling them unsavory political names, thereby consigning them to illegitimate political categories ("outside agitators," "nonstudents," "anarchists," etc.) or by contending that the "real purpose" of the protest is not to change a particular policy but to destroy American democratic institutions.

(4) They present themselves as defenders of civil liberties and law and order, all the while characterizing protesters as lawless and irrational, bent on using a pretense, a defense of constitutional liberties, to destroy them for others.

(5) They predict dire and terrible consequences should the protestors win in this symbolic test of power.[17]

Thus, dialectic, once thought by Aristotle to be the counterpart of rhetoric, becomes the centerpiece of administrative rhetoric.

What is remarkable is that administrators frequently resorted to these arguments even before protesters moved to confrontation and radicalism. For example, on September 30, 1964, (before the arrest of Weinberg and a month before the sit-ins at Sproul Hall), Chancellor Edward Strong stated:

The University cannot allow its facilities to be so used [for political action and solicitation of money] without endangering its future as an independent educational institution. The issue now has been carried far beyond the bounds of discussion by a small minority of students. These students should recognize the fullness of the privileges extended to them by the University, and ask themselves whether they wish to take further actions damaging to the University.

The University cannot and will not allow students to engage in deliberate violation of law and order on campus.[18]

These arguments were used to avoid discussing the particular merits of the issues dissidents had raised. Yet, they were used persistently and with increasing harshness to describe the *meaning* of the protest, the symbolic war between the credibility of the institution and the destructiveness of the protesters' petitions. Thus, on November 2 Chancellor Strong argued: "[T]here is the problem of keeping the University true to its role and purpose in society. We cannot permit the University to be used or exploited for purposes not in accord with its charter as an educational institution."[19] To protesters, this statement was bitterly ironic in the light of Kerr's praise for the university's adapting itself to purposes other than educational in his lectures *The Uses of the University*. Strong continued by adding: "The functioning of any society requires that authority be vested in some individuals, be they judges, legislators, or executives. Arbitrary exercise of authority is always to be challenged, but defamation of authority duly exercised undermines respect for high offices and demoralizes a society."[20]

What is greatly obscured in this statement is the fact that students believed the administration had acted capriciously by banning the traditional use of Bancroft-Telegraph area for political advocacy, and they had in fact challenged what they believed to be the "arbitrary exercise of authority," something Strong said was *always* to be challenged. After all, Dean Towle had not consulted with student organizations before issuing the ban, and students were the ones most directly effected. Students had responded by petitioning the university to lift the ban, in other words, by challenging the arbitrary action.[21]

But it was left to President Clark Kerr to voice the principal topics that constitute administrative rhetoric. In a major statement on December 3, a critical time when students were occupying Sproul Hall, Kerr stated:

> The protest has had the slogan of "free speech;" it has had the substance of a demand for on-campus political action and this substance has been granted within the limits of the law; but it has now become an instrument of anarchy and of personal aggrandizement. . . .
>
> The university is an institution whose primary obligation is to educate its students. It has shown patience. This patience has been met with impatience and with violation of the law. The university has shown tolerance. This tolerance has been met with intolerance and distortion of the truth. The university has shown reasonableness. This reasonableness has been met with irrationality and intransigence. The university has shown decency. This decency has been met with indecency and ill-will.
>
> When patience and tolerance and reasonableness and decency have been tried, yet democratic processes continue to be forsaken by the FSM in favor of anarchy, then the process of law enforcement takes over. This nation is devoted to freedom under the law, not to anarchy under a willful minority, whether that minority be radical students in the north or white supremacists in the south. The ends of neither group justify the means they employ. Freedom can only exist within a rule of law and this is just as true when the attack is from the radical left as when it is from the Ku Klux Klan.[22]

Kerr's statement reflected the full range of administrative rhetoric. From the outset officials of the university had reacted more to the symbolism they believed the protests represented than to the original specific issues about Bancroft-Telegraph and freedom of speech. In other words, they continually changed the meaning of the protest to issues of authority and credibility. Once this change occurred, they began attacking the ethos of protesters, portraying them as illegitimate participants in academic matters. The choice to describe them as *anarchists* could be understood as typical hyperbole of such rhetoric. But it meant more than that. For administrators, the challenge posed by protesters meant a challenge to their rules and their rule. As administrators saw it, such a challenge could lead only to abolition of such rules, therefore—anarchy.

The critic must ask how there can be a reasonable resolution of an issue when administrative figures transform issues into dialectic confrontations between reasonableness and unreasonableness, truth and falsehood, right and wrong, credibility of authority versus illegitimacy of protest. And how can reasonable discussion proceed when one group claims to have truth, righteousness, and authority on its side while portraying its opponents as irrational, wrong, and illegitimate?

In fact, what administrators at Berkeley did was use the form and arguments of ideological rhetoric to attack what they perceived as an ideological attack on procedures. Thus, in defense of the sanctity of procedures, they resorted to an ideological response to deliberative requests for reconsideration of policies concerning those very procedures.

Other Uses of Administrative Rhetoric

Administrative rhetoric would be used repeatedly by Presidents Johnson and Nixon in defending their policies against protestors opposed to the war in Vietnam. In the beginning stages of America's escalation of its involvement in the war, members of the administration recognized that the war was not fought for military objectives but for the more abstract goals of reputation and credibility.[23]

Credibility and maintenance of authority would be, as they were at Berkeley, the central issues of the administration's defense of the war in Vietnam. Upon escalating the war, President Johnson stated that the United States had two goals in Vietnam: (1) "to convince the Communists that we cannot be defeated by force of arms or by superior power"; and (2) "once the Communists know, as we know, that a violent solution is impossible, then a peaceful solution is inevitable."[24] Johnson attacked protesters as "Nervous Nellies" who "will become frustrated and bothered and break ranks under the strain, and some will turn on their leaders, and on their country, and on our own fighting men."[25]

Nixon would rely on administrative rhetoric even more than Johnson. He would extend the range of opponents to include congressional critics and the news media. In his speech at the Air Force Academy on June 4, 1969, Nixon divided ideas about foreign policy into two mutually exclusive schools of thought: the neo-isolationists' and his own. He attributed a number of policy positions to the neo-isolationists—including unilateral disarmament, downgrading of American alliances with allies, and weakening American defenses. In so doing Nixon elevated specific policy criticisms to larger issues of America's place in the world and the credibility of American power. He stated: "Imagine . . . what would happen to this world if America were to become a dropout in assuming the responsibility for defending peace and freedom in the world. As every world leader knows, *and as even the most outspoken critics of America would admit,* the rest of the world would live in terror."[26] In this excerpt from the speech, Nixon placed his critics in the incredible position of advocating specific policies that he charged these critics knew in advance were irresponsible and disastrous.

Vice President Spiro Agnew's celebrated attack on the media also falls into this same rhetorical category. In his speech at Des Moines, Iowa, on November 13, 1969, he described the television networks as controlled by a "small group of men," "a handful of men," or "small band."[27] He accused them of being biased and unrepresentative: "The views of this fraternity do *not* represent the views of America." Agnew practically accused Averell Harriman, former chief negotiator at the Paris peace talks and ABC's guest commentator on the evening of Nixon's November 3, 1969, speech, of treason.[28] Once again, the central issue, as it always is when administrative rhetoric is used, was the credibility of authorities and institutions. Agnew stated it succinctly in attacking television newspeople: "A raised eyebrow, an inflection of the voice, a caustic remark dropped in the middle of a broadcast can raise doubts in a million minds about the veracity of a public official or the wisdom of government policy."

The last thing most administrators want is anyone asking questions or raising doubts about the "veracity of a public official or the wisdom of a government policy." Thus, the extensive use of administrative rhetoric.

Conclusion

The main effect of the use of administrative rhetoric is to ignore the specific issues that originally aroused protest and instead to switch the terms for argument, to change the meaning of protest. Administrators contend their institution is under severe attack and demand unconditional support in this time of peril, regardless of the correctness or reasonableness of the policy they have enacted and are now seeking to enforce. They see themselves as standing at the ramparts defending the last remnants of Western civilization against the uncivilized hordes who would destroy them and their authority.[29] They believe that if they are defeated, the cause of freedom will also be defeated. It is not therefore remarkable that authorities predict catastrophic consequences should they lose in this great symbolic war.

What is important to note is the problem of political participation. Protesters at Berkeley and many elsewhere believed in democratic myths, most pertinently, that every citizen has the right to petition for redress of grievances, to be listened to attentively, and thus to participate—to some degree—in policy making. Administrators, on the other hand, had a different view. They saw themselves as the only legitimate decision makers with legitimate power to *make* and enforce regulations. Once these elite officials made decisions, it was the duty of others to support them: "Those in the best position to guide the destiny of the nation [or university] were those selected as leaders by the system. The judgment of these leaders could be questioned, but only verbally."[30] At this point the issue shifted again, this time to political participation: Who should be allowed to have a voice in decisionmaking, and what weight should be given to those voices? Thus, Savio's condemnation of speech without consequences becomes even more poignant. When officials were attacked for not responding to the specific issues that aroused the protest in the first place, administrators overreacted and predicted horrendous consequences if they were to relent. In so doing, administrators used the form of ideological rhetoric to defend their cherished procedures and to discredit protesters.

Of course, the actual consequences turned out to be much different from those wild and unrestrained imaginings. The Free Speech Movement eventually won not only the right to engage in politics at Bancroft-Telegraph but many other rights as well.[31] Despite the repeated predictions by the administration, the university was not destroyed. In the same vein, the U.S. defeat in the

American-Vietnamese war did not result in the catastrophes for American power or prestige that the architects of the war contended. Nor has the growing influence of the media destroyed fundamental American institutions. These predictions were as exaggerated as the smears of protesters were debasing.

But the use of administrative rhetoric did have one profound effect. It convinced some protesters that procedural means for protest were a sham. Some believed that new methods were needed, and with these new methods would come new definitions of the political meaning of protest and therefore new rhetorical forms to justify those meanings.

9

The Dynamics of Ideology and Forms of Ideological Rhetoric

American politics is unique. Unlike many other countries, Americans have no sustained radical tradition.[1] But in times of severe psychic shock to the civic body, in times of extreme social disruptions or political displacements, ideologies—like charismatic movements—arise.[2] In fact, such social turmoil may be imperative for the emergence of ideologies. Thus, it was so in the mid-1960s. Frustrated by their inability to end the war or angered by their inability to curb racial injustice or outraged by the refusal of authorities to engage in civilized debate on crucial issues in the manner they anticipated, protesters sought to find explanations for what appeared to them to be a breakdown in democratic processes. What that meant for some was a move from procedural politics to ideology, from deliberative rhetoric to ideological rhetoric in one of its various forms.

It should be stressed that those who turned to ideology remained a minority among the protesters, albeit in the words of Richard Nixon, a very "vocal minority." Most who protested various policies or injustices remained within the perimeters of procedural politics and deliberative rhetoric. However, in many circles, those who cast their lots with ideologues were viewed as the majority, and some even believed that if they were not now a majority among protesters, they soon would be.

Insurgent ideologues among the protesters gained such publicity or notoriety because they represented a different way of thinking and speaking about politics and policies. They represented a distinct break in the protest movements. If we are to understand the ideologue's rhetoric, we must first briefly review the nature of ideology, especially as it differs from procedural politics. This inquiry and review concentrates on ideology within left protest movements. It should be noted, however, that the anticommunist ideology that governed much of American foreign policy shared many of the premises and arguments with left ideologues.[3] Part of that kind of ideological rhetoric has been examined in the previous chapter on Johnson's rhetoric. The focus in the remainder of this chapter, after the review of the nature of ideology, is on the development of different forms of ideological rhetoric among the leftists.

The Nature of Ideology Reviewed

Every classical ideology strives for universality, for harmony, for completeness, for piety, for intellectual purity. The ideologue merges politics with philosophy (or theology). In essence, the ideologue attempts to capture social reality in total, in a complete and comprehensive intellectual form that will account for all types of political and historical thought and action. The ideologue proposes to build a political and social architectonic structure thoroughly grounded in experience and history—not speculation nor idealism —in which the motion of history can be arrested and therefore known, in which all human purposes can be determined and acted upon.[4]

Ideology is an attempt to fit the facts of political, social, and economic relations into coherent patterns as a critique of current circumstances and as a plan of action for the future. For adherents to understand a particular ideology requires a new consciousness. A new consciousness requires a new language, for there is no political consciousness without language, which is the essence of consciousness:

Social consciousness, awareness of how multifarious and contradictory social action can be, changes only in this way: by *acquiring new terms and idioms* (i.e. ideological rhetoric) *to supplant obsolete linguistic structures* (i.e. deliberative rhetoric). Thus it is not language that generates what people say. Language does not possess this magical power or possesses it only fitfully and dubiously. What people say derives from praxis—from the performance of task, from the division of labor—arises out of real actions, real struggles in the world. What they actually do, however, enters consciousness only by way of language, *by being said.* Ideologies mediate between praxis and consciousness (i.e. language).[5]

Lefebvre underestimated the creative power of language, even if one agrees with his notion about the origins of such language. Language is not merely mediative, but creative as well. A new language creates a new rhetoric and new rhetorical genres. Every ideology generates its own language, intended to order perceptions, organize thought, shape responses, and incorporate a full philosophy of being and doing. It legitimizes one set of motives, values, and ideals and at the same time banishes all others from its reality.

The language of ideologial rhetoric is one of truth explained in dialectical fashion through deterministic categories. The purpose of the arguments is to gain solidarity among adherents, to recognize that it is not a particular policy they are agitated about, but an oppressive system that has persistently exploited them. Thus, the ideologue transforms dissidents and authorities into *oppressed* and *oppressor*, *exploited* and *exploiter*. These are further identified by economic, sexual, political, or racial categories: proletariat and bourgeois, liberated feminist and male chauvinist, black slave and white racist. The two conflicting classes, according to the ideologue, are engaged in a dialectic struggle rooted in the historical development of these classes and their inherent antagonisms. The central issues shift from *ideas* advocated by people to *interests* represented by classes. Since each class acts not out of reason, but out of self-interest, the oppressive class is immune to reasonable persuasion. Therefore, members of the oppressed class must join together to act against the oppressors, for actions—not words—are the only things oppressors understand. The pertinent assumption of ideology is that advocates believe that what they say is true, not probable. Their ideas, they claim, are products of objective readings of historical circumstances, not personal insights.

The Structure of Ideological Rhetoric

The model for the *form* or *structure* of ideological rhetoric comes from *The Communist Manifesto*.[6] In later ideologies the *content* of the ideology may change, but the *form* remains the same. Therefore, to understand this form as distinct from the form of deliberative rhetoric, we must pause in the narrative of rhetorical protests to examine the structure of ideological rhetoric by briefly analyzing the argumentative structure of the *Manifesto*.

The *Manifesto* is divided into four sections: (1) bourgeois and proletarians; (2) proletarians and communists; (3) socialist and communist literature; and (4) position of the communists in relation to the various existing opposition parties.

In the first section Marx and Engels begin with the basic assumption (the truth) of the communist ideology: "The history of all hitherto existing society is the history of class struggles." That *truth* guides all other arguments used in the *Manifesto*, both in analysis of history and of the then current situation, and in recommendations about what had to be done. Any evidence or particular example is fitted into that truth. Marx and Engels next describe the current historical epoch: the class warfare between the proletariat and the proletariat bourgeoisie. The bourgeoisie has become, they contend, the oppressing class and the proletariat the oppressed. The result of this oppression is that the bourgeoisie has gained power but also corrupted societal institutions: "The bourgeoisie has stripped of its halo every occupation hitherto honoured and looked up to with reverent awe. It has converted the physician, the lawyer, the priest, the poet, the man of science, into its paid wage-laborours." And it has made slaves of the proletariat, who suffer alienation from work, family, and the institutions of society.

The purpose of this first section is to raise the consciousness of the proletariat to see its problems and miseries for what they really are: products of a continual class struggle. The oppressing class is corrupt; the oppressed class is exploited. The bourgeoisie is vulnerable to attack; the proletariat is now revolutionary, the new agent of revolutionary development and change. The instances of bourgeois corruption are specified; the examples of proletariat suffering are emphasized. The inability of the ruling class to reform itself (because classes always act only in their own interests) is proclaimed; the need for the exploited class to rise up in battle for its own interests is directed.

The second section concentrates on the relationship of communists to proletarians. Marx and Engels argue: "The Communists do not form a separate party opposed to other working-class parties. They have no interests separate and apart from those of the proletariat as a whole." The purpose of this statement is to gain solidarity and identification with followers: all differences melt when the interests of the class surface. Marx and Engels then present a list of programmatic changes they would institute in society were communists, acting as agents for the proletariat, to seize power: abolition of property, free education, credit in the hands of the state, and so forth. These changes, they charge, would result in "an association, in which the free development of each is the condition for the free development of all." The basic appeal of this section is the need for solidarity now with the communists so that completed freedom can be assured in the future.

The third section concentrates on criticism or condemnation of competing ideologies for the allegiance of the proletariat. This section is peculiar to ideologues but inherent in ideological thought. Since other ideological groups share some common ideas with the communists and because ideologues insist that they alone have truth, ideologues must eventually condemn others, especially the reformers. There are three reasons for this set of arguments. First, ideologues seek to consolidate all radicals behind one organization. Competing organizations or parties splinter the movement and therefore must be discredited. Second, ideologues must condemn reformist groups because as long as people hold hopes that the system will reform itself (or that it can be reformed), they will not join a movement that calls for a new political and social structure. In essence, ideologues must destroy hope in the existing system and in reformist parties so as to create hope in their platform and party. Third, ideologues believe they alone in their particular ideology have truth, and that truth is not arguable. All other truth-claims are illegitimate and must be discredited. Unlike procedural politicians who presume truth emerged out of the marketplace of argument, ideologues presume basic truths for themselves and denounce those who would question them about basic premises. The only arguable topics are topics of strategy and tactics. Thus it is that only an ideologue can argue with another ideologue, because they alone have similar forms of thinking.

The final section of the *Manifesto* demands that workers now act on the new consciousness the authors have created: "Let the ruling classes tremble at a Communistic revolution. The proletarians have nothing to lose but their chains. They have a world to win. WORKING MEN OF ALL COUNTRIES, UNITE!"

The structure of ideological rhetoric lies in the following arguments.

First, *the issue in dispute signifies a struggle for power between two mutually exclusive classes.* This line of argument is central to creating political solidarity and to destroying sympathy and empathy for opponents.

Second, *one class is an oppressor, the other oppressed.* These characterizations, "oppressor" and "oppressed," carry heavy moral content. To "oppress" another is to impose unjust burdens upon others through a cruel or unreasonable abuse of power. To be oppressed is to suffer injustice, cruelty, and unreasonable abuse. Thus, oppressors become morally malignant and the oppressed, innocent victims.

Third, *the oppressor is corrupt politically, morally, and intellectually; the oppressed have suffered too long from this corruption.* It is not enough to name the oppressors as morally culpable; they must be shown to be beyond redemption. Thus, the ideologue describes the history of examples of that corruption and its immediate applications to current life. By citing the suffering of the oppressed, the ideologue exalts them above the oppressor, and that exaltation of moral superiority is absolutely necessary to any rhetoric of revolt so that ends may justify means.

Fourth, *the oppressor acts only in self-interest; therefore, the oppressed should recognize its own interests and act accordingly.* (Paradoxically, ideologues present themselves as teachers of the truth who have no historically conditioned interests, or if they have, their interests are solely with the oppressed.) Ideologues must persuade supporters that all acts by oppressors are intended to further maintain or expand the oppressors' superior class status and privileges. Even acts of kindness or benevolence must be "unmasked" through attribution of base motives to demonstrate that these actions are not what they seem; in other words, they are not acts to relieve oppression, but "masks" intended to fool the oppressed for the furtherance of the goals of oppressors. The oppressed therefore must recognize the inherent corruption of their oppressors as well as any hidden motives behind any reformist rhetoric or actions in order to recognize that their own interests are in direct conflict with those of their exploiters.

Fifth, *since oppressors act only in their own interests, they are not susceptible to reason; thus, means other than reason must be used to cause change.* This line of argument helps explain why the original protest did not result in changed policies or an end to exploitation. Indeed, the use of administrative rhetoric may be cited as further evidence of the imperviousness of authorities to reason. This coordinated line of argument also prepares the oppressed for immediate or future action to replace reliance on discourse as a means for change.

Sixth, *the organization the oppressed can trust is the one the ideologue belongs to; all other organizations are primarily reformist and therefore serve consciously or unconsciously the interests of the oppressing class.* Empirical reasoning must be attacked and discredited as only another instrument used by oppressors to mask their real interests. In the same fashion, competing ideologies or parties must be discredited as not representing the true or real interests of the oppressed. These arguments are essential to gain avid converts to one's own ideology.

Finally, *ideologues express absolute faith that the oppressors will*

eventually be crushed and the oppressed will achieve justice be-
cause history is on the side of the exploited, not the exploiters. This
optimistic interpretation of history is essential to motivating rebellion. People do not revolt for lost causes or causes whose out-
come is in doubt. If the possibility of immediate success is not
apparent, the ideologue must develop a secondary theme of sacrificing now for success in the future. Such an argument has an altruistic
appeal consistent with the altruism of the ideologue-teacher. Such a
theme will be only as persuasive as the ideologue has been in convincing converts to accept class solidarity and political cohesiveness
through the other topics of ideological rhetoric.

The form of ideological rhetoric is deductive. Examples and instances are selected to substantiate the generalizations inherent in
the rhetoric. Motives are attributed along lines consistent with the
ideology. The ideologue directs these arguments not toward opponents in hopes of resolving differences but toward potential supporters in hopes of converting them. They ignore what rhetoricians
traditionally call "common ground."[7] Class polarization, not common ground, is sought. Should someone deny that the examples are
representative or that the motives are actual, the ideologue must
"unmask" that person by attributing base motives of deception or
treachery to that dissenter. Since ideologues begin with the belief
that their ideology is true, any protestations to the contrary regarding analysis, motive, or method must either be mistaken or an act of
deception. Thus, the ideologue must correct such false impressions
by unmasking the real motives behind such statements. By exposing
the "real" motives, the radical gains the strategic advantage of placing the opponent on the defensive to prove that the attributed
motives are not true. Furthermore, the ideologue maintains control
over the definition of issues and the motives of opponents, and the
one who controls the definition of terms in an argument can usually
win it. Much of this unmasking then becomes self-fulfilling prophecy. But it is typical of an ideological rhetoric. Louis Halle noted:
"When we devise a conceptual order to explain the existential world
of past or present, we may suppose that it is based on a record of
actual observation. But a conceptual order that undertakes to explain the future is bound to be *a priori*. It describes existential circumstances before they have come into being, depending for its
ultimate vindication either on the operations of some historical ne-
cessity or on the tendency of prophecy to be self-fulfilling."[8] This
unmasking process is the hallmark of an ideologue. Thus, to summarize, ideologues seek not to adjust ideas to people and people to
ideas, but rather to adjust people and events to ideology.

As one demonstration of the formal consistency of ideological rhetoric we may cite an example from another era. The Preamble to the Constitution of the Industrial Workers of the World provides a succinct example of classical ideological rhetoric:

The working class and the employing class have nothing in common. There can be no peace so long as hunger and want are found among millions of working people and the few, who make up the employing class, have all the good things of life.

Between these two classes a struggle must go on until the workers of the world organize as a class, take possession of the earth and the machinery of production, and abolish the wage system.

We find that the centering of the management of industries into fewer and fewer hands makes the trade unions unable to cope with the ever growing power of the employing class. The trade unions foster a state of affairs which allows one set of workers to be pitted against another set of workers in the same industry, thereby helping defeat one another in wage wars. Moreover, the trade unions aid the employing class to mislead the workers into the belief that the working class have interests in common with their employers. . . .

It is the historic mission of the working class to do away with capitalism. The army of production must be organized, not only for the every-day struggle with capitalists, but also to carry on production when capitalism shall have been overthrown. By organizing industrially we are forming the structure of the new society within the shell of the old.[9]

Ideological rhetoric is the superimposition of political theory upon fact so as to create a social coherence and political meaning beyond a specific issue, and it is a call to action for constituents beyond traditional protest. It is "a mystifying representation of social reality, or the process of change, of its latent tendencies and its future."[10]

In the 1960s each of the protest movements developed an ideological dimension, a group of radicals who split from traditional protest of deliberative rhetoric and embraced an ideological analysis and rhetoric to cope with what they saw as the growing political crisis in the United States. That change caused not only a change in rhetoric but a radical change in identity, purpose, methods, and politics.

Ideological Rhetoric in Protest Movements

A new language. A new way of thinking. Thus, a new set of meanings for events, politics, and people.

To dissidents of the 1960s a new language meant an entirely new direction. Tom Hayden encouraged it: "Could we not make the dialogue in the country drastically different from that at the Defense Department and the LBJ Ranch?"[11] Arthur Smith analyzed it: "Their [black ideologues'] rhetoric also becomes a rhetoric of re-definition as they grapple with terms like *Negritude*, Negro, Afro-Americans, black natural, and brother. In the identity crisis, each revolutionist has to hew out his own definition from the forest of cultural possibilities in an effort to elicit response from his audience when he appeals to them on the basis of this new definition."[12] Members of the SDS experienced it when the ideologues trans-formed that organization: "When PL [Progressive Labor] fought for its politics, it had the advantage of disciplined organization and greater facility with Marxist terminology over its loosely organized ideologically heterogeneous SDS counterparts. Even more impor-tant, PL had a self-conscious concept of an anti-imperialist student organization and a vague idea about how those students could even-tually become a cadre in a working-class movement."[13] Some femi-nists, after the Miss America protest in 1968, adopted a radical ideological stance. The "Redstockings Manifesto" embodied it: "Women are an oppressed class," it read. "Our oppression is total, affecting every facet of our lives. We are exploited as sex objects, breeders, domestic servants, and cheap labor. We are considered in-ferior beings, whose only purpose is to enhance men's lives. Our humanity is denied. Our prescribed behavior is enforced by the threat of physical violence."[14] This "Manifesto" is a classic of mod-ern ideological rhetoric. The oppressed are identified; their oppres-sion briefly described, and, finally, the oppressors:

We identify the agents of our oppression as men. Male supremacy is the oldest, most basic form of domination. All other forms of exploitation and oppression (racism, capitalism, imperialism, etc.) are extensions of male su-premacy: men dominate women, a few men dominate the rest. All power structures throughout history have been male-dominated and male-oriented. Men have controlled all political, economic and cultural institu-tions and backed up this control with physical force. They have used their power to keep women in an inferior position. *All men* receive economic, sexual and psychological benefits from male supremacy. *All men* have op-pressed women. . . .

We identify with all women. We define our best interests as that of the poorest, most brutally exploited woman. . . .

We call on all our sisters to unite with us in struggle.

We call on all men to give up their male privileges and support women's liberation in the interest of our humanity and their own.

In fighting for our liberation we will always take the side of women against their oppressors. We will not ask what is "revolutionary" or "re-formist," only what is good for women.[15]

Here the Redstockings presented ideological rhetoric in pristine form: a dialectical battle between men and women in which the sexual classes are mutually exclusive. It is a rhetoric of conversion, not persuasion. But the audience for this manifesto was not men, but women: "Our chief task at present is to develop female class consciousness through sharing experiences and publicly exposing the sexist foundation of all our institutions. Consciousness raising is not 'therapy,' which implies the existence of individual solutions and falsely assumes that the male-female relationship is purely personal, but the only method by which we can ensure that our program for liberation is based on the concrete realities of our lives."[16] Some time ago, in another context, Everett Lee Hunt observed that the acceptance of an ideology "orders all our conflicts, divides our writers neatly into schools, explains all their failures and fills us with a long unfelt glow"[17]—the glow, I might add, of knowing truth absolutely.

With the move to ideology, protest proceeds not dialectically, but geometrically. The rhetorical situation becomes more complex. It changes from a debate model of those who affirm a policy against those who oppose it to a new model, one more akin to a gigantic chess board with several games going at once, each intimately related to the others. Deliberative rhetors continue to engage each other in statement-counterstatement, retort-counterretort, as they debate specific policies in dispute. Ideologues denounce deliberative rhetors' efforts as futile because those still working within the system believe that policies can actually change without changing structures and institutions. Typical of this development was Ti-Grace Atkinson's resignation from NOW. She stated: "The leader of NOW Betty Friedan . . . said, 'I want to get women into position of power.' Some of the rest of us saw this statement as representative of the opposite side of our differences. We said, each in our own way, 'We want to destroy the positions of power.'" Therefore, she concluded, since she had "failed to get rid of the power position I hold, I have no choice but to step out of it."[18] Conversely, Friedan later denounced Atkinson: "Also, I never told anyone, but very early Ti-Grace Atkinson took me to lunch in Philadelphia with the wife of a top C.I.A. official, who offered to help us. I told Ti-Grace we didn't want any help from the C.I.A. Sometime in 1968, we heard that 200 women had been trained by the F.B.I. or C.I.A. to infiltrate the women's movement—as it is known was done by the F.B.I in the student and radical movements."[19] These denunciations among people—sometimes former comrades—within the same movement are typical of the denunciations that fly between deliberative rhetors and ideological rhetors. They are part of the sectarian battles.

Furthermore, reactionaries cite the emergence of ideologues as concrete proof that traditional values are being systematically destroyed by subversives who are "coddled" by liberal bureaucrats and politicians. Liberal politicians, who are astonished, angry, or afraid of ideologues, make alliances with procedural protestors as models of legitimate protest. Even conservatives find a Martin Luther King preferable to a Malcolm X. In sum, one of the major effects that ideologues have on others is to legitimize procedural protest.

But among radical groups there is a different effect. Once ideologies emerge, they begin to split into factions, in which they vie with one another for possession of truth, power, and allegiances.

Factions and Sectarian Debates

Factionalism (or sectarianism) is a dirty word among radicals. It always has been. But factions within radical movements are as predictable as the rising of the sun. Factionalism stems from the belief of ideologues that they alone possess truth, or that, at least, their ideology is an intellectual and political representation of truth. But different ideologues make different truth claims. During the 1960s. Progressive Labor claimed that the essence of the struggle was economic class warfare between the working class and imperial capitalists. Other radicals claimed otherwise. Marxist humanists saw the conflict as one between liberal bureaucrats and radical humanists. Black radicals saw the problems as one that placed blacks and whites in direct confrontation. Feminists, at least some of them, contended that the real issue was not race, nor economics, nor anything other than the corrupt dominance of American institutions by males who oppressed females. Furthermore, these "content" issues were confounded by strategic and tactical disputes.

Factionalism within ideological movements comes from the differing answers ideologues give to important questions of strategy and tactics. *Who best represents the constituency and can muster enough muscle to achieve ideological goals?* Black and white, or blacks only? Men and women, or women only? Working class or minorities or students or intellectuals—all, some, or whom? *What is the current state of the movement and what are its prospects?* Is the time ripe for revolution? Should radicals devote most of their energies to raising consciousness in preparation for the revolution later on? Or should they be concentrating on making the revolution happen now? Indeed, can a revolution actually happen? Should one settle for a social rather than a political revolution? *What are the best means for achieving ideological change, that is, changes in the primary structures and institutions of society?* This issue basically boils down to a question of what role violence should play in the movement. *What is the appropriate relation between radicals and procedural protesters?* Should radicals join with nonideological, reformist groups to achieve short-term tactical goals, or should radicals remain separate, pursuing separate goals? Should ideological doctrine be adjusted or compromised to join with these groups, or should doctrine remain pure? In earlier radical movements when unions played a significant role, these questions were posed as a debate over "boring from within" versus dual unionism.[20]

What is important here is not only that the left becomes wrecked by factionalism, but that it also develops different arguments to substantiate and justify its different perceptions of its current status and hopes for the future. Radical blacks divided among separatists (Black Muslims), pan-Africanists (followers of Malcolm X), and advocates of black power (Stokely Carmichael, H. Rap Brown, and the Black Panthers). The antiwar movement splintered on its radical side among Progressive Labor, the Revolutionary Youth Movement, and Weatherpeople.[21] Radical feminists split among the New York Radical Women, Redstockings, Radical Lesbians, and so on.[22] As these sects emerged with competing ideologies, radicals developed competing forms of ideological rhetoric to express distinctive ideological commitments. There are, essentially, three such forms: *consciousness raising, revolutionary,* and *lamentation.* What binds these is a more or less common language and common *topoi* associated with ideological rhetoric. What distinguished them from one another is the use each makes of ideological rhetoric and the specific *topoi* that define each form.

Three Forms of Ideological Rhetoric

Consciousness Raising

In his play *Waiting for Lefty* Clifford Odets depicted a meeting of taxi drivers in the 1930s who, threatened with another salary cut, come together to discuss whether to strike or not. In a series of flash-back scenes, several of them describe how their own particular circumstances have resulted in economic and personal deprivation, alienation, and deep feelings of individual helplessness. At the climax of the play Agate Keller, the most ideologically sophisticated of the group, binds up these individual cases into a collective experience of working-class oppression. His explanation of their predicament and his call for action are so persuasive, the taxi drivers join in a show of class solidarity by shouting in unison for a strike.

The solidarity achieved by the characters in *Lefty* is the effect that advocates using consciousness raising[23] also seek. *They attempt to transform individual experiences of frustration, discrimination, or alienation into a general ideological knowledge of their collective oppression as a class by another class or by the system.* To achieve these results they must change the language people use to describe their experiences so as to change the perceptions and interpretations of those experiences. Consciousness raising, thus, is a prelude to action, a prerequisite of initiation into the collective consciousness of the ideology.

Kathie Sarachild, one of the early formulators of consciousness-raising sessions among feminists, described the main topics to be included in meetings or speeches. (1) *"Ongoing consciousness expansion"*:[24] individual experiences are related and testimonies are given regarding personal feelings of discrimination or alienation; these are discussed and then related to the generalities of the ideology. This process of becoming *aware* is one designed to demonstrate that others within the gender have had the same experiences or that their experiences have the same meaning. This sharing of examples of mutual misery is the first important step toward class or gender solidarity. (2) *"Classic forms of resisting consciousness, or How to avoid facing the awful truth"*: discussions of existing personal perceptions or individual traits that inhibit the acceptance of the truth is a process that requires the banishing of personal resistances.[25] (3) *"'Starting to stop'—overcoming repressions and delusions"*: initiates must be convinced that their misery springs not from personal failures or individual flaws, but rather from an antagonistic gender or system that seeks to oppress all members of a gender or class. This process is one of *absolution.* One must be purged of the delusion that the first cause for misery comes from oneself and understand instead that the real cause is an oppressive, antagonistic class, gender, or system. (4) *"Understanding and developing radical feminist theory. Using the above techniques to begin to understand our oppression"*: This step requires the initiate to accept the ideological interpretation of oppression as opposed to a personal, individualistic interpretation. This process is one of *conversion* to the ideology. (5) *"Consciousness-raiser (organizer) training—so that every woman in a 'bitch session' cell group herself becomes an 'organizer' in turn, of other groups"*: Once one has achieved ideological consciousness, then one must witness one's commitment by *proselytizing*.

In sum, the rhetoric of consciousness raising transforms personal experiences of discrimination or alienation into a collective knowledge of the oppression shared by all members of the class or gender so as to achieve ideological cohesion within the class or gender. The language is changed from that of deliberative rhetoric to one of radicalism, and therefore the *meaning* of these experiences and one's identity is also changed remarkably. Those who resort to consciousness raising do not believe they have sufficient strength with constituencies to cause significant change. Therefore, they seek to enlist more and more into the constituencies by educating members of the class or gender they represent as a prerequisite to political or radical action. To demonstrate commitment to this form of rhetoric, they commit symbolic acts consistent with it, *that is*, that confirm class or gender or racial solidarity. They may exclude from meetings anyone who is not a member of the class, gender, or race. They may begin to dress alike to distinguish themselves from others. They may develop their own forums, operated by themselves for their own constituencies. For example, Robin Morgan, leader in the Women's Liberation Movement, wrote in the introduction to her *Sisterhood Is Powerful*: "This book is an action. It was conceived, written, edited, copy-edited, proofread, designed, and illustrated by women. (The process broke down for the first time at the printer's, that industry being one of the man which are all but completely closed to women.)"[26] Such actions are symbolic confirmations of conversion to the ideology. Consciousness raising, then, is the building of an ideological constituency as preparation for action and is the most widely used form of ideological rhetoric.

Revolutionary Rhetoric

The revolutionary wants action. In addition to the usual topics of ideology, revolutionaries infuse their messages with lines of argument intended to emphasize the urgency for revolutionary action. Using excerpts from a letter by Timothy Leary, we can trace these characteristic *topoi*.

First, *the revolutionary attempts to destroy all hope in the existing political system and to transfer that hope instead to the revolution that will bring about a free or equal society.* Leary wrote: "I declare that World War III is now being waged by short-haired robots whose deliberate aim is to destroy the complex web of free wild life by the imposition of mechanical order. Listen. There is no choice left but to defend life by all and every means possible against the genocidal machine. Listen. There are no neutrals in genetic war. There are no noncombatants at Buchenwald, My Lai or Soledad. You are part of the death apparatus or you belong to the network of free life."[27] This line of argument is intended to raise the issue to an apocalyptic battle between the agents of revolution (invariably characterized as on the side of freedom) and the agents of oppression (invariably characterized as on the side of death).

Second, *the revolutionary portrays the oppressor as evil, devoid of any human thoughts or feelings:*

If you fail to see that we are victims—defendants of genocidal war you will not understand the rage of blacks, the fierceness of the browns, the holy fanaticism of the Palestinians, the righteous mania of the Weathermen, and the pervasive resentment of the young.

Listen Americans. Your government is an instrument of total lethal evil. . . .

Listen. There is no compromise with a machine. You cannot talk peace and love to a humanoid robot whose every Federal Bureaucratic impulse is soulless, heartless, lifeless, loveless.

Revolutionaries turn opponents into objects or categories. They describe opponents as "robots," "machines," or in other circumstances "pigs," "gooks," "fascist imperialists," and so on. The psychology is rather simple. Except out of rage or insanity, people will not kill someone who is a recognizable human being. Thus, opponents must be turned into nonhuman objects. Militarists have long known this psychology and use the same techniques in training civilians to become military personnel. These arguments also function to assert the moral superiority of revolutionaries by proclaiming their humanity vis-à-vis the absolute ("soulless, heartless, lifeless, loveless") inhumanity of the opposition. Leary even described revolutionaries as "holy" and "righteous." Again, the psychology is not difficult to understand. Convinced that one represents a higher morality threatened by inhuman objects, the revolutionary is prepared to kill.[28] And it has occurred in the past that in this name of superior morality—be it ideological purity, Aryan superiority, religious fanaticism, or America's sacred commitments and beliefs—revolutionaries have killed wantonly.

Finally, *the revolutionary wants action.* Leary wrote: "Resist physically, robot agents who threaten life must be disarmed, disabled, disconnected by force . . . . Arm yourself and shoot to live . . . . Life is never violent. To shoot a genocidal robot policeman in the defense of life is a sacred act." The moral imperative to kill for the sake of the revolution is cloaked in the language of a "sacred act" and "self-defense." After all, revolutionaries kill in defense of life, whereas the robots "threaten life" and must be "disconnected."

However, the revolution did not happen. The government was not overthrown. To avoid having their revolutionary rhetoric ridiculed as "mere rhetoric," these radicals forcibly occupied buildings, bombed selected symbolic targets, and went underground. The riots, the bombings, particularly by Weatherpeople, represented symbolic, existential commitments to the revolutionary rhetoric.[29] To make certain others understood their earnestness, they sent letters after bombings claiming responsibility. If they could not make the revolution actually happen, they could at least demonstrate a willingness to commit symbolic acts of revolution. In so doing they achieved not an overthrow of the government, but a personal, existential authenticity that separated them from those who only talked revolution.

Lamentation

The lamentation[30] is absolutely moral. It is informed by a tragic vision: "when the *lamenteur* takes pen in hand, it is often to construct a two-valued picture of reality. Too effective a communicator to leave no way out, the writer leaves the 'way out' somewhat far out—at least by present lights. In other words, the usual probabilities of rhetorical exchange are transformed for the most part into a polemics and hyperbole of prophecy."[31]

In his *American Power and the New Mandarins*, Noam Chomsky relied upon this rhetorical form to express his outrage over the American-Vietnamese war. The starting point for this form, from which all other arguments flow, is the rhetor's belief that his or her position is right *and moral* and thus not open to dispute. Those who lament also believe those they condemn are absolutely wrong and immoral. Chomsky wrote: "There may have been a time when American policy in Vietnam was a debatable matter. This time is long past. It is no more debatable than the Italian war in Abyssinia or the Russian suppression of Hungarian freedom. The war is simply an obscenity, a depraved act by weak and miserable men, including all of us, who have allowed it to go on and on with endless fury and destruction—all of us who would have remained silent had stability and order been secured."[32]

The rhetorical consequences of this position are clear and staggering. If such rhetors are right and their opponents are not only wrong but depraved, how can one engage in argument? Chomsky realized this and eschewed debate with "weak and miserable" opponents:

> By entering into the arena of argument and counter-argument, of technical feasibility and tactics, of footnotes and citations, by accepting the presumption of legitimacy of debate on certain issues, one has already lost one's humanity. This is the feeling I find almost impossible to repress when going through the motions of building a case against the American war in Vietnam. Anyone who puts a fraction of his mind to the task can construct a case that is overwhelming; surely this is now obvious. In an important way, by doing so he degrades himself, and insults beyond measure the victims of our violence and our moral blindness.[33]

The lamentation thus begins with a belief in the absolute righteousness of one's cause and in the absolute corruption of one's opponents.

If one cannot argue the merits of an issue without debasing oneself and if there is not solution to the problem, what is one left to argue? There are three lines of argument left to those who elect to use this rhetorical form, three that characterize the lamentation.

First, *the advocate persistently condemns the society and people as depraved and corrupt for bringing this moral catastrophe to pass.* The *lamenteur* shares this condemnation with other ideologues. However, the language is more moral than political. Several examples from Chomsky may serve to illustrate the difference. Chomsky wrote: "I suppose this is the first time in history that a nation has so openly and publicly exhibited its own war crimes. Perhaps this shows how well our free institutions function. Or does it simply show how immune we have become to suffering? Probably the latter."[34] Or: "When we lament over the German conscience, we are demanding of them a display of self-hatred—a good thing, no doubt. But for us the matter is infinitely more serious. It is not a matter of self-hatred regarding sins of the past."[35] This voice is not that merely of an ideologue decrying oppression. It is the echo of an Old Testament prophet grieving over a people and a nation in the most uncompromising moral language, a people and a nation that has turned away from the path of righteousness.

Second, *the advocate recites the moral history of critical incidents, influential ideas, and prominent figures who have brought on this moral crisis.* The list cited by Chomsky is too extensive to be recited here. However, figuring most prominently in his moral history are incidents demonstrating an historic American imperialism toward the rest of the world (especially smaller nations); American responsibility for the development of the cold war; and liberal pragmatists and objective intellectuals, who are blistered rhetorically for their ideas and actions. The purpose of this *topos* is to illuminate the causes that have brought the nation to the brink of the apocalypse.

Finally, *the advocate calls for a purgation of this corruption through a confession of one's civic sins as a means of seeking civic salvation through public redemption.* Early in his book Chomsky confessed that his activities in 1965 in the antiwar protest came ten or fifteen years too late, but he vowed to make up for that lost time (or lost vision?) by working exhaustively against the war. The most pressing problem Chomsky confronted was deciding what action should be taken to end the war. Nothing less than total confession and cleansing was required:

> What can one say about a country where a museum of science in a great city can feature an exhibit in which people fire machine guns from a helicopter at Vietnamese huts, with a light flashing when a hit is scored. What can one say about a country where such an idea can even be considered? You have to weep for this country.
>
> These and a thousand other examples testify to moral degeneration on such a scale that talk about the "normal channels" of political action and protest become meaningless or hypocritical. We have to ask ourselves whether what is needed in the United States is dissent—or denazification. The question is a debatable one. Reasonable people may differ. The fact that the question is even debatable is a terrifying thing. To me it seems that what is needed is a kind of denazification.[36]

Chomsky rejected both patient persuasion and militant confrontation; the former on moral grounds, the latter on moral and practical grounds.[37] Rather, through self-hatred ("a good thing, no doubt") redemption might be found: recognition of the immorality of the war and a conscious decision to resist it personally and collectively. Throughout his book Chomsky insisted that only through people's recognizing the moral issues could anything positive emerge from the tragedy of the American-Vietnamese war.

Chomsky's tone is neither optimistic nor pessimistic. It is tragic, a tone befitting the lamentation. He focused again and again on the human tragedies of the war. Occasionally, he seemed to suggest that it would never end. When finally asserting that it would eventually conclude, he sadly noted that it might do so for all the wrong reasons, for example, for economic or political reasons instead of moral reasons.

The lamentation lacks the optimism, the thrills, even sometimes the clear political analyses of the rhetoric of other ideologues. Instead, the advocate concentrates on moral issues and thus reminds us of the Old Testament prophets, especially Amos:

Hear ye this word which I take up against you, *even* a lamentation O house of Israel.

The virgin of Israel is fallen; she shall no more rise: she is forsaken upon her land; *there is* none to raise her up.

For thus saith the Lord God; the City that went out by a thousand shall leave an hundred, and that which went but *by* a thousand shall leave an hundred, and that which went forth *by* an hundred, shall leave then; to the house of Israel. . . .

Seek the Lord, and ye shall live; lest he break out like fire in the house of Joseph, and devour *it*, and *there* be none to quench it in Bethel.

Ye who turn judgment to wormwood, and leave off righteousness in the earth.[38]

In using the lamentation Noam Chomsky presented himself as a latter-day prophet calling upon Americans to redeem themselves by confessing their political sins and returning to the path of righteousness embodied in the original democratic ideal.

Conclusion

The move to ideological politics among some protesters represented a move to a different kind of thinking about politics and policies. The catalyst for that change was the escalation of the war in Vietnam. For some, that escalation symbolized the futility of using procedural means for protest and deliberative rhetoric for voicing that protest. Moreover, they believed they needed a new political framework and a new political language to interpret the refusal of authorities to change politics as quickly as they thought they ought to be changed. Thus, some turned away from procedural politics to ideological politics in protesting the war. Soon, others in other protest groups—those opposed to racial discrimination or sexual discrimination—joined this transition. They named the system as the cause of their problems and focused on denouncing authorities or advocating overthrow of the system. Specific problems and policies became only examples of the architectonic corruption of the overall system of government.

As this transition from procedural politics to ideological politics proceeded, protesters changed from deliberative rhetoric to ideological rhetoric to accommodate that transition. Ideology changed the purpose, nature, and topics of protest rhetoric and, in doing so, changed the meaning of both the protest and the rhetoric. The purpose was to convert adherents to the truth of the ideology. The nature of this rhetoric changed from using examples to redress faulty policies to using the same examples to denounce the all-pervading corruption of the system. The transformation of purpose and the nature of the rhetoric created a new set of topics to be addressed. Discrimination became oppression. Faulty policy became not mistaken judgments, but a logical extension of a corrupt and oppressive government. Elected officials were discredited even as the authority of the ideology was proclaimed.

These powerful changes planted the seeds for schisms within movements. People who embraced ideology denounced those who clung to procedural politics as naive, as "Uncle Toms" of the ruling class. Conversely, those who believed in reforming the system denounced ideologues for splintering the movement by setting class against class, race against race, and gender against gender. But this was only the first level of schisms.

The second level occurred within the ideological groups themselves. They disagreed about the current state of the crises, about the agents who would address the crises, and about the means for carrying forward the ideological agenda. Factionalism raged within ideological circles. As each faction arose, a new rhetoric to justify that faction arose with it. Eventually, most of the radical groups dissolved, not only because authorities cracked down on them, but also from the sheer weight of their own internal dissensions. Each of the ideological movements disbanded or became ineffective in different ways. Such factionalism should not have been surprising. All radical movements have been plagued by internal factionalism. Nearly every radical movement in America since the nineteenth century has suffered the pangs of factionalism. Usually weaker groups have been destroyed by the stronger or more disciplined groups. Or radical ideas have been assimilated into procedural politics.

What, then, can we say about the radicalism that so exhilarated some and frightened so many others? Given the crises of the decade and the political fervor of protesters, radicalism was a predictable development. When the political order seems unresponsive or is unresponsive to demands of relatively large numbers of people who believe they have legitimate and pressing grievances, radicalism emerges as a means for explaining that unresponsiveness, that failure of authorities to act upon those crises as rapidly as protesters believe they should. Ideology provides an intellectual and architectonic explanation not only for a single failed policy, but more important, for a flawed and doomed system. It provides intellectual clarity of political issues on the largest scale possible.

But it should also be noted that radicalism apparently has little sustaining influence, except for a few. The American system of government was not overthrown, nor was it changed radically. Some radical ideas actually became political realities. Some discriminatory laws against blacks and women were removed. Participation in the electoral process was expanded. The war in Vietnam ended. Radicals demonstrated the extent of problems and the passion that some people felt about them. But without a sustaining tradition, radicalism remained an existential commitment rather than a political force in American society. Those radicals who understood that their politics were existential, not practical, that they were critiques not guides to action, understood their positive place in American politics. Those who actually believed radicalism would produce a revolution or usher in a new order were soon disillusioned. Some of these drifted back into procedural politics. Others, near the end of the decade, sought another way of thinking about politics and society, a third way different from both procedural and ideological politics. These few—as is always the case—produced cynicism.

10

The Diatribe or
the Subversion of Delicacy

Cynic, n. A blackguard whose faulty vision sees things as they
are, not as they ought to be. Hence the custom among the
Scythians of plucking out a cynic's eyes to improve his vision.
—Ambrose Bierce, *The Devil's Dictionary*

Once again, we return to the free speech battle at Berkeley, this time
to introduce the cynic. Just as the first stirrings of student protest
and radicalism erupted at Berkeley, so too did the first well-
publicized appearance of a cynic. On March 3, 1965, as the Berkeley
free speech controversy was winding down, John Thomson, a non-
student from New York, walked on campus and sat down on the
Student Union steps near the street. He held a 5-by-8-inch piece of
notebook paper in front of his chest. On the paper he had written
one word:
FUCK.
He was quickly arrested.
This seemingly bizarre incident led to predictable responses, and
they came in two waves. The first wave included a predictable rallying around Thomson's action by student activists. An "obscenity
rally" was held. Protesting students asked why Thomson should be
arrested when nothing comparable had happened to Alpha Epsilon
Phi fraternity when it had sponsored a "Miss Pussy Galore" contest
only shortly before.[1] A "Fuck Defense Fund" was created, and those
who set up tables to solicit money for the fund were arrested. An
attempt was made to give some respectability to this new development when some said that "FUCK" was an acronym for "Freedom
Under Clark Kerr."
Authorities soon began referring to the Berkeley Filthy Speech
Movement, and that label quickly caught on. Newspapers in the

area printed front-page stories about the obscenity rallies, and some began equating the Free Speech Movement with Filthy Speech.

The second wave of responses were denunciations by both the administration and the Free Speech Movement itself. Acting Berkeley chancellor Martin Meyerson issued a statement denouncing this affront to public sensitivities: "The four-letter-word signs and utterances had a significance beyond their shock impact; they also symbolized intolerance for the rights and feelings of others . . . . What might have been regarded earlier as childish bad taste has become to many the last straw of contempt."[2] The executive committee of FSM agreed and issued a statement separating itself from those who used obscenities: "Only in the recent controversy over 'obscene' words can students be said not to have acted responsibly. The FSM did not initiate or support this controversy. We regret . . . that the students involved acted in an unfortunate manner."[3] Thus, the typical cynical condition: condemned by both the right and the left, a social and political outcast, a "metaphysical outlaw" (to borrow a description from Tom Robbins)—and in this particular case, all over one word: Fuck. There was a whole metaphysical world wrapped up in that little word, a new world that appalled and even frightened others regardless of their political differences.

What in the World . . . ?

In the protests of the 1960s a third way of thinking arose in contrast to that of procedural protesters and ideologues. When President Johnson escalated the war in Vietnam, young people opposed to the war grew desperate. They invented simplistic slogans such as "Hey! Hey! LBJ! How many kids did you kill today?" While respectable critics continued a conventional rhetoric of protest and ideologues offered ideological analyses of the causes of American political events, some young people used obscenities and bizarre acts to describe their outrage and frustrations over what they considered an obscene war. Indeed, obscenities became commonplace. A writer in *Rat*, an underground newspaper, wrote: "What difference can there be between shoving liberty up the ass of Vietnam and giving America love in the same way? (When you're up against a wall the gun may loom larger than the man and a penis without a human context loses the power of creation.)"[4] Profanities used in speeches were seldom broadcast or published in the reporting of protest rallies. We can understand the reluctance of conventional newspapers to print them and of television stations to broadcast them.

However, many of us who attended antiwar rallies recall the vehemence with which speakers used obscenities to describe their outrage at the war. I remember vividly a young man who developed his ideas quite reasonably until he reached the climax of his speech. Then everything he attacked he called "shit." The policy was shit. The leaders were shit. People who supported the war were shit. The effect was striking and drew repeated applause and cheers.

These profanities shocked even those supporting the peace movement. Why this language? Why alienate your audience? Why deliberately offend potential supporters? How can a moral protest be reconciled with the use of obscenities? Beyond these questions, do not obscenities render speakers vulnerable to attacks on questions unrelated to the protest? Do not these become counterproductive politically and rhetorically?

But obscenities were only the most visible (or audible) trait exhibited. In fact, profanities were only a small part of a larger picture. Some protesters insisted on flaunting a new lifestyle. In so doing they extended the scope of protest beyond language to life, beyond politics to American culture. Some adopted hippie garb; others imitated the revolutionary dress of Castro or even American Revolutionary soldiers. Che Guevara and W. C. Fields became folk heroes. "Counter-culture" people ridiculed and then deserted the affluent, middle-class families from which they came. Many lived communally. Some among them advocated dropping dope and found Dr. Timothy Leary's call to "Tune in, turn on, and drop out" as significant as anything Karl Marx ever wrote. Each act seemed to backfire in the protest movements: each provided a powerful rhetorical aid to supporters of the war and created an embarrassment to opponents of the war.

These activities converged in the rhetoric and antics of the Youth International Party, the "Yippies." The Yippies added frivolity and jest—"put-ons"—that amazed, confounded, and angered both friends and foes. Observing their activities at the Democratic national convention in Chicago in 1968, at which time the Yippies nominated Pigasus for president and adopted the slogan: "Why take a half a hog when you can have the whole hog?" a bewildered Theodore H. White concluded that their nickname, "Crazies," aptly described them. He thought they were sad, naive people and that they appealed only to groups willing to exploit them: "The police; television; and those calculating organizers who can manipulate them as a skirmish line into the forefront of confrontation."[5] These sentiments, echoed by journalists and scholars, became the conventional wisdom about such protests. If the protesters' only source of power was public opinion, how are we to understand these acts that seem not only counter-productive but absurd as well?

They were absurd, but there was reason to such absurdities. In fact, a long tradition. To gain perspective we must hark back to the archetypal moral protesters of ancient Greece, the cynics, and to the distinctive rhetorical form they created, the diatribe. In so doing I intend to establish the following: (1) a long historical tradition lies behind these antics, a tradition informed by the cynical way of life; (2) the cynics created the diatribe, a unique rhetorical form that was a product of their intellectual and moral commitments, commitments that precluded traditional strategies for expression and protest; and (3) the Yippies were political heirs to that tradition, which they expressed during the late stages of the protests against the war.

At this point, I ask for the reader's patience. What follows is a long digression into the world of ancient Greece where the original cynics first flourished. Much time will be spent among them to understand Diogenes (their patron saint), the basic beliefs of cynics, the diatribe (their unique rhetorical form), and typical criticism of them by others. I take the reader on this digression for three reasons. It does provide a more enriched perspective on the third way of thinking and on the protest of the Yippies. Second, the original cynics were philosophic and therefore developed the ideas of cynicism more fully than their contemporary political counterparts, the Yippies. The contrast between Diogenes and Plato illuminates contemporary cynical contempt for idealism and ideology. Finally, the criticisms of the original cynics are examined because they represent critiques of this third way of thinking that have dogged them down through the ages. These criticisms are more accessible than contemporary critiques, even as they are the same charges that were made against Yippies. This excursion is necessary if we really want to understand cynicism and its modern heirs, the Yippies.

Diogenes: Patron Saint

Cynics began to appear in the fourth century in Athens but did not flourish as a sect until the second century. They were products of the Hellenistic age, "a time when old standards had been discarded, and the individual was left to the mercy of capricious but irresistible forces."[6] They were also a product of authorities' attempting to enforce a conformity to deal with these capricious forces of history.

Diogenes of Sinope (413–327) was the most renowned, although Hegisias of Sinope and Crates of Thebes also gained some repute. Hipparchia, the wife of Crates, became so famous for her adherence to the cynical way of life that she was nicknamed the "female philosopher," one of few women in antiquity to be accorded such respect. Despite the claim that Antisthenes, an eccentric and gentle Socratic, formed the cynical tradition and the fact that cynicism developed as a "school" two hundred years after the death of Diogenes, Diogenes became the most famous cynic, indeed, its patron saint.

Diogenes cut an unconventional swath throughout Athens. Apparently, he arrived there when he was well into his middle years. Legend has it that he went into exile from his native Sinope because his father counterfeited money, was caught, and disgraced his family. Another legend says Diogenes himself did it. For our purposes, a better story is that Diogenes consulted an oracle and was told that his purpose in life was to remint the currency. Taking the oracle's word literally rather than symbolically, that's what he did and was thus forced into exile when he got caught.[7] That was the turning point in his life. He had done what the oracle said and got punished for it. Little wonder Diogenes became bitter. If you can't trust an oracle, who can you trust?

But trust he did, except that thenceforth he began to interpret the oracle's statement metaphorically rather than literally. From that point on his sole aim in life would be to "remint the civic currency" on a much larger scale by revaluating all values. Gilbert Murray remarked that Diogenes "would deface all the coinage current in the world. Every conventional stamp was false. The men stamped as generals and kings; the things stamped as honour and wisdom and happiness and riches; all were base metal with lying superscription."[8]

Arriving in Athens, Diogenes attached himself to Antisthenes, the pupil of Socrates who took his master's teachings on virtue and simplicity explicitly. To this end, Antisthenes lived the simple life, indeed, a life indifferent to worldly cares, he being content to have one garment only, a staff to lean on, and a wallet (or beggar's bag, which became the sure symbol of the cynic). As Bertrand Russell remarked: "He believed in a 'return to nature,' and carried this belief very far. There was to be no government, no private property, no marriage, no established religion. He was not exactly an ascetic, but he despised luxury and all pursuit of artificial pleasure of the senses."[9] Supposedly, he even attacked the law of noncontradiction ("a thing cannot be itself and its opposite at the same time"), the foundation for Western thought. But he seems not to have explored this very modern idea with anything approaching thoroughness. He taught that ill repute and pain were often good things. But saying that he "taught" about such matters is misleading. He had little use for formal teaching or pupils. (After all, if one believes in the natural life, how can one "teach" except by example? Thus, when he believed virtue could be "taught," he meant this in a very much different sense than the sophists, who also believed virtue could be taught. Sophists taught by rules. Antisthenes and the cynics who followed "taught" by example.)[10] So, the old man relented and accepted Diogenes, little knowing perhaps that his pupil would turn his gentle teachings about simplicity and self-sufficiency into a wholesale, bitter attack on all conventional ways of living and thinking.

Diogenes was the first modern intellectual: a heroic antihero. In classical Athens he made a spectacle of himself. He walked barefoot in the snow, slept in abandoned jars and in the portals of the temple. He was known to have lighted a lamp in broad daylight, announcing "I am looking for a man."[11] Once he went into the theater after the festival had finished and upon meeting those coming out, stated: "This is what I practise doing all my life."[12] He ate whenever and wherever he felt like it. At one dinner people kept throwing bones to him as they would to a dog. So, Diogenes acted in that manner and urinated on them. Diogenes and his followers "never washed, never had their hair cut, wrapped themselves in rags and lived on alms like beggars."[13] They broke with society, lived as strangers under the protection of laws they despised, and offended fellow citizens by gross rudeness and shameless indecencies.

Diogenes sought freedom. A real and complete freedom. And he believed the only road to that freedom lay in absolute humanism; that is, as Diogenes Laertius related, he allowed "no such authority as he allowed to natural right, and [he asserted] that the manner of life he lived was the same as that of Heracles when he preferred liberty to everything."[14] Absolute freedom, personal absolute freedom was Diogenes' goal. And he found freedom not in civilized laws nor in abstract ideologies, but in nature, in the natural self, in the concrete experiences of living.[15] Diogenes made nature the standard for human conduct. And he carried this belief to logical extremes. When accused of acting lewdly by masturbating in public, he replied that he wished it "were as easy to banish hunger by rubbing the belly."[16] He even went to the point of using animals as models for behavior. It was said that he learned ways of adapting to whatever circumstances he faced by watching a mouse scurrying about "not looking for a place to lie down in, not afraid of the dark, not seeking any of the things which are considered to be dainties."[17] Adaptation to circumstances, to whatever life (which is natural) presented to him became a part of the practical preparation for cynical living. He believed that nothing could succeed without strenuous training, and one had to be fully trained to face and endure the hardships of life. This was doubly important for someone so eccentric as Diogenes, who not only spoke bluntly but lived in defiance of all social niceties. He was occasionally arrested, beaten, and even sold into slavery. For such a life, one needs to be hardy, or, as Diogenes once said, have a helmet. Little wonder that Cicero in his *De Officiis* noted: "A great many arguments to the same purpose are maintained by these [cynical] philosophers in the subversion of delicacy."

Diogenes was the real gadfly of Athens, much more so than Socrates, who spent his leisure time with young aristocrats whose values he so frequently reinforced. Diogenes attacked just about everyone. Once, upon seeing the officials of the temple leading a thief away, he observed: "The great thieves are leading away the little thief." He called an ignorant rich man a "sheep with the golden fleece." He chastised the orators of Athens for making a persistent fuss about justice without ever practicing it in their own lives.

But the one he took the most pleasure in irritating and ridiculing was Plato. Plato represented everything that Diogenes opposed: idealism, philosophic pride, intellectual speculation separated from practical living. At one time, he called Plato's lectures a waste of time. He heckled Plato and heaped comical scorn upon him. When Plato discoursed on his ideal forms such as "tablehood" and "cuphood," Diogenes replied: "Table and cup I see; but your tablehood and cuphood, Plato, I can no wise see."[18] When Plato defined man as an animal, biped and featherless, Diogenes plucked a chicken and brought it to Plato's lecture announcing: "Here is Plato's Man."[19] Indeed, he attacked all speculative reasoning. And he attacked not by engaging in speculative refutation, but by existential acts: "To one who by argument had proved conclusively that he had horns, [Diogenes] said, touching his forehead, 'Well, I for my part don't see any.' In like manner, when somebody declared that there is no such thing as motion, he got up and walked about. When some one was discoursing on celestial phenomena, 'How many days,' asked Diogenes, 'were you in coming from the sky?'"[20] The radical individualism, the practical reasoning for living—both caused Diogenes to attack and reject completely all speculative thought. He was the philosopher of living, not a theoretical speculator about Life. When asked who would bury him when he died, he replied, "Whoever wants the house."[21] Persistently, he attacked the hypocrisy of those who said one thing and then did the opposite. He had no faith in laws or rules to right wrongs. Being treated well or badly were natural conditions of life, and thus they were things to be endured or ridiculed rather than protested. Instead, he demanded that people right themselves before they proposed to right the ills of others.

But all of this was done with humor, a humor as often bitter as it was ironical, as we have seen. He apparently was in the habit of giving people the finger whenever he felt like it. He observed that the finger one chose to stick out made all the difference. People became mad, he said, when it was the middle finger. But when one stretched out the little finger, no one cared.

He called money the "mother-city of all evils." He recognized that to have to work to get money required a person to accept the rules of the workplace, which meant that one could not speak out freely nor act as one wished. And once one acquires money, one begins to acquire the amenities of life, which then become more important than life itself. One becomes a slave to one's acquisitions, hoarding them, protecting them, and always wanting more and more. Thus, one's freedom is severely restricted, as one becomes a slave to one's possessions. And the more one acquires, the more restrictions on freedom one accepts. (The song "Me and Bobby McGee" expresses Diogenes' view exactly: "Freedom's just another word for nothing left to lose.") Thus, Diogenes extolled poverty and took to begging. On one occasion he begged alms from a statue, which others thought was absurd. But Diogenes had a quite practical reason for doing so. When asked, he said he did it: "to get practice in being refused."[22]

Diogenes' cynicism was not what we think of today when we speak of someone's being cynical. Diogenes was a misanthropic idealist, and his cynicism was fiercely ethical. He demanded that people truly be themselves, and not what society said they should be. He saw all customs and conventions as falsifications of life requiring people to do unnatural things. Bertrand Russell observed that he "had an ardent passion for 'virtue,' in comparison with which he held worldly good of no account."[23] He was strict and uncompromising in that passion. He said of himself that he was like the trainer of choruses who set a note a little high to insure that the rest should hit the right note.

His eccentric way of living and speaking and his stringent commitment to virtue to the exclusion of all else led some (probably Plato) to call him a "Socrates gone mad." It is a charge that repeatedly has been made against cynics: madness, insanity. Diogenes sought to turn all of Athenian life upside down, and he attacked all that was considered speculative or sophistic, social or civilized. His radical individualism contrasted sharply with the delicate appointments of the comfortable life. His shamelessness horrified. His bluntness in all matters, his speaking the truth regardless of consequences, was not only unbecoming but shocking as well. His emphasis on the "self," the private person and private life, certainly was foreign to the decorous Athenians, who glorified public life and had little interest in or even an intellectual conception of a private "self."[24] Surely, his status as a metaphysical outlaw, a social misfit, a political outcast—all by his own choice—makes it understandable that some would believe him mad since Diogenes rejected all civic restraints and recognized only the restraints imposed by nature.

But Diogenes turned the charge of madness upon those who made it. He believed they were insane for living false lives, lives defined and controlled by society's conventions and customs. Such a life, Diogenes believed, falsified self and thus meant a life of madness. These are the true counterfeits, for the natural person is defaced, the natural person's thinking is corrupted, and the reality of life is distorted.

For all his eccentricities, Diogenes was honored and loved (at least when he wasn't urinating on someone, giving them the finger, or masturbating in public). His highest honor came from Alexander in their famous meeting when he searched out and found Diogenes sunning himself. Alexander introduced himself as Alexander the Great, to which Diogenes introduced himself as Diogenes the Dog. Alexander is supposed to have said that he so admired Diogenes that he told him that anything he wanted he could have. Diogenes' only request was that Alexander stand aside because he was casting a shadow over him and interfering with his sunbathing. Perhaps Alexander had never met anyone who did not ask for something from him. According to legend, he came away saying: "Had I not been Alexander, I should have liked to be Diogenes."[25] And Diogenes' fame spread internationally. During his triumphs in India, Alexander met wise men in Taxila who inquired after three wise men from Greece: Socrates, Pythagoras, and Diogenes.[26] When Diogenes died, Athenians raised a marble statue of a dog over his grave.

The dog was Diogenes' symbol, as it was to be for all cynics. But the dog he admired was the wandering, ownerless dog who went wherever he pleased.[27] When asked why people called him a dog, Diogenes answered: "I fawn on those who give me anything. I yelp at those who refuse, and I set my teeth in rascals."[28]

When Diogenes died, he had inaugurated a new way of thinking, and that way was called cynicism.

Cynicism: The Third Way

The cynics left no authoritative body of writings that explained or developed their philosophy in any systematic way. But from various stories about them, especially about Diogenes, and from the fragments they left we can piece together basic premises of their thought.

One can begin to understand any great body of thought by asking a simple question: Where do the thinkers believe Truth lies? Plato scorned finding it in people, saying that people lived lives governed by appearances, not truth. Thus, he devised his ideal forms, external to people, as the source of truth. Aristotle found truth in this world waiting to be discovered through observation and systematic categorization. Others have found truth in history, in particular social classes, in public opinion, in authoritative books (the Bible, for instance), and in a variety of other places.

Cynics share with Plato the belief that most people live lives of appearances and lies. But the cynics attributed that condition to the fact that people live by societal conventions that are life deforming and thought distorting. Cynics find truth in a radical individualism, in stripping away all conventions and living the natural life. Truth, then, is to be found in self, but a self freed from the restricting conventions of both the civic and civilized life.

Cynics took the admonition "Know thyself" literally and made it the self-sufficient source of truth. And if truth is the source for reality and morality, cynics created an extreme form of individuality to seek that truth which marked them off from all others of ancient times, with the exception of some Eastern Oriental thinkers. Equally important, if truth lies in each person, then there must be a multitude of truths, and many of these cynical truths inevitably will conflict with and contradict one another, while still being true: thus, the cynical attack on the law of noncontradiction and their acceptance of the intellectual contradictions of natural life.

Diogenes Laertius observed of the cynics: "They are content . . . to do away with the subjects of Logic and Physics and to devote their whole attention to Ethics."[29] For cynics, every question is an ethical question. Each problem, they contended, when stripped of its veneer of self-interest, reveals a fundamental moral issue. They sought absolute freedom, and they defined that freedom as freedom from societal conventions that counterfeit life. They sought absolute virtue, which they found not in rules or logic, but in being true to one's nature and in harmony with the natural essentials of life. To achieve these goals, they advocated living life on the minimum so as not to be distracted from the pursuit of virtue nor to be impeded by fear of losing one's possessions or status when speaking the truth. They were realists recognizing that their peculiar way of living would bring scorn upon themselves, and they took it with ironic, though often bitter, humor.

This moralistic posture pointed directly to a particular lifestyle. As Diogenes said, philosophy taught him to be prepared for every fortune. Thus, the cynical philosophy was not solely a search for truth, though indeed it was that, but also a preparation for living once that truth was found. Thought and action could not be separated.

These commitments begat a way of living that many found disturbing. Diogenes Laertius wrote: "They also hold that we should live frugally, eating food for nourishment only and wearing a single garment. Wealth and fame and high birth they despise. Some at all events are vegetarians and drink cold water only and are content with any kind of shelter or tub, like Diogenes, who used to say it was the privilege of gods to need nothing and of god-like men to want but little."[30] But such acts served symbolic purposes.

First, cynics took their beliefs out of the abstract and made them part of their lives. In this sense, they were the first existentialists. They did what they professed, especially when it came to money. They recognized that to earn money meant to accept conventional means for getting money and, beyond that, to adopt conventional modes of living to keep their money. According to Diogenes, any compromise with society is a compromise of ethics. To live by other people's conventions is to embrace the death of person, of self; to defy society and all its conventions is to embrace life and commit oneself to living. The choice is clear-cut. One can have no truck with customs regardless of the disguises they wear: laws, civil authority, political institutions, social mores. In taking this position, cynics divorced themselves from the normal flow of society by rejecting both the civic and the civilized life, even as they wandered freely within the city taking full advantage of the civil and civilized life. They made a clear distinction between humanity and society. The former is natural and truthful; the latter unnatural and corrupt. Thus, Farrand Sayre concluded: "Disregard of honor and reputation . . . was developed into open defiance of public opinion by shamelessness."[31]

Second, the cynics did not possess power and by all accounts did not seek political influence. They were cultural critics, not politicians. If anything, they were the original anarchists. But they were no defenders of the downtrodden, nor did they seek to redress any grievances the poor may have felt. Instead, they celebrated poverty as a condition necessary to achieve freedom. In fact, it appears that the cynics had little to do with the poor other than to "preach" their philosophy among them. (But why would they have much to do with such people? Cynics made their way by begging. And one begs from people who have money, not from the poor who by definition are indigent.)

Third, cynics were extremists. Crates earned his nickname, the "door-opener," through his habit of walking into any house and criticizing its inhabitants for their foolhardy ways. Crates and Hipparchia followed nature to the point of fornicating in public. Diogenes urinated on others and masturbated in public. He found no impropriety in stealing from the temple. To steal from the temple or another corrupt institution is to commit no crime, for society's institutions are immoral. Each of these acts had meaning to the cynics. Each was an attack on convention, especially that of privacy, and imitated the "dog" nature of complete honesty and shamelessness. Each act, moreover, was intended to shock sensibilities, to scandalize public opinion by profaning societal customs, to challenge what existential theologians describe as one's pre-understanding about how one should talk and respond to ideas and actions.[32] Furthermore, cynics argued that each act was natural: something everyone would do were he or she not inhibited by corrupt social customs, or something everyone would be able to do were conventional institutions replaced by the community of natural men and women.

Fourth, the cynics were the first to celebrate the universal brotherhood of humankind.[33] Living outside society, they contended they served a higher purpose—the human community, which knows no race, creed, or nationality. Thus, they renounced marriage (unless it was a matter of free agreement between consenting adults), parental rights to children, and citizenship. The natural community of humankind transcends these ethereal concerns. They were cosmopolitan, usually solitary wandering preachers proclaiming the falsity of all conventional life and proclaiming the freedom to be found in the being natural. Their lifestyles represented an alternative way of living that others—depressed by the compromises that politics and politeness demand—could embrace as an escape from the repression of society to the freedom of cynicism. Conversely, cynics established counterconventions, sometimes as rigid as those they denounced, that functioned as a protest against society's norms.

Dedicating their lives to virtue, they cultivated their own particular set of virtues: ruggedness, apathy, indifference, endurance, idleness, poverty, contempt for the opinions of others. To the conventional mind, such attitudes represent a socially useless and indolent human being. Seen through the lens of socially conforming beliefs, these "virtues" are the very vices that children are taught to avoid. But that is exactly the cynical point! Each of these attitudes has the virtue of sustaining the cynical life among people who are overwhelmingly conventional. One has to be rugged to suffer the slings and arrows of outraged public opinion. One has to be apathetic to overcome the social conditioning (that all are subjected to from childhood on) that demands everyone be a productive member of society. One has to learn indifference to be able to suffer the denunciations others will heap upon the cynic. Idleness is a prerequisite to being able to live with oneself, for most people work to avoid having to see themselves as they are. Contempt for the opinions of others is the occupational hazard of philosophers. Every philosopher has contempt (or pity) for those who do not share that philosophy, and cynics are no exception. The only difference is that some philosophers are more adroit at concealing that contempt. But as in all other matters, cynics concealed little and took their contempt to the extreme.

The cynics were critics of conventions, gadflies of culture, censors of people who separated their beliefs from their actions. Moralistic to the point of misanthropy, they gave expediency little place in their body of thought. Every action, they believed, should be guided by moral principles founded upon a belief in absolute humanism. Most people make distinctions between moral problems and political problems, between professional responsibilities and personal commitments, between the demands of truth and the demands of politeness, between morals and mores. Cynics denied, even condemned these distinctions as artificial, as products of societal conditioning that had corrupted people's minds and sense of reality. The cynics would not admit that any institution had any legitimate authority unless it was based on natural rights.

When stripped of their more bizarre actions, the cynics were distinctively modern. They were the original romantics believing as they did in the noble savage, but they were not as naive as the romantics in believing the noble savage was inherently good. Only natural. They were the original anarchists, but in modern times they would probably have felt more at home with the singing Wobblies than with the more philosophic and serious anarchist thinkers such as Proudhon. In fact, they surely would have ridiculed his attempts at liberation of the poor and powerless. After all, they prided themselves on being practical. The virtues they cultivated bear a remarkable resemblance to those endorsed by early Christians and even some of the more fundamentalist modern Christians. The difference between the two, however, lies in the fact that Christians believed that observing such pieties would lead them to salvation, whereas the cynics believed they were necessary to survive on this earth.[34]

The roots for existentialism, for part of the joyful wisdom of Nietzsche, and for the argument, structure, and style of Dostoyevsky's *Notes from the Underground* can be traced back to cynicism. In sum, this long neglected band of holy barbarians represents a distinct intellectual tradition in contradistinction to idealism and ideology.[35]

The Diatribe: Rhetorical Form of the Cynics

The cynics' moralistic posture led to a dilemma. If society is a priori immoral, how are cynics to live within it without compromising themselves? Conversely, if cynical truth is important, does it not deserve to be shared with others? The answers to these questions led to two distinct rhetorical postures.

One could decide that the only thing to do in an immoral society was to withdraw into private contemplation, neither to accept nor to ask anything from others and thereby preserve one's personal purity. The rhetorical import of silence and withdrawal is obvious. They are symbolic acts; both affirm and legitimize private commitments, thus enhancing the ethos of the cynic. Moreover, few can resist the curiosity to ask why one has withdrawn and why one remains silent. To ask these questions sincerely is to suspend habitual presuppositions about cynics and thereby to establish a new common ground the cynics can use to voice their criticisms of society. However, withdrawal would be very uncharacteristic of Greeks, who saw themselves as a part of society, even if they condemned the society in which they lived.

Cynics did not withdraw, and they decidedly were not silent. Some wrote satires, thus retreating into the literary life. Others sought civic salvation by wandering about delivering diatribes to whomever would listen. When asked what was the greatest freedom, Diogenes unhesitatingly replied: "Freedom of speech." Unlike professional speakers, however, cynics did not aim at persuasion by traditional means. Audiences would have to experience the totality of their wrongs, much as contemporary existentialists believe people will not realize their condition until they have experienced existential shock. Thus, cynics sought to dramatize their criticism of society through the diatribe, an extemporaneous sermon often filled with invective. The goal was the popular presentation of their practical philosophy. Its invention, as all invention is, was based on themes drawn from their own beliefs: The ancient Greek diatribe

is a monologue, usually in verse, but often also in prose or in prose mingled with verse, which is informal and is apparently improvised. It appears to be perfectly spontaneous and to have no set logical structure, but to spring from a momentary impulse, a casual occurrence, a passing remark. It is marked by constant variety of tone and shifts of subject-matter, and it is enlivened by wit, humor, parody, paradox, word-play, and other decorations. It is of course non-fictional, non-narrative. It deals with a theme of general interest, but it illustrates its subject by personal references, topical allusions, and character-sketches, and it introduces fiction in the form of anecdotes and fables.[36]

Highet goes on to remark that its tone was improvisational and generally inappropriate to the gravity of its subject. Frequently, the cynic's diatribe was flippant, ironic, shocking, sarcastic, and often filled with bitter humor and ridicule. The most serious subject was treated with sarcastic flippancy, the lighter subjects with a grave ironic humor.

The diatribe is the rhetorical version of the philosophic dialogue; much the same way a conventional speech is a rhetorical version of a philosophic disquisition.[37] It is an attempt to criticize, to entertain, to present cynical themes and apply them to real life, to shock, and to convey bitterly humorous impressions of public figures, all in one.

But the diatribe is to the conventional speech what Alice's adventures in Wonderland are to conventional life. Logic is inverted; assumptions are reversed; the unexpected becomes expected. It demands more creativity from the speaker than any other form of rhetoric. Most speeches are intended to persuade by drawing upon the beliefs of the audience as resources for proofs. The speaker tries to appeal to reason, emotion, conventional beliefs or attitudes, or conscience by not offending traditional beliefs or feelings. Speakers attempt to establish their ethos by reflecting the ethos of the audience. In other words and in one way or another, speakers seek identification with their constituencies.

Cynics rejected these strategies as compromises with an immoral society. People's consciences, their logic and emotions, their perspectives and attitudes have all been corrupted by immoral and unreal institutions. Thus, to reflect the ethos of society is to reflect civic corruption. The cynic must attack, criticize, ridicule the very corruption that lies deep in the body of the sick commonwealth. To this end, cynics attack the basic societal values to which conventional speakers would customarily appeal. The diatribe, then, is absurdist moral dramaturgy intended to assault sensibilities, to turn thought upside down, to turn social mores inside out, to commit in language the very barbarisms one condemns in society.[38] But the cynics did not attempt to persuade in the sense that we usually think of persuasion of others. The only persuasion cynics believed in was self-persuasion, with perhaps the cynic showing the way by example.

An important purpose of the diatribe is shock, which serves two purposes. First, it gathers an audience when orthodox speeches will not. Diogenes Laertius recorded the following incident: "When one day he [Diogenes] was gravely discoursing and nobody attended to him, he began whistling, and as people clustered about him, he reproached them with coming in all seriousness to hear nonsense, but slowly and contemptuously when the theme was serious."[39] Whistling was unusual, unexpected, logically meaningless. Given the Greeks' sense of decorum, it might have been considered shocking. Yet, whistling served a rhetorical purpose. The inventive ways the cynics used to gain an audience would remain throughout the centuries a controversial part of their dissemination of their beliefs.

Beyond attracting attention, shock also functions as the first step toward rearranging perspectives. People seldom become concerned about problems until they are shocked. Shock may lead to self-examination. The diatribe is intended to produce shock by satirizing fundamental values and expectations and by dramatizing the chasm that exists between ideals and practices, between language and actions, between principles and actualities, between using words and meaning them. By bizarre uses of language (but bizarre only by conventional standards of the use of language) and through symbolic, offensive acts, cynics challenged the traditional form of rhetorical and cultural transactions, ridiculed basic values, and created a new form of rhetoric.

Through the diatribe cynics parodied the rhetorical situation. The themes they treated were personal freedom, personal courage, personal endurance—all to be found in the natural life. These are indeed dignified topics. Yet the cynics' style, marked by obscenity and slang, was far from dignified. Instead of reflecting the ethos of an audience, cynics scorned or laughed at it by dressing as they did, by acting as they did, by speaking as they did.

Opposed to conventional morality, cynics proposed a counter-morality. Issues should be argued in terms of how they would promote freedom, regardless of political or economic consequences. What contributes to greater freedom from society's restrictions is good; what reinforces societal conventions or institutions is evil. The natural right of a person to live a natural life without interference from society forms the basis for this morality.

The diatribe is to rhetoric what satire is to literature.[40] Each attempts to reduce conventional beliefs to the ridiculous, thereby making those who support orthodoxy seem contemptible, hypocritical, or stupid. Each seeks laughter, but not for its own sake. The laughter of the cynic is a bitter laughter, an uncomfortable laughter, the uneasy laughter of one who is seeing a frightful truth or a different reality, but presented in flippant or comic form.[41] Laughter is spontaneous, sometimes the spontaneous recognition of a unique truth. Furthermore, cynics recognized that comedy often forces one to think, and sometimes the result of serious thinking must be relieved by laughter, or else one may dissolve into tears. Cynical laughter is intended to serve as a cleansing force to purge preconceptions about ideas, to provide spontaneous insights, to deflate pomposity, to challenge conventional assumptions, to confront the human consequences of ideas and policies, to ridicule the "business as usual" mentality. Exaggeration, parody, puns, incongruity, and burlesque typify both diatribe and satire. If the listener is to respond appropriately, the listener must realize what the cynic or satirist *intends*. One does not take Swift's *A Modest Proposal* literally. One has to rearrange one's expectations and the way one reads the *Proposal* to recognize the bitter despair that Swift feels over the starvation in Ireland. So, too, to appreciate diatribe, one has to rearrange one's expectations and perspectives. But both these forms create problems since the *text* does not reveal—and sometimes does not even give any explicit clues to—the sincerity of the author. And sincerity is important if one is to believe another. What one says about the *Proposal* is: "Oh, he couldn't *really* mean that." Thus, one uses other standards external of the text to understand the intent and meaning of the satire (diatribe). Add to this abdication of an explicit serious intent, the bitterly comic spirit of both satire and diatribe, and the naive listener or reader has difficulty in knowing how to respond, other than to be offended by the grossness or exhibitionism of the cynic.

But the diatribe is a rhetorical genre distinct from satire. Satirists do not have to act or provide symbolic proofs for what they believe. They are literary artists, and their writings are sufficient in themselves. Cynics—as practical philosophers—must act to legitimize their diatribes. Thus, preposterous acts become part of the legitimizing process for this rhetoric, proof positive the cynics mean what they say. These acts also leave them open to ad hominem charges, logically irrelevant to the issues at hand, but rhetorically potent in destroying the cynic's ethos.

The greatest weakness of the diatribe is that its effectiveness is limited. What if shock leads to repulsion rather than self-examination? To this the cynic has no answer, and indifference becomes a virtue (or rationalization) for the cynic to react to such responses. Moreover, once attention has been gained and criticism voiced, the usefulness of the diatribe diminishes. People demand serious remedies seriously treated. Moral dramaturgy must eventually give way to a conventional rhetorical form of serious reforms. Of course, cynics reply that people will never really listen to them and give up their comfortable conventional ways of living, and therefore there will always be a time and place for cynics with their bitter, spontaneous, laughing diatribes.

Criticism of the Cynics

Critics have dealt harshly with cynics. Two leading criticisms have been raised, which W. W. Tarn summarizes: "It [cynicism] was not a philosophy, like those of the four schools with a body of doctrine; it was a way of life, a mode of thought, and was entirely negative; you were to discard everything on which civilization had been built up, and often enough, unless you were a Crates or a Demona, you ended by finding nothing at the bottom but mere animalism. It never *constructed* anything, anything which affected men otherwise than as individuals."[42]

These criticisms have merit but miss the point. If cynicism is not a philosophy because it does not have a "body of doctrine," then the pre-Socratics—especially Heraclitus—must be banished from the canons of philosophic inquiry for the same reason. Defending themselves, cynics would reply that to judge them by conventional standards is to admit that one is so bound up in conventions that one cannot entertain new ideas or possibilities.

To say cynics are totally negative is to echo a charge made against them throughout the centuries. True, the main thrust is negative, a misanthropic criticism of customs. But for cynics this assault is essential if people are ever to see how much their lives are controlled by society's mores, ever to see how unauthentic their lives are because they are defined by attitudes and standards coming from others, not themselves. Cynics would contend that each criticism they make is intended to lead to personal freedom. That cynics treat people only as individuals, they would claim, is no fault, for that is precisely how people ought to be treated. "Physician, heal thyself!"

Cynics, as critics or protesters, believe it futile to attempt to change policies or systems. They seek to change people, to expose the falseness of their individual lives. They attack, but they propose no new rules of conduct other than to be one's natural self.

Finally, it is charged that it is not a philosophy but a way of life. That's an interesting charge, and it is true in part. Cynicism does require certain ways of living. But does such a charge, which has been leveled against cynics since the time of Plato, mean that philosophy and ways of living must be separated? Does it mean philosophy has nothing to do with ways of living? Does philosophy then separate thinking from living? The cynic would say that is most certainly true of the ways in which most philosophies function: a sterile eristic unrelated to the practical problems of life. After all, what democrat—not to mention what poet—after reading Plato's *Republic* would ever want Plato to rule or even advise a ruler? Then, the cynic asks: Of what use is Plato's *Republic* except as an idle eristic? After all, what modern cynic after reading Marx and Engels and seeing the Soviet state would ever want Marx or his descendants to rule him? Then, the modern cynic asks: Of what use is ideology except to replace one form of oppression with another form of oppression?

What are we to say about cynicism? Tarn is essentially correct when he says it is a way of life. It is a rhetorical anti-rhetorical movement, a standing protest qua protest against the hypocrisy and corruption that attends civic life. The diatribe, limited though it may be, is intended to illuminate and to purge corruption when other methods fail. Cynicism is the lifestyle of outsiders who choose to alienate themselves from societal life and who discover a morality in personal experience to replace that founded on metaphysics. The diatribe contains many elements found in fundamentalist Christian sermons,[43] though the diatribe promises freedom in this life, not salvation in the next life. Cynics oppose the compartmentalization of life into neat pigeonholes that allow people to act one way on one occasion and a contradictory way on another, all the while pompously insisting that they firmly believe in some higher, consistent principles. Instead, cynics celebrate the unity of life. We live, they proclaim, in a universe, not a multiverse. Thought, language, and action are intimately related. Without language there is no thought. And language conditions thought. Each is empty of real content if people do not act upon what they believe.

But always there is laughter. The gentle laughter that comes from continued observation of the follies of humankind; the bitter laughter of free spirits who find themselves enslaved by society's conventions; the witty laughter intended to puncture hypocrisy and pomposity; the paradoxical laughter of turning language and life upside down just for the hell of it. In this sense, cynics were the first existentialists, more in the mold, however, of Ionesco than Sartre or Camus.

Roots of a Modern Cynicism

Donald R. Dudley concluded his book on cynics and cynicism in 1937 by suggesting that we shall probably never see their kind again. His judgment was premature. The tradition was resurrected by the Beat Generation of the 1950s with Jack Kerouac's novel *On the Road* and Allen Ginsberg's great cynical dog-poem, "Howl." At about the same time in England, John Osborne created a modern cynical anti-hero in Jimmy Porter in his play *Look Back in Anger*, while in Ireland J. P. Donleavy was creating still another rollicking cynical hero in the form of Sebastian Dangerfield in his novel *The Ginger Man*. With his unique and usually crisp poems, Richard Brautigan resurrected the gentle cynical spirit of Saroyan. Lenny Bruce turned his unique vision of contemporary life into cynical humor (in contrast with Mort Sahl, who was the more conventional satirist). In the 1960s Ken Kesey and the Merry Pranksters transformed the prevailing cynicism from solitary literary acts into group ridicule of prevailing culture. Eventually, Jerry Rubin and Abbie Hoffman created the Yippies, their attempt at a political form of cynicism.

We have spent so much time preparing the intellectual background for the modern cynics because the cynical tradition is so different from other intellectual traditions, and because its criticism of others and the criticism it brought upon itself was repeated—in different terms—in the protests of the 1960s. Since we have spent so much time on this tradition, perhaps we should review how protests had developed and where they stood when the Yippies emerged. The war in Vietnam proved the crucible for renewal of the cynical tradition. Young people's opposition to the war was not merely intellectual; it was painfully real and urgent. At the outset of the anti-war movement protesters relied on traditional forms of protest: speeches, essays, peaceful demonstrations. These failed to change policies as quickly as protesters wanted. The war grew, and they grew weary of traditional form.

In the eyes of many young people, Joseph Heller's *Catch 22* had become a terrifying reality. Even as President Johnson approved of dissent, he also denounced dissenters as "Nervous Nellies" and accused them of speaking from paranoid frustrations and even cowardice. Protesters could say they objected to the war on moral grounds, only to learn that this would not protect them from the draft. Some sought refuge in the Nuremberg principles, that private people have a responsibility to act against governments that violate political morality. But the refuge was hardly a sanctuary. The very government that sanctioned that principle—indeed, enforced it at the Nazi trials—was the very same government that would jail protesters for acting against its policies in Vietnam. According to many protesters, each of these acts added up to a consuming hypocrisy in American life. The ground was fertile for the emergence of cynicism. And recognition of this corruption led some to a realization that new rhetorical strategies would have to be developed. To do so, they had to understand why they had failed when they had protested through conventional channels using conventional means.

First, language. The administration had attempted to placate people into supporting the war by using a Newspeak that turned people into "personnel," horrible deaths into weekly statistics, defeats into victories, and a repressive military dictatorship into a democratic government in power through "free elections." Each concrete event—whether favorable or unfavorable to the U.S. government—was transformed into an example that proved an abstract principle, belief, or assumption of the prevailing anticommunist ideology, an ideology that blinded most decision makers to the concrete actualities of the Vietnam war. The existential theory of objectification certainly found verification in this administrative rhetoric.

The original protesters used the prevailing language of American politics and seemingly (to them) lost their cause. Jerry Rubin described their problem in a speech in Cincinnati, Ohio: "When they control the words, they control everything, and they got the words controlled. They got 'war' meaning 'peace'; they got 'fuck' being a 'bad word' they got 'napalm' being a good word—they got 'decency' that to me is indecent. The whole thing is like backwards, and we gotta turn it around."[44] A new language had to be created to express new ideas, new perspectives, new attitudes. But what language?

They realized that their second mistake lay in their idealistic belief that reasoned, academic discourse in the tradition of pragmatic liberalism would be respected and would change Johnson's Vietnam policy. Instead, the administration deserted pragmatic language about Vietnam and resorted to the administrative rhetoric of anticommunism to justify its policies. Furthermore, a liberal president ignored arguments against the war even as he patronized dissent, a doubly cruel blow. Finally, the teach-ins and peaceful demonstrations lost force as they became commonplace. Protesters realized that new forums and new forms would have to be created if the momentum of the antiwar movement was to be sustained. But what new forums and what new forms? And how should they be created?

Providing answers to these questions led to divisions within the antiwar movement. Most continued traditional methods for protest and began looking toward the 1968 election as a means for ending American participation in the war by changing leaders. These people treated the war in Vietnam as a policy to be reversed, even as they admitted greater issues were involved, by using convenional resources of political and rhetorical protest.

Ideologues viewed the war as an illustration of a higher principle, a symptom of a disease in the body politic. But they disagreed among themselves about the diagnosis that should be drawn from the symptoms, and what treatment should be prescribed for the patient. Thus, some became pacifists opposed to all wars; others embraced Marxism or Maoism as an alternative to capitalistic welfare-statism; some joined the Weatherpeople and went underground in hopes of overthrowing the American government; still others formed the Yippies. Frequently, they fought among one another as vigorously as they fought with supporters of the war.[45]

Yippies as Cynics

Yippies rejected the procedural protests that conventional people used. Yippies also rejected the ideological solutions to American problems that Marxists, anarchists, Weatherpeople, and others advocated. They based their beliefs on absolute individualism: "There are no ideological requirements to be a yippie. Write your own slogan. Protest your own issue. Each man his own yippie."[46] Using the cynical technique of imagining an interview between a straight journalist and himself, Abbie Hoffman addressed the issue of ideology:

[Q] Do you have an ideology?
[A] No. Ideology is a brain disease.
[Q] Do you have a movement?
[A] Yes, it's called dancing.
[Q] Isn't that a put-on?
[A] No.
[Q] Can you explain that?
[A] Suppose we start the questions again.
[Q] OK. Do you have an ideology?
[A] We are for peace, equal rights, and brotherhood.
[Q] Now I understand.
[A] I don't. That was a put-on. I don't understand what I said.
[Q] I'm getting confused.
[A] Well, let's go on.
[Q] Are you for anything? Do you have a vision of this new society you talk of?
[A] Yes. We are for a free society.
[Q] Could you spell that out?
[A] F-R-E-E.[47]

This radical individualism marked the Yippies as a unique faction within the antiwar movement. Yet, they did hold a loosely knit set of beliefs that falls into the tradition of cynicism.

Yippies contended that people are not free because they have been conditioned and defiled by corrupt institutions. As Jerry Rubin said; "We are not protesting 'issues': we are protesting Western civilization."[48] People who believe in these institutions, according to the Yippies, initiate and perpetuate wars, racism, and oppression through conventions they have established. Yippies sought freedom from oppressive conventions and societal restrictions. "Free is the essence of Yippie!"[49] Like the cynics of Greece, they cherished personal freedom. Unlike other factions within the peace coalition that sought to transform institutions to fit ideological concerns, Yippies sought to do away with institutions altogether.

Furthermore, unlike some militants who resorted to violence, Yippies generally relied on ridicule and "put-ons." The hearings of the House Committee on Un-American Activities in 1966 are instructive. Some protesters denounced the hearings as invasions of their privacy and refused to testify on constitutional grounds. More radical members denounced the hearings as fascist and condemned the committee's star "friendly witness," Phillip Abbot Luce, as a "fink." (Luce had formerly been a leading figure in the Progressive Labor Party, had organized trips to Cuba to help with the sugar harvest, and had at one time toured the country denouncing HUAC. The cancellation of his scheduled appearance at Ohio State University in 1962 led to the Free Speech Protest at that university. But he had switched sides and become a reactionary right-winger who testified at committee hearings.) But such protests were not the way of Yippies and especially not Jerry Rubin. He showed up wearing an American Revolutionary War uniform complete from the three-cornered hat down to the buckled shoes. And he demanded to testify. So much so that when the hearings were called off before his testimony, he had to be ushered from the room to *keep* him from testifying. (At a subsequent HUAC hearing, Rubin showed up wearing a bright red Santa Claus suit.)

At the great march on the Pentagon the Yippies joined devout worshippers in chanting Hari Krishna and intoned sustained sounds of "Ommmmmmmmmmmmmm" as attempts to exorcise the evil "vibrations" arising from the military establishment. Rubin was eventually arrested at this march for urinating on a Pentagon wall: "It satisfied an immediate need and made a profound moral statement," Rubin wrote. "I demanded they charge me with 'urinating on the Pentagon,' a political-sexual crime. Instead they booked me for 'loitering,' and I got 30 days in jail."[50]

Yippies mounted a full-scale attack on the "mother-city of all evil"—money. "Money is a drug. Amerika is a drug culture, a nation of crazy addicts," Rubin observed. Echoing the cynics, he stated: "All money represents theft. To steal from the rich is a sacred and religious act."[51] On August 24, 1967, Rubin and Hoffman went to the balcony of the New York Stock Exchange and began to throw dollar bills over the ledge as an attempt to "introduce a little reality into their fantasy lives."[52] (This is not as silly as it sounds when one thinks about it. What Rubin and Hoffman were throwing was real money to people who deal in paper exchanges of monetary value that can change from day to day, depending on fluctuations within the market. When one billionaire was told after the October 1987 stock market crash that he had lost millions, he shrugged it off, saying it was all on paper—both the value and the loss.) Yippies also burned money at a socialist meeting, only to learn that the socialists were as outraged as the capitalists of Wall Street over their action. "How can you burn money when poor people in the ghetto need it?" the socialists cried.

Yippies rejected the work ethic and advocated "ripping off" conventional institutions. People should be freed from the drudgery of work so they can celebrate life, be creative, and enjoy sex. In their eyes each of these activities is a natural function that has been suppressed by corrupt customs, especially the obsession with money. Thus, public sexual acts serve as political-rhetorical metaphors signaling liberation from conventions even as they protest conventions. Underlying these acts is a firm belief that although sex is natural and creative, war and money-grubbing are unnatural and destructive. To commit public sexual acts is to attempt to shock people into recognizing that the very same customs that suppress sex also sustain wars and exploitation. Until those customs are discarded and the institutions that perpetuate them are destroyed, people will continue to feel guilty about sex and proud to make wars.

Mixed with these general beliefs were specific political demands: disarmament, an immediate end to the war in Vietnam, community control, and so on. These were the Yippies' concession to the protests of the 1960s and marked them off somewhat from the original cynics. But in typical cynical fashion they also included a plank advocating the "abolition of all money" and a blank line (No. 18) so that one could fill in anything one wanted to add to the manifesto.[53] This grab-bag of cultural criticism, political demands, and ridiculous antics led to attacks on Yippies from all sides. The left denounced them as acid-heads, freaks, and hippies who were diverting energies from the revolution. Hippies denounced them as Marxists in disguise who used rock music, dope, and psychedelics to seduce "flower people" into political action.[54] In fact, both were right and both were mistaken.

Yippies were the heirs of cynicism, which they transformed into a rhetorical movement intended to ridicule civic life in America. They sought to change perspectives rather than impose ideologies on people. "Yippies believe there can be no social revolution without a head revolution and no head revolution without a social revolution."[55]

The Diatribes of the Yippies

Jerry Rubin's book *Do It!* provides an excellent example of modern cynical rhetoric. Rubin not only indulges in diatribes, he also comments on the purposes of his strategies. The theme of the book is the need to liberate people from oppressive institutions. Therefore, Rubin ridicules both traditional politics and the ideological politics of the right and the new left as mirror images of one another. Each still supports political institutions. They just disagree about what the content and form of those institutions ought to be. Thus, one chapter is entitled "George Wallace is Bobby Kennedy in Drag." But their chief charge against all other political people was that they are boring: "The Left drives people away almost as fast as Nixon drives people toward us. Ideological hassles on theoretical bullshit, boring meetings—is this the life of a revolutionary?"[56] The same charge is leveled against traditional peace protesters. In fact, they treat all opponents with comical disregard. Instead of condemning President Johnson as a source of secular evil among the power elite of America (as ideologues did) or treating him with some respect in hopes that he would change his policies (as procedural protesters did), Rubin called Johnson the "creeping meatball" and coined the slogan "Rise up and abandon the creeping meatball."[57] Of course, he meant more than LBJ. Everyone who is not a Yippie is a "creeping meatball."

Do It! is loosely strung together, as the author jumps from topic to topic recounting his life and the evils of society. It is filled with devices traditionally used in diatribes to evoke laughter, repulsion, and, oddly enough for the conventional mind, reflection. However, the hallmark of this rhetoric is obscenity and lewdness. Photographs of nudes present natural man or woman (or both) to the reader. Profanities are repeated page after page. These serve to undermine any language of good manners or polite forms by making public that which previously had been confined to locker rooms. They are used to shock. Rubin states that the "more people you alienate, the more people you reach. If you don't alienate people, you're not reaching them."[58] In a subsequent book Rubin wrote: "A speech is a public celebration. We live together on the streets. A speech is not an exchange of information—it is an emotional event with everyone touching each other. It is a revival meeting. We are charged emotionally. The speaker tries to get the audience to react. A good speaker polarizes, forcing the white racists to expose their racism, the liberals to squirm nervously and the liberated to start dancing."[59]

Beyond the need to shock, Yippies used obscenities to mark the hypocrisy of society, a hypocrisy symbolized by those who support the war without pangs of conscience but who, were they to see a person walk nude through the streets, would rise up in moral indignation. By shouting and writing profanities, Yippies named the war "The Great Obscenity" and thus waved the bloody shirt of misplaced values in the faces of business-as-usual Americans, classes-as-usual academics.

Symbolic Acts

The diatribe cannot be considered apart from the antics of the Yippies, for each is a part of the rhetorical process. Here a distinction must be made between those in government and those outside. If a people in power are to confirm their rhetoric, they must enact policies that are reasonably consistent with positions they have taken. Otherwise, their credibility may be questioned. People out of power must invent symbolic acts that confirm their beliefs, or they are open to the charge of hypocrisy. For example, Rubin disparaged radicals for this: "The ideological left is made up of part-time people whose lifestyle mocks their rhetoric. There's a thousand miles between their actions and their ideology. How can you be a revolutionary going to school during the day and attending meetings at night?"[60] Thus, the antics of the Yippies were not only symbolic protests, but also symbolic confirmations of their ideas that enhance ethos among their supporters even as they repel their opponents.

Refusing to live within conventional society, Yippies adopted unconventional dress—Indian costumes, Revolutionary War uniforms, Santa Claus suits—as marks of identification for their movement and as means of attracting coverage by the media. Media was essential to the Yippies: "You can't be a revolutionary today without a television set—it's as important as a gun."[61] Rubin and Hoffman dressed in court justice robes and challenged Attorney General John Mitchell to a boxing match to settle their legal issues man-to-man. They wore their hair long and sometimes took off their clothes in public. Rubin summarized the intention of these acts: "We're living

TV commercials for the revolution. We're walking picket signs. Every response to long-hairs creates a moral crisis for straights. We force adults to bring all their repressions to the surface, to expose their real feelings."[62] To produce this "moral crisis" they profaned traditional symbols that the majority considered sacred. They attempted to arouse emotions by forcing the public to experience secular (and in some cases, religious) sacrilege.

Desecration of the American flag and waving the Viet Cong flag became the leading symbolic acts in this process.[63] Tom Wolfe had Ken Kesey, a novelist and cynic, explain the rhetorical purposes of desecrating traditional symbols (Kesey seizes an American flag and grinds his foot on it): "[D]on't just describe an emotion, but arouse it, make them experience it, by manipulating the symbol of the emotion, and sometimes we have to come into awareness through the back door."[64] Much of the rhetoric of the cynics and Yippies is an attempt to rebuild the house of society by stealing in through the back door. These absurd acts—sexual and otherwise—were attempts to manipulate symbols by repudiating and profaning their traditional, conventional meanings, thus producing horror among people who have never examined their reasons for responding as they had toward these symbols. This strategy culminates in the cynical tradition of the wonderland "politics of experience." Don't argue about corrupt ideas, ridicule them. Don't placate degenerate emotions; provoke them, bring them to the surface. Don't merely criticize society, create a countersociety of radically different individuals. Recognize the truth of Dostoyevsky's observation: "the whole work of man really seems to consist in nothing but proving to himself every minute that he is a man and not a piano key."[65] Do It!

Effects

The effects of the diatribe are mixed. Even as Yippies assaulted traditional myths, they created myths about themselves that did not attract a wide following.

The bizarre antics of Yippies gained them a forum on television out of all proportion to their actual numbers or influence. Jerry Rubin and Abbie Hoffman became instant electronic celebrities, and their inventiveness in discovering new means for getting public and television attention set the highest standards for all other protesters. Yet, when they used profanities or carried symbolic acts too far, they lost access to media. The pubic in general did not react positively to them. Though no survey was taken to ascertain the public's response to Yippies, in particular, there were studies of reactions to "protesters" at the time. In 1968 the Survey Research Center of the University of Michigan found that nearly 75 percent of the people reacted negatively to protesters. Among those who favored complete withdrawal from Vietnam, as many as 53 percent reacted negatively.[66] We can assume with some degree of safety that the percentages would have been higher in reaction to Yippies.

On the other hand, the Yippies and other extreme groups among the antiwar movement contributed to making respectable the political critics of the war who worked within the system. In contrast to the popular images of the obscenity-shouting Yippies and the bomb-hurling Weatherpeople, Senators Fulbright, Kennedy, Church, and McGovern seemed models of responsible criticism. Just as Stokely Carmichael legitimized the moderate, nonviolent posture of Martin Luther King, Jr., so, too, the violent acts of the Weatherpeople and the absurd acts of the Yippies contributed to the acceptance of traditional criticism of the war and enhanced the ethos of those critics who held positions of power or remained within the traditional mainstream of protest.

Conclusion

The rhetorical mood of the Vietnam war was frenzied and fervent. Unlike World Wars I and II, the Vietnam war seemed not to have been fought for a higher, moral purpose. Critics did not believe that it would "make the world safe for democracy" or preserve the "arsenal of democracy," certainly not in South Vietnam. Critics saw it as a dirty war fought for obscure purposes, at best, or evil ends, at worst. In opposing the war they had, as Thomas Mann once observed, two choices: to take a position that is either ironic or radical.

Yippies chose an extreme form of irony, the diatribe. They revived, probably unknowingly, the cynical tradition of protesting a war and a society that supported that war. In doing so, they alienated from their cause as many, if not more, than they drew to it.

Yippies rejected the civic society and did everything within their power to identify themselves as outcasts—metaphysical, linguistic, comical outcasts. They took a stance that was purely critical. Few were immune from their satirical criticism. It was frolicking criticism that was their compass and guide. They offered few programmatic solutions, no policy solutions, no ideological solutions. They merely said people should be free.

And always there was laughter, the ridiculous and sometimes bitter laughter of the cynic. They contended they really joined the "revolution" because that's where the fun was, and they meant to have fun. But beneath the veneer of fun was the motive to cause change: to end the war, to eradicate discrimination, to create a society in which people can be free. However, in their calls for an end to poverty in America, they betrayed an optimism more American than cynical.

11

Postscript to a Decade

In his 1955 book *The Liberal Tradition in America*, Louis Hartz concluded that "the age of purely domestic crisis apparently is over."[1] At the midpoint of that decade such a conclusion probably seemed secure. A Republican had been elected president, but he had not overturned the New Deal. Instead, Eisenhower had further institutionalized it by accepting rather than rejecting it. By 1955 the scourge of McCarthyism was on its way out after the Army-McCarthy hearings. The Supreme Court had ruled that segregated schools were unconstitutional and had mandated an orderly transition to integrated schools. The economy was strong, and America was not at war. Little wonder Hartz felt so comfortably optimistic about the future. The Age of Political Enlightenment had finally dawned in America.

But a decade later much had changed, and certainly optimism had dimmed. Instead of the era of civil tranquility Hartz imagined, the 1960s turned into a time of enormous domestic upheavals, a decade of crises.

President Kennedy, the first president born in the twentieth century, saw crises everywhere: from Cuba to Berlin to Vietnam; from price hikes to civil rights (although quite belatedly on this last issue). He shifted political fears in foreign affairs from the issue of confrontation with the Soviet Union to exaggerated concern for smaller nations in the world that he thought would become the new battleground between communism and the free world. He changed defense policy from sole reliance on massive retaliation to counterinsurgency and the use of counterrevolutionary forces such as the Green Berets.

Lyndon Johnson inherited this legacy and sought to continue the commitments Kennedy had made. Therefore he acted promptly on civil rights. But he also acted in foreign policy by committing the United States to fight the war in Vietnam, a commitment that had tragic consequences for his administration. And the domestic turmoil increased.

By the end of the decade there was a "crisis of liberalism," variously called a "credibility crisis" or a "crisis of confidence." The decade had been wracked (and for some, wrecked) by war, protests, confrontations, and violence. One president was dead from an assassin's bullet. Another president had been forced by events and circumstances not to seek reelection. Kennedy inaugurated the era by calling it a time of "maximum danger," and so it seemed to become, but in ways very different from what Kennedy envisioned.

From out of the dustbin of the once discredited 1950s, a new Nixon arose to preside over the end of the war in Vietnam and eventually over his own self-destruction as president. There were ironies aplenty in the election of Richard Nixon in 1968, the man who had been defeated for president at the dawning of the decade, now elected to govern amid the after-shocks of the decade. Not the least of these ironies was that this staunch anticommunist ended a war fought to contain communism and then "opened the doors" to one communist colossus, the People Republic of China, and negotiated the SALT agreements with the other. This dramatic change was motivated, I believe, more by the rhetorical psychology that drove his career than by any ideology that he had publicly espoused over the years. Indeed, it may have been that this psychology was the very structure that allowed him to move from his extremely conservative positions on the cold war to the progressive initiatives toward other superpowers.

If the 1950s were supposed to be the beginning of an Age of Political Enlightenment, the 1960s, were to be an Age of the Liberal Triumph. Intellectuals proclaimed an "end to ideology" and the victory of liberal political procedures. All that was now needed, after Eisenhower, was a liberal white knight to turn government's concern toward the dispossessd in American society and to move America from the strident anticommunism of the Dulles-McCarthy period. The new ideal of the 1960s was to be a cool, pragmatic ethos that would initiate a new era of orderly change.

Authorities and protesters mystified each other. Those in power could not understand why dissidents did not yield to standard operating procedures. They were amazed that people would take to the streets rather than wait patiently at the supplication tables to voice their dissent from prevailing policies or urge new policies upon authorities. They were confounded that these people did not pay proper respect to those in authority but instead demanded to share some authority with them. Mystification gave way to anger and then to denunciation.

But protesters were equally mystified. They believed they had a constitutional right to petition their government for redress of grievances. They had been taught that a democracy was a great marketplace of competing ideas where everyone's ideas were treated equally. They believed that ideas mattered and that rational discourse would be respected. Thus, the original protesters went into the great "marketplace of ideas" to peddle their grievances, filled with idealistic expectations that finally the marketplace would be open to them. What they found was much different. Those who administered the marketplace questioned their "peddler's permits" and, finding them wanting, attempted to expel them from the marketplace. When they did not go peaceably, they were denounced and attacked for presuming to peddle their wares without the appropriate permits or credentials. They responded with denunciations of their own and with equal anger.

The decade that began with a proclamation of the "end of ideology" exposed a set of official ideologies and produced a proliferation of protesting ideologies. In the rush of events and in the rhetoric of administrative responses to these events, officials who denounced "ideologies" resorted to a harsh ideological rhetoric to sustain their positions or policies. The administrative reactions to campus protests revealed an administrative ideology as rigid as the "subversive" ideologies they denounced. Supporters of the war in Vietnam rolled out the anticommunist ideology to justify involvement in that war.

So, too, with protesters. Orderly protest soon changed into disorderly confrontations. When dissidents did not get expected responses from administrators and the protests accelerated, they resorted to ideological analyses of America's various troubles. By the end of the 1960s these ideologues found only disillusionment. Those who had placed their hopes on arousing a radicalized working class in America found themselves in direct confrontation with "hard-hats," who preferred to break their heads rather than join their ranks. Whites who hoped for an alliance among minorities, students, and intellectuals found themselves shut out by the calls for all-black organizations devoted to black goals, and by a majority of students who preferred beer blasts to radical blasts against the establishment. Feminists went their own way searching for their own history and producing their own sustaining organizations. Above all, radicals found themselves doing battle with one another as much as with their adversaries. In the end, almost all—the feminist movement being the most notable exception—declined and faded away, only a nostalgic memory from a turbulent decade.[2]

The result of all these was another "crisis of confidence" among Americans.[3] In official circles, it resulted in critiques of the prevailing anticommunist ideology and in diminished acceptance of administrative authority. The effect was profound. An American presidency was broken; the Vietnam war had to be given up; and the authority of authorities was in disarray. By the end of the decade the old anticommunist ideology had lost part of its force to justify the carnage at home and abroad. And during the next two decades a new generation that had come of age in the 1960s would be replacing the "Munich" analogy with the "Vietnam" analogy and substituting the "quagmire" metaphor for the "domino" theory.

The "crisis of confidence" extended also to protesters. Radicals used their own ideologies to critique American politics and society and to produce a revolution. But their ideologies produced neither a practical guide to action nor the broad-based constituency they dreamed of as an agent of change. The critique was intellectually satisfying but lacked what it needed most: a critique of the critique.[4] What followed during the next two decades was an intensive reexamination of the concept of ideology that has produced new ideological perspectives and methods for those who still clung to the nostalgic radicalism of the 1960s. Others returned to procedural politics or gave up political action altogether. Still others found in cynicism a comfortable intellectual residence from which to observe the next decade.

What then can we say of the protests? They did not end the war. They did not eliminate racism or sexism. They did not produce a generation of radicals. But the truth is that they had no power to do the first two and were unable to do the third.[5] Only officials could act to end the war or to relieve institutional racism or sexism. But it cannot be emphasized enough that because of the protests—urgent and demanding as they were—these issues captured public attention and eventually required those in power to respond to them. For those who deplore the excesses of some protesters, one has to ask where this country might now be had it not been for the protests.

Finally, what can be said about the "resounding rhetoric" of the period? During a brief decade people both in and out of power ran through a variety of forms of political discourse. In the end they not only exhausted these forms, they exhausted themselves. And what was left was the rhetoric of self, exemplified by Nixon's psychological rhetoric in official circles, and by the cynic's rhetoric among protesters.

The decade that began with Kennedy's clarion call to "ask what you can do for your country" ended with Nixon's denunciations of the "inflated rhetoric," the "angry rhetoric," the "bombastic rhetoric that postures rather than persuades."[6] The resounding rhetoric of the 1960s gave way to admonitions to "watch what we do, not what we say" in the 1970s. The self-absorbed Nixon seemed to be the perfect president to usher in a new "Me Generation."

And what of the protest rhetoric? Historians of rhetoric have long referred to the "rhetoric of the open hand" and the "rhetoric of the closed hand."[7] From this examination of protest in the 1960s, one might conclude by saying that procedural discourse is the rhetoric of the open hand. Administrative discourse is the rhetoric of the closed hand. Ideological discourse is the rhetoric of the clenched fist raised high above the head. And finally, there is the diatribe—or the rhetoric of the extended middle finger offered to one and all by the laughing cynic.

Notes

Preface

1. Richard A. Joslyn, "Keeping Politics in the Study of Political Discourse," in Herbert W. Simons and Aram A. Agharazian, eds., *Form, Genre, and the Study of Political Discourse* (Columbia: University of South Carolina Press, 1986), pp. 336–337.

2. Ibid., pp. 314–315. I reworked the final question from a declarative statement made by Joslyn in his critique of Roderick Hart's essay. I think I do no violence to Joslyn's intent by this rewording of his statement.

3. See Karlyn Kohrs Campbell and Kathleen Hall Jamieson, eds., *Form and Genre: Shaping Rhetorical Action* (Falls Church, Va.: Speech Communication Association, [1978]).

4. Henri Lefebvre, *The Sociology of Marx*, trans. Norbert Guterman (New York: Pantheon Books, 1968), p. 56.

5. For a discussion of the concept and its many meanings, see John Plamentz, *Ideology* (New York: Praeger, 1970). For a detailed criticism of the uses of the concept of ideology, see Walter Carlanes, *The Concept of Ideology and Political Analysis* (Westport, Conn.: Greenwood Press, 1981). For an extensive bibliography of works on the concept of ideology, see Martin Seliger, *Ideology and Politics* (New York: Free Press, 1976) and Colin Sumner, *Reading Ideologies* (New York: Academic Press, 1979). For an excellent essay review of pertinent works on ideology and its relation to rhetoric, see Ray E. McKerrow, "Marxism and a Rhetorical Conception of Ideology," *Quarterly Journal of Speech* 69 (1983): 192–205.

This note could go on almost indefinitely, given all that has been written in scholarly circles about this elusive political idea, but these references should provide the flavor of the controversy. In the aftermath of the 1960s there was a "crisis" of ideology among ideologues that produced a critique of ideology. See Alvin W. Gouldner, *The Two Marxisms: Contradictions and Anomalies in the Development of Theory* (New York: Oxford University Press, 1980), and Goran Therborn, *Science, Class and Society* (London: New Left Books, 1976). In addition, the idea of ideology has been adapted and expanded to account for a variety of political beliefs and values that traditionally were not studied as ideology. In other words, the concept of ideology has been adapted to other uses for political analysis. For example, see Michael H. Hunt, *Ideology and U.S. Foreign Policy* (New Haven, Conn.: Yale University Press, 1987). A similar adaptation has occurred within the rhetorical field, specifically in the works of Michael C. McGee and Philip Wander. See Michael Calvin McGee, "The Ideograph: A Link Between Rhetoric and Ideology," *Quarterly Journal of Speech* 66 (February 1980): 1–16; and Philip Wander, "The Rhetoric of American Foreign Policy," *Quarterly Journal of Speech* 70 (November 1984): 339–361.

6. Gouldner, *The Two Marxisms*, esp. pp. 32–63.

7. Michael J. Parenti, *The Anti-Communist Impulse* (New York: Random House, 1969), pp. 3–4.

1. Presidential Rhetoric: Perspectives

1. For a more extensive elaboration of presidential rhetoric and its relation to power, see my essay, "Presidential Rhetoric: Definition of a Discipline of Study," in Theodore Windt and Beth Ingold, eds., *Essays in Presidential Rhetoric*, 2nd ed. (Dubuque, Iowa: Kendall/Hunt, 1987), pp. xv– xliii.

2. See Samuel Kernell, *Going Public* (Washington, D.C.: Congressional Quarterly, 1986); George C. Edwards III, *The Public Presidency: The Pursuit of Popular Support* (New York: St. Martin's Press, 1983); Theodore J. Lowi, *The Personal President* (Ithaca, N.Y.: Cornell University Press, 1985); William K. Muir, Jr., "Ronald Reagan: The Primacy of Rhetoric," in Fred I. Greenstein, ed., *Leadership in the Modern Presidency* (Cambridge: Harvard University Press, 1988), pp. 260–295.

3. Cf. Joseph C. Spear, *Presidents and the Press* (Cambridge: MIT Press, 1986).

4. Steven Weisman, "Reagan Quoted as Assailing TV Coverage of the Recession," *New York Times*, March 18, 1982, B–16.

5. Giandomenico Majone, "Policy Analysis and Public Deliberation," in Robert B. Reich, ed., *The Power of Public Ideas* (Cambridge: Ballinger Publishing, 1988), p. 157. In the same volume see the following essays: Steven Kelman, "Why Public Ideas Matter," pp. 31–54; Mark Moore, "What Sort of Ideas Become Public Ideas," pp. 55–84; and Philip B. Heymann, "How Government Expresses Public Ideas," pp. 85–108.

6. Cf. David Green, *Shaping Political Consciousness: The Language of*

Politics in America from McKinley to Reagan (Ithaca, N.Y.: Cornell University Press, 1987).

7. Quoted in Thomas E. Cronin, "The Textbook Presidency and Political Science" (Paper prepared for delivery at the 66th Annual Meeting of the American Political Science Association, Los Angeles, California, September 7–12, 1970), p. 5. Cf. John E. Mueller, "Presidential Popularity from Truman to Johnson," *American Political Science Review* 64 (March 1970): pp. 18–34. Using public opinion polling data, Mueller demonstrated that on occasions that presidents call "critical" public support increases dramatically. What he also shows is that support drops off just as quickly once the crisis is over or within a very short period of time if the crisis is not resolved.

8. Quoted in James Madison, *Notes of Debates in the Federal Convention of 1787*, with an introduction of Adrienne Koch (New York: Norton Library, 1969), p. 45.

9. Clinton Rossiter, *The American Presidency*, rev. ed. (New York: New American Library, 1960), p. 17.

10. James M. Burns and Jack W. Peltason, *Government by the People*, 5th ed. (Englewood Cliffs, N.J.: Prentice Hall, 1964), pp. 434–435. Emphasis added.

11. In recent years the news media have attempted to balance presidential statements with opposing views for the public. In reporting presidential statements, news media, particularly television, have relied on someone's supporting an opposing view to answer the president in order to achieve balance in reporting the "truth" about situations or actions. More recently, television and newspapers have pooled their resources to commission polls that confirm or deny presidential statements about public support for policies. Thus, if the president calls upon the public to support him or says that he has public support on an issue, immediately the networks commission a poll to demonstrate whether such public support exists.

12. George E. Reedy, *The Twilight of the Presidency* (New York: World Publishing, 1970), pp. 40–41.

13. In his essay "Corrupt Rhetoric: President For and the Mayaguez Affair," Professor Dan Hahn based part of his criticism of Ford's action on this premise. He wrote: "Nowhere in that enumeration [of presidential powers in Article II of the Constitution] is found the power to engage in military operations outside a declaration of war." Hahn, "Corrupt Rhetoric," in Windt and Ingold, eds., *Essays in Presidential Rhetoric*, p. 321.

14. Quoted by Clinton Rossiter, *The Supreme Court and the Commander in Chief*, with an introductory note and additional text by Richard P. Longaker (Ithaca, N.Y.: Cornell University Press, 1976), p. 71.

15. "Authority of the President to Repel the Attack in Korea," *Department of State Bulletin* 23 (1950): 173–174, quoted by Rossiter, *The Supreme Court*, pp. 134–135. Secretary of State Dean Acheson extended this power several months later when he noted: "Not only has the President the authority to use the Armed Forces in carrying out the broad foreign policy of the United States and implementing treaties, but it is equally clear that this authority may not be interfered with by the Congress in the exercise of powers which it has under the Constitution." *National Commitments, Sen-*

ate Committee on Foreign Relations, 90th Cong., 1st sess. (1967), S. Rept. 797, p. 17, quoted in *The Supreme Court*, Rossiter, p. 135.

16. Ibid.

17. For a summary of the development of these powers up to and through the War Powers Act of 1973, see Rossiter, *The Supreme Court*, esp. pp. 65–102 and 133–219.

18. Quoted in ibid., p. 77.

19. See Lyndon Johnson's justifications for responding to the incidents in the Gulf of Tonkin in August 1964 and for sending the Marines into the Dominican Republic in April and May of 1965. See Nixon's justification for the invasion of Cambodia in May 1970 as well as Ford's rationale for his actions in the Mayaguez incidents. It was the same argument invoked by Reagan to justify the invasion of Grenada.

20. Cf. Jeffrey K. Tulis, *The Rhetorical Presidency* (Princeton, N.J.: Princeton University Press, 1987), pp. 173–193; Kathleen Hall Jamieson, *Eloquence in the Electronic Age* (New York: Oxford University Press, 1988), pp. 201–237.

21. Roderick P. Hart, *The Sound of Leadership* (Chicago: University of Chicago Press, 1987), pp. 211–212.

22. Ibid., p. 200.

23. Donald T. Regan, *For the Record* (San Diego: Harcourt Brace Jovanovich, 1988), p. 142.

24. On Johnson's "credibility gap," see Hugh Sidey, *A Very Personal Presidency: Lyndon Johnson in the White House* (New York: Atheneum, 1968), pp. 159–195.

25. "The White House Horrors," in Theodore Windt, ed., *Presidential Rhetoric: 1961 to the Present*, 4th ed. (Dubuque: Kendall/Hunt, 1987), pp. 171–179. On the reasons for the House Judiciary Committee's votes on impeachment charges, see J. Anthony Lukas, *Nightmare* (New York: Viking: 1976), pp. 515–569.

26. One of the chief strategies of journalists at presidential press conferences is to question the president about conflicting statements made by members of his administration or conflicts between what the president has said and what one of his advisers had said on a pertinent issue. See Carolyn Smith, "Toward a Rhetoric of Presidential Press Conferences" (Ph.D. diss., University of Pittsburgh, 1987), pp. 422–424.

27. See Bradley H. Patterson, Jr., "Communication Directors: The Rule of HPCQ," *The Ring of Power. The White House Staff and Its Expanding Role in Government* (New York: Basic Books, 1988), pp. 177–190. For the frustrations that some journalists experience with this consistency, see Mark Hertsgaard, *On Bended Knee: The Press and the Reagan Presidency* (New York: Farrar Straus Giroux, 1988), pp. 3–100. The problem with Hertsgaard's criticism of the Reagan administration is that he does not understand the administration's rhetorical perspective on communicating with the public or the press. Quite simply, some influential members of the Reagan administration, especially Michael Deaver and David Gergen, took a positive rhetorical stance toward communicating information to the press. They sought to release information and arguments that bolstered the case for Reagan's

policies and his image as a leader and left it to others to build cases against those policies and that leadership. Like lawyers defending a client, they did not see their responsibilities as building the contrary case for the prosecution.

28. Hart, *The Sound of Leadership,* p. 210. Emphasis added.

29. For his recollection of how the speech was written and what went through his mind as he composed it, see Richard N. Goodwin, *Remembering America* (Boston: Little, Brown, 1988), pp. 324–339. What is most interesting about Goodwin's account is that he says he drew upon his own experiences to give fire and feeling to the speech. Johnson called him only once while he was writing, and he called to mention to Goodwin that his first job had been teaching Mexican-Americans in Cotulla, Texas. Johnson thought Goodwin might want to make reference to that experience in the speech.

30. As a professional speechwriter, I can attest to this reluctance. It is only recently that I decided to write about the speechwriting process as I have experienced it. And in doing so, I used only one example from the experiences I had, that of writing for Richard L. Thornburgh almost ten years ago. For those interested, see my essay "Speech Writing in Campaigns for Governor" in Michael Margolis and Gary Mauser, eds., *Manipulating Public Opinion* (Pacific Grove, Calif.: Brooks/Cole, 1989), pp. 47–69.

31. Goodwin, *Remembering America,* pp. 328–329.

32. For a description of the presidential speechwriting process, see Patterson, "Judson Welliver and Successors: The Speechwriting and Research Office [of the Presidency]," *The Ring of Power,* pp. 191–199.

Hart's description of "speeches for hire" extends a long tradition of criticizing speechwriters for getting paid for their work. But most speechwriters take comfort by recalling the words of Dr. Samuel Johnson: "No man but a blockhead ever wrote except for money," quoted as preface by Larry L. King, *None but a Blockhead. On Being a Writer* (New York: Viking, 1986).

33. William E. Connolly, "Preface to the First Edition," *The Terms of Political Discourse,* 2nd ed. (Princeton, N.J.: Princeton University Press, 1983), n.p.

34. Michael H. Hunt, *Ideology and U.S. Foreign Policy* (New Haven, Conn.: Yale University Press, 1987), p. 15.

35. Ibid.

2. The Crisis Rhetoric of President John F. Kennedy: The First Two Years

1. Theodore C. Sorensen, *Kennedy* (New York: Harper and Row, 1965), pp. 292–293.

2. John F. Kennedy, "Annual Message to Congress on the State of the Union, January 30, 1961," *Public Papers of the President: John F. Kennedy, 1961* (Washington, D.C.: Government Printing Office, 1962), 1:22.

3. Sorensen, *Kennedy,* p. 329.

4. See Theodore Otto Windt, Jr., "The Kennedy-Nixon Debates," in Robert V. Friedenberg, ed., *Rhetorical Studies of National Political Debates*, (New York: Praeger, 1990).

5. "Senator John F. Kennedy and Vice President Richard M. Nixon; First Joint Radio-Television Broadcast, September 26, 1960, Originating CBS, Chicago, Ill., All Networks Carried," *The Joint Appearances of Senator John F. Kennedy and Vice President Richard M. Nixon, Presidential Campaign of 1960* (Washington, D.C.: Government Printing Office, 1961), p. 73. Emphasis added.

6. "Speech of Senator John F. Kennedy, Cincinnati, Ohio, Democratic Dinner, October 6, 1960," ibid., pp. 510–511.

7. "Text of a Statement on Cuba by Senator John F. Kennedy, October 20, 1960," ibid., p. 681. For Nixon's reactions in the campaign, see his *Six Crises* (New York: Pyramid Books, 1968), pp. 380–384.

8. See Sorensen, *Kennedy*, pp. 240–248.

9. "Let Us Begin," inaugural address in Theodore Windt, ed., *Presidential Rhetoric: 1961 to the Present*, 4th ed. (Dubuque: Kendall/Hunt, 1987), p. 9. All subsequent quotations come from this publication of the speech.

10. Patrick Anderson, *The Presidents' Men* (Garden City, N.Y.: Doubleday, Anchor ed., 1969), p. 346.

11. James L. Golden, "Perspectives on the Legacy of John F. Kennedy," in Lawrence W. Hugenberg, ed., *Rhetorical Studies Honoring James L. Golden*, (Dubuque, Iowa: Kendall/Hunt, 1986), p. 80.

12. Garry Wills, *The Kennedy Imprisonment* (Boston: Little, Brown, 1982), p. 301. For an analysis of the style of Kennedy's address, see Edward P. J. Corbett, "Analysis of the Style of John F. Kennedy's Inaugural Address," reprinted in Theodore Windt and Beth Ingold, eds., *Essays in Presidential Rhetoric*, 2nd ed. (Dubuque, Iowa: Kendall/Hunt, 1987), pp. 95–104.

13. For an example of such a parody, see Oliver Jensen, "The Gettysburg Address in Eisenhowerese," in Dwight Macdonald, ed., *Parodies* (New York: Modern Library, 1965), pp. 448–449. Instead of being parodied, Kennedy engaged in self-parody. For example, at a dinner on the anniversary of his inaugural, he parodied his inaugural address in this manner: "We observe tonight not a celebration of freedom but a victory of party, for we have sworn to pay off the same party debt our forebears ran up nearly a year and three months ago." For the complete text, see *Public Papers: Kennedy*, 1:41.

14. Carl Sandburg, "Foreword," *To Turn the Tide*, ed. John W. Gardner (New York: Harper and Brothers, 1962), p. xi. For other analyses, see Dan F. Hahn, "Ask Not What a Youngster Can Do for You: Kennedy's Inaugural Address," *Presidential Studies Quarterly* 14 (1984): 78–86; Sam Meyer, "The John F. Kennedy Inauguration Speech: Function and Importance of Its 'Address System,'" *Rhetoric Society Quarterly* 12 (Fall 1982): 239–250. For a perspective on Kennedy's address within the tradition of inaugural addresses, see Karlyn Kohrs Campbell and Kathleen Hall Jamieson, "Inaugurating the Presidency," *Presidential Studies Quarterly* 15 (Spring 1985): 394–411.

15. Cf. Tom Wicker, *JFK and LBJ. The Influence of Personality upon Politics* (Baltimore: Penguin, 1968), pp. 15–148.

16. For the fullest account of this event, see Peter Wyden, *Bay of Pigs* (New York: Simon and Schuster, 1979); cf. Trumbull Higgins, *The Perfect Failure: Kennedy, Eisenhower, and the CIA at the Bay of Pigs* (New York: W. W. Norton, 1987).

17. Because of public concern over the fiasco, Sorensen had to write a draft of this speech overnight.

18. "Lessons to be Learned from the Bay of Pigs Invasion," in Windt, ed., *Presidential Rhetoric*, p. 12. All subsequent quotations are from this transcript of the speech.

19. Cf. Wyden, *Bay of Pigs*, pp. 65–288.

20. Richard J. Walton, *Cold War and Counterrevolution. The Foreign Policy of John F. Kennedy* (New York: Viking Press, 1972), p. 53.

21. Cf. *Khrushchev's "Mein Kampf,"* with background by Harrison E. Salisbury (New York: Belmont Books, 1961).

22. For one analysis of Khrushchev's speech, see *Two Communist Manifestoes*, with an introduction by Charles Burton Marshall (Washington, D.C.: Washington Center of Foreign Policy Research, 1961).

23. "The President and the Press," in Windt, ed., *Presidential Rhetoric*, p. 16. All subsequent quotations are from this transcript.

24. Quoted in the *New York Times*, April 28, 1961, C–30.

25. Ibid.

26. Ibid.

27. *New York Times*, May 10, 1961, p. 10.

28. Sorensen, *Kennedy*, pp. 319–320. Cf. Benjamin C. Bradlee, *Conversations with Kennedy* (New York: W. W. Norton, 1975).

29. For an extended treatment of Kennedy and the press, although it omits much discussion of the aftermath of the Bay of Pigs adventure, see Montague Kern, Patricia W. Levering, and Ralph B. Levering, *The Kennedy Crises: The Press, the Presidency, and Foreign Policy* (Chapel Hill: University of North Carolina Press, 1983).

30. Clifton Daniel, "The Press and National Security," a lecture delivered on June 1, 1966 and reprinted in Appendix B of William McGaffin and Erwin Knoll, *Anything but the Truth* (New York: G. P. Putnam's Sons, 1968), p. 205. This speech also contains Daniel's recollections about how and why the *New York Times* decided to suppress information about the Bay of Pigs invasion.

31. Ibid.

32. Sorensen, *Kennedy*, p. 308; Arthur M. Schlesinger, Jr., *A Thousand Days: John F. Kennedy in the White House* (Boston: Houghton Mifflin, 1965), p. 297.

33. See Roger Hilsman, *To Move a Nation: The Politics of Foreign Policy in the Administration of John F. Kennedy* (New York: Dell, 1967), pp. 50–60.

34. John Kennedy, "Meetings with Khrushchev and de Gaulle," in Windt, ed., *Presidential Rhetoric*, p. 20.

35. Quoted in Thomas J. Schoenbaum, *Waging Peace and War: Dean*

Rusk in the Truman, Kennedy and Johnson Years (New York: Simon and Schuster, 1988), p. 336.

36. Ibid. For a description of Kennedy's mood after coming out of this meeting, as it was picked up by the press, see Kern et al., *The Kennedy Crises*, pp. 60–88.

37. Nikita S. Khrushchev, "Speech at Friendship Meeting of Polish People's Republic and the Soviet Union," November 10, 1958, in *For Victory in Peaceful Competition with Capitalism* (New York: International Arts and Sciences Press, 1960), pp. 727–746.

38. "Proposals of the Soviet Government on the Berlin Question," November 27, 1959, in ibid., pp. 758–771.

39. Dwight D. Eisenhower, *Waging Peace, 1956–1961* (Garden City, N.Y.: Doubleday, 1961), p. 331. On Eisenhower's handling of the 1958–1959 problem of Berlin, see pp. 329–360.

40. See my "Rhetoric of Peaceful Coexistence: A Criticism of Selected American Speeches by Nikita S. Khrushchev" (Ph.D. diss., Ohio State University, 1965). I maintained that Khrushchev used the Berlin situation to provoke the United States into negotiating on other issues. I believe that Khrushchev would have been elated if he had been able to secure Allied agreement to a peace treaty that would have recognized the two separate Germanys because that would have been a diplomatic coup for him. But I am convinced that he knew the United States—at least at that time in the cold war—would not agree to such a treaty. Therefore, I believe he used the threat of signing a separate one to provoke the United States into responding on some other issues.

41. Arthur M. Schlesinger, Jr., *A Thousand Days*, p. 391. In an interview with James Wechsler of the *New York Post* Kennedy demonstrated that he also took the Berlin crisis personally. "If Khrushchev wants to rub my nose in the dirt, it's all over." Quoted in Schlesinger, p. 391. For more detailed information on the "crisis," see R. M. Slusser, *The Berlin Crisis of 1961: Soviet-American Relations and the Struggle for Power in the Kremlin, June–November, 1961* (Baltimore: Johns Hopkins University Press, 1973).

42. "Meetings with Khrushchev and deGaulle," in Windt, ed., *Presidential Rhetoric*, p. 22. Emphasis added.

43. Schlesinger wrote: "The President was meanwhile fighting his way through the thicket of debate [over Berlin] to his own conclusions. Cuba and Laos had been side issues. But Berlin threatened a war which might destroy civilization, and he thought about little else that summer [1961]." Schlesinger, *A Thousand Days*, p. 390.

44. The Acheson group included Foy Kohler, assistant secretary of state; Paul Nitze, assistant secretary of defense; Vice President Johnson; columnist Joseph Alsop; the German Desk at the State Department; and the Joint Chiefs of Staff. The Schlesinger group included Ambassador Llewellyn Thompson; Charles Bohlen, Kennedy's Soviet affairs adviser; Senator J. William Fulbright; Henry Kissinger, still a professor at Harvard but also an ad hoc adviser to the Kennedy administration; and columnist Walter Lippmann.

45. On July 5, as the situation was heating up, Schlesinger met with a

Soviet friend of his, Kornienko of the Soviet embassy, who said he was puzzled over the U.S. reaction to Khrushchev's proposals and suggested that if the president did not like them, that he come up with an alternative that could be discussed. See Schlesinger, *A Thousand Days*, pp. 385–390.

46. Acheson's belief that the Soviets were testing the new president became conventional wisdom about Soviet actions during the early days of a new administration, so much so that it is now taken as fact, rather than a product of Acheson's imagination, which it was. The Soviets had not tested Truman when he first assumed power because the Soviet Union and the United States were allies at the time. The Soviets had not tested Eisenhower in the early days because Stalin died in March 1953 and they were concerned with internal governing problems for the next two years, that is, until Malenkov resigned and Khrushchev triumphed. Thus, Acheson's contention that Kennedy was being tested was the first instance of this "theory" and set the precedent, largely unexamined by political figures, for the imaginative belief that the Soviet leadership deliberately "tests" new American presidents early in their administration, a test to which the president must react (or in most cases, overreact) forcefully.

47. Schlesinger, *A Thousand Days*, p. 391.

48. "Second Joint Radio-Television Broadcast [Debate], October 7, 1960," *The Joint Appearances of Kennedy and Nixon*, p. 159. Emphasis added. Looking back on this statement as well as other similar ones made by Kennedy during the campaign and upon the events of the summer of 1961, psychologists might call Kennedy's Berlin crisis an incident of self-fulfilling prophecy.

49. "The Berlin 'Crisis'," in Windt, ed., *Presidential Rhetoric*, p. 24. All subsequent quotations are from this text.

50. Schlesinger, *A Thousand Days*, p. 391.

51. The $3.47 billion additional monies for defense raised the Defense budget by some $6 billion since Kennedy had taken office. That was $6 billion more than Eisenhower had requested for his last budget, which was in effect during the first year of Kennedy's administration. Kennedy's lavish spending on the military during his tenure led Sorensen to cite as a major achievement of the Kennedy administration, "the largest and fastest military buildup in our peacetime history." Sorensen, *Kennedy*, p. 759. Little wonder that twenty years later President Reagan would repeatedly contrast his lavish spending on the military with Kennedy's as a defense against accusations by liberal Democrats that the spending was not necessary.

One could argue that Kennedy created the Berlin crisis as a means for getting more money for conventional forces. There is some circumstantial evidence to support this interpretation of the crisis. When Kennedy assumed office, he found American conventional forces in a state of decline because of the Eisenhower-Dulles doctrine of massive retaliation and its reliance on our nuclear arsenal. Kennedy immediately sought to rebuild those conventional forces so as to possess a more flexible means of responding to Soviet military challenges, especially in Third World nations where our nuclear strength would be inappropriate and ineffective. But Kennedy, like all first-year presidents, was stuck with his predecessor's budget and would not be able to propose these increases until the next fiscal budget. Kennedy's impatience can be imagined. In this scenario, the Berlin crisis would provide an excellent pretext to increase military spending dramatically.

However, this scenario is inadequate as an explanation for the widespread fear produced by the speech, for the intensity of the speech, or as the leading cause of the crisis. More likely, the great increase in defense spending that Kennedy got as a result of the speech was more a by-product than a cause.

52. Sorensen, *Kennedy*, p. 591.

53. Following Kennedy's July 25 speech, Khrushchev gave an equally belligerent speech in response. The day after the speech, according to Schlesinger (*A Thousand Days*, p. 392), Khrushchev told John J. McCloy that Kennedy had declared preliminary war on the Soviet Union. Subsequently, on August 7, Khrushchev rattled his rockets at the United States and suggested calling up *his* reserves. Schlesinger called the two speeches by Kennedy and Khrushchev "mirrors" of one another in that they bore "curious resemblances" to each other. Given that Kennedy had threatened Khrushchev because he believed Khrushchev had threatened him over Berlin, it is not "curious" that Khrushchev should threaten Kennedy in return.

54. Kennedy's symbolic actions set the precedent for presidents Carter and Reagan. When the Soviets invaded Afghanistan, Carter reacted symbolically by canceling American participation in the Olympic games and by placing an embargo on shipments of grain to the Soviet Union. When the Soviets shot down Korean Air Lines flight number 007, Reagan did the same by a series of symbolic acts that demonstrated our condemnation of that Soviet act by suspending Aeroflot flights into the United States and limiting cultural, scientific, and diplomatic exchanges. Certainly, these actions were tepid in comparison with Soviet actions, but the alternatives were worse: doing nothing or unleashing a nuclear war. Within that context, such tepid but prudent symbolic actions express our condemnation of the Soviet Union in concrete ways and also maintain our role as a responsible nuclear power.

55. Quoted in Schlesinger, *A Thousand Days*, pp. 390–391.

56. For a brief but good examination of the steel crisis, see Grant McConnell, *Steel and the Presidency, 1962* (New York: W. W. Norton, 1963). For the "crisis" as a political crisis for Kennedy, see Richard Godden and Richard Maidment, "Anger, Language, and Politics: John F. Kennedy and the Steel Crisis," in Windt and Ingold, eds., *Essays in Presidential Rhetoric*, pp. 105–134.

57. "The Steel Crisis," in Windt, ed., *Presidential Rhetoric*, p. 31.

58. Sorensen, *Kennedy*, p. 450.

59. When Kennedy was later quoted as saying "My father always told me that steel men were sons of bitches, but I never realized till now how right he was," the remark was widely quoted in newspapers and magazines as representing Kennedy's antibusiness attitude. Ibid., p. 449.

60. Cf. McConnell, *Steel*, pp. 13–33.

61. Political language can be divided into three types: *literal, promissory,* and *therapeutic.* By *literal,* we mean the president means exactly what he

says and intends his audience to interpret his words exactly. By *promissory*, we mean the president promises to do something but wants his audience to understand that he may have to compromise in order to achieve his goal. For example, a president may promise to fight for a tax cut of 30 percent across the board for Americans but eventually only gets a 25 percent tax cut. In this case, the president has promised to do something and achieved it by compromising part of the original promise. This type of language and rhetoric is most indicative of a democratic society in which power is shared among various parts of government. Usually, the public understands that the president cannot fulfill his promise literally because the democratic system requires negotiation and compromise. One might also call this type of language, the language of negotiation or bargaining, as Murray Edelman does in *The Symbolic Uses of Politics* (Urbana: University of Illinois Press, 1964). By *therapeutic*, we mean language that reaffirms values or positions but cannot be realized in fact immediately or in the near future. In the case of the steel crisis, the executives could have interpreted Kennedy's words against them as therapy to keep his union constituencies satisfied that the president was angry about the price increase, felt betrayed, shared the concern and outrage of the union, but could not act to rescind the price increase. Therefore, the executives could have told themselves and others that they understood the president had to say such things about the steel companies, but it was only words or "mere rhetoric." In this case, Kennedy wanted no misunderstanding about how his words should be interpreted.

62. Schlesinger, *A Thousand Days*, p. 586.

63. Henry Fairlie, *The Kennedy Promise* (New York: Dell, 1974), pp. 162–164.

64. Schlesinger, *A Thousand Days*, p. 639.

65. Charles A. Reich, "Another Such Victory . . . The President's Short War Against Steel," *New Republic*, April 30, 1962, p. 8.

66. "Remarks at the White House Correspondents and News Photographers Associations Dinner," April 27, 1962, *Public Papers: Kennedy, 1962*, 1:344–345.

67. Schlesinger, *A Thousand Days*, p. 728.

68. Quoted in Tony Hendra, *Going Too Far (The Rise and Demise of Sick, Gross, Black, Sophomoric, Weirdo, Pinko, Anarchist, Underground Anti-Establishment Human)* (New York: Doubleday, 1987), p. 152.

69. On the crisis, see: Elie Able, *The Missile Crisis* (Philadelphia: Lippincott, 1966); Graham T. Allison, *Essence of Decision: Explaining the Cuban Missile Crisis* (Boston: Little, Brown, 1971); Hilsman, *To Move a Nation*, pp. 159–232; Robert F. Kennedy, *Thirteen Days:* (New York: W. W. Norton, 1969); Nikita S. Khrushchev, *Khrushchev Remembers*, trans. and ed. Strobe Talbott (New York: Bantam, 1971), pp. 540–558; David L. Larson, ed., *The "Cuban Missile Crisis" of 1962. Selected Documents and Chronology* (Boston: Houghton Mifflin, 1963); Schlesinger, *A Thousand Days*, pp. 795–841; Sorensen, *Kennedy*, pp. 667–718; Michel Tatu, *Power in the Kremlin from Khrushchev to Kosygin*, trans. Helen Katel (New York: Viking, 1967), pp. 230–297: James G. Blight and David A. Welch, *On the Brink: Americans and Soviets Reexamine the Cuban Missile Crisis* (New York: Hill and Wang,

1989); McGeorge Bundy, *Danger and Survival* (New York: Random House, 1988), pp. 358–462.

70. Sorensen, *Kennedy*, pp. 676–678. For edited transcripts of two important meetings (October 16 and October 27) held by the Executive Committee, see McGeorge Bundy, transcriber, and James G. Blight, ed., "White House Tapes and Minutes of the Cuban Missile Crisis," *International Security* 10, (Summer 1985): 164–203, and David A. Welsh and James G. Blight, "The Eleventh Hour of the Cuban Missile Crisis: An Introduction to the ExComm Transcripts," and McGeorge Bundy, transcriber, and James G. Blight, ed., "October 27, 1962: Transcripts of the Meetings of the ExComm," *International Security* 12, (Winter 1987/88): 5–92.

71. Sorensen, *Kennedy*, p. 678.

72. On this genre of presidential rhetoric, see Theodore Otto Windt, Jr., "The Presidency and Speeches on International Crises: Repeating the Rhetorical Past," in Windt and Ingold, eds., *Essays in Presidential Rhetoric*, pp. 125–134.

73. "The Cuban Missile Crisis," in Windt, *ed., Presidential Rhetoric*, p. 36. All subsequent quotations are from this text.

74. Sorensen admitted that according to the president the missiles in Cuba did not alter the balance of power *in fact*, but *in appearance*, and that those appearances would affect American will and leadership in the world. Sorensen, *Kennedy*, p. 678.

75. David Detzer, *The Brink: Cuban Missile Crisis, 1962* (New York: Thomas Y. Crowell, 1979), pp. 237–239. The recently published transcripts of the October 27 meeting of the Executive Committee demonstrate that Kennedy was much more willing to negotiate and to avoid war than previous memoirs indicated. Dean Rusk added to this new view of the president in the written letter to the Hawk's Cay conference. In it, Rusk revealed that President Kennedy had said he would not allow the missiles in Turkey to become a stumbling block to resolving the crisis. According to Rusk, the president even would call Andrew Cordier at Columbia University and dictate a letter to him that would be made by Secretary General U Thant of the United Nations, and that would propose "the removal of both the Jupiters [missiles in Turkey] and the missiles in Cuba." J. Anthony Lukas, "Class Reunion: Kennedy's Men Relive the Cuban Missile Crisis," *New York Times Magazine*, August 30, 1987, p. 58.

76. Quoted in Jim Heath, *Decade of Disillusionment: The Kennedy-Johnson Years* (Bloomington: Indiana University Press, 1976), p. 131. Cf. B. J. Bernstein, "The Cuban Missile Crisis," in L. H. Miller and R. W. Pruessen, eds., *Reflections on the Cold War: A Quarter Century of American Foreign Policy*, (Philadelphia: Temple University Press, 1974), pp. 130–133; "The Week We Almost Went to War," *Bulletin of Atomic Scientists*, February 1976, pp. 13–21; Louise FitzSimons, *The Kennedy Doctrine* (New York: Random House, 1972); and Walton, *Cold War*.

77. "Excerpt from Statement by Cuban President Osvaldo Dorticos Torrado Before the U.S. General Assembly," in Larson, ed., *The "Cuban Missile Crisis"*, pp. 33–36. The speech by President Dorticos was summarized in an article by the *New York Times* on October 9, 1962. Ambassador Stevenson

referred to that speech in a statement to the press on October 23, the day after Kennedy's announcement of the crisis. See *Department of State Bulletin* 47 (November 12, 1962): 450.

78. Arthur Schlesinger, Jr., *Robert Kennedy and His Times* (Boston: Houghton Mifflin, 1978), p. 512.

A four-day conference on the Cuban missile crisis was held on the 25th anniversary of the crisis on March 5–8, 1987, at Hawk Channel in Florida. Participating were eight members of the Kennedy administration and various interested scholars. This conference is especially important in light of the new or revised views that were presented by former members of the Kennedy administration. See Lukas, "Class Reunion," pp. 22–27, 57, 61. See also, Robert A. Pollard, "The Cuban Missile Crisis: Legacies and Lessons," *Wilson Quarterly* 6 (Autumn 1982): 148– 158. I agree with Pollard's conclusion that few scholars these days view the missile crisis as a great triumph for the Kennedy administration.

79. For examples:

On September 7, Sen. Everett Dirksen and Rep. Charles Hallack, minority leaders in Congress, issued a statement urging a stronger U.S. policy toward Cuba and proposed giving the president authority to use troops, if necessary, to defeat communism in Cuba.

On September 16, Sen. Barry Goldwater charged the administration with a "do nothing" policy in Cuba and that it had virtually given the communists a free rein there.

On September 17, senators Hugh Scott and Kenneth Keating urged some form of a military and/or economic blockade of Cuba to halt Soviet military assistance.

On September 18, Richard Nixon, Republican candidate for governor of California, called for a "quarantine" of Cuba to halt Soviet shipments of arms.

Add to this that during the first two years of the Kennedy administration the coalition of Republicans and conservative Democrats held a majority in Congress, particularly in the Senate. Rep. Richard Bolling (D-Missouri) estimated that the coalition had a 224–213 majority in the House during Kennedy's first two years. See Randall B. Ripley, "Kennedy and Congress," *University Programs Modular Studies* (Morristown, N.J.: General Learning Press, 1972), p. 8.

Pierre Salinger, Kennedy's press secretary, made a similar point after the Moscow meetings of American, Cuban, and Soviet surviving participants. See Salinger, "Gaps in the Cuban Missile Crisis Story," *New York Times*, February 5, 1989, E–5.

80. Schlesinger, *Robert F. Kennedy*, p. 530.

3. The Crisis Rhetoric of President John F. Kennedy: The Final Year

1. Roger Hilsman, *To Move a Nation: The Politics of Foreign Policy in the Administration of John F. Kennedy* (New York: Dell, 1967), pp. 340–357.

2. Ibid., p. 351

3. Ibid., p. 350.

4. Ibid., p. 351.

5. Ibid., pp. 356–357. Of course, by the time the speech was delivered, Lyndon Johnson, not Kennedy, was president. Johnson was attempting to bring the executive branch under his control and probably thus had precious little time for a major change in policy toward China.

6. Theodore C. Sorensen, *Kennedy* (New York: Harper and Row, 1965), p. 730. Sorensen contended that Soviet opposition to "on-site" inspections provided the greatest stumbling block to negotiations over limiting nuclear testing. Frequently, this opposition to inspections was used in American cold war rhetoric as demonstrative proof of the closed nature of the Soviet system. But it had been an ongoing argument between the two nations, with each country shifting positions as it suited each. See Allen W. Dulles, "Disarmament in the Atomic Age," *Foreign Affairs* 25 (January 1947): 204–217.

7. Sorensen, *Kennedy*, p. 731.

8. John F. Kennedy, "Peace," in Theodore Windt, ed., *Presidential Rhetoric: 1961 to the Present*, 4th ed. (Dubuque, Iowa: Kendall/Hunt, 1987), p. 41. All subsequent quotations are taken from this text. To appreciate fully the change in assumptions and language Kennedy was attempting, one should compare this speech with President Truman's speech on aid to Greece and Turkey (later called the "Truman Doctrine"), delivered to Congress on March 12, 1947. Truman's speech, as much as any other, helped to establish the strident anticommunist language and rhetoric that would prevail until Kennedy attacked it directly in his American University speech.

9. Cf. Walter Lippmann, *Public Opinion* (New York: Pelican Books, 1946), pp. 59–96.

10. During his 1959 visit to the United States, Chairman Nikita S. Khrushchev persisted in making the same distinction as he sought peaceful coexistence with the United States. See the collection of his American speeches, *Khrushchev in America* (New York: Crosscurrents Press, 1960), esp. his address to the American people over national radio and television, pp. 198–207.

11. Walter Lippmann, *Public Opinion* (New York: Pelican Books, 1946), p. 81. See also, Amitai Etzioni, "The Kennedy Experiment," *Psychology Today* 3 (December 1969): 43–45, 62–63.

12. In this instance, Kennedy appropriated the language of the right to use against the right. William Safire defined *defeatist* as an "attack word against those urging caution, or withdrawal from what they consider indefensible positions." See Safire, *Safire's Political Dictionary* (New York: Ballantine Books, 1978), p. 161.

13. Khrushchev's agreement to participate in these discussions arrived only a day before the speech was delivered and was inserted into the speech at the last minute. For an intensive examination of the treaty, see Glenn T. Seaborg (with the assistance of Benjamin S. Loeb), *Kennedy, Khrushchev and the Test Ban* (Berkeley: University of California Press, 1981).

14. Amitai Etzioni, "Can JFK Peace Psychology Tactics Work for Nixon?" *Washington Post*, December 7, 1969, C–2.

15. Ibid.

16. See Sorensen, *Kennedy*, p. 733.

17. See, in particular, Kennedy's news conference at the Foreign Ministry in Bonn on June 24 and his "Address in the Assembly Hall at the Paulskirche in Frankfurt," on June 25 in *Public Papers of the Presidents of the United States: John F. Kennedy, 1963* 3: (Washington, D.C.: Government Printing Office, 1962–1964), 505–511, 516–521.

18. "Ich Bin Ein Berliner," in Windt, ed., *Presidential Rhetoric*, p. 50.

19. Kenneth P. O'Donnell and David Powers with Joe McCarthy, *Johnny We Hardly Knew Ye. Memories of John Fitzgerald Kennedy* (New York: Pocket Books, 1973), p. 417.

20. The theory and some details of this two-track policy had already been laid out by Henry Kissinger and Gen. Maxwell Taylor, an important adviser to Kennedy. See their books: Kissinger, *Nuclear Weapons and Foreign Policy* (New York: Harper and Brothers, 1958), esp. his chapters on "limited wars"; and Taylor, *The Uncertain Trumpet* (New York: Harper and Brothers, 1959). General Taylor even suggested the creation of an Office for Limited Wars in the White House to coordinate these military adventures. Kennedy thought that might be going too far in institutionalizing that part of his foreign policy.

21. Cf. George E. Reedy, *The Twilight of the Presidency* (New York: World Publishing, 1970), pp. 41–42.

22. Kennedy, "Radio and Television Address to the American People on the Nuclear Test Ban Treaty," *Public Papers: Kennedy, 1963*, 3:601–606.

23. For one discussion of many about the politics surrounding the ratification of the treaty, see Sorensen, *Kennedy*, pp. 734–746.

24. Quoted by ibid., p. 733.

25. Quoted in Theodore H. White, *The Making of the President 1960* (New York: Atheneum, 1961), p. 323.

26. Ibid.

27. Only Adlai Stevenson in 1956 got less when he got only 61 percent of the vote. In 1952 Stevenson got 79 percent; in 1964 Johnson got 94 percent; in 1968 Humphrey got 85 percent; in 1972 McGovern got 87 percent; in 1976 and1980 Carter got 85 percent and 86 percent; and in 1984 Mondale got 93 percent. See Richard A. Watson, "Vote by Groups in Presidential Elections Since 1952," *The Presidential Contest* (New York: John Wiley and Sons, 1984), p. 86. Surely, Sorensen was dealing with mythology and not facts when he wrote that the Negro community "voted overwhelmingly for Kennedy." Sorensen, *Kennedy*, p. 216. One should remember that in 1960 it was not only southern Protestants who opposed Kennedy because he was a Catholic. Many black Protestants opposed him for the same reason, and that undoubtedly held down the traditionally Democratic black vote for him. Stevenson's percentage of the black vote dropped to 61 percent primarily because it was during the Eisenhower administration (in 1954) that the *Brown v. Board of Education* decision was handed down by the Supreme Court, with a chief justice who was a Republican writing the majority opinion.

28. In his recollection in the Oral History section of the Kennedy Library,

Burke Marshall said that Kennedy later ruefully recalled that remark jokingly and wondered, "Who put those words in my mouth?" Burke Marshall, Oral History, May 29, 1964, John F. Kennedy Library, Boston, Mass., p. 55, cited in Robert E. Gilbert, "John F. Kennedy and Civil Rights for Black Americans," *Presidential Studies Quarterly* 12 (Summer 1982): 398. For a collaborating view of these incidents, see Harris Wofford, *Of Kennedys and Kings* (New York: Farrar, Straus, Giroux, 1980), pp. 124–177.

29. Harry Golden, *Mr. Kennedy and the Negroes* (New York: World Publishing, 1964), p. 269.

30. "In other words, Kennedy's civil rights activities were, for the most part, a response to the dynamics of the situation—the protests and demonstrations of the early Sixties." Victor S. Navasky, *Kennedy Justice* (New York: Atheneum, 1970), p. 443. "John Kennedy's record on civil rights contained failures that ran far deeper than his successes." Bruce Miroff, *Pragmatic Illusions: The Presidential Politics of John F. Kennedy* (New York: David McKay, 1976), p. 269. "At a time when John Kennedy should have been anxious not to destroy the credit of the moderate leaders among their increasingly impatient followers [in the civil rights movement], he recklessly did so. He neither gave them what they needed, nor allowed them to stand apart from him, able to criticize the slowness and the inadequacy of his actions." Henry Fairlie, *The Kennedy Promise* (New York: Dell, 1974), p. 204.

31. For a brief but balanced assessment of the Kennedy administration's efforts in civil rights, see Gilbert, "Kennedy and Civil Rights," pp. 386–399; for an analysis of Kennedy's rhetoric, see Steven R. Goldzwig and George N. Dionisopoulos, "John F. Kennedy's Civil Rights Discourse: The Evolution from 'Principled Bystander' to Public Advocate," *Communication Monographs* 56 (September 1989): 179–198.

32. For a summary of those political obstacles, see Gilbert, "Kennedy and Civil Rights," pp. 393–397.

33. The best study of the integration of the University of Mississippi is Walter Lord's *The Past that Would Not Die* (New York: Harper and Row, 1964). See also Harold Fleming, "The Federal Executive and Civil Rights: 1961–1965," *Daedalus* 94 (Fall 1965); and Donald Francis Sullivan, "The Civil Rights Programs of the Kennedy Administration: A Political Analysis" (Ph.D. diss., University of Oklahoma, 1965). For the conversations between the U.S. Justice Department, especially Attorney General Robert Kennedy, and Governor Ross Barnet of Mississippi, see Navasky, *Kennedy Justice*, pp. 160–242.

34. "Desegregation at the University of Mississippi: A Legal Issue," televised report to the nation, September 30, 1962, in Windt, ed., *Presidential Rhetoric*, p. 34. All subsequent quotations are from this text.

35. Sorensen, *Kennedy*, p. 487.

36. Navasky, *Kennedy Justice*, p. 167. Neither President Kennedy nor his brother, the attorney general, seemed to have much "feel" for the urgency of blacks in the civil rights movement. At a celebrated meeting on May 24, 1963, attended by Robert Kennedy, James Baldwin, and black artists Baldwin had assembled at Kennedy's request, the lack of understanding became painfully apparent. Baldwin and his group lectured the attorney general on the need for immediate action. Robert Kennedy lectured them on how the

system worked, on the difficulties of getting things done. The meeting was acrimonious, and neither side demonstrated much understanding of the other. See Arthur M. Schlesinger, Jr., *Robert Kennedy and His Times* (Boston: Houghton Mifflin, 1978), pp. 961–963 for one account of this meeting. What is important to understanding the Kennedys on civil rights is that this meeting took place in 1963, less than a month before Kennedy was thrust into the turmoil of the movement by the events at the University of Alabama.

37. Quoted in Sorensen, *Kennedy*, p. 492.

38. Sorensen, *Kennedy*, p. 495.

39. "Civil Rights: A Moral Issue," report to the nation, June 11, 1963, in Windt, ed., *Presidential Rhetoric*, pp. 46–47. All subsequent quotations are from this text. Sorensen wrote that in the larger sense Kennedy had been preparing this speech for some time. Sorensen, *Kennedy*, p. 495. In fact, it was a return to his 1960 campaign speaking on the issue. In his opening statement at the first television debate with Vice President Nixon, Kennedy stated: "I'm not satisfied until every American enjoys his full constitutional rights. If a Negro baby is born, and this is true also of Puerto Ricans and Mexicans in some of our cities, he has about one-half as much chance to get through high school as a white baby. He has one-third as much chance to get through college as a white student. He has about a third as much chance to be a professional man, and about half as much chance to own a house. He has about four times as much chance that he'll be out of work in his life as the white baby." *The Joint Appearances of Senator John F. Kennedy and Vice President Richard M. Nixon: Presidential Campaign of 1960* (Washington, D.C.: Government Printing Office, 1961), p. 74.

40. On June 3, 1963, as Kennedy was preparing civil rights legislation, Johnson telephoned Theodore Sorensen to give his thoughts on how civil rights and the attendant legislation should be handled. His conversation, which was later transcribed, offers a fascinating insight into Johnson's attitudes about the issue and his frustrations about the way in which the Kennedy administration had handled the issue. See Herbert S. Parmet, *JFK: The Presidency of John F. Kennedy* (New York: Dial, 1983), pp. 268–271.

41. Dwight D. Eisenhower, "Farewell to the American People, January 17, 1961," in Craig Allen Smith and Kathy B. Smith, eds., *The President and the Public. Rhetoric and National Leadership* (Lanham, Md.: University Press of America, 1985), pp. 311–312.

42. Sorensen lists fifteen "selective [major] accomplishments" of the presidency of John F. Kennedy, *Kennedy*, pp. 761–762.

43. Richard J. Walton, *Cold War and Counterrevolution: The Foreign Policy of John F. Kennedy* (New York: Viking Press, 1972), p. 233.

4. Americanizing the Vietnam War: President Johnson's Press Conference of July 28, 1965

1. Cf. "Remarks in New York City Before the American Bar Association," *Public Papers of the President. Lyndon B. Johnson, 1963–1964* (Washington, D.C.: Government Printing Office, 1966), 2:952–955.

2. "Address at Johns Hopkins University: 'Peace Without Conquest,'" *Public Papers: Johnson, 1965*, 1:394–399. For an excellent and perceptive analysis of the development, writing, and delivery of this address, see Kathleen J. Turner, *Lyndon Johnson's Dual War* (Chicago: University of Chicago Press, 1985), pp. 111–133. Turner's analysis of Johnson's "dual war" is so compelling that this current essay is little more than a footnote to her work.

3. Lyndon B. Johnson, "The Great Society," commencement address at the University of Michigan, May 22, 1964, in Theodore Windt, ed., *Presidential Rhetoric: 1961 to the Present*, 4th ed. (Dubuque, Iowa: Kendall/Hunt, 1987), p. 63.

4. Cf. Turner, *Johnson's Dual War*, pp. 144–152; Richard E. Neustadt and Ernest R. May, *Thinking in Time: The Use of History for Decision Makers* (New York: Free Press, 1986), pp. 75–90.

5. Lyndon B. Johnson, "Let Us Continue," speech to Joint Session of Congress, November 27, 1963, in Windt, ed., *Presidential Rhetoric*, p. 53.

6. Lyndon B. Johnson, "War: The Gulf of Tonkin," August 4, 1964, in Windt, ed., *Presidential Rhetoric*, p. 65. For one analysis of this speech, see Richard A. Cherwitz, "Lyndon Johnson and the 'Crisis' of Tonkin Gulf: A President's Justification of War," *Western Journal of Speech Communication*, 41 (Spring 1978): 93–104. Cherwitz's title is misleading since Johnson was not justifying a "war" but a retaliatory attack on North Vietnam. On the larger question of declaring war, see Robert L. Ivie, *Congress Declares War* (Kent, Ohio: Kent State University Press, 1983).

7. Johnson, "Remarks in New York City before the American Bar Association," in *Public Papers: Johnson, 1963–1964*, 2:953.

8. "The U.S. Marine Force will not, repeat will not, engage in day to day actions against the Viet Cong." Quoted in Herbert Y. Schandler, *Lyndon Johnson and Vietnam. The Unmaking of a President* (Princeton, N.J.: Princeton University Press, 1977), p. 19.

9. Cf. Turner, *Johnson's Dual War*, pp. 111–133.

10. Johnson, "Address at Johns Hopkins," *Public Papers, Johnson, 1965*, 1:397.

11. Lyndon B. Johnson, *The Vantage Point* (New York: Pocket Books, 1971), p. 149. Johnson explicitly mentioned only three options, but as they developed there were five different options that were discussed. For another description of the discussions leading up to the decision, see Jack Valenti, *A Very Human President* (New York: W. W. Norton, 1975), pp. 322–353.

12. Johnson, *The Vantage Point*, p. 149.

13. Ambassador Maxwell Taylor specifically stated this in his long cable to the president on January 6, 1965: "To take this decision would in effect change the basis of our conduct of the war." Ambassador Taylor to the President, "Evaluation of present situation in SVN, causes of troubles and what can be done," National Security File History, box 40, Lyndon B. Johnson Library Archives.

14. "Memorandum, Possible Items for Discussion, July 22, 1965," quoted in Turner, *Johnson's Dual War*, p. 150.

15. Cf. ibid., p. 145

16. Johnson, *The Vantage Point*, p. 153.

17. "Memorandum, Bundy to Johnson, July 21, 1965," quoted in Turner, *Johnson's Dual War*, p. 150.

18. Cf. Rowland Evans and Robert Novak, *Lyndon B. Johnson: The Exercise of Power* (New York: New American Library, 1966), pp. 510–529.

19. "Memorandum to the President," Press Office File, box 73, LBJ Library Archives.

20. Lyndon B. Johnson, "The Vietnam War Becomes the American-Vietnamese War," news conference, July 28, 1965, in Windt, ed., *Presidential Rhetoric*, pp. 79–85.

21. Johnson, "Address at Johns Hopkins," *Public Papers: Johnson, 1965*, 1:394.

22. On the use of historical analogies in justifying foreign policy decisions, see Ernest R. May, *"Lessons" of the Past: The Use and Misuse of History in American Foreign Policy* (New York: Oxford University Press, 1973). On the influence of the Munich analogy on Johnson's decision-making process prior to the press conference, as well as another historical analogy he might have chosen to use, see Neustadt and May, *Thinking in Time*, pp. 75–90 and 157–171.

23. President Eisenhower had coined the "domino" metaphor in 1954 in trying to explain his decision to send economic aid to South Vietnam: "You have a row of dominoes set up" and "you knock over the first one, and what will happen to the last one is that it will go over very quickly." For a full-scale critique of the domino theory as well as most other arguments that were used to support the war in Vietnam, see Michael J. Parenti, *The Anti-Communist Impulse* (New York: Random House, 1969).

24. Polls demonstrated that the public overwhelmingly supported Johnson's increase in American troops in Vietnam at this time. The Harris poll indicated that 65 percent supported Johnson's policies in Vietnam. At the time of Johnson's press conference, Samuel Lubell reported that 75 percent believed "we have no other choice than to send in more troops." *Time*, August 6, 1965, p. 32.

25. James McNaughton, "Draft for McNamara on Proposed Course of Action," in *The Pentagon Papers* (New York: Bantam Books, 1971), p. 432.

26. McNaughton, "Further McNaughton Memo on Factors in Bombing Decision," in ibid., pp. 491–492.

27. Jonathan Schell, *The Time of Illusion* (New York: Alfred A. Knopf, 1976), pp. 9–10. Schell's book is indispensable in understanding not only the doctrine of credibility (see esp. pp. 335–387) but how embracing this doctrine effected domestic policy as well as foreign policy. For an elaborate theoretical exposition and advocacy of the doctrine, see its major architect, Henry Kissinger, *Nuclear Weapons and Foreign Policy* (New York: Harper and Brothers, 1957).

28. McNaughton, "Further McNaughton Memo," p. 492.

29. Johnson, "The President's News Conference of July 28, 1965," *Public Papers: Johnson, 1965*, 2:801.

5. Understanding Richard Nixon: A Psycho-Rhetorical Analysis

1. Quoted from Jules Witcover, *The Resurrection of Richard Nixon* (New York: G. P. Putnam's Sons, 1970), p. 21.

2. See James Keogh, *President Nixon and the Press* (New York: Funk and Wagnalls, 1972), pp. 38–60.

3. Earl Mazo and Stephen Hess, *Nixon: A Political Portrait* (New York: Popular Library, 1968), pp. 170–171.

4. Richard Nixon, *Six Crises* (New York: Pyramid Books, 1968), p. xxiv.

5. It would be more to the point to say that *Six Crises* represents what Nixon wanted people to believe about what he thought, what he felt, how he reacted, rather than being a candid confessional autobiography. After all, the book was written in preparation for the 1962 gubernatorial campaign in California and was then reissued in preparation for the 1968 presidential campaign. Nonetheless, this remarkable book contains some invaluable insights into how his mind works when writing with the public clearly and distinctly in that mind. It is drama, the drama of Richard Nixon as he faced six crises in his political career.

6. David Abrahamsen, *Nixon v. Nixon: An Emotional Tragedy* (New York: New American Library, 1978); Eli S. Chesen, *President Nixon's Psychiatric Profile* (New York: Peter H. Wyden, 1973); Bruce Mazlish, *In Search of Nixon: A Psycho-Historical Inquiry* (Baltimore: Penguin Books, 1973); and Fawn M. Brodie, *Richard Nixon: The Shaping of His Character* (Cambridge: Harvard University Press, 1983) Pioneered by Freud in his study of Leonardo de Vinci, psychobiography has grown into a scholarly discipline of its own. It has had its ups and downs, from the disgraceful Freud and William C. Bullitt's *Thomas Woodrow Wilson* to the sublime, Erik H. Erikson's *Young Man Luther*. Cf. Mazlish, "The Psycho-Historical Approach" in *In Search of Nixon*, pp. 151–170; and Erikson, "On the Nature of Psycho-Historical Evidence," *Daedalus* 97 (Summer 1968): 695–730.

One of the interesting problems—which also raises questions about the political biases of psychiatrists in making judgments about the character of a political figure—comes from Meyer Zeligs's book, *Friendship and Fratricide*, a study of the Hiss-Chambers controversy. Zeligs contended that Hiss was innocent and that Chambers acted against him out of personal, paranoid motives. Zeligs recounted the well-known traumatic childhood and adolescence of Chambers to conclude that Chambers was a paranoid capable of inventing stories about Hiss as a spy. Allen Weinstein in his almost definitive book about Hiss and Chambers noted the problems with this kind of psychobiography in describing the ways in which Chambers's personality was analyzed. He wrote: "Neither the two psychiatrists [Zeligs or Dr. Carl Binger, who testified at one of the Hiss trials about Chambers's psychological make-up] nor Smith [John Chabot Smith, author of *Alger Hiss: The True Story*] went into Hiss's own traumatic youth as having possibly induced distortions of normal personality growth such as those they detected in Chambers. Thus, in Hiss's case, the fact that his father slit his throat when Alger was three, that his mother may have neglected him, that Hiss's older and revered brother died after a wasted youth, and that his favorite sister poisoned herself—all of this, according to Binger and Zeligs, produced a splendid character strengthened by adversity, while, by contrast, bizarre family experiences in Chambers's case purportedly unhinged the latter's moral sensibilities." Weinstein, *Perjury: The Hiss-Chambers Case* (New York: Alfred A. Knopf, 1978), p. 584. Regardless of whether one believes in Hiss's innocence, one is disturbed by this kind of psychoanalysis, and by Weinstein's critique of it makes it even more disturbing.

7. Abrahamsen, *Nixon v. Nixon*, p. 124. Emphasis added.

8. Stephen E. Ambrose, *Nixon: The Education of a Politician 1913–1962* (New York: Simon and Schuster, 1987), pp. 32–33.

9. Abrahamsen, *Nixon v. Nixon*, p. 17.

10. Ibid., pp. 17–18.

11. Ibid., p 23.

12. Ibid.

13. Ibid., p. 24.

14. Ibid., p. 126.

15. Ibid., pp. 21–22.

16. James David Barber, *The Presidential Character* (Englewood Cliffs, N.J.: Prentice-Hall, 1972), pp. 388–394.

17. Ibid., p. 385.

18. Ibid.

19. Quoted in Ambrose, *Nixon*, p. 140. Ambrose, a sympathetic biographer, is astonished by Nixon's lie: "That was a breathtaking assertion, reckless in its disregard of the truth, outrageous in its denial of the facts, as was Nixon's further claim that he had never implied that Voorhis was a Communist or raise the issue of Communism in the campaign." In the eighteen pages that precedes this, Ambrose documented how great a role the issue of communism played in that campaign.

20. Richard Nixon, *RN: The Memoirs of Richard Nixon* (New York: Grosset and Dunlap, 1978), p. 41.

21. Garry Wills, *Nixon Agonistes: The Crisis of the Self-Made Man* (Boston: Houghton Mifflin, 1970), pp. 79–80.

22. One of Nixon's close friends from high school and college remarked about the change in Nixon when he entered politics: "There was never anything ruthless about Dick when we were growing up. If it was a fair fight, anything went . . . but not anything dirty. That's why I could never understand the positions he took in campaigns." Quoted in Ambrose, *Nixon*, p. 139.

23. Cf. Alfred Steinberg, *Sam Johnson's Boy* (New York: Macmillan, 1968); Merle Miller, *Lyndon: An Oral Biography* (New York: G. P. Putman's Sons, 1980); and Doris Kearns, *Lyndon Johnson and the American Dream* (New York: Harper and Row, 1976).

24. Chotiner discussed many of Nixon's campaigning strategies and tactics in a speech he delivered to Republican candidates throughout the coun-

try in 1955: "Fundamentals of Campaign Organization," unpublished manuscript.

25. "President's News Conference of November 4, 1966," *The Public Papers of the President: Lyndon B. Johnson, 1966* (Washington, D.C.: Government Printing Office, 1967), 2:1317.

26. Herbert M. Blau and William B. Ross, *Politics Battle Plan* (New York: Macmillan, 1968), p. 2. The dust jaket identifies the authors as having worked in the advertising and public relations business "since 1946" and having worked primarily for Republicans, especially for Richard M. Nixon in 1960.

27. Cf. Murray Edelman's descriptions of "hortatory" and "bargaining" language in *The Symbolic Uses of Politics* (Urbana: University of Illinois Press, 1964), pp. 134–138 and 145–151.

28. William Costello, *The Facts About Nixon: An Unauthorized* Biography (New York: Viking Press, 1960), p. 182. On Nixon as a campaigner and politician, see pp. 37–264. A "friendly" biography published at the same time paints a similar picture but with different strokes. See Bela Kornitzer, *The Real Nixon: An Intimate Biography* (New York: Rand McNally, 1960).

29. Nixon, *RN*, pp. 33–113. Interestingly, after describing the Senate campaign and why he won it, Nixon drops the subject of the Senate altogether and immediately begins writing about what he thought about the 1952 presidential campaign.

30. Wills, *Nixon Agonistes*, p. 128. Wills added: "The Vice-President was given the thankless task of campaigning for every Republican in America on off-years, when the ticket, without Eisenhower's magic name at the top, took woeful beatings."

31. Emmet John Hughes, *The Ordeal of Power. A Political Memoir of the Eisenhower Years* (New York: Atheneum, 1963), p. 134.

32. For the best account of Nixon's campaign activities during the years 1962–1968, see Jules Witcover, *The Resurrection of Nixon*, pp. 13–170.

33. It is not insignificant that Nixon was on the trip to the Soviet Union when it was jointly announced in Washington and Moscow that Premier Khrushchev and President Eisenhower would exchange visits with one another. Nixon knew nothing about the negotiations for this exchange and did not learn about it until it was publicly announced, even though he was in Moscow meeting with Khrushchev at the time. Instead, President Eisenhower trusted his brother Milton, who accompanied Nixon on the trip, with the information about the exchange of visits.

34. See Weinstein, *Perjury*, pp. 3–59, 271–284.

35. Hughes, *Ordeal of Power*, pp. 117–118.

36. Transcript of a seminar with John Ehrlichman on the Nixon administration at the University of Pittsburgh, September 28, 1978, p. 24. Ehrlichman went on to say: "I was totally in charge of environmental problems because he was persuaded that nobody ever cast a ballot in this country on an environmental problem, except a few kooks who didn't make any difference. And so I could do anything I wanted, unless it got in the way of something else."

Nixon's passion for seeing policy issues as campaign issues caused one brilliant member of his 1968 campaign staff to resign. See Richard J. Whalen, *To Catch a Falling Flag* (Boston: Houghton Mifflin, 1972).

37. Lynn Hinds and Carolyn Smith, "Nixspeak: Rhetoric of Opposites," *Nation*, February 16, 1970, pp. 172–174. Cf. William Safire's chapter, "'Us' Against 'Them'" in *Before the Fall* (New York: Belmont Tower, 1975), pp. 307–316. The habit of dividing all issues into either-or issues may have stemmed from Nixon's high school and college debating career. See William Lee Miller, "The Debating Career of Richard M. Nixon," *The Reporter*, April 19, 1956, pp. 11–17.

38. Meg Greenfield, "The Prose of Richard Nixon," *The Reporter*, September 29, 1960, p. 17.

39. Quoted in *RN*, p. 35. One must wonder how one can talk to *returning* veterans in foxholes. If Nixon meant that during the war he talked to soldiers (presumably under fire if they were in foxholes) about the pros and cons of the American political system, one also finds that hard to believe under such conditions.

40. "Student Revolutionaries," in Theodore Windt, ed., *Presidential Rhetoric: 1961 to the Present*, 4th ed. (Dubuque, Iowa: Kendall/Hunt, 1987), pp. 115–121.

41. "The Importance of Military Power," ibid., pp. 122–127.

42. "The War in Viet Nam," ibid., p. 134.

43. See Robert P. Newman, "Under the Veneer: Nixon's Vietnam Speech of November 3, 1969," *Quarterly Journal of Speech* 56 (April 1970): 168–178.

44. Chotiner, "Fundamentals of Campaign Organization," p. 2. The fundamental strategy involved in this advice is to keep your candidate always on the offensive and your opponent on the defensive. However, if the opponent launches an attack against your candidate that cannot be ignored, Chotiner advised that "you answer it . . . with an attack of your own against the opposition for having launched it in the first place." Chotiner cited Nixon's "Checkers Speech" as the "classic that will live in all political history" as the prime example of this technique (p. 10).

45. Jeb Stuart Magruder, *An American Life* (New York: Atheneum, 1974), p. 73. The president elaborated on this idea in a longer memorandum, dated September 22, 1969, that Magruder published in its entirety, pp. 74–76.

46. Andrew A. King and Floyd Douglas Anderson, "Nixon, Agnew, and the 'Silent Majority': A Case Study in the Rhetoric of Polarization," *Western Journal of Speech Communication* 35 (Fall 1971): 247.

47. From a half-page ad in October 18, 1946, *Corvina Argus-Citizen*, quoted in Costello, *The Facts About Nixon*, pp. 54–55. These charges were false or misleading. See Frank Mankiewicz, *Perfectly Clear: Nixon from Whittier to Watergate* (New York: Quadrangle, 1973), pp. 31–45.

48. Quoted in Costello, *The Facts About Nixon*, p. 65. Costello does an admirable job of putting these charges about the voting records in context on pp. 65–67,

49. Barnet Baskerville, "The New Nixon," *Quarterly Journal of Speech* 43 (February 1957): 36–39. See also Baskerville, "The Illusion of Proof," *Western Journal of Speech* 25 (Fall 1961): 236–242.

50. "Student Revolutionaries," in Windt, ed., *Presidential Rhetoric*, p. 119.

51. "The Importance of Military Power," in ibid., p. 123.

52. "Acceptance Speech," in 1968 edition of *Six Crises*, p. vi.

53. Arthur Schlesinger, Jr., *Kennedy or Nixon: Does It Make Any Difference?* (New York: Macmillan, 1960), pp. 3–4.

54. See Wills, "The Politics of Resentment" in *Nixon Agonistes*, pp. 55–71.

55. "Acceptance Speech," in *Six Crises*, p. vii. Emphasis added.

56. The two major exceptions are his support for the Marshall Plan and his support for Taft-Hartley during his years as representative. The latter led to his first debates with another freshman congressman, John F. Kennedy, in McKees Rocks, Pa., in 1947.

57. Quoted in Costello, *The Facts about Nixon*, p. 55.

58. Quoted in ibid., pp. 68–69.

59. Quoted in Mankiewicz, *Perfectly Clear*, p. 67. For a discussion of the fraudulence of the Committee for the Preservation of the Democratic Party in California, see ibid., pp. 66–75 and Appendix 5, pp. 219–232.

60. See Magruder, *An American Life*, p. 208.

61. "Student Revolutionaries," in Windt, ed., *Presidential Rhetoric*, p. 119.

62. "The Importance of Military Power," in ibid., p. 123.

63. See Vice President Agnew's speeches: "Impudence in the Streets," "The Responsibilities of Television," and "Dangers of the Media" in *Frankly Speaking* (Washington, D.C.: Public Affairs Press, 1970), pp. 44–51, 62–72, 73–77. The rhetorical strategy for Nixon to follow during the 1970 campaign was set by Nixon prior to the campaign. See Rowland Evans, Jr., and Robert D. Novak, *Nixon in the White House: The Frustration of Power* (New York: Random House, 1971), pp. 327–331.

64. Nixon, *RN*, p. 411.

65. "The Importance of Military Power," in Windt, ed., *Presidential Rhetoric*, p. 123.

66. "The War in Vietnam," in ibid., p. 129.

67. Ibid., p. 130.

68. Greenfield, "The Prose of Richard Nixon," p. 18

69. Quoted in Mankiewicz, *Perfectly Clear*, p. 52. Again, Nixon has his facts wrong. When Nixon "exposed" Alger Hiss, Hiss had already been out of the State Department for two years and was president of the Carnegie Foundation for Peace, hardly a position to "influence the foreign policy of the United States."

70. Quoted in Greenfield, "The Prose of Richard Nixon," p. 18.

71. Safire, *Before the Fall*, p. 315.

72. "The War in Vietnam," in Windt, ed., *Presidential Rhetoric*, p. 134.

73. "The Cambodian Invasion," in ibid., p. 141.

74. "Student Revolutionaries," in ibid., pp. 118–119.

75. "The Importance of Military Power," in ibid., p. 123. The critic will find it hard to believe that any politician would advocate policies that he or she knew would be catastrophic. Politicians just do not work that way. Cer-

tainly, Nixon knew that when he made the charge. Therefore, one has to conclude that Nixon made this absurd charge to delegitimize his opponents further.

76. "Statement by the President Regarding Nominations to the Court," *Weekly Compilation of Presidential Documents* (April 13, 1970), p. 505.

77. See Richard E. Vatz and Theodore Otto Windt, Jr., "The Defeats of Judges Haynsworth and Carswell: Rejection of Supreme Court Nominees," *Quarterly Journal of Speech* 60 (December 1974): pp. 477–488.

78. Quoted in J. Anthony Lukas, *Nightmare: The Underside of the Nixon Years* (New York: Viking Press, 1976), p. 272.

79. Quote from John Dean as published in ibid., p. 278.

80. See Lukas; Theodore H. White, *Breach of Faith* (New York: Atheneum, 1975); Elizabeth Drew, *Washington Journal* (New York: Random House, 1974); John J. Sirica, *To Set the Record Straight* (New York: W. W. Norton, 1979); Arthur Schlesinger, Jr., *The Imperial Presidency* (Boston: Houghton Mifflin, 1974). See also the forty-two volumes of *Hearings Before the Committee on the Judiciary, House of Representatives Ninety-Third Congress, Pursuant to H. Res. 803*, 42 vols. (Washington, D.C.: Government Printing Office, 1974).

81. "Farewell," in Windt, ed., *Presidential Rhetoric*, p. 217. Nixon ignored the fact that former Vice President Agnew had pleaded no contest to a charge of income tax evasion for taking kick backs while he was governor and later vice president. But then again, Nixon was speaking extemporaneously on this occasion of his leaving the White House.

82. Walter Goodman, rev. of Fawn Brodie's *Richard Nixon. The Shaping of His Character*, *New York Times Book Review* (October 4, 1981), p. 18.

6. A Rhetorical Sketch of Protests: Perspectives

1. For an elaboration on this distinction, see Ernest Barker, *Greek Political Theory* (New York: Barnes and Noble, 1960).

2. Walter Lippmann, *The Public Philosophy* (New York: Little, Brown, 1955), p. 65.

3. John H. Bunzel, *Anti-Politics in America* (New York: Alfred A. Knopf, 1967), p. 128.

4. Edward Shils, *The Intellectuals and the Powers and Other Essays* (Chicago: University of Chicago Press, 1972), pp. 26–27.

5. Lippmann, *The Public Philosophy*, p. 70.

6. Quoted in Patrick Anderson, *The President's Men* (Garden City, N.Y.: Doubleday, 1969), p. 31. Emphasis added.

7. Richard E. Neustadt, *Presidential Power: The Politics of Leadership* (New York: John Wiley and Sons, 1961), p. 162. Emphasis added.

8. Garry Wills, *Nixon Agonistes: The Crisis of the Self-Made Man* (Boston: Houghton Mifflin, 1970), pp. 558–575. Much of what follows in my description of the intellectual and political ethos of this time comes from Wills.

9. The writings that contributed to this "de-ideologizing" of American thought in the 1950s and early 1960s are too extensive to list here. But some of the more prominent works noted in the text include: [social psychology] Vance Packard's *The Hidden Persuaders* (New York: David McKay, 1957) and *The Status Seekers* (New York: David McKay, 1959); William H. Whyte, Jr., *The Organization Man* (New York: Simon and Schuster, 1955); [sociology] David Riesman's *Individualism Reconsidered* (Glencoe, Ill.: Free Press, 1954) and (with Nathan Glazer and Reuel Denney), *The Lonely Crowd*, abridged ed. (New Haven, Conn.: Yale University Press, 1961); [higher education] Clark Kerr, *The Uses of the University* (Cambridge: Harvard University Press, 1964); [religion] Reinhold Niebuhr, "The Triumph of Experience Over Dogma," in *The Irony of American History* (New York: Charles Scribner's Sons, 1952) and Niebuhr's *The Self and the Dramas of History* (New York: Charles Scribner's Sons, 1955); Harvey Cox, "The Style of the Secular City," in *The Secular City* (New York: Macmillan, 1965).

As overviews of the 1950s that set the stage for the decade to come, one might consult any number of general histories of the period. One that serves as a good guide is Douglas T. Miller and Marion Nowak, *The Fifties: The Way We Really Were* (Garden City, N.Y.: Doubleday, 1977).

10. See Marian J. Morton, *The Terrors of Ideological Politics. Liberal Historians in a Conservative Mood* (Cleveland, Ohio: The Press of Case Western Reserve University, 1972).

11. Zbigniew Brzezinski and Samuel Huntington, *Political Power: USA/USSR* (New York: Macmillan, 1963). George F. Kennan made a similar distinction in his *Memoirs* (Boston: Little, Brown, 1967), p. 341.

12. Daniel Bell, *The End of Ideology. On the Exhaustion of Political Ideas in the Fifties*, rev. ed. (New York: Free Press, 1965).

13. Chaim I. Waxman, "Introduction," in Waxman, ed., *The End of Ideology Debate*, (New York: Simon and Schuster, 1969), pp. 7–8. Waxman's words were written ironically and thus are taken out of his context. But I believe they were written to express, even with irony, the kind of person who would necessarily evolve from the "end of ideology" thesis.

14. Bernard Crick, *In Defense of Politics*, rev. ed. (Baltimore: Penguin Books, Pelican, 1964), p. 18. Emphasis added.

15. Seymour Martin Lipset and Earl Raab, *The Politics of Unreason* (New York: Harper and Row, 1970), p. 3.

16. Ibid., p. 4.

17. Quoted in Jules Witcover, *The Resurrection of Richard Nixon* (New York: G. P. Putnam's Sons, 1970), p. 119.

18. Michael J. Parenti, *The Anti-Communist Impulse* (New York: Random House, 1969), p. 4. Parenti's book is an analysis of the principal assumptions and beliefs that constitute this ideology and what he considered its tragic results. But notice the date of his book, 1969. The recognition that anticommunism was an ideology came late in the 1960s and has been agreed upon only by some. Others maintain the doctrine of containing communism is merely a reasonable policy, not an ideology. However, even in the early days of the cold war, there were critics of impassioned anticom-

munism. See Thomas G. Patterson, ed., *Cold War Critics*, (Chicago: Quadrangle, 1971).

19. Philip Wander called this development that of "technocratic realism." See his essay, "The Rhetoric of American Foreign Policy," *Quarterly Journal of Speech* 70 (November 1984): 349–361. Cf. David Halberstam, *The Best and the Brightest* (New York: Random House, 1972); Walter Isaacson and Evan Thomas, *The Wise Men* (New York: Simon and Schuster, 1986); and Strobe Talbott *The Master of the Game: Paul Nitze and the Nuclear Peace* (New York: Alfred A. Knopf, 1988).

20. *The Rhetoric and Poetics of Aristotle*, trans. W. Rhys Roberts (New York: Modern Library, 1954), I.8.1365, pp. 54–55.

21. Henri Lefebvre, *The Sociology of Marx*, trans. Norbert Guterman (New York: Pantheon Books, 1968), p. 81.

22. Alvin W. Gouldner, *The Two Marxisms: Contradictions and Anomalies in the Development of Theory* (New York: Oxford University Press, 1980), p. 168.

23. Donald C. Bryant, "Rhetoric: Its Function and Scope," rpt. in Joseph Schwartz and John A. Recenga, eds., *The Province of Rhetoric*, (New York: Ronald Press, 1965), p. 19.

24. Charles Sears Baldwin, *Ancient Rhetoric and Poetic* (Gloucester, Mass.: Peter Smith, 1959), p. 5. The relationship of truth to rhetoric and vice versa has become an issue of hot contention among rhetorical scholars, beginning with Robert L. Scott, who sparked the debate with "On Viewing Rhetoric as Epistemic," *Central States Speech Journal* 18 (February 1967): 9–17. The writings on this problem have become too extensive to cite in detail here. For a different position from Scott's and an extensive bibliography on the topic, see Richard A. Cherwitz and James W. Hikins, *Communication and Knowledge: An Investigation in Rhetorical Epistemology* (Columbia: University of South Carolina Press, 1986).

25. Ralph R. Smith and Russell R. Windes, "The Innovational Movement: A Rhetorical Theory," *Quarterly Journal of Speech* 61 (December 1975): 143.

26. The classic statement of the relationship of religion and rhetoric is found in Saint Augustine's *On Christian Doctrine*. The first three books are devoted to the ways of interpreting biblical truth. Book four is concerned with the rhetorical means for adapting that truth to believers. See *On Christian Doctrine*, trans. D. W. Robertson, Jr. (New York: Liberal Arts Press, 1958).

27. For the controversy over ideology in rhetorical criticism, see Philip Wander and Steve Jenkins, " Rhetoric, Society, and the Critical Response," *Quarterly Journal of Speech* 58 (December 1972): 441–450; Lawrence W. Rosenfield, "The Experience of Criticism," ibid. 60 (December 1974): 489–496; Michael C. McGee, "In Search of 'The People': A Rhetorical Alternative," ibid. 61 (October 1975): 248–258; Michael Calvin McGee, "'Not Men, but Measures': The Origins and Import of an Ideological Principle," ibid. 64 (April 1978): 141–154; Michael Calvin McGee, "The 'Ideograph': A Link Between Rhetoric and Ideology," ibid. 66 (February 1980): 1–16; Philip Wander, "Cultural Criticism," in Dan D. Nimmo and Keith R. Sanders, eds.,

Handbook of Political Communication (Beverly Hills, Calif.: Sage, 1981), pp. 495–505; Philip Wander, "The Ideological Turn in Modern Criticism," *Central States Speech Journal* 34 (Spring 1983), 1–18; Lawrence W. Rosenfield, "Ideological Miasma," ibid. 34 (Summer 1983): 119–121; Forbes Hill, "A Turn Against Ideology: Reply to Professor Wander," ibid. 34 (Summer 1983): 121–126; Karlyn Kohrs Campbell, "Response to Forbes Hill," ibid. 34 (Summer 1983): 126–127; Allan Megill, "Special Report: Responses to Wander: Heidegger, Wander, and Ideology," ibid. 34 (Summer 1983): 114–119; Philip Wander, "The Third Persona: An Ideological Turn in Rhetorical Theory," ibid. 35 (Winter 1984): 197–216; Robert Francesconi, "Heidegger and Ideology: Reflections of an Innocent Bystander," ibid. 35 (Spring 1984): 51–53; Michael Calvin McGee, "Another Phillippic: Notes on the Ideological Turn in Criticism," ibid. 35 (Spring 1984): 43–50; Farrel Corcoran, "The Widening Gyre: Another Look at Ideology in Wander and his Critics," ibid. 35 (Spring 1984): 54–56.

28. This problem is one that Gouldner suggested when he wrote in 1980 that Marxism needed to be subjected to a Marxist critique itself. That he proceeded to do in *The Two Marxisms*. See esp. pp. 3–89.

29. See Sidney Lens, *Radicalism in America* (New York: Thomas Y. Crowell, 1966), p. 1.

30. Of course, this point is controversial, and rhetorical scholars line up on either side of how to interpret "rhetorical situations." Cf. Lloyd F. Bitzer, "The Rhetorical Situation," *Philosophy and Rhetoric* 1 (Winter 1968): 1–14; and Richard E. Vatz, "The Myth of the Rhetorical Situation," ibid. 6 (Summer 1973): 154–161. Although a variety of other scholars have contributed to and refined the debate over the "rhetorical situation," these two essays present the differences in bald contrast. My own inclination is to side with Vatz when it comes to political rhetoric, where choices for defining issues and acting must be taken quickly without the time for reflection that others in other activities have.

31. Sonja K. Foss, *Rhetorical Criticism: Exploration and Practice* (Prospect Heights, Ill.: Waveland Press, 1989), p. 112. I have drawn on Foss's excellent summary for defining these three elements in generic criticism. For additional statements on the theory of genres, see Karlyn Kohrs Campbell and Kathleen Hall Jamieson, eds., *Form and Genre: Shaping Rhetorical Action* (Falls Church, Va.: Speech Communication Association, [1978]); Jackson Harrell and Wil A. Linkugel, "On Rhetorical Genre: An Organizing Perspective," *Philosophy and Rhetoric* 11 (Fall 1978): 263–264; Herbert W. Simons and Aram A. Aghazarian, eds., *Form, Genre, and the Study of Political Discourse*, (Columbia: University of South Carolina Press, 1986).

32. Cf. Richard B. Gregg, "The Ego-Function of the Rhetoric of Protest," *Philosophy and Rhetoric* 4 (Spring 1971): 71–91. I take the use of symbolic acts a bit further than Gregg and insist that they are the standards by which one judges political authenticity.

33. Richard Hofstadter, *The Paranoid Style in American Politics and Other Essays* (New York: Alfred A. Knopf, 1965), p. 189.

34. Leland M. Griffin, "The Rhetoric of Historical Movements," *Quarterly Journal of Speech* 38 (April 1952): 184–188. Cf. Griffin, "A Dramatistic

Theory of the Rhetoric of Movements," in William H. Rueckett, ed., *Critical Responses to Kenneth Burke* (Minneapolis: University of Minnesota Press, 1969), p. 462.

35. Herbert A. Simons, "Requirements, Problems, and Strategies: A Theory of Persuasion for Social Movements," *Quarterly Journal of Speech* 56 (February 1970): 1–11. Cf. Simons, Elizabeth Mechling and Howard N. Schrier, "Functions of Communication in Mobilizing for Collective Action from the Bottom Up: The Rhetoric of Social Movements," in Carroll C. Arnold and John Waite Bowers, eds., *Handbook of Rhetorical and Communication Theory* (Boston: Allyn and Bacon, 1983).

36. Robert S. Cathcart, "New Approaches to the Study of Movements: Defining Movements Rhetorically," *Western Journal of Speech Communication* 36 (Spring 1972): 82–88.

37. The most notable attempt to synthesize various theories and methods is the work by Charles Stewart, Craig Smith, and Robert E. Denton, Jr., *Persuasion and Social Movements* (Prospect Heights, Ill.: Waveland Press, 1984). However, it did not produce the consensus they desired, and critical pluralism in regard to studying the rhetoric of movements still reigns.

38. Cf. the entire issue of *Central States Speech Journal* 31 (Winter 1980), which was devoted to different approaches to social movements. For an extensive but selected bibliography of persuasion and social movements, see Stewart, Smith, and Denton, *Persuasion and Social Movements*, pp. 201–219.

39. "Special Report: Social Movements," ed. Bernard L. Brock, *Central States Speech Journal* 34 (Spring 1983): 67–82.

40. The reasons for these changes are various. One reason, however, bears special mention: the influence of mass media, particularly television. As striking news events occurred, television swooped down on someone who seemed to represent a new idea or who had coined a new slogan and demanded to know what the person or organization stood for on a national basis. As Maria Varela, who worked with both SDS and SNCC, explained the problem: "We had been sort of thrust into the national picture and . . . we weren't ready for it. We didn't have a philosophy or a strategy for working nationally . . . . And we were winging it." Quoted in Todd Gitlin, *The Whole World Is Watching* (Berkeley: University of California Press, 1980), p. 163. For the critical role television played in creating celebrity leaders, stereotyping organizations, and provoking ad hoc national political statements, see Gitlin's excellent account.

As faculty adviser of the United Afro-American Students Organization at the University of Texas at El Paso, I can attest to the pressure television brought to producing such statements. When a local television station learned that black students had banded together to form an all-black organization (and this was in 1967, a while before such organizations became commonplace), it rushed its top reporter out to do a story on the organization. When the reporter found out that the faculty adviser was white, he chose to interview me rather than the leaders of the organization. And he questioned me about everything from my "philosophy" of racial relations to what the formation of this organization meant to blacks and whites nationally. Initially, I refused to answer any of these questions except in the most disingenuous manner until he and I reached a professional (and private) agreement about how he would pursue news stories in relation to the organization. But even under these conditions, the reporter, who stayed with the story right through the assassination of Dr. Martin Luther King, Jr., repeatedly asked questions of me and of the leaders of the organization that went far beyond any issues that had been discussed within the organization.

41. Robert C. Tucker, "The Theory of Charismatic Leadership," *Daedalus* 98 (Summer 1968): 736.

42. Peter Sloterdijk, *Critique of Cynical Reason*, trans. Michael Eldred (Minneapolis: University of Minnesota Press, 1987), p. 91. See Part I, pp. 3–133, for his philosophic examination of the progress from Enlightenment to Ideology to Cynicism.

7. Liberal Protest: Procedural Politics and Deliberative Rhetoric

1. Cf. Theodore Otto Windt, Jr., "Roots for the Idea of 'Common Ground' in Classical Rhetoric," *Pennsylvania Speech Annual* 26 (1969): 1–8.

2. Hans J. Morgenthau, "Political Folklore in Vietnam," first address at the National Teach-In, abridged version in Louis Menashe and Ronald Radosh, eds., *Teach-Ins: U.S.A.* (New York: Frederick A. Praeger, 1967), p. 159.

3. Cf. Sidney Lens, *The Labor Wars: From the Molly Maguires to the Sitdowns* (Garden City, N.Y.: Anchor Press/Doubleday, 1974).

4. Cf. Charles Stewart, Craig Smith, and Robert E. Denton, Jr., *Persuasion and Social Movements* (Prospect Heights, Ill.: Waveland Press, 1984). See their selected bibliography, pp. 201–219.

5. "Quaker Resolution Against Slavery, 1652," in Joanne Grant, ed., *Black Protest: History, Documents and Analyses, 1619 to the Present* (New York: Fawcett, 1969), p. 26.

6. John H. Thurber and John L. Petelle, "The Negro Pulpit and Civil Rights," *Central States Speech Journal* 19 (Winter 1968), 273–278.

7. See David M. Jabusch, "The Rhetoric of Civil Rights," *Western Journal of Speech* 30 (Summer 1966): 176–183; David M. Hunsaker, "The Rhetoric of *Brown v. Board of Education*: Paradigm for Contemporary Social Protest," *Southern Speech Communication Journal* 43 (1978), 91–109.

8. Martin Luther King, Jr., *Stride Toward Freedom: The Montgomery Story* (New York: Harper and Row, 1958), p. 48. For additional information about the events and rhetoric surrounding the bus boycott, I am indebted to Jeffrey J. Leech, "Martin Luther King: The Montgomery Bus Boycott and the Rhetoric of Non-Violent Protest" (term paper, University of Pittsburgh, 1969), 22 pp. Cf. Donald H. Smith, "Martin Luther King, Jr.: In the Beginning at Montgomery," *Southern Speech Communication Journal* 34 (Fall 1968): 2–8.

9. King, "Non-Violence and Racial Justice," *Christian Century*, February 6, 1957, p. 166.

10. Philip C. Wander, "The John Birch and Martin Luther King Symbols in the Radical Right," *Western Journal of Speech* 35 (Winter 1971): 4–14.

11. Julius Lester, "Cleaver, Carmichael and the Politics of Black Liberation," in Dotson Rader, ed., *Defiance 1*, (New York: Paperback Library, 1970), pp. 78–79.

12. Compare, for example, Dr. King's famous "Letter from a Birmingham Jail" to Eldridge Cleaver's "A Letter from Jail," printed in *Ramparts*, June 15, 1968. Cf. Richard P. Fulkerson, "The Public Letter as a Rhetorical Form: Structure, Logic, and Style in King's 'Letter from Birmingham Jail,'" *Quarterly Journal of Speech* 65 (April 1979): 121–136.

13. Cf. Aristotle, *Rhetoric*, I. 9. 1366a–1376b.

14. King, "I Have a Dream," in Wil A. Linkugel, R. R. Allen, and Richard L. Johannessen, eds., *Contemporary American Speeches* (Belmont, Calif.: Wadsworth, 1969), pp. 293–294. Black protest had its roots in the church and therefore used religious language and the black religious rhetorical tradition persistently. Seldom were other movements able to use this powerful connection between religious symbols and protest rhetoric. For example, the Rev. William Sloan Coffin, a prominent religious opponent of the war, gave only *one* sermon on the war and instead confined his protest rhetoric to traditional rhetorical means and topics. See William Carl III, "Old Testament Prophecy and the Question of Prophetic Preaching: A Perspective on Ecclesiastical Protest to the Vietnam War and the Participation of William Sloane Coffin, Jr." (Ph.D. diss., University of Pittsburgh, 1977).

15. At the march on Washington, march organizers persuaded John Lewis to alter his speech only moments before delivering it because they thought the original version would be counterproductive to the movement's goals. Certainly, at this time, Lewis was no radical in comparison with the Muslims or Malcolm X.

16. On Malcolm X's rhetoric, see Thomas W. Benson, "Rhetoric and Autobiography: The Case of Malcolm X," *Quarterly Journal of Speech* 60 (February 1974): 1–13.

17. Nigel Young, *An Infantile Disorder? The Crisis and Decline of the New Left* (Boulder, Colo.: Westview Press, 1977), p. 115.

18. C. Eric Lincoln, *The Black Muslims in America* (Boston: Beacon Press, 1963), p. 145.

19. "Death of a Desperado," *Newsweek*, March 8, 1965, p. 24.

20. "Malcolm X," *Nation*, March 8, 1965, p. 239.

21. Betty Friedan, *The Feminine Mystique* (New York: Dell Publishing, 1963). I am indebted to a series of unpublished papers on the feminist movement by Roxanne Tucci Davidson for part of the work in this section.

22. Friedan, *Feminine Mystique*, p. 10.

23. "NOW (National Organization for Women) Bill of Rights," in Robin Morgan, ed., *Sisterhood Is Powerful* (New York: Vintage Books, 1970), p. 512.

24. Betty Friedan, "Up From the Kitchen Floor," *New York Times Magazine*, March 4, 1973, p. 30.

25. Cf. Morgan, "Introduction," *Sisterhood Is Powerful*, pp. xxi–xxii.

26. Ibid., pp. xxi–xxviii.

27. Jo Freeman, "On the Origins of Social Movements," in Jo Freeman, ed., *Social Movements of the Sixties and Seventies* (White Plains, N.Y.: Longman, 1983), pp. 20–21.

28. Kathie Sarachild, "The Power of History," in Sarachild, ed., *Feminist Revolution* (New York: Redstockings of the Women's Liberation Movement, 1978), pp. 13–43.

29. "Excerpts from the SCUM (Society for Cutting Up Men) Manifesto," in Morgan, ed., *Sisterhood Is Powerful*, p. 518.

30. Ibid., p. 514.

31. See Morgan's brief biographical sketch of Solanis and the apologia for her, ibid., p. 600.

32. This is not to say that there wasn't an overall peace movement prior to the war. There was. A. J. Muste was one of its leaders, and in 1961 there was the San Francisco-to-Moscow Walk for Peace. But it was the escalation of the war in Vietnam that provided the impetus for the broad-based antiwar movement of the 1960s.

33. Morgenthau, "Political Folklore in Vietnam," p. 164.

34. See J. Robert Cox, "Perspectives on Rhetorical Criticism of Movements: Antiwar Dissent, 1964–1970," *Western Journal of Speech Communication* 38 (Fall 1974): 254–268. Cox demonstrated that even after some protestors turned to radicalism, most of the speeches given at large meetings in Washington remained well within the deliberative genre. For amplification of this essay, see his Ph.D. dissertation, "The Rhetorical Structure of Mass Protest: A Criticism of Selected Speeches of the Vietnam Anti-War Movement" (University of Pittsburgh, 1973).

35. See Howard H. Martin, "The Rhetoric of Academic Protest," *Central States Speech Journal* 17 (November 1966): 244–250.

36. I. F. Stone. "The White House Outsmarted Itself and Put the Spotlight on the Teach-In . . . ," *I. F. Stone's Weekly*, May 25, 1965, p. 3.

37. Cf. Meg Greenfield, "After the Washington Teach-In," in Menashe and Radosh, eds., *Teach-Ins*, p. 183.

38. Anyone who writes on the development of the rhetoric of the new left owes a deep debt of gratitude to Leland M. Griffin, "The Rhetorical Structure of the 'New Left' Movement: Part I," republished in Robert L. Scott and Bernard L. Brock, eds., *Methods of Rhetorical Criticism: A Twentieth-Century Perspective* (New York: Harper and Row, 1972), pp. 352–383. There are a variety of books devoted to analyzing the ideological development of the new left. On the influence of Mills on SDS and the writing of the Port Huron Statement, see James Miller, *"Democracy Is in the Streets": From Port Huron to the Siege of Chicago* (New York: Simon and Schuster, Touchstone Books, 1987), pp. 78–154. For the most even-handed summary of these ideological influences, not only on the new left but on other radical organizations and advocates of this period, see Young's *An Infantile Disorder?*

39. C. Wright Mills, *The Power Elite* (New York: Oxford University Press, 1959), p. 335. For a critique of his views, see William Domhoff and Hoyt B.

Ballard, eds., *C. Wright Mills and The Power Elite* (Boston: Beacon Press, 1968).

40. Mills *The Power Elite*, pp. 335–336.

41. "The Port Huron Statement," republished in Paul Jacobs and Saul Landau, *The New Radicals: A Report with Documents* (New York: Vintage, 1966), p. 151.

42. Ibid., p. 155. The sexist language is in the original and is indicative of the ways even progressive thinkers thought at the time.

43. Milton Viorst, *Fire in the Streets* (New York: Simon and Schuster, 1979), p. 190.

44. For penetrating critiques of Kennedy's "conservative default" written by those not mesmerized by "Camelot," see Richard J. Walton, *Cold War and Counterrevolution: The Foreign Policy of John F. Kennedy* (New York: Viking Press, 1972); and Henry Fairlie, *The Kennedy Promise* (New York: Dell, 1974).

45. Alan Adelson, *SDS. A Profile* (New York: Charles Scribner's Sons, 1972), p. 208. Cf. Jack Newfield, "SDS: From *Port Huron* to *La Chinoise*," *Evergreen Review* 73 (1969): pp. 15–17; and Greg Calvert and Carol Neiman, *A Disrupted History: The New Left and the New Capitalism* (New York: Random House, 1971), pp. 3–40.

46. "The Port Huron Statement," in Miller, *"Democracy Is in the Streets"*, p. 350. For the development of this critique in the statement, see pp. 350–358. Even socialists, led by Michael Harrington, were dismayed that the statement did not stress a vigilant anticommunism. Gitlin quotes Harrington as saying that it "seemed to imply the United States was the prime source of evil in the Cold War." See Todd Gitlin, *The Sixties: Years of Hope, Days of Rage* (New York: Bantam Books, 1987), pp. 110–126.

47. *The Politics of Protest: Violent Aspects of Protest and Confrontation: A Staff Report to the National Commission on the Causes and Prevention of Violence*, prepared by Jerome Skolnick (Washington, D.C.: Government Printing Office, 1969), p. 76.

8. The Administrative Rhetoric of Credibility: Changing the Issues

1. Max Heirich, *The Beginning: Berkeley 1964* (New York: Columbia University Press, 1970), p. 1. For antecedent student protests, see Julian Foster and Durward Long, eds., *Protest! Student Activism in America*, (New York: William Morrow, 1970), pp. 345–361 in particular.

2. The most easily accessible source for documents is Seymour Martin Lipset and Sheldon S. Wolin, eds., *The Berkeley Student Revolt: Facts and Interpretations* (Garden City, N.Y.: Anchor Books, 1965). This volume includes a helpful "Chronology of Events: Three Months of Crisis," written by the editors of the *California Monthly*. Also valuable is Michael V. Miller and Susan Gilmore, eds., *Revolution at Berkeley: The Crisis in American Education* (New York: Dial Press, 1965). One might also want to consult

Christopher G. Katope and Paul G. Zolbrod, eds., *Beyond Berkeley* (Cleveland: World Publishing, 1966). To place the free speech battle within the context of protest during the 1960s, one might consult Ronald Frazer, ed., *1968: A Generation in Revolt* (New York: Pantheon Books, 1988), pp. 89–99. Also, Todd Gitlin has scattered references to the controversy in *The Sixties: Years of Hope, Days of Rage* (New York: Bantam Books, 1987). I believe Heirich's *The Beginning* presents the most balanced interpretation of what occurred.

3. For the significant parts of Dean Towle's statement, see "Chronology of Events" in Lipset and Wolin, eds., *The Berkeley Student Revolt*, pp. 100–101.

4. Heirich estimated the crowd at 4,000 to 5,000. All quotations from Savio's speech, "An End to History," are taken from the copy reprinted in ibid., pp. 216–219.

5. Quoted in Heirich, *The Beginning*, p. 81.

6. For examples, see Jerry Farber, *The Student as Nigger* (New York: Pocket Books, 1970); Naomi Weisstein, "Woman as Nigger," in Leslie B. Tanner, ed., *Voices from Women's Liberation* (New York: Signet, 1971), pp. 296–303; and François Dupuis, "From a White Nigger to a Quebec Separatist," in *Defiance 3*, ed. by Dotson Rader (New York: Paperback Library, 1971), pp. 134–147.

7. Savio, "An End to History," p. 217.

8. Miller and Gilmore, *Revolution at Berkeley*, p. 85.

9. C. Wright Mills, "The Politics of Responsibility," in Carl Oglesby, ed., *The New Left Reader* (New York: Grove Press, 1969), p. 23.

10. Weber's most important writings on this subject may be found in *Theories of Social and Economic Organization* (New York: Free Press, 1947) and *Charisma and Institution Building* (Chicago: University of Chicago Press, 1968).

11. Savio insisted on the relationship of speech to action but made a distinction between a "radical" speech (one that advocates "changes so radical as to be irrelevant in the foreseeable future") and his advocacy of sit-ins to bring about "changes in discriminatory hiring practices," which he undoubtedly thought was comparable to what members of the Free Speech Movement had done.

12. Heirich, *The Beginning*, p. 87.

13. For another interpretation of administrative responses to protest, see John Waite Bowers and Donovan J. Ochs, *The Rhetoric of Agitation and Control* (Reading, Mass.: Addison-Wesley, 1971), pp. 39–56. Bowers and Ochs present a more elaborate pattern of administrative responses, including avoidance, suppression, adjustment, and capitulation, which the authors then explain in terms of tactics adopted by administrators that achieve or result in each of these. They concentrate on each political and bureaucratic stance administrators take more than on the rhetoric to justify these stances. Their analysis is valuable and should be consulted in conjunction with the analysis presented here.

14. Cf. Michael W. Miles, *The Radical Probe: The Logic of Student Rebellion* (New York: Atheneum, 1971), pp. 63–109.

15. William Peterson, "What is Left at Berkeley," originally published in *Columbia University Forum* and reprinted in Lipset and Wolin, eds., *The Berkeley Student Revolt*, p. 369.

16. John Searle, *The Campus War* (New York: World, 1971), p. 9. Emphasis added. Searle's book is an invaluable aid to understanding the mind-set of some liberal academicians and administrators.

17. Compare this form of rhetoric to Kennedy's use of domestic crisis rhetoric and to the form of Nixon's rhetoric in Chapter Two and Chapter Five, respectively.

18. Statement issued by Chancellor Strong on September 30 and quoted from Lipset and Wolin, eds., *The Berkeley Student Revolt*, p. 109.

19. Address to the Town and Gown Club by Chancellor Strong on November 2, ibid.

20. Ibid.

21. See Heirich, *The Beginning*, pp. 49–97; and "Chronology of Events," pp. 99–108.

22. Statement by President Clark Kerr on December 3 in Lipset and Wolin, eds., *The Berkeley Student Revolt*, pp. 246–247.

23. Cf. Chapter Three and the memoranda of James McNaughton quoted in that chapter.

24. "The Vietnam War Becomes the American-Vietnamese War," in Theodore Windt, ed., *Presidential Rhetoric: 1961 to the Present*, 4th ed. (Dubuque, Iowa: Kendall/Hunt, 1987), pp. 81–82.

25. "Nervous Nellies," ibid., p. 92.

26. "The Importance of Military Power," ibid., p. 123. Emphasis added.

27. *Collected Speeches of Spiro Agnew* (New York: Audubon Books, 1971), pp. 85, 96, 89. All subsequent quotations from Agnew's speech are from this publication of the speech. For an incisive criticism, see Karlyn Kohrs Campbell, *Critiques of Contemporary Rhetoric* (Belmont, Calif.: Wadsworth, 1972), pp. 78–110.

28. Agnew accused Harriman of swapping "some of the greatest military concessions in the history of warfare for an enemy agreement on the shape of a bargaining table." Ibid., p. 86.

29. In analyzing the protests at Birmingham, Alabama, in 1963, Bowers and Ochs pointed out that the white supremacists and racists took this same position in response to the demonstrations by Dr. Martin Luther King, Jr. See Bowers and Ochs, *Rhetoric of Agitation*, pp. 122–125.

30. Ibid., p. 59.

31. See Heirich, *The Beginning*, pp. 251–285.

9. The Dynamics of Ideology and Ideological Rhetoric

1. Neither the Socialist nor the Communist party has been able to gain a significant following in the United States, except in periods of severe distress. See Sidney Lens, *Radicalism in America* (New York: Thomas Y. Crowell, 1966). Also, one need only consult where the leading radicals of the

1960s are today to see the lack of a sustained radical temperament or politics.

2. See Robert C. Tucker, "The Theory of Charismatic Leadership," *Daedalus* 98 (Summer 1968): 731–756; and Edward Shils, *The Intellectuals and the Powers and Other Essays* (Chicago: University of Chicago Press, 1972), pp. 29–31.

3. For a detailed examination of the idea of the anticommunist ideology, see Michael J. Parenti, *The Anti-Communist Impulse* (New York: Random House, 1969), pp. 160–161, and Charles E. Osgood, *An Alternative to War or Surrender* (Urbana: University of Illinois Press, 1962), pp. 139 *passim*. See also: Barnet Baskerville, "The Cross and the Flag: Evangelists of the Far Right," *Western Journal of Speech*, 27 (Fall 1963): 197–206; Thomas G. Goodnight and John Poulakos, "Conspiracy Rhetoric: From Pragmatism to Fantasy in Public Discourse," *Western Journal of Speech Communication*, 45 (Fall 1981): 299–316; Craig Allen Smith, "The Hofstadter Hypothesis Revisited: The Nature of Evidence in Politically 'Paranoid' Discourse," *Southern Speech Communication Journal* 42 (Spring 1977): 274–289. On the broader issue of doctrinaire rhetoric, see Roderick P. Hart, "The Rhetoric of the True Believer," *Speech Monographs* 38 (November 1971): 249–271.

4. Henri Lefebvre, *The Sociology of Marx*, trans. Norbert Guterman (New York: Pantheon Books, 1968), pp. 59–122. Lefebvre contends that the critics purposefully "study the emergence of forms, the way forms react on contents, structure on processes" (p. 56) as the major function of criticizing ideological rhetoric. If he is correct, as I believe he is, he presents the rhetorical critic with another far-reaching purpose in doing criticism, especially in view of Lefebvre's emphasis on the importance of language's influencing structure, process, and even content. In fact, Lefebvre is the starting point for my outline of the different kinds of ideological rhetoric that follow.

5. Ibid., pp. 72–73.

6. All subsequent quotations from the "Manifesto" are taken from "The Communist Manifesto" in William Lutz and Harry Brent, eds., *On Revolution* (Cambridge, Mass.: Winthrop, 1971), pp. 3–23.

7. The classical notion of "common ground" is not based on class but on reason and common interests (or enlightened self-interests, as liberals prefer to call it). See Theodore O. Windt, "Roots for the Idea of 'Common Ground' in Classical Rhetoric," *Pennsylvania Speech Annual* 26 (September 1969): 5–15.

8. Louis J. Halle, *The Society of Man* (London: Chatto and Windus, 1965), p. 103.

9. The Preamble is reprinted in Patrick Renshaw, *The Wobblies: The Story of Syndicalism in the United States* (New York: Anchor Books, 1968), facing p. 102.

10. Lefebvre, *The Sociology of Marx*, p. 87.

11. Tom Hayden, "A Protest Against the Draft and Death of Intellect," in Louis Menashe and Ronald Radosh, eds., *Teach-Ins: U.S.A.*, (New York: Frederick A. Praeger, 1967), p. 336. Throughout the war both the Johnson and Nixon administrations sought to control the language describing events

in Vietnam. Although this example comes from a later time (1970), it aptly demonstrates this attempt to control language and thus to control thinking about the war. The U.S. Command in Vietnam issued its briefing officers a "guidance" directive entitled "Let's Say It Right" that noted "Incorrect Terms" and "Correct Terms":

Incorrect Terms	Correct Terms
National Liberation Front	Vietcong or V.C.
V.C. tax collectors	V.C. extortionists
Hearts and minds of the people	Develop community spirit
U.S. Troop withdrawal	Redeployment or replacement
Mercenary	Civilian irregular Defense Group (or C.I.D.G.) soldier (or volunteer)
Search and destroy	Search and clear

Source: "Let's Say It Right," *New York Times*, January 11, 1970, E–5.

12. Arthur L. Smith, *Rhetoric of Black Revolution* (Boston: Allyn and Bacon, 1969), p. 7. Cf. Diane Schaich Hope, "Redefinition of Self: A Comparison of the Rhetoric of the Women's Liberation and Black Liberation Movements," *Today's Speech* 23 (Winter 1975): 17–25.

13. "Introduction," Harold Jacobs, ed., *Weatherman* (n.p.: Ramparts Press, 1970), pp. 3–4.

14. "Redstockings Manifesto," in Leslie B. Tanner, ed., *Voices from Women's Liberation* (New York: New American Library, 1970), p. 109.

15. Ibid., pp. 109–111.

16. Ibid., p. 110.

17. Everett Lee Hunt, "The Social Interpretation of Literature," *English Journal* 24 (March 1935): 214. Hunt was replying to Granville Hicks's call for a communist or marxist interpretation of literature.

18. Ti-Grace Atkinson, ed., *Amazon Women* (New York: Links Books, 1974), p. 11.

19. Betty Friedan, "Up from the Kitchen Floor," *New York Times Magazine*, March 4, 1973, p. 33. For further examples of this kind of factionalism within the women's liberation movement, see the following essays: Kathie Sarachild, "The Power of History"; Carol Hanisch, "The Liberal Takeover of Women's Liberation"; Ellen Willis, "The Conservatism of Ms."; and Redstockings, "The Pseudo-Left/Lesbian Alliance Against Feminism," all published in Sarachild, ed., *Feminist Revolution* (New York: Redstockings of the Women's Liberation Movement, 1978).

20. Cf. Theodore Draper, *The Roots of American Communism* (New York: Viking Press, 1957), pp. 11–35. Draper contended that attempting to answer these questions led to factionalism in practically every historical radical movement. For other historical examples of sectarianism in ideological politics, see Philip S. Foner, *The Industrial Workers of the World, 1905–1917* (New York: International Publishers, 1973), pp. 60–80, 415–434; and Isaac Deutscher, *The Prophet Unarmed. Trotsky; 1921–1929* 2 (London: Oxford University Press, 1959), pp. 164–394.

21. For one brief account of the split in SDS, see Jacobs, *Weatherman*, pp. 1–13.

22. For one account of this split, see Kathie Sarachild, "The Power of History," in *Feminist Revolution*, pp. 13–43.

23. Cf. James W. Chesebro, John F. Cragan, and Patricia McCullough, "The Small Group Technique of the Radical Revolutionary: A Synthetic Study of Consciousness Raising," *Communication Monographs* 40 (June 1973): 136–146; Brenda Robinson Hancock, "Affirmation by Negation in the Women's Liberation Movement," *Quarterly Journal of Speech* 58 (October 1972): 264–271.

24. Each subsequent quotation on consciousness-raising is from "Introduction," Robin Morgan, ed., *Sisterhood Is Powerful* (New York: Vintage Books, 1970), pp. xxiii–xxiv.

25. Cf. Irene Peslikis, "Resistances of Consciousness," in ibid., pp. 337–339.

26. Ibid., p. xiii.

27. Each subsequent quotation is from Timothy Leary, "Letter From Timothy Leary," in Jacobs, *Weatherman*, pp. 517–519. Leary may seem an odd choice to represent the revolutionary. But his "Letter" is representative.

28. Cf. Howard S. Erlich, "'. . . And by Opposing, End Them.' The Genre of Moral Justification for Legal Transgressions," *Today's Speech* 23 (Winter 1975): 13–16.

29. Cf. Robert J. Doolittle, "Riots as Symbolic: A Criticism and Approach," *Central States Speech Journal* 27 (Winter 1976): 310–317.

30. Cf. William L. Burke. "Notes on a Rhetoric of Lamentation," *Central States Speech Journal* 30 (Summer 1979): 109–121; and Sacvan Bercovitch, *The American Jeremiad* (Madison: University of Wisconsin Press, 1978).

31. Burke, "Rhetoric of Lamentation," p. 120.

32. Noam Chomsky, *American Power and the New Mandarins* (New York: Pantheon Books, 1969), p. 9. The equivalent of Chomsky's lamentation over the war in the black movement is to be found in some sermons and in the "blues" musical tradition.

33. Ibid.,

34. Ibid., p. 10.

35. Ibid., p. 169.

36. Ibid., p. 31.

37. Ibid., pp. 367–400. Throughout this book Chomsky distinguished between confrontation and resistance, between political resistance and moral resistance. These distinctions, too extensive to detail here, set Chomsky apart in my mind from other ideologues when it comes to those symbolic acts that legitimize his rhetoric.

38. Amos 5:1–3, 6–7.

10. The Diatribe or the Subversion of Delicacy

1. Max Heirich recorded a conversation with someone who had been critical of the entire Free Speech Movement and who tried to make a distinction between the actions of the fraternity and Thomson. Heirich quoted

him as saying: "That was just a bunch of fraternity boys blowing off steam. You know that when it's all over they're going to return to take their place as respectable members of society. But these people are out to deliberately break every rule they can, to try to tear down society." Heirich, *The Beginning: Berkeley 1964* (New York: Columbia University Press, 1970), p. 259. For a report on most of the major incidents and responses to Thomson's action, see pp. 256–263.

2. Quoted in ibid., p. 260.

3. Ibid., p. 261

4. Quoted in Stephen Spender, *The Year of the Young Rebels* (New York: Vintage Books, 1969), p. 8.

5. Theodore H. White, *The Making of the President 1968* (New York: Atheneum, 1969), p. 286. Cf. David Lewis Stein, *Living the Revolution: The Yippies in Chicago* (Indianapolis: Bobbs Merrill, 1969).

6. Donald R. Dudley, *A History of Cynicism* (London: Methuen, 1937), pp. ix–x.

7. All of these stories are found in "Diogenes Laertius," *Lives of Eminent Philosophers*, ed. R. D. Hicks, vol. 2 (Cambridge: Harvard University Press, 1965), p. 23. The only book-length "biography" of Diogenes is Farrand Sayre, *Diogenes of Sinope: A Study of Greek Cynicism* (Baltimore: J. H. Furst, 1938).

8. From Gilbert Murray, *Fives Stages of Greek Religion*, quoted by Bertrand Russell, *A History of Western Philosophy* (New York: Simon and Schuster, Touchstone Books, 1972), p. 231.

9. Russell, *A History of Western Philosophy*, p. 231.

10. "Diogenes Laertius," p. 25.

11. Ibid., p. 43. Usually this statement reads "looking for an honest man." The insertion of "honest" probably occurred sometime during the seventh century to make it consistent with Christian theology. *Courageous* or *hardy* would have been more appropriate, as either would have been consistent with Greek style and Diogenes' thinking.

12. Ibid., p. 67.

13. H. I. Marrou, *A History of Education in Antiquity*, trans. George Lamb (New York: Mentor Books, 1964), p. 292.

14. "Diogenes Laertius," p. 73.

15. The idea was not entirely new. "The antithesis between nature and convention seems to have originated with Hippias." Everett Lee Hunt, "Plato and Aristotle on Rhetoric and Rhetoricians," in Raymond F. Howes, ed., *Historical Studies of Rhetoric and Rhetoricians*, (Ithaca, N.Y.: Cornell University Press, 1961), p. 24. But Diogenes made it the cornerstone of his doctrine of freedom and natural rights as well as the motivating force in his way of living.

16. "Diogenes Laertius," p. 71.

17. Ibid., p. 25.

18. Ibid., p. 55.

19. Ibid., p. 43. The attack on the idealism of Socrates and Plato became a persistent theme in cynical diatribes. In the *Superiority of the Cynic Life*, Maximus of Tyre wrote: "I am ready indeed to praise Socrates; but then his

words occur to me: 'I obey the law and go voluntarily to gaol, and take the poison voluntarily.'—O Socrates, do you not see what you are saying? Do you then yield voluntarily, or are you an involuntary victim of fortune?— 'Obeying the law.'—What law? For if you mean the law of Zeus, I commend the law; but if you mean Solon's law, in what was Solon better than Socrates? Let Plato answer to me for philosophy, whether it saved him from the perturbation when Dio fled, when Dionysius threatened, when he was compelled to sail back and forth over the Sicilian and Ionian seas . . . . Wherefore I say that from this tyranny of circumstance the only liberation is in that life which raised Diogenes above Lycurgus and Solon and Artaxerxes and Alexander, and made him freer than Socrates himself." Quoted in Paul Elmer More, *Hellenistic Philosophies* (Princeton, N.J.: Princeton University Press, 1923), p. 295.

20. "Diogenes Laertius," p. 41.

21. Ibid., p. 55.

22. Ibid., p. 51.

23. Russell, *A History of Western Philosophy*, p. 231.

24. See John O. Lyons, *The Invention of the Self: The Hinge of Consciousness in the Eighteenth Century* (Carbondale: Southern Illinois University Press, 1978), pp. 18–74.

25. "Diogenes Laertius," p. 35.

26. Robin Lane Fox, *The Search for Alexander* (Boston: Little Brown, 1980), p. 321.

27. Cf. Lawrence Ferlinghetti's poem, "Dog," *A Coney Island of the Mind* (New York: New Directions, 1959), pp. 67–68.

28. "Diogenes Laertius," p. 63.

29. Ibid., p. 107.

30. Ibid., p. 109. For a fuller explanation of cynical philosophy, see Peter Sloterdijk, *Critique of Cynical Reason*, trans. Michael Eldred (Minneapolis: University of Minnesota Press, 1987). Sloterdijk draws almost solely on European sources, however, and places his exposition of and argument from cynicism totally within the European context. For a hostile scholarly treatment of cynicism, see Farrand Sayre, *The Greek Cynics* (Baltimore: J. H. Furst, 1948).

31. Sayre, *The Greek Cynics*, p. 17.

32. See John MacQuarrie, *The Scope of DeMythologizing: Bultmann and His Critics* (New York: Harper Torchbooks, 1966), pp. 45–53.

33. Some scholars find this conclusion debatable. See W. W. Tarn, "Alexander, Cynics and Stoics," *American Journal of Philology* 60 (January 1939): 41–70.

34. For brief, in fact all too brief, glosses on this connection between Christianity and cynicism, see Dudley, *A History of Cynicism*, pp. 209–213; and More, *Hellenistic Philosophies*, pp. 281–303.

35. Sloterdijk makes this same point emphatically and elaborates upon it, but again almost solely within the European intellectual tradition.

36. Gilbert Highet, *The Anatomy of Satire* (Princeton, N.J.: Princeton University Press, 1962), pp. 40–41. For a philological history of the diatribe, see Barbara Wallach, "A History of the Diatribe from its Origin up to the

First Century B.C. and a Study of the Influence of the Genre upon Lucretius III, 830–1094 (Ph.D. diss. University of Illinois, 1974). See also Oltamare, *Les Origines de la Diatribe Romaine* (Paris: n.p., 1926).

37. Dudley, *A History of Cynicism*, p. 111.

38. For a theory of the dadaist form of cynical dramaturgy, see Tristan Tzara, *Seven Dada Manifestos and Lampisteries*, trans. Barbara Wright (New York: Riverrun Press, n.d.); and "Lecture on Dada (1922)," in Robert Motherwell, ed., *The Dada Painters and Poets: An Anthology* (Boston: G. K. Hall, 1981).

39. "Diogenes Laertius," p. 29.

40. In fact, diatribe is the father of satire. Bion of Borysthenes (third century B.C.) supposedly created the diatribe as a distinct rhetorical genre, from which it developed into Roman satire. See Highet, *Anatomy of Satire*, pp. 24–66; C. W. Mendell, "Satire as Popular Philosophy," *Classical Philology* 33 (1920): 138–157.

41. Mary A. Grant, *Ancient Rhetorical Theories of the Laughable*, University of Wisconsin Studies in Language and Literature 21 (Madison, 1924), pp. 53–61. Cf. Tony Hendra, *Going Too Far (The Rise and Demise of Sick, Gross, Black, Sophomoric, Weirdo, Pinko, Anarchist, Underground, Anti-Establishment Human)* (New York: Doubleday, 1987); Jacob Brackman, *The Put-On: Modern Fooling and Modern Mistrust* (Chicago: Henry Regnery, 1967); Neil Schaeffer, *The Art of Laughter* (New York: Columbia University Press, 1981), pp. 59–80 ("Lenny Bruce and Extreme Comedy.")

42. W. W. Tarn, "Alexander, Cynics and Stoics," p. 42.

43. See W. Barnett Pearce, Stephen W. Littlejohn, Alison Alexander, "The New Christian Right and the Humanist Response: Reciprocated Diatribe," *Communication Quarterly* 35 (Spring 1987): 171–192; and Roderick P. Hart, "An Unquiet Desperation: Rhetorical Aspects of 'Popular' Atheism in the United States," *Quarterly Journal of Speech* 64 (February 1978): 33–46. Rudolph Bultmann, the great German theologian, saw the connection between the cynic diatribe and early Christian preaching in much more expansive terms. His was one of the original studies to draw direct connections between Christianity's preaching and the cynical diatribe and way of life. See his *Der Stiil der paulinischen Predigt u. die kynisch-stoische Diatribe*, Forschugen zur Religion u. Kultur des Alten u. Neuen Test. 13 (Gottingen, 1910). For additional studies in this relationship, see W. Wuellner, ed., *Diatribe in Ancient Rhetorical Theory*, protocol of the twenty-second colloquy (Berkeley: Center for Hermeneutical Studies in Hellenistic and Modern Culture, 1976).

44. Jerry Rubin, "Do It!" in Peter Babcox, Deborah Babcox, and Bob Abels, eds., *The Conspiracy* (New York: Dell Books, 1969), p. 214.

45. The internal schisms in the feminist movement have already been cited in the chapter on ideologies. Within the black movement there were charges that procedural protesters were "Uncle Toms" and "Aunt Jemimas." SDS finally split apart because of sectarianism within. On that final breakup of SDS, see Todd Gitlin, *The Sixties: Years of Hope, Days of Rage* (New York: Bantam Books, 1987), pp. 377–419. Yippies attacked almost everyone else and were, in turn, attacked by almost everyone. See the sections in

Do It! entitled "Ideology Is a Brain Disease," pp. 113–116 ("The Yippies are Marxists. We follow in the revolutionary tradition of Groucho, Chico, Harpo, and Karl"); "I Agree With Your Tactics, I Don't Know About Your Goals," pp. 125–130; and "George Wallace is Bobby Kennedy in Drag," pp. 144–148.

46. Jerry Rubin, *Do It!* (New York: Ballantine Books, 1970), p. 84.

47. Free [Abbie Hoffman], *Revolution for the Hell of It* (New York: Pocket Books, 1970), p. 60.

48. Rubin, *Do It!*, p. 105.

49. [Hoffman], *Revolution for the Hell of It*, p. 153.

50. Rubin, *Do It!*, p. 80.

51. Ibid., pp. 120, 122.

52. Ibid., p. 117.

53. [Hoffman], *Revolution for the Hell of It*, pp. 173–174.

54. Rubin, *Do It!*, p. 83.

55. Ibid., p. 84.

56. Ibid., p. 115. See also pp. 117 and 119.

57. Ibid., p. 84.

58. Ibid., p. 127.

59. Jerry Rubin, *We Are Everywhere* (New York: Harper and Row, 1971), p. 222. To appreciate the full force of fun involved in the Yippie's diatribe, listen to the audio tape of Abbie Hoffman's "Wake Up America," issued by Big Toe Records.

60. Rubin, *Do It!* p. 114.

61. Ibid., p. 108.

62. Ibid., p. 95.

63. Cf. Richard J. Goodman and William I. Gorden, "The Rhetoric of Desecration," *Quarterly Journal of Speech* 57 (February 1971): pp. 23–31.

64. Quoted in Tom Wolfe, *The Electric Kool-Aid Acid Test* (New York: Bantam Books, 1969), p. 166.

65. Feodor Mikhailovich Dostoyevsky, *Notes from the Underground*, trans. Bernard Guilbert Guerney, in *Short Novels of the Masters* ed. Charles Neider (New York: Rinehart, 1952), p. 146.

66. Philip E. Converse and Howard Schuman, " 'Silent Majorities' and the Vietnam War," *Scientific American*, June, 1970, p. 24. For a more detailed study of the public's reaction to protest against the war, see Milton J. Rosenberg, Sidney Verba, and Philip E. Converse, *Vietnam and the Silent Majority: The Dove's Guide* (New York: Harper and Row, 1970).

11. Postscript to a Decade

1. Louis Hartz, *The Liberal Tradition in America* (New York: Harcourt, Brace & World, Harvest ed., 1955), p. 283.

2. There are a number of volumes on what happened to the various protest organizations. For concise examinations, the following in one volume are instructive. On the decline of the SDS see Frederick D. Miller, "The End

of SDS and the Emergence of Weatherman: Demise Through Success," in Jo Freeman, ed., *Social Movements of the Sixties and Seventies* (New York: Longman, 1983), pp. 279–297; on the civil rights movement, see Douglas McAdam, "The Decline of the Civil Rights Movement," in ibid., pp. 298–319; on SNCC, see Emily Stoper, "The Student Non-Violent Coordinating Committee: Rise and Fall of a Redemptive Organization," in ibid., pp. 320–334.

3. See, for example, Arthur Schlesinger, Jr., *The Crisis of Confidence: Ideas, Power and Violence in America* (Boston: Houghton Mifflin, 1969).

4. See Alvin W. Gouldner, *The Two Marxism. Contradictions and Anomalies in the Development of Theory* (New York: Oxford University Press, 1980), and Goran Therborn, *Science, Class and Society* (London: New Left Books, 1976).

5. J. Justin Gustainis and Dan F. Hahn call the antiwar protests a "failure" for not being instrumental in bringing the American-Vietnamese war to an end. They cite *intrinsic* factors (identification with the counterculture, immoderate protest tactics, violence, attacks on capitalism, use of obscenity, and desecration of the flag) and *extrinsic* factors (anticommunism, opposition to protest in any form, violence by opponents of protest, media coverage, and polarization by political figures) as reasons for their failures. But their analysis presumes that protest rhetoric could be instrumental in achieving this goal. And it seems to presume that if protesters had not used these strategies and tactics ("intrinsic factors"), they might have been more influential. Much of my work directly contradicts Gustainis and Hahn in these respects. See Gustainis and Hahn, "While the Whole World Watched: Rhetorical Failures of Anti-War Protest," *Communication Quarterly* 36 (Summer 1988): 203–216.

6. Richard Nixon, "Inaugural Address," *Setting the Course*, commentaries by Richard Wilson (New York: Funk and Wagnalls, 1970), p. 5.

7. The actual formulation had rhetoric as an "open hand" and logic as a "closed hand." See Wilbur Samuel Howell, *Logic and Rhetoric in England, 1500–1700* (Princeton, N.J.: Princeton University Press, 1956).

Bibliography

Books

Able, Elie. *The Missile Crisis*. Philadelphia: Lippincott, 1966.

Abrahamsen, David. *Nixon v. Nixon: An Emotional Tragedy*. New York: New American Library, 1978.

Adelson, Alan. *SDS: A Profile*. New York: Charles Scribner's Sons, 1972.

Allison, Graham T. *Essence of Decision. Explaining the Cuban Missile Crisis*. Boston: Little, Brown, 1971.

Ambrose, Stephen E. *Nixon: The Education of a Politician, 1913–1962*. New York: Simon and Schuster, 1987.

Anderson, Patrick. *The Presidents' Men*. Garden City, N.Y.: Doubleday, Anchor ed., 1969.

Atkinson, Ti-Grace, ed. *Amazon Women*. New York: Links Books, 1974.

Augustine, Saint. *On Christian Doctrine*. Trans. D. W. Robertson, Jr. New York: Liberal Arts Press, 1958.

Babcox, Peter, Deborah Abels, and Bob Abels, eds. *The Conspiracy*. New York: Dell Books, 1969.

Baldwin, Charles Sears. *Ancient Rhetoric and Poetic*. Gloucester, Mass.: Peter Smith, 1959.

Barber, James David. *The Presidential Character*. Englewood Cliffs, N.J.: Prentice-Hall, 1972.

Barker, Ernest. *Greek Political Theory*. New York: Barnes and Noble, 1960.

Bell, Daniel. *The End of Ideology. On the Exhaustion of Political Ideas in the Fifties*. rev. ed. New York: Free Press, 1965.

Bercovitch, Sacvan. *The American Jeremiad*. Madison: University of Wisconsin Press, 1978.

Blau, Herbert M., and William B. Ross. *Politics Battle Plan*. New York: Macmillan, 1968.

Blight, James G., and David A. Welch. *On the Brink. Americans and Soviets Reexamine the Cuban Missile Crisis*. New York: Hill and Wang, 1989.

Bowers, John Waite, and Donovan Ochs. *The Rhetoric of Agitation and Control*. Reading, Mass.: Addison-Wesley, 1971.

Brackman, Jacob. *The Put-On: Modern Fooling and Modern Mistrust*. Chicago: Henry Regnery, 1967.

Bradlee, Benjamin C. *Conversations with Kennedy*. New York: W. W. Norton, 1975.

Brzezinski, Zbigniew, and Samuel Huntington. *Political Power: USA/USSR*. New York: Macmillan, 1963.

Brodie, Fawn M. *Richard Nixon: The Shaping of His Character*. Cambridge: Harvard University Press, 1983.

Bultmann, Rudolph. *Der Still der paulinischen Predigt u. die Kynisch-stoisch Diatribe*. Forschugen zur Religion u. Kultur des Alten u. Neuen Test. 13. Gottingen, 1910.

Bundy, McGeorge. *Danger and Survival*. New York: Random House, 1988.

Bunzel, John H. *Anti-Politics in America*. New York: Alfred A. Knopf, 1967.

Burns, James M., and Jack W. Peltason. *Government by the People*. 5th ed. Englewood Cliffs, N.J.: Prentice Hall, 1964.

Calvert, Greg, and Carol Neiman. *A Disrupted History: The Left and the New Capitalism*. New York: Random House, 1971.

Campbell, Karlyn Kohrs. *Critiques of Contemporary Rhetoric*. Belmont, Calif.: Wadsworth, 1972.

Campbell, Karlyn Kohrs, and Kathleen Hall Jamieson, eds. *Form and Genre: Shaping Rhetorical Action*. Falls Church, Va.: Speech Communication Association, [1978].

Carl, William III. "Old Testament Prophecy and the Question of Prophetic Preaching: A Perspective on Ecclesiastical Protest to the Vietnam War and the Participation of William Sloane Coffin, Jr." Ph.D. dissertation, University of Pittsburgh, 1977.

Carlanes, Walter. *The Concept of Ideology and Political Analysis*. Westport, Conn.: Greenwood Press, 1981.

Cherwitz, Richard A., and James W. Hikins. *Communication and Knowledge: An Investigation in Rhetorical Epistemology*. Columbia: University of South Carolina Press, 1986.

Chesen, Eli S. *President Nixon's Psychiatric Profile*. New York: Peter H. Wyden, 1973.

Chomsky, Noam. *American Power and the New Mandarins*. New York: Pantheon Books, 1969.

Collected Speeches of Spiro Agnew. New York: Audubon Books, 1971.

Connolly, William E. *The Terms of Political Discourse*. 2nd ed. Princeton, N.J.: Princeton University Press, 1983.

Costello, William. *The Facts about Nixon. An Unauthorized Biography*. New York: Viking Press, 1960.

Cox, Harvey. *The Secular City*. New York: Macmillan, 1965.

Cox, J. Robert. "The Rhetorical Structure of Mass Protest: A Criticism of

Selected Speeches of the Vietnam Anti-War Movement." Ph.D. dissertation, University of Pittsburgh, 1973.

Crick, Bernard. *In Defense of Politics*. rev. ed. Baltimore: Penguin Books, Pelican, 1964.

Detzer, David. *The Brink: Cuban Missile Crisis, 1962*. New York: Thomas Y. Crowell, 1979.

Deutscher, Isaac. *The Prophet Unarmed. Trotsky, 1921–1929*. Vol. 2. London: Oxford University Press, 1959.

"Diogenes, Laertius." *Lives of Eminent Philosophers*. Ed. R. D. Hicks. Vol. 2. Cambridge: Harvard University Press, 1965.

Domhoff, William, and Hoyt B. Ballard, eds. *C. Wright Mills and The Power Elite*. Boston: Beacon Press, 1968.

Draper, Theodore. *The Roots of American Communism*. New York: Viking Press, 1957.

Drew, Elizabeth. *Washington Journal*. New York: Random House, 1974.

Dudley, Donald R. *A History of Cynicism*. London: Methuen, 1937.

Edelman, Murray. *The Symbolic Uses of Politics*. Urbana: University of Illinois Press, 1964.

Edwards, George C. III. *The Public Presidency: The Pursuit of Popular Support*. New York: St. Martin's Press, 1983.

Eisenhower, Dwight D. *Waging Peace, 1956–1961*. Garden City, N.Y.: Doubleday, 1965.

Evans, Rowland, and Robert Novak. *Lyndon B. Johnson: The Exercise of Power*. New York: New American Library, 1966.

———. *Nixon in the White House: The Frustration of Power*. New York: Random House, 1971.

Fairlie, Henry. *The Kennedy Promise*. New York: Dell, 1974.

Farber, Jerry. *The Student as Nigger*. New York: Pocket Books, 1970.

FitzSimons, Louise. *The Kennedy Doctrine*. New York: Random House, 1972.

Foner, Philip S. *The Industrial Workers of the World, 1905–1917*. New York: International Publishers, 1973.

For Victory in Peaceful Competition with Capitalism. New York: International Arts and Sciences Press, 1960.

Foss, Sonja K. *Rhetorical Criticism: Exploration and Practice*. Prospect Heights, Ill.: Waveland Press, 1989.

Foster, Julian and Durward Long, eds. *Protest! Student Activism in America*. New York: William Morrow, 1970.

Fox, Robin Lane. *The Search for Alexander*. Boston: Little Brown, 1980.

Frankly Speaking. Washington: Public Affairs Press, 1970.

Frazer, Ronald, ed. *1968: A Generation in Revolt*. New York: Pantheon Books, 1988.

Free [Abbie Hoffman]. *Revolution for the Hell of It*. New York: Pocket Books, 1970.

Freeman, Jo, ed. *Social Movements of the Sixties and Seventies*. White Plains, N.Y.: Longman, 1983.

Friedan, Betty. *The Feminine Mystique*. New York: Dell, 1963.

Gardner, John W., ed. *To Turn the Tide.* with a Foreword by Carl Sandburg New York: Harper and Brothers, 1962.

Gitlin, Todd. *The Whole World Is Watching.* Berkeley: University of California Press, 1980.

Gitlin, Todd. *The Sixties: Years of Hope, Days of Rage.* New York: Bantam Books, 1987.

Golden, Harry. *Mr. Kennedy and the Negroes.* New York: World Publishing, 1964.

Goodwin, Richard N. *Remembering America.* Boston: Little, Brown, 1988.

Gouldner, Alvin W. *The Two Marxisms: Contradictions and Anomalies in the Development of Theory.* New York: Oxford University Press, 1980.

Grant, Joanne, ed. *Black Protest: History, Documents, and Analysis, 1619 to the Present.* New York: Fawcett, 1989.

Grant, Mary A. *Ancient Rhetorical Theories of the Laughable.* University of Wisconsin Studies in Language and Literature 21. Madison, Wis., 1924.

Green, David. *Shaping Political Consciousness. The Language of Politics in America from McKinley to Reagan.* Ithaca, N.Y.: Cornell University Press, 1987.

Greenstein, Fred I., ed. *Leadership in the Modern Presidency.* Cambridge: Harvard University Press, 1988.

Halberstam, David. *The Best and the Brightest.* New York: Random House, 1972.

Halle, Louis J. *The Society of Man.* London: Chatto and Windus, 1965.

Hart, Roderick P. *The Sound of Leadership.* Chicago: University of Chicago Press, 1987.

Hartz, Louis. *The Liberal Tradition in America.* New York: Brace & World, Harvest ed., 1955).

Hearings Before the Committee on the Judiciary House of Representatives Ninety-Third Congress Pursuant to H. Res. 803. 42 vols. Washington, D.C.: Government Printing Office, 1974.

Heath, Jim. *Decade of Disillusionment. The Kennedy-Johnson Years.* Bloomington: Indiana University Press, 1976.

Heirich, Max. *The Beginning: Berkeley 1964.* New York: Columbia University Press, 1970.

Hendra, Tony. *Going Too Far (The Rise and Demise of Sick, Gross, Black, Sophomoric, Weirdo, Pinko, Anarchist, Underground, Anti-Establishment Human)* New York: Doubleday, 1987.

Hertsgaard, Mark. *On Bended Knee: The Press and the Reagan Presidency.* New York: Farrar Straus Giroux, 1988.

Higgins, Trumbull. *The Perfect Failure: Kennedy, Eisenhower, and the CIA at the Bay of Pigs.* New York: W. W. Norton, 1987.

Highet, Gilbert. *The Anatomy of Satire.* Princeton, N.J.: Princeton University Press, 1962.

Hilsman, Roger. *To Move a Nation. The Politics of Foreign Policy in the Administration of John F. Kennedy.* New York: Dell, 1967.

Hoffman, Abbie. *See* Free.

Hofstadter, Richard. *The Paranoid Style in American Politics and Other Essays.* New York: Alfred A. Knopf, 1965.

Howell, Wilbur Samuel. *Logic and Rhetoric in England, 1500–1700*. Princeton, N.J.: Princeton University Press, 1956.

Hugenberg, Lawrence W., ed. *Rhetorical Studies Honoring James L. Golden*. Dubuque, Iowa: Kendall/Hunt, 1986.

Hughes, Emmet John. *The Ordeal of Power: A Political Memoir of the Eisenhower Years*. New York: Atheneum, 1963.

Hunt, Michael H. *Ideology and U.S. Foreign Policy*. New Haven, Conn.: Yale University Press, 1987.

Isaacson, Walter, and Evan Thomas. *The Wise Men*. New York: Simon and Schuster, 1986.

Ivie, Robert L. *Congress Declares War*. Kent, Ohio: Kent State University Press, 1983.

Jacobs, Harold, ed. *Weatherman*. N.p.: Ramparts Press, 1970.

Jacobs, Paul, and Saul Landau. *The New Radicals: A Report with Documents*. New York: Vintage, 1966.

Jamieson, Kathleen Hall. *Eloquence in the Electronic Age*. New York: Oxford University Press, 1988.

Johnson, Lyndon B. *The Vantage Point*. New York: Pocket Books, 1971.

The Joint Appearances of Senator John F. Kennedy and Vice President Richard M. Nixon: Presidential Campaign of 1960. Washington, D.C.: Government Printing Office, 1961.

Katope, Christopher G., and Paul G. Zolbrod, eds. *Beyond Berkeley*. Cleveland: World Publishing, 1966.

Kearns, Doris. *Lyndon Johnson and the American Dream*. New York: Harper and Row, 1976.

Kennan, George F. *Memoirs*. Boston: Little, Brown, 1967.

Kennedy, Robert F. *Thirteen Days: A Memoir of the Cuban Missile Crisis*. New York: W. W. Norton, 1969.

Keogh, James. *President Nixon and the Press*. New York: Funk and Wagnalls, 1972.

Kern, Montague, Patricia W. Levering, and Ralph B. Levering. *The Kennedy Crises: The Press, the Presidency, and Foreign Policy*. Chapel Hill: University of North Carolina Press, 1983.

Kernall, Samuel. *Going Public*. Washington, D.C.: Congressional Quarterly, 1986.

Kerr, Clark. *The Uses of the University*. Cambridge: Harvard University Press, 1964.

Khrushchev in America. New York: Crosscurrents Press, 1960.

Khrushchev's 'Mein Kampf', with background by Harrison E. Salisbury. New York: Belmont Books, 1961.

Khrushchev Remembers, trans. and ed. Strobe Talbott. New York: Bantam, 1971.

King, Larry L. *None but a Blockhead. On Being a Writer*. New York: Viking, 1986.

King, Jr., Martin Luther. *Stride Toward Freedom: The Montgomery Story*. New York: Harper and Row, 1958.

Kissinger, Henry. *Nuclear Weapons and Foreign Policy*. New York: Harper and Brothers, 1958.

Kornitzer, Bela. *The Real Nixon. An Intimate Biography.* New York: Rand McNally, 1960.

Larson, David L., ed. *The "Cuban Missile Crisis" of 1962: Selected Documents and Chronology.* Boston: Hougton Mifflin, 1963.

Lefebvre, Henri. *The Sociology of Marx.* Trans. Norbert Guterman. New York: Pantheon Books, 1968.

Lens, Sidney. *The Labor Wars: From the Molly Maguires to the Sitdowns..* Garden City, N.Y.: Anchor Press/Doubleday, 1974.

————. *Radicalism in America.* New York: Thomas Y. Crowell, 1966.

Lincoln, C. Eric. *The Black Muslims in America.* Boston: Beacon Press, 1963.

Linkugel, Wil A., R. R. Allen, and Richard L. Johannessen, eds. *Contemporary American Speeches.* Belmont, Calif.: Wadsworth, 1969.

Lippmann, Walter. *Public Opinion.* New York: Pelican Books, 1946.

————. *The Public Philosophy.* New York: Little, Brown, 1955.

Lipset, Seymour Martin, and Earl Raab. *The Politics of Unreason.* New York: Harper and Row, 1970.

Lipset, Seymour Martin, and Sheldon S. Wolin, eds. *The Berkeley Student Revolt: Facts and Interpretations.* Garden City, N.Y.: Anchor Books, 1965.

Lord, Walter. *The Past that Would Not Die.* New York: Harper and Row, 1964.

Lowi, Theodore J. *The Personal President.* Ithaca, N.Y.: Cornell University Press, 1985.

Lukas, J. Anthony. *Nightmare: The Underside of the Nixon Years.* New York: Viking, 1976.

Lutz, William, and Harry Brent, eds. *On Revolution.* Cambridge, Mass.: Winthrop, 1971.

Lyons, John O. *The Invention of the Self: The Hinge of Consciousness in the Eighteenth Century.* Carbondale: Southern Illinois University Press, 1978.

McConnell, Grant. *Steel and the Presidency, 1962.* New York: W. W. Norton, 1963.

Macdonald, Dwight, ed. *Parodies.* New York: Modern Library, 1965.

McGaffin, William, and Erwin Knoll. *Anything but the Truth.* New York: G. P. Putnam's Sons, 1968.

MacQuarrie, John. *The Scope of DeMythologizing: Bultmann and His Critics.* New York: Harper Torchbooks, 1966.

Madison, James. *Notes of the Debates in the Federal Convention of 1787,* with an introduction by Adrienne Koch. New York: Norton Library, 1969.

Magruder, Jeb Stuart. *An American Life.* New York: Atheneum, 1974.

Mankiewicz, Frank. *Perfectly Clear. Nixon From Whittier to Watergate.* New York: Quadrangle, 1973.

Margolis, Michael, and Gary Mauser. *Manipulating Public Opinion: Essays on Public Opinion as a Dependent Variable.* Pacific Grove, Calif.: Brooks/Cole, 1989.

Marrou, H. I. *A History of Education in Antiquity.* Trans. George Lamb. New York: Mentor Books, 1964.

May, Ernest R. *"Lessons" of the Past: The Use and Misuse of History in American Foreign Policy.* New York: Oxford University Press, 1973.

Mazlish, Bruce. *In Search of Nixon: A Psycho-Historical Inquiry.* Baltimore: Penguin Books, 1973.

Mazo, Earl, and Stephen Hess. *Nixon. A Political Portrait.* New York: Popular Library, 1968.

Menashe, Louis, and Ronald Radosh, eds. *Teach-Ins: U.S.A.* New York: Frederick A. Praeger, 1967.

Miles, Michael W. *The Radical Probe: The Logic of Student Rebellion.* New York: Atheneum, 1971.

Miller, Douglas T., and Marion Nowak. *The Fifties: The Way We Really Were.* Garden City, N.Y.: Doubleday, 1977.

Miller, James. *"Democracy Is in the Streets": From Port Huron to the Seige of Chicago.* New York: Simon and Schuster, Touchstone Books, 1987.

Miller, L. H., and R. W. Pruessen, eds. *Reflections on the Cold War: A Quarter Century of American Foreign Policy.* Philadelphia: Temple University Press, 1974.

Miller, Merle. *Lyndon: An Oral Biography.* New York: G. P. Putnam's Sons, 1980.

Miller, Michael V., and Susan Gilmore, eds. *Revolution at Berkeley: The Crisis in American Higher Education.* New York: Dial Press, 1965.

Mills, C. Wright. *The Power Elite.* New York: Oxford University Press, 1959.

Miroff, Bruce. *Pragmatic Illusions: The Presidential Politics of John F. Kennedy.* New York: David McKay, 1976.

More, Paul Elmer. *Hellenistic Philosophies.* Princeton, N.J.: Princeton University Press, 1923.

Morgan, Robin, ed. *Sisterhood Is Powerful.* New York: Vintage Books, 1970.

Morton, Marian J. *The Terrors of Ideological Politics. Liberal Historians in a Conservative Mood.* Cleveland: The Press of Case Western Reserve University, 1972.

Motherwell, Robert, ed. *The Dada Painters and Poets: An Anthology.* Boston: G. K. Hall, 1981.

Navasky, Victor S. *Kennedy Justice.* New York: Atheneum, 1970.

Neustadt, Richard E. *Presidential Power: The Politics of Leadership.* New York: John Wiley and Sons, 1961.

————, and Ernest R. May. *Thinking in Time: The Use of History for Decision Makers.* New York: Free Press, 1986.

Niebuhr, Reinhold. *The Irony of American History.* New York: Charles Scribner's Sons, 1952.

————. *The Self and the Dramas of History.* New York: Charles Scribner's Sons, 1955.

Nimmo, Dan D. and Keith Sanders (eds.). *Handbook of Political Communication.* Beverly Hills, Calif.: Sage, 1981.

Nixon, Richard. *RN: The Memoirs of Richard Nixon.* New York: Grosset and Dunlap, 1978.

————. *Six Crises.* New York: Pyramid Books, 1968.

O'Donnell, Kenneth P., and David Powers with Joe McCarthy. *Johnny We*

Hardly Knew Ye: Memories of John Fitzgerald Kennedy. New York: Pocket Books, 1973.

Oglesby, Carl, ed. *The New Left Reader.* New York: Grove Press, 1969.

Oltamare. *Les Origines de la Diatribe Romaine.* Paris: n. p., 1926.

Osgood, Charles E. *An Alternative to War or Surrender.* Urbana: University of Illinois Press, 1962.

Packard, Vance. *The Hidden Persuaders.* New York: David McKay, 1957.

———. *The Status Seekers.* New York: David McKay, 1959.

Parenti, Michael J. *The Anti-Communist Impulse.* New York: Random House, 1969.

Parmet, Herbert S. *JFK: The Presidency of John F. Kennedy.* New York: Dial, 1983.

Patterson, Jr., Bradley H. *The Ring of Power. The White House Staff and Its Expanding Role in Government.* New York: Basic Books, 1988.

Patterson, Thomas G., ed. *Cold War Critics.* Chicago: Quadrangle, 1971.

The Pentagon Papers. New York: Bantam Books, 1971.

Plamentz, John. *Ideology.* New York: Praeger, 1970.

The Politics of Protest: Violent Aspects of Protest and Confrontation: A Staff Report to the National Commission on the Causes and Prevention of Violence. Prepared by Jerome Skolnick. Washington, D.C.: Government Printing Office, 1969.

Public Papers of the President: John F. Kennedy. 3 vols. Washington, D.C.: Government Printing Office, 1962–1964.

Public Papers of the President: Lyndon B. Johnson. 10 vols. Washington, D.C.: Government Printing Office, 1964–1969.

Reedy, George E. *The Twilight of the Presidency.* New York: World Publishing, 1970.

Regan, Donald T. *For the Record.* San Diego: Harcourt Brace Jovanovich, 1988.

Reich, Robert B. *The Power of Public Ideas.* Cambridge: Ballinger Publishing, 1988.

Reisman, David. *Individualism Reconsidered.* Glencoe: Free Press, 1954.

———, with Nathan Glazer and Reuel Denney. *The Lonely Crowd.* Abridged ed. New Haven, Conn.: Yale University Press, 1961.

Renshaw, Patrick. *The Wobblies: The Story of Syndicalism in the United States.* New York: Anchor Books, 1968.

The Rhetoric and Poetics of Aristotle. Trans. W. Rhys Roberts. New York: Modern Library, 1954.

Rosenberg, Milton J., Sidney Verba, and Philip E. Converse. *Vietnam and the Silent Majority: The Dove's Guide.* New York: Harper and Row, 1970.

Rossiter, Clinton. *The American Presidency.* Rev. ed. New York: New American Library, 1960.

———. *The Supreme Court and the Commander in Chief,* with an introductory note and additional text by Richard P. Longaker. Ithaca, N.Y.: Cornell University Press, 1976.

Rubin, Jerry. *Do It!* New York: Ballantine Books, 1970.

———. *We Are Everywhere.* New York: Harper and Row, 1971.

Russell, Bertrand. *A History of Western Philosophy*. New York: Simon and Schuster, Touchstone Books, 1972.

Safire, William. *Before the Fall*. New York: Belmont Tower, 1975.

———. *Safire's Political Dictionary*. New York: Ballantine Books, 1978.

Sarachild, Kathie, ed. *Feminist Revolution*. New York: Redstockings of the Women's Liberation Movement, 1978.

Sayre, Farrand. *Diogenes of Sinope: A Study of Greek Cynicism*. Baltimore: J. H. Furst, 1938.

———. *The Greek Cynics*. Baltimore: J. H. Furst, 1948.

Schaeffer, Neil. *The Art of Laughter*. New York: Columbia University Press, 1981.

Schandler, Herbert Y. *Lyndon Johnson and Vietnam: The Unmaking of a President*. Princeton, N.J.: Princeton University Press, 1977.

Schell, Jonathan. *The Time of Illusion*. New York: Alfred A. Knopf, 1976.

Schlesinger, Jr., Arthur M. *The Crisis of Confidence. Ideas, Power, and Violence in America*. Boston: Houghton Mifflin, 1969.

———. *The Imperial Presidency*. Boston: Houghton Mifflin, 1974.

———. *Kennedy or Nixon: Does It Make Any Difference?* New York: Macmillan, 1960.

———. *Robert Kennedy and His Times*. Boston: Houghton Mifflin, 1978.

———. *A Thousand Days: John F. Kennedy in the White House*. Boston: Houghton Mifflin, 1965.

Schoenbaum, Thomas J. *Waging Peace and War: Dean Rusk in the Truman, Kennedy and Johnson Years*. New York: Simon and Schuster, 1988.

Scott, Robert L., and Bernard L. Brock, eds. *Methods of Rhetorical Criticism: A Twentieth-Century Perspective*. New York: Harper and Row, 1972.

Seaborg, Glenn T. (with the assistance of Benjamin S. Loeb). *Kennedy, Khrushchev, and the Test Ban*. Berkeley: University of California Press, 1981.

Searle, John. *The Campus War*. New York: World, 1971.

Seliger, Martin. *Ideology and Politics*. New York: Free Press, 1976.

Shils, Edward. *The Intellectuals and the Powers and Other Essays*. Chicago: University of Chicago Press, 1972.

Sidey, Hugh. *A Very Personal Presidency: Lyndon Johnson in the White House*. New York: Atheneum, 1968.

Simons, Herbert W., and Aram A. Agharazian, eds. *Form, Genre, and the Study of Political Discourse*. Columbia: University of South Carolina Press, 1986.

Sirica, John J. *To Set the Record Straight*. New York: W. W. Norton, 1979.

Sloterdijk, Peter. *Critique of Cynical Reason*. Trans. Michael Eldred. Minneapolis: University of Minnesota Press, 1987.

Slusser, R. M. *The Berlin Crisis of 1961: Soviet-American Relations and the Struggle for Power in the Kremlin, June–November, 1961*. Baltimore: Johns Hopkins University Press, 1973.

Smith, Arthur L. *Rhetoric of Black Revolution*. Boston: Allyn and Bacon, 1969.

Smith, Carolyn. "Toward a Rhetoric of Presidential Press Conferences." Ph.D. dissertation, University of Pittsburgh, 1987.

Smith, Craig Allen, and Kathy B. Smith, eds. *The President and the Public: Rhetoric and National Leadership.* Lanham, Md.: University Press of America, 1985.

Sorensen, Theodore C. *Kennedy.* New York: Harper and Row, 1965.

Spear, Joseph C. *Presidents and the Press.* Cambridge: MIT Press, 1986.

Spender, Stephen. *The Year of the Young Rebels.* New York: Vintage Books, 1969.

Stein, David Lewis. *Living the Revolution: The Yippies in Chicago.* Indianapolis: Bobbs Merrill, 1969.

Steinberg, Alfred. *Sam Johnson's Boy.* New York: Macmillan, 1968.

Stewart, Charles, Craig Smith, and Robert E. Denton, Jr. *Persuasion and Social Movements.* Prospect Heights Ill.: Waveland Press, 1984.

Sullivan, Donald Francis. "The Civil Rights Programs of the Kennedy Administration: A Political Analysis." Ph.D. dissertation, University of Oklahoma, 1965.

Sumner, Colin. *Reading Ideologies.* New York: Academic Press, 1979.

Talbott, Strobe. *The Master of the Game: Paul Nitze and the Nuclear Peace.* New York: Alfred A. Knopf, 1988.

Tanner, Leslie B., ed. *Voices from Women's Liberation.* New York: Signet, 1971.

Tatu, Michel. *Power in the Kremlin from Khrushchev to Kosygin,* Trans. Helen Katel. New York: Viking, 1967.

Taylor, Marxwell. *The Uncertain Trumpet.* New York: Harper and Brothers, 1959.

Therborn, Goran. *Science, Class and Society.* London: New Left Books, 1976.

Tulis, Jeffrey K. *The Rhetorical Presidency.* Princeton, N.J.: Princeton University Press, 1987.

Turner, Kathleen J. *Lyndon Johnson's Dual War.* Chicago: University of Chicago Press, 1985.

Two Communist Manifestoes, with an introduction by Charles Burton Marshall. Washington, D.C.: Washington Center of Foreign Policy Research, 1961.

Tzara, Tristan. *Seven Dada Manifestos and Lampisteries.* Trans. Barbara Wright. New York: Riverrun Press, n.d.

Valenti, Jack. *A Very Human President.* New York: W. W. Norton, 1975.

Viorst, Milton. *Fire in the Streets.* New York: Simon and Schuster, 1979.

Wallach, Barbara. "A History of the Diatribe from its Origins up to the First Century B.C. and a Study of the Influence of the Genre upon Lucretius III, 830–1094. Ph.D. dissertation, University of Illinois, 1974.

Walton, Richard J. *Cold War and Counterrevolution. The Foreign Policy of John F. Kennedy.* New York: Viking Press, 1972.

Watson, Richard A. *The Presidential Contest.* New York: John Wiley and Sons, 1984.

Waxman, Chaim I., ed. *The End of Ideology Debate.* New York: Simon and Schuster, 1969.

Weber, Max. *Charisma and Institution Building*. Chicago: University of Chicago Press, 1968.

———. *Theories of Social and Economic Organization*. New York: Free Press, 1947.

Weinstein, Allen. *Perjury: The Hiss-Chambers Case*. New York: Alfred A. Knopf, 1978.

Whalen, Richard J. *To Catch a Falling Flag*. Boston: Houghton Mifflin, 1972.

White, Theodore H. *Breach of Faith*. New York: Atheneum, 1975.

———. *The Making of the President 1960*. New York: Atheneum, 1961.

———. *The Making of the President 1968*. New York: Atheneum, 1969.

Whyte, Jr., William H. *The Organization Man*. New York: Simon and Schuster, 1955.

Wicker, Tom. *JFK and LBJ. The Influence of Personality upon Politics*. Baltimore: Penguin Books, 1969.

Wills, Gary. *The Kennedy Imprisonment*. Boston: Little, Brown, 1982.

———. *Nixon Agonistes: The Crisis of the Self-Made Man*. Boston: Houghton Mifflin, 1970.

Windt, Theodore, ed. *Presidential Rhetoric: 1961 to the Present*. 4th ed. Dubuque, Iowa: Kendall/Hunt, 1987.

———. "The Rhetoric of Peaceful Coexistence: A Criticism of Selected American Speeches by Nikita S. Khrushchev." Ph.D. dissertation, Ohio State University, 1965.

Windt, Theodore and Beth Ingold, eds. *Essays in Presidential Rhetoric*. 2nd ed. Dubuque, Iowa: Kendall/Hunt, 1987.

Witcover, Jules. *The Resurrection of Richard Nixon*. New York: G. P. Putnam's Sons, 1970.

Wofford, Harris. *Of Kennedy and Kings*. New York: Farrar, Straus, Giroux, 1980.

Wolfe, Tom. *The Electric Kool-Aid Acid Test*. New York: Bantam Books, 1969.

Wuellner, W., ed. *Diatribe in Ancient Rhetorical Theory: Second Colloquy*. Berkeley: Center for Hermeneutical Studies in Hellenistic and Modern Culture, 1976.

Wyden, Peter. *Bay of Pigs*. New York: Simon and Schuster, 1979.

Young, Nigel. *An Infantile Disorder? The Crisis and Decline of the New Left*. Boulder, Colo.: Westview Press, 1977.

Articles

Baskerville, Barnet. "The Cross and the Flag: Evangelists of the Far Right." *Western Journal of Speech* 27 (Fall 1963): 197–206.

———. "The Illusion of Proof." *Western Journal of Speech* 25 (Fall 1961): 236–242.

———. "The New Nixon." *Quarterly Journal of Speech* 53 (February 1957): 36–39.

Benson, Thomas W. "Rhetoric and Autobiography: The Case of Malcolm X." *Quarterly Journal of Speech* 60 (February 1974): 1–13.

Bitzer, Lloyd F. "The Rhetorical Situation." *Philosophy and Rhetoric*, 1 (Winter 1968): 1–14.

Brock, Bernard L., ed. "Special Report: Social Movements." *Central States Speech Journal* 34 (Spring 1983): 67–82.

Bryant, Donald C. "Rhetoric: Its Function and Scope." Rpt. in Joseph Schwartz and John A. Recenga, eds., *The Province of Rhetoric*, pp. 3–35. New York: Ronald Press, 1965.

Bundy, McGeorge, ed. "White House Tapes and Minutes of the Cuban Crisis." *International Security* 10 (Summer 1985): 164–203.

Bundy, McGeorge, transcriber, and James G. Blight, ed. "October 27, 1962: Transcripts of the Meetings of the ExComm." *International Security* 12 (Winter 1987/88): 30–92.

Burke, William L. "Notes on a Rhetoric of Lamentation." *Central States Speech Journal* 30 (Summer 1979): 310–317.

Campbell, Karlyn Kohrs. "Response to Forbes Hill." *Central States Speech Journal* 34 (Summer 1983): 126–127.

Campbell, Karlyn Kohrs, and Kathleen Hall Jamieson. "Inaugurating the Presidency." *Presidential Studies Quarterly* 15 (Spring 1985): 394–411.

Cathcart, Robert S. "New Approaches to the Study of Movements: Defining Movements Rhetorically." *Western Journal of Speech* 36 (Spring 1972): 82–88.

Cherwitz, Richard A. "Lyndon Johnson and the 'Crisis' of Tonkin Gulf: A President's Justification of War." *Western Journal of Speech Communication* 41 (Spring 1978): 93–104.

Chesebro, James W., John F. Cragan, and Patricia McCullough. "The Small Group Technique of the Radical Revolutionary: A Synthetic Study of Consciousness Raising." *Communication Monographs*, 40 (June 1973): 136–146.

Cleaver, Eldridge. "A Letter from Jail." *Ramparts*, June 15, 1968, pp. 18–21.

Converse, Philip E., and Howard Schuman. " 'Silent Majorities' and and the Vietnam War." *Scientific American*, June 1970, pp. 17–25.

Corcoran, Farrel. "The Widening Gyre: Another Look at Ideology in Wander and His Critics." *Central States Speech Journal* 35 (Spring 1984): 54–56.

Cox, J. Robert. "Perspectives on Rhetorical Criticism of Movements: Antiwar Dissent, 1964–1970." *Western Journal of Speech* 38 (Fall 1974): 254–268.

Cronin, Thomas E. "The Textbook Presidency and Political Science." A paper prepared for delivery at the 65th Annual Meeting of the American Political Science Association, Los Angeles, California, September 7–12.

Doolittle, Robert J. "Riots as Symbolic: A Criticism and Approach." *Central States Speech Journal* 27 (Winter 1976): 310–317.

Dulles, Allen W. "Disarmament in the Atomic Age." *Foreign Affairs* 25 (January 1947): 204–217.

Dupuis, François. "From a White Nigger to a Quebec Separatist." In Dotson Rader, ed., *Defiance 3*, pp. 134–147. New York: Paperback Library, 1971.

Erikson, Erik H. "On the Nature of Psycho-Historical Evidence." *Daedalus* 97 (Summer 1968): 695–730.

Erlich, Howard S. "'. . . And by Opposing, End Them.' The Genre of Moral Justification for Legal Transgressions." *Today's Speech* 23 (Winter 1975): 13–16.

Etzioni, Amitai. "The Kennedy Experiment." *Psychology Today* 3 (December 1969): 43–45, 62–63.

Fleming, Harold. "The Federal Executive and Civil Rights: 1961–1965." *Daedalus* 94 (Fall 1965): 921–948.

Francesconi, Robert. "Heidegger and Ideology: Reflections of an Innocent Bystander." *Central States Speech Journal* 35 (Spring 1984): 51–53.

Friedan, Betty. "Up from the Kitchen Floor." *New York Times Magazine*, March 4, 1973, pp. 8–9, 28 passim.

Fulkerson, Richard P. "The Public Letter as a Rhetorical Form: Structure, Logic, and Style in King's 'Letter from Birmingham Jail.'" *Quarterly Journal of Speech* 65 (April 1979): 121–136.

Gilbert, Robert E. "John F. Kennedy and Civil Rights for Black Americans." *Presidential Studies Quarterly* 12 (Summer 1982): 386–399.

Goldzwig, Steven R., and George N. Dionispoulos. "John F. Kennedy's Civil Rights Discourse: The Evolution from 'Principled Bystander' to Public Advocate." *Communication Monographs* 56 (September 1989): 179–198.

Goodman, Richard J., and William I. Gorden. "The Rhetoric of Desecration" *Quarterly Journal of Speech* 57 (February 1971): 23–31.

Goodman, Walter. Review of Fawn Brodie's *Richard Nixon. The Shaping of His Character, New York Times Book Review,* October 4, 1981, p. 18.

Goodnight, Thomas G., and John Poulakos. "Conspiracy Rhetoric: From Pragmatism to Fantasy in Public Discourse." *Western Journal of Speech Communication* 45 (Fall 1981): 229–316.

Greenfield, Meg. "The Prose of Richard Nixon." *The Reporter*, September 29, 1960, pp. 15–20.

Gregg, Richard B. "The Ego-Function of the Rhetoric of Protest," *Philosophy and Rhetoric* 4 (Spring 1971): 71–91.

Griffin, Leland M. "A Dramatistic Theory of the Rhetoric of Movements." In William H. Rueckett, ed., *Critical Responses to Kenneth Burke.* Minneapolis: University of Minnesota Press, 1969.

———. "The Rhetoric of Historical Movements." *Quarterly Journal of Speech* 38 (April 1952): 184–188.

Hahn, Dan F. "Ask Not What a Youngster Can Do for You: Kennedy's Inaugural Address." *Presidential Studies Quarterly* 14 (1984): 239–250.

Hahn, Dan F., and Justin Gustainis. "While the Whole World Watched: Rhetorical Failures of Anti-War Protest." *Communication Quarterly* 36 (Summer 1988): 203–216.

Hancock, Brenda Robinson. "Affirmation by Negation in the Women's Liberation Movement." *Quarterly Journal of Speech* 58 (October 1972): 264–271.

Harrell, Jackson, and Wil A. Linkugel. "On Rhetorical Genre: An Organizing Perspective." *Philosophy and Rhetoric* 11 (Fall 1978): 263–264.

Hart, Roderick P. "The Rhetoric of the True Believer." *Speech Monographs* 38 (November 1971): 249–271.

———. "An Unquiet Desperation: Rhetorical Aspects of 'Popular' Atheism in the United States." *Quarterly Journal of Speech* 64 (February 1978): 33–46.

Hill, Forbes. "A Turn Against Ideology: Reply to Professor Wander." *Central States Speech Journal* 34 (Summer 1983): 121–126.

Hinds, Lynn, and Carolyn Smith. "Nixspeak: Rhetoric of Opposites." *Nation*, February 16, 1970, pp. 172–174.

Hope, Diane Schaich. "Redefinition of Self: A Comparison of the Rhetoric of Women's Liberation and Black Liberation Movements." *Today's Speech* 23 (Winter 1975): 17–25.

Hunsaker, David M. "The Rhetoric of *Brown v. Board of Education*: Paradigm for Contemporary Social Protest." *Southern Speech Communication Journal* 43 (1978): 91–109.

Hunt, Everett Lee. "Plato and Aristotle on Rhetoric and Rhetoricians." In Raymond F. Howes, ed., *Historical Studies in Rhetoric and Rhetoricians*, pp. 19–65. Ithaca, N.Y.: Cornell University Press, 1961.

———. "The Social Interpretation of Literature." *English Journal* 24 (March 1935): 214–219.

Jabusch, David M. "The Rhetoric of Civil Rights." *Western Journal of Speech* 30 (Summer 1966): 176–183.

King, Andrew A., and Floyd Douglas Anderson. "Nixon, Agnew and the 'Silent Majority': A Case Study in the Rhetoric of Polarization." *Western Journal of Speech Communication* 35 (Fall 1971): 243–255.

King, Martin Luther, Jr. "Non-Violence and Racial Justice." *Christian Century*, February 6, 1957, p. 166.

Lester, Julius. "Cleaver, Carmichael and the Politics of Black Liberation." In Dotson Rader, ed., *Defiance 1*, pp. 78–79. New York: Paperback Library, 1970.

Lukas, J. Anthony. "Class Reunion: Kennedy's Men Relive the Cuban Missile Crisis." *New York Times Magazine*, August 30, 1987, pp. 22–27, 51 passim.

MGee, Michael C. "Another Phillippic: Notes on the Ideological Turn in Criticism." *Central States Speech Journal* 35 (Spring 1984): 43–50.

———. "The Ideograph: A Link Between Rhetoric and Ideology." *Quarterly Journal of Speech* 66 (February 1980): 1–16.

———. "In Search of 'The People': A Rhetorical Alternative." *Quarterly Journal of Speech* 61 (October 1975): 235–249.

———. "'Not Men, but Measures': The Origins and Import of an Ideological Principle." *Quarterly Journal of Speech* 64 (April 1978): 141–154.

McKerrow, Ray E. "Marxism and a Rhetorical Conception of Ideology." *Quarterly Journal of Speech* 69 (1983): 192–205.

Martin, Howard. "The Rhetoric of Academic Protest," *Central States Speech Journal* 17 (November 1966): 244–250.

Megill, Allan. "Special Report: Responses to Wander: Heidegger, Wander, and Ideology." *Central States Speech Journal* 34 (Summer 1983), 114–119.

Mendell, C. W. "Satire as Popular Philsophy," *Classical Philology* 33 (1920): 138–157.

Meyer, Sam. "The John F. Kennedy Inauguration Speech: Function and Importance of Its 'Address System.'" *Rhetoric Society Quarterly* 12 (Fall 1982): 239–250.

Miller, William Lee. "The Debating Career of Richard M. Nixon." *The Reporter,* April 19, 1956, p. 17.

Morgenthau, Hans J. "Political Folklore in Vietnam." In Louis Menashe and Ronald Radosh, eds., *Teach Ins: U.S.A.,* pp. 158–164. New York: Frederick A. Praeger, 1967.

Mueller, John E. "Presidential Popularity from Truman to Johnson" *American Political Science Review* 64 (March 1970): 18–34.

Newfield, Jack. "SDS: From *Port Huron* to *La Chinoise.*" *Evergreen Review* 73 (1969): 15–17.

Newman, Robert P. "Under the Veneer: Nixon's Vietnam Speech of November 3, 1969." *Quarterly Journal of Speech* 56 (April 1970): 168–178.

Pearce, W. Barnett, Stephen W. Littlejohn, and Alison Alexander. "The New Christian Right and the Humanist Response: Reciprocated Diatribe." *Communication Quarterly* 35 (Spring 1987): 171–192.

Pollard, Robert A. "The Cuban Missile Crisis: Legacies and Lessons." *Wilson Quarterly* 6 (Autumn 1982): 22–27, 57, 61.

Reich, Charles A. "Another Such Victory . . . The President's Short War Against Steel." *New Republic,* April 30, 1962, pp. 8–10.

Ripley, Randall B. "Kennedy and Congress." *University Programs Modular Studies.* Morristown, N.J.: General Learning Press, 1972.

Rosenfield, Lawrence W. "The Experience of Criticism." *Quarterly Journal of Speech* 60 (December 1974): 489–496.

———. "Ideological Miasma." *Central States Speech Journal* 34 (Summer 1983): 119–121.

Salinger, Pierre. "Gaps in the Cuban Missile Crisis Story." *New York Times,* February 5, 1989, E–5.

Scott, Robert L. "On Viewing Rhetoric as Epistemic." *Central States Speech Journal* 18 (February 1967): 9–17.

Simons, Herbert A. "Requirements, Problems, and Strategies: A Theory Persuasion for Social Movements." *Quarterly Journal of Speech* 56 (February 1970): 1–11.

———, Elizabeth Mechling, and Howard N. Schrier. "Functions of Communication in Mobilizing for Collective Action from the Bottom Up: The Rhetoric of Social Movements." In Carroll C. Arnold and John Waite Bowers, eds., *Handbook of Rhetorical and Communication Theory.* Boston: Allyn and Bacon, 1983.

Smith, Craig Allen. "The Hofstadter Hypothesis Revisited: The Nature of Evidence in Politically 'Paranoid' Discourse." *Southern Speech Communication Journal* 42 (Spring 1977): 274–289.

Smith, Donald H. "Martin Luther King, Jr.: In the Beginning at Montgomery." *Southern Speech Communication Journal* 34 (Fall 1968): 2–8.

Smith, Ralph R., and Russell R. Windes. "The Innovational Movement: A

Rhetorical Theory." *Quarterly Journal of Speech* 61 (December 1975): 140–153.

Stone, I. F. "The White House Outsmarted Itself and Put the Spotlight on the Teach-In . . . ." *I. F. Stone's Weekly*, May 25, 1965, p. 3.

Tarn, W. W. "Alexander, Cynics and Stoics," *American Journal of Philology* 60 (January 1939): 41–70.

Thurber, John H., and John L. Petelle. "The Negro Pulpit and Civil Rights." *Central States Speech Journal* 19 (Winter 1968): 273–278.

Tucker, Robert C. "The Theory of Charismatic Leadership." *Daedalus* 98 (Summer 1968): 731–756.

Vatz, Richard E. "The Myth of the Rhetorical Situation" *Philosophy and Rhetoric* 6 (Summer 1973): 154–161.

Wander, Philip. "The Ideological Turn in Modern Criticism." *Central States Speech Journal* 34 (Spring 1983), 1–18.

———. "The John Birch and Martin Luther King Symbols in the Radical Right." *Western Journal of Speech* 35 (Winter 1971): 4–14.

———. "The Rhetoric of American Foreign Policy." *Quarterly Journal of Speech* 70 (November 1984): 339–361.

———. "The Third Persona: An Ideological Turn in Rhetorical Theory." *Central States Speech Journal* 35 (Winter 1984): 197–216.

———, and Steve Jenkins. "Rhetoric, Society and the Critical Response." *Quarterly Journal of Speech* 58 (December 1972): 441–450.

Weisman, Steven. "Reagan Quoted as Assailing TV Coverage of the Recession." *New York Times*, March 18, 1981, B–16.

Welch, David A., and James G. Blight. "The Eleventh Hour of the Cuban Missile Crisis: An Introduction to the ExComm Transcripts." *International Security* 12 (Winter 1987/88): 5–92.

Windt, Jr. Theodore O. "Administrative Rhetoric: An Undemocratic Response to Protest." *Communication Quarterly* 30 (1982): 245–250.

———. "The Diatribe: Last Resort for Protest." *Quarterly Journal of Speech* 58 (February 1972): 1–14.

———. "The Kennedy-Nixon Debates." In Robert V. Friedenberg, ed., *Rhetorical Studies of National Political Debates*. New York: Praeger, 1990.

———. "Roots for the Idea of 'Common Ground' in Classical Rhetoric." *Pennsylvania Speech Annual* 26 (September 1969): 1–8.

———. "Seeking Detente with Superpowers: John F. Kennedy at American University. In Theodore Windt and Beth Ingold, eds., *Essays in Presidential Rhetoric*, pp. 71–84. Dubuque: Kendall/Hunt, 1983.

"The Week We Almost Went to War," *Bulletin of Atomic Scientists* 32 (February 1976): 13–21.

Index

Goodwin, Richard, 13, 34, 96
Gouldner, Alvin, xiv, 149
Greenfield, Meg, 121, 129–130
Griffin, Leland M., 156

Halle, Louis, 196
Hamisch, Carol, 169
Hamlet (Shakespeare), 132–133
Hart, Roderick, 9–13
Hartz, Louis, 240
Hayden, Tom, 145, 172, 197–198
Heirich, Max, 182
Highet, Gilbert, 224–225
Hilsman, Roger, 62–63, 68
Hinds, Lynn, 121
Hipparchia, 214–215, 222
Hiss, Alger, 113, 118, 120, 130, 264–265
Hoffman, Abbie [Free], 230, 234, 237; on ideology, 232
Hofstadter, Richard, 155
"Howl," 230
Hughes, Emmet John, 118, 120
Hunt, Everett Lee, 199
Hunt, Michael H., 14, 16

Ideological rhetoric, xiii–xv, 190–210, 231–232, 242, 244; contrasted with presidential rhetoric, xiii; problems of criticizing, xiii–xiv; compared with religious rhetoric, 150–151; and administrative rhetoric, 183, 186, 188; structure of, 192–197; forms of, 201–208; accused of hypocrisy by Yippies, 236. *See also* Consciousness-raising; Diatribe; Ideology
Ideology, xiv, 190–210, 242; defined, xiv, 191–192, 245 (n. 5); problems with definition, xiv, 245–246 (n. 5); anticommunist, 55, 103–104, 147, 173, 191, 231, 243; contrasted with procedural politics, 140–148; and religion, 149–150; factionalism of, 200–201, 209–210; as a "brain disease," 235, 236
In Defense of Politics (Crick), 145

Johnson, Lyndon B., 11, 12–13, 15, 43, 59, 84, 88–105, 116, 117, 134, 169, 186, 212, 230, 231, 235, 241; and Vietnam escalation, 88–105; speech at Johns Hopkins University, 88, 92, 98, 102; speech at Syracuse University, 89; speech before American Bar Association, 89; reviews policy in Vietnam,

92–95; press conference on July 28, 1965, 96–98; arguments justifying escalation in Vietnam, 98–102; war aims in Vietnam, 102; on Kennedy's civil rights program, 261 (n. 40)
Joslyn, Richard A., ix–x

Kefauver, Estes, 49–50
Kennedy, John F., xi, xii, 5, 13, 14–15, 17–87, 90, 93, 97, 99, 102, 104, 108, 112, 116, 172, 173, 240, 241, 244; importance of his speeches, 18–19; and the 1960 presidential campaign, 19–21; and civil rights, 21–22, 61, 71–72, 76–84, 259 (n. 27), 260 (n. 30); inaugural address, 22–24, 27; Bay of Pigs, 24–35; Berlin crisis, 35–44, 253–254 (n. 51); steel crisis, 44–52; humor of, 50–52, 250 (n. 13); Cuban missile crisis, 52–60, 256 (n. 75), 257 (n. 79); nuclear test-ban treaty, 61–76, 258 (n. 6); speech at Berlin wall, 72–73, 76; forms of rhetoric, 85; sets themes for a generation, 85; accomplishments of, 86–87
Kennedy, Joseph, 51
Kennedy, Robert F., 51, 57, 76, 235, 260–261 (n. 36)
Kennedy Imprisonment, The (Wills), 23
Kerouac, Jack, 229
Kerr, Clark, 144, 180, 181, 183, 185–187, 211
Kesey, Ken, 230, 237
Khrushchev, Nikita S., 28, 35, 43–44, 60, 70–71, 75, 120; speech on January 6, 1961, 28–29; meets Kennedy in Vienna, 35; proposes German peace treaty, 36–39, 44, 252 (n. 40), 254 (n. 53); and Cuban missile crisis, 52, 56–57; on Kennedy's speech at American University, 75
King, Martin Luther, Jr., 23, 76, 81, 163–166, 200, 238

Lamentation, 205–208
Language. *See* Political language
Leary, Timothy, 203–205, 213
Lefebvre, Henri, xii, 148–149, 191–192, 280 (n. 4)
Lester, Julius, 164
Liberal Tradition in America, The (Hartz), 144, 240
Lippmann, Walter, 94, 140–141
Lodge, Henry Cabot, 89, 93

ministrative rhetoric; Domestic crisis rhetoric; Foreign crisis rhetoric; Johnson, Lyndon B.; Kennedy, John F.; Nixon, Richard M.

Presidents: and definitions, 4–6; and ethos, 6–9; and foreign policy, 8–9; and warmaking powers, 8–9, 247 (n. 15), 248 (n. 18). *See also* Johnson, Lyndon B.; Kennedy, John F.; Nixon, Richard M.; Roosevelt, Franklin D.; Truman, Harry S.

Prize cases, 8–9

Procedural politics, 140–147, 160–176, 194; and FSM, 178–180; Aristotle on, 140, 148; Lippmann on, 140; Bunzel on, 141. *See also* Ideology; Political language; Political definitions; Politics

Progressive Labor Party (PL), 198, 200, 207, 233

Psychobiography, 15, 109–113, 133–134, 264–265 (n. 6)

Public Philosophy, The (Lippmann), 140

Radical: defined, 152; relation to procedural protesters, 162, 175–176; factionalism, 200–210

Reactionary: defined, 152

Reagan, Ronald, 11, 86, 103

Reedy, George, 7

Regan, Donald, 10

Republic, The (Plato), 229

Rhetoric: and politics, 148; defined by Baldwin, 150; defined by Bryant, 150; and political movements, 155–159. *See also* Political rhetoric; Presidential rhetoric

Rhetoric of Aristotle, The, 148, 152

RN (Nixon), 118, 127

Robbins, Tom, 212

Robert Kennedy and His Times (Schlesinger), 58

Roosevelt, Franklin D., 6, 48, 53, 143

Rossiter, Clinton, 7, 8

Rostow, Walter W., 34

Rubin, Jerry, 230, 231, 233–234, 237; and money, 233–234; and diatribe, 235; on speeches, 235–236; ridicules Marxists, 285–286 (n. 45)

Rusk, Dean, 43

Russell, Bertrand, 215, 218

Safire, William, 130

Sahl, Mort, 51, 230

Sandburg, Carl, 24

Sarachild, Kathie, 202

Savio, Mario, 145, 180–182, 188, 278 (n.11)

Sayre, Farrand, 221

Schell, Jonathan, 100, 101, 263 (n. 27)

Schlesinger, Arthur M., Jr., 17, 34, 38–40, 49, 51, 58, 60, 125, 143, 253 (n. 46)

Searle, John, 183

Simons, Herbert A., 156

Sisterhood Is Powerful (Morgan), 203

Six Crises (Nixon), 108, 113, 119, 264 (n. 5)

Slave, The (Baraka), 166, 167

Sloterdejk, Peter, 159

Smith, Arthur, 198

Smith, Carolyn, 121, 248 (n. 26)

Society for Cutting Up Men (SCUM), 169

Socrates, 215, 217, 218, 219; diatribe against, 283–284 (n. 19)

Solanis, Valeria, 169

Sorensen, Theodore, 17, 18, 22, 28, 33, 34, 42, 64–65, 80, 82, 251 (n. 17)

Speechwriting, 9–14, 249 (n. 29, n. 30, n. 32). *See also* Goodwin, Richard; Sorensen, Theodore

Stevenson, Adlai, 124, 130

Stewart, Charles, 157

Strategic Arms Limitation Treaty I (SALT I), 73, 106, 241

Strong, Edward, 183–185. *See also* Berkeley Free Speech Movement

Students for a Democratic Society (SDS), 168, 171–174, 175; and Port Huron Statement, 172

Symbolic acts: importance of, xi–xii, 45; in Berlin crisis, 42–43; in steel crisis, 49–50; in Cuban missile crisis, 57–58; in seeking detente, 63, 70–71; and rhetorical genres, 155; in black civil rights movement, 164–165; and consciousness-raising, 203; and revolutionaries, 205; and Greek cynics, 222, 227; and Yippies, 236–237. *See also* Political symbolism

Tarn, W. W., 228, 229

Teach-ins, 91–92, 104, 161, 169–171, 231

Television, 107, 236–237, 247 (n. 11), 273 (n. 40)

Thomson, John, 211. *See also* Berkeley Filthy Speech Movement

About the Series

STUDIES IN RHETORIC AND COMMUNICATION
General Editors:
E. Culpepper Clark, Raymie E. McKerrow, and David Zarefsky

The University of Alabama Press has established this series to publish major new works in the general area of rhetoric and communication, including books treating the symbolic manifestations of political discourse, argument as social knowledge, the impact of machine technology on patterns of communication behavior, and other topics related to the nature or impact of symbolic communication. We actively solicit studies involving historical, critical, or theoretical analyses of human discourse.

About the Author

Theodore Otto Windt, Jr., is Associate Professor of Political Rhetoric at the University of Pittsburgh and a political commentator for KDKA-TV. He received his doctorate from Ohio State University.